I've Got the Light of Freedom

CHARLES M. PAYNE

I've Got the Light of Freedom

The Organizing Tradition and the
Mississippi Freedom Struggle

With a New Preface

UNIVERSITY OF CALIFORNIA PRESS

BERKELEY   LOS ANGELES   LONDON

University of California Press, one of the most distinguished university presses in the
United States, enriches lives around the world by advancing scholarship in the humanities,
social sciences, and natural sciences. Its activities are supported by the UC Press Foundation
and by philanthropic contributions from individuals and institutions. For more information,
visit www.ucpress.edu.

University of California Press
Berkeley and Los Angeles, California

University of California Press, Ltd.
London, England

First Paperback Printing 1996

Library of Congress Cataloging-in-Publication Data

Payne, Charles M.
   I've got the light of freedom : the organizing tradition and the Mississippi freedom struggle,
   with a new preface / Charles M. Payne.
      p.   cm.
   "A Centennial book."
   Includes bibliographical references and index.
   ISBN-13 978-0-520-25176-2 (pbk. : alk. paper)
   1. Civil rights movements—Mississippi—History—20th century.   2. Civil rights workers—
   Mississippi—History—20th century.   3. Afro-Americans—Civil rights—Mississippi.
   4. Mississippi—Race relations.   5. Civil rights movements—Mississippi—Greenwood—
   History—20th century.   6. Greenwood (Miss.)—Race relations.
   I. Title.
   E185.93.M6P39   2007
   323'.09762—dc22

Printed in the United States of America

16

10   9   8   7

The paper used in this publication meets the minimum requirements of ANSI/NISO
Z39.48-1992 (R 1997) (*Permanence of Paper*).

For my grandparents,
William Smith from Claxton, Georgia,
Anna Mae Smith from Fitzgerald, Georgia,
and Rachel Payne
from Cambridge, Maryland

Holly
Springs

TUNICA

PANOLA   Oxford

COAHOMA
Clarksdale   QUITMAN

YALOBUSHA

TALLAHATCHIE

BOLIVAR
              Ruleville
Cleveland

SUNFLOWER   LEFLORE
              Greenwood
Indianola   Winona
              Itta
              Bena   CARROLL
Greenville

WASHINGTON   HOLMES
         Belzoni
                   Mileston
         HUMPHREYS

SHARKEY   Philadelphia

ISSAQUENA   YAZOO

                   Canton

              Tougaloo
              Jackson

         Vicksburg
WARREN

Natchez

         Liberty   McComb
                    PIKE WALTHALL
         AMITE   Hattiesburg

☐ Mississippi Delta
▨ Southwest Mississippi

N
W ✦ E
S

Mississippi

Gulfport
Biloxi

CONTENTS

Whenever you find yourself on the side of the majority,
it is time to pause and reflect.

MARK TWAIN

I've Got the Light of Freedom was published a year after John Dittmer's *Local People: The Struggle for Civil Rights in Mississippi* (Illinois, 1994) and at about the same time as Adam Fairclough's *Race & Democracy: The Civil Rights Struggle in Louisiana, 1915–1972* (Georgia, 1995). In retrospect, the publication of the three books relatively close together marked a turning point of sorts in civil rights scholarship. In different ways, all three works represented a departure from what Julian Bond calls the Master Narrative of the civil rights movement. That narrative, so familiar as to constitute almost a form of civic religion, goes:

> Traditionally, relationships between the races in the South were oppressive. Many Southerners were very prejudiced against Blacks. In 1954, the Supreme Court decided this was wrong. Inspired by the court, courageous Americans, Black and white, took protest to the street, in the form of sit-ins, bus boycotts, and Freedom Rides. The nonviolent protest movement, led by the brilliant and eloquent Reverend Martin Luther King, aided by a sympathetic federal government, most notably the Kennedy brothers and a born-again Lyndon Johnson, was able to make America understand racial discrimination as a moral issue. Once Americans understood that discrimination was wrong, they quickly moved to remove racial prejudice and discrimination from American life, as evidenced by

the Civil Rights Acts of 1964 and 1965. Dr. King was tragically slain in 1968. Fortunately, by that time the country had been changed, changed for the better in some fundamental ways. The movement was a remarkable victory for all Americans. By the 1970s, Southern states where Blacks could not have voted ten years earlier were sending African Americans to Congress. Inexplicably, just as the civil rights victories were piling up, many Black Americans, under the banner of Black Power, turned their backs on American society.

One college student recently came up with an even briefer version. "One day, a nice old lady, Rosa Parks, sat down on a bus and got arrested. The next day, Martin Luther King Jr. stood up, and the Montgomery bus boycott followed. And sometime later, King delivered his famous 'I Have a Dream' speech and segregation was over."[1]

The last decade has witnessed a remarkable flowering of movement scholarship, much of it trying to dismantle the mainstream narrative, assertion by assertion. Scholars are questioning the top-down and triumphal underpinnings of the narrative; the overemphasis on the South as a site of struggle; the extent of nonviolence; the character of white resistance, including the idea that it was mostly a problem of the South; the continued marginalization of women; the chronology; the role of liberals; the equation of Black Power with the end of the movement; the separation between civil rights history and labor history; and the related tendency to underemphasize the economic goals of the movement. Even the language used to describe the movement is a point of contestation. Was it "segregation" or "white supremacy"? The "civil rights movement" or the "freedom struggle"? Mind you, all of this is argument among magi; popular understanding of the movement continues to be organized around Kennedy and King, around nonviolence and that speech.[2]

Still, even if we don't know who is listening, the scholarly literature has expanded and changed in ways that could not have been foreseen just a decade ago. Ideas which were oppositional then have a hint of a new orthodoxy about them now. Reviewing that literature is too large a task to attempt here, but we can look at some of the subsequent work on the rural South, situating *Light of Freedom* in the work that came after (although just doing that now can be seen as controversial).

Among the many works which argue that the movement's beginnings need to be sought long before *Brown* or the Montgomery bus boycott, Paul Ortiz's *Emancipation Betrayed: The Hidden History of Black Organizing and White Violence in Florida from Reconstruction to the Bloody Election of 1920* (California, 2005) is especially interesting because he couches the point in a study of a largely forgotten struggle, the post–World War I fight for the franchise and better economic conditions in Florida. He makes a very strong case for the salience of historical memory. He attributes much of the vibrancy of the Florida movement to the ability of activist leaders to ritually mobilize memories of successful Black struggle in the context of the Civil War and Reconstruction. He also stresses the importance of networks, not so much church-based groups as women's clubs, fraternal organizations, labor unions, and mutual-aid societies. Only a wave of state-sanctioned violence, in the context of utter national indifference, brought the movement to an end.

Looking at the movement in rural Louisiana over a seventy-year period, Greta De Jong's *A Different Day: African American Struggles for Justice in Rural Louisiana, 1900–1970* (North Carolina, 2002) finds that the activists there always had a conception of goals broader than the Master Narrative envisions. At all points, they were concerned with economic independence, political participation, education, and safety from violence. In the 1960s, CORE activists coming into the parishes she studies found people who were not so much interested in desegregating local facilities as in economic justice and the right to vote, an experience similar to that of SNCC in Mississippi. As in Mississippi, the most receptive people tended to be land-owning farmers and young people, and the most reluctant, teachers and preachers. Fraternal orders like the Masons and Knights of Pythias, which were crucial to the campaign Ortiz describes in Florida, were also significant in Louisiana. Individuals who were interested in working with CORE were not necessarily interested in its message of nonviolence: "The most common response of African Americans to the numerous drive-by shootings and bombings carried out by white supremacists in black neighborhoods was to reach for their firearms" (p. 189).

In *Let The People Decide: Black Freedom and White Resistance Move-*

ments in Sunflower County, Mississippi, 1945–1986 (North Carolina, 2004), Todd Moye demonstrates that, even within a single county, the course of the movement could be very different from one town to another. He also contends that the movement almost certainly saved the county from economic disaster by creating a climate that made business investment possible. In the course of telling that story, he also tells the story of Jack Harper, a former leader of the Citizen's Council who has been repeatedly elected to public office in a Black majority county, apparently by delivering a high level of service to constituents he once tried to keep from voting. We are only beginning to think about how Southern white people understand their own adjustments to a post-movement world, a story which needs to be told at multiple levels. Joseph Crespino's *In Search of Another County: Mississippi and the Conservative Counterrevolution* (Princeton, forthcoming) tells one part of the story, detailing the ways political elites, after early legislative and judicial losses, began learning to cut their losses, in part by taking strategic advantage of racial antipathies in the rest of the country, saying in effect that they would desegregate the schools of Mississippi one day after the schools of New York desegregated. This kind of analysis is part of a larger, ongoing effort to see the defenders of white supremacy as something more than one-dimensional, cardboard racists.

It seems somehow fitting that white supremacists and black radicals are both being, if not rehabilitated, then at least considered through more complex lenses. The emerging literature on Black Power sees its advocates as more than hate-filled nihilists; rather, they were rational political actors whose work grew naturally out of the earlier movement and helped reshape the American political landscape, including the character of Black leadership.[3] Part of what is involved in the reconsideration of Black Power is a reexamination of the idea that Civil Rights and Black Power represented fundamentally different movements, the one to be lionized—at least in retrospect—the other vilified. This involves an ongoing reexamination of the meaning of nonviolence. Rather than seeing attitudes toward violence as one of the sharpest differences between the two phases of the movement, the new scholarship emphasizes the continuities, arguing that philosophical commitment to nonviolence was always rare and became more so over time; that support for self-defense was always widespread; and that, in the South, many movement participants saw little tension between nonviolence as they understood it and self-defense.[4] Worth Long, a SNCC activist quoted by Todd Moye, may have said it best: Black people, were, by and large, "unviolent" (p. 232).

The new Black Power literature intersects with what may be the most interesting revisionist theme, a call for more attention to African American movements for racial justice outside of the South.[5] As soon as one does that, the Master Narrative is pretty much done for. Now one has to rethink the role of the church, the nature of militance, the role of left radicalism, and how McCarthyism reconfigured the movement. Looking at the North gives us a different way to think about the limits of liberalism, and of antidiscrimination as the end-all of racial policy. Some of the most interesting work, including Rhonda Williams's *The Politics of Public Housing: Black Women's Struggles against Urban Inequality* (Oxford, 2004) and Felicia Kornbluh's *A Right to Welfare? Poor Women, Professionals, and Poverty Programs, 1935–1975* (Pennsylvania, forthcoming), focuses on the struggles of low-income urban women around welfare or public housing. They raise questions that fundamentally challenge our conception of what it means to be a citizen. What works for the sharecropper doesn't work for them. In modern America, does citizenship entail a right to some minimum level of consumption? Can you be a citizen without access to some kind of credit?

While there is no doubt that some of the most interesting work will come from this "Up South" school, the Southern vein is hardly mined out. A recent work which demonstrates that is Emilye Crosby's *A Little Taste of Freedom: The Black Freedom Struggle in Claiborne County, Mississippi* (North Carolina, 2005). The movement in Claiborne County, where Crosby grew up, started later than in much of the rest of the state, largely after the 1965 Voting Rights Act. Using over 140 interviews, in addition to the files of the Sovereignty Commission (Mississippi's state agency for the defense of white supremacy), FBI files, and local police files, as well as, one imagines, her personal knowledge of the county, she is able to perform the rare feat of analyzing the evolution of a complex social movement in both the white and Black communities and of doing it at the level of personality, comparable in this respect to William Hinton's *Fanshen*. One can see Black people growing more confident, partly in response to the leadership of Rudy Shields, a remarkable organizer even by the standards of the Mississippi movement, and white people growing more frustrated and uncertain. One can see that at all points in the process there are divisions among both Blacks and whites that do not become part of the public transcript. Crosby offers one of the most extensive discussions available of the price individual Black people paid for their activism and of the thoroughness with which movement opponents were able to turn instruments of government to their ends, even in a county where the sheriff was relatively even-handed and respected by both sides.

There is a real temptation for bottom-up history to sing praises to the agency, courage, and wisdom of the poor and look no further. In fact, it is probably a good idea to assume that people are formed by the society they struggle against and carry some of its flaws within them. By far, the chapter of *Light of Freedom* which has been least commented upon by reviewers is chapter 12 with its discussion of various corruptions within the movement. To its credit, there are no plaster saints in *A Little Taste of Freedom*. The movement in Claiborne County relied heavily on boycotts, and Crosby describes in detail the way activists enforced discipline against Black people who failed to support the boycotts, ranging from ostracism to physical violence. That the way Black activists enforced group discipline paralleled the way the Citizen's Council enforced it was an irony lost on few. At the same time, Crosby is able to say something about how boycott violators understood what they were doing. Claiborne County is in the part of the state in which Charles Evers was most influential, and no one better reflects moral ambiguity than Evers—able to command intense loyalty from his constituents while steadily enriching himself, setting himself up as an autocrat willing to rule with force and intimidation when charisma wouldn't do, and all the while maintaining cozy relationships with the defenders of white supremacy.

Perhaps no idea was dearer to the young people who worked in Mississippi in the 1960s than the idea that they were building for the long haul, doing work that would continue in some form long after they themselves were no longer around. In *Freedom Is a Constant Struggle: The Mississippi Civil Rights Movement and Its Legacy* (Chicago, 2004), Kenneth Andrews argues that experience shows they were largely right. Comparing those Mississippi counties which developed a high level of movement infrastructure in the 1960s to those which did not, he finds that, two decades later, Blacks from movement counties still enjoyed a higher level of some public goods—more political participation, more Black officeholders, more influence over social welfare policies.[6] "In the face of resistance, movements built infrastructures and propelled changes in an array of local institutions and those efforts have had an enduring legacy in Mississippi" (p. 200).

What can be said at this point about work currently in the pipeline is that it will definitely put the Southern movement more closely in dialogue with struggles in the rest of the country, not all of them African American. It will focus on what happened in the South after national attention turned elsewhere, which will include a reevaluation of the role of federal government and market forces, as well as a reevaluation of class tensions within Black communities. If the previous wave of revisionism pushed discussion of the movement's origins back before the mid-fifties, the next will challenge the idea that the movement ended in the mid-sixties. There will be continued interest in the role the movement played in pushing the country's political center rightward. (Recall that Lyndon Johnson, signing the Voting Rights Act, commented sadly that he was signing the country over to the Republicans for the foreseeable future.) Hasan Jeffries' forthcoming work on the Alabama movement promises to be an extensive analysis of how the rural movement shaped Black Power. One hopes, with all the forthcoming work on Black Power, that it will not just use the movement as a way to think about relationships between Blacks and whites, but as a way to think about relationships among Blacks. That is one way to step outside the terms of received discourse. There is growing interest in how memories of the movement are constructed—see, especially, Renee C. Romano and Leigh Raiford, *The Civil Rights Movement in American Memory* (Georgia, 2006)—but little of that interest has yet focused on Black Power in any depth. Once we get beyond describing the obvious ways in which the movement was distorted, this is another very promising avenue of analysis.

In his interview with me, Bob Moses noted that part of what was important about SNCC is that it provided a context and a culture in which young people could grow.[7] The women of SNCC are currently preparing a collection of essays (*Hands on the Plow,* edited by Martha Prescod Norman and Judy Richardson) that will illuminate the processes of growth. It is a remarkable collection, lyrical and self-critical in a way that memoirs seldom are, and very much in the tradition of African American humanism.

It is still true that every way of seeing is a way of not seeing. Bottom-up analysis carries its own temptations, beyond the temptation of seeing only virtue in the oppressed—or, for that matter, seeing only oppression in the oppressed. Every historical parallel isn't a case of historical continuity. There really was something special about the period from the mid-fifties to the mid-sixties, if only in the degree of attention paid to race nationally and in the changed nature of acceptable public discourse. Thinking from a purely bottom-up perspective makes sense only for a limited number of questions. Understanding the consequences of the movement requires understanding national actors and institutions.[8]

All that acknowledged, it remains true that scholars trying to understand the world through the eyes of its subaltern classes do not bear primary responsibility for the fact that most Americans profoundly misunderstand the nature of the movement. Partly because of that misunderstanding, teaching movement history as a critique of the Master Narrative is a profoundly rewarding experience. Students of all backgrounds come away with an awareness of how perspectives embedded in the way they understand the past affect their understanding of the present. Black students, in addition, say that this kind of history makes them think differently about their forebears. They mean that they learn to think more respectfully about previous generations of Black people. They have absorbed images about the past which imply—and are more powerful because they imply, rather than state—the historical irrelevance of Black people, their massive passivity. A history that challenges that is, of course, useful, but doing that doesn't require any embellishment. Hagiographic history is going to be attacked sooner or later. As James Baldwin noted: "To accept one's past—one's history—is not the same thing as drowning in it; it is learning how to use it. An invented past can never be used; it cracks and crumbles under the pressures of life like clay in a season of drought."[9] Giving young people a history that they can use doesn't require any bending of the record. Quite the contrary. The more precisely and complexly we can render the history, the longer it will be useful.

Durham, North Carolina
August 2006

1. Emilye Crosby, *A Little Taste of Freedom: The Black Freedom Struggle in Claiborne County, Mississippi* (Chapel Hill: University of North Carolina Press, 2005), p. xiii.

2. One exception is the growing interest in Southern states in civil rights tourism. As this is written, a discussion is taking place in Philadelphia, Mississippi, on setting up a museum about the murder of Schwerner, Chaney, and Goodman, raising obvious questions about the balance between opportunism and commemoration.

3. See Peniel Joseph, *The Black Power Movement: Rethinking the Civil Rights–Black Power Era* (New York: Routledge, 2006); and Peniel Joseph, *Waiting 'Til the Midnight Hour: A Narrative History of Black Power in America* (New York: Henry Holt, 2006). See also Jeffrey Ogbar, *Black Power: Radical Politics and African American Identity* (Baltimore: Johns Hopkins University Press, 2004); and Komozi Woodard, *A Nation within a Nation: Amiri Baraka (Leroi Jones) and Black Power Politics* (Chapel Hill: University of North Carolina Press, 1999). Of course, the best earlier literature anticipated some of the points being made in the new Black Power literature; see William Chafe, *Civilities and Civil Rights: Greensboro, North Carolina, and the Black Struggle for Freedom* (New York: Oxford University Press, 1980). Although it is not specifically about Black Power, Steve Estes *I Am a Man: Race, Manhood, and the Civil Rights Movement* (Chapel Hill: University of North Carolina Press, 2005)

raises questions about the masculinist underpinnings of the entire movement which will be crucial to future analyses of Black Power. Stokely Carmichael's autobiography makes several contributions to this discussion; see Carmichael with Ekweume Michael Thelwell, *Ready for Revolution: The Life and Struggles of Stokely Carmichael (Kwame Ture)* (New York: Scribner, 2003). As to the attitude of SNCC toward Malcolm X, an issue raised in the bibliographic essay in this volume, Carmichael/Ture treats him as an exemplar in every respect. In terms of questions about intellectual gatekeeping and the shaping of historical memory, it is important to note that almost every one of the mainstream media that reviewed Carmichael's book chose a white reviewer to do it.

4. Christopher Strain, *Pure Fire: Self-Defense as Activism in the Civil Rights Era* (Athens: University of Georgia Press, 2005); Akinyele Umoja, "1964: The Beginning of the End of Nonviolence in the Mississippi Freedom Movement," *Radical History Review* 85 (Winter 2003), pp. 201–226; Akinyele Umoja, " 'We Will Shoot Back': The Natchez Model and Paramilitary Organization in the Mississippi Freedom Movement," *Journal of Black Studies* 32 (January 2002), pp. 267–290; Emilye J. Crosby, " 'This Nonviolent Stuff Ain't No Good—It'll Get Ya Killed': Teaching about Self-Defense in the African American Freedom Struggle," in Julie Buckner Armstrong et al., eds., *Teaching the American Civil Rights Movement: Freedom's Bittersweet Song* (New York: Routledge, 2002); Timothy B. Tyson, *Radio Free Dixie: Robert F. Williams and the Roots of Black Power* (Chapel Hill: University of North Carolina Press, 1999); Lance E. Hill, *The Deacons for Defense: Armed Resistance and the Civil Rights Movement* (Chapel Hill: University of North Carolina Press, 2004).

5. The clarion call is Jeanne Theoharis, Komozi Woodard, and Matthew Countryman, eds., *Freedom North: Black Freedom Struggles Outside the South, 1940–1980* (New York: Palgrave MacMillan, 2003); but see also Martha Biondi, *To Stand and Fight: The Struggle for Civil Rights in Postwar New York City* (Cambridge, Mass.: Harvard University Press, 2003); Matthew Countryman, *Up South: Civil Rights and Black Power in Philadelphia* (Philadelphia: University of Pennsylvania Press, 2005); and Robert Self, *American Babylon: Race and the Struggle for Postwar Oakland* (Princeton: Princeton University Press, 2005).

6. The pattern does not hold for school desegregation. There, counties with more movement infrastructure saw less desegregation over time, presumably a function of the fact that stronger movements generated stronger opposition in an area where the federal government wasn't going to intervene. Whether Black office-holding is in fact a collective "good" for Blacks, is, of course, a point of contestation.

7. For the Moses interview, see Charles Payne and Stephen Lawson, *Debating*

the Civil Rights Movement, 2nd ed. (Lanham, Md.: Rowman and Littlefield, 2006).

8. Let us note, too, that some criticism of bottom-up theory and of work on the Southern movement tries to hold that work accountable for questions it is not trying to address.

9. James Baldwin, *The Fire Next Time* (New York: Dial Press, 1963), p. 368.

organizers represented a coalition of civil rights groups, but most owed their primary allegiance to the Student Nonviolent Coordinating Committee (SNCC, pronounced *snick*), the organization that had, under the watchful eye of Ella Baker, grown out of the sit-ins of 1960.

Wherever they were sent, the civil rights activists found that their initial reception by local Blacks was less than enthusiastic. The movement was generally dismissed as "dat mess." Reprisals were virtually certain. Those who were even thought to be interested in the movement might lose their jobs. Those who did join could expect to be shot at and to have their churches bombed and their homes targeted by arsonists. People who were able to survive the winter months only because of surplus commodities from the federal government could expect to lose them. Farmers who needed loans to get their crops started in the spring could expect their credit to be withdrawn. People who needed medical care could expect it to be refused. As one white landowner said, with completely unintended irony, to a Black family as he kicked them off his land, "Your food, your work and your very lives depend on good-hearted white people."[2]

Nonetheless, a significant number of the Black residents in towns across the state eventually chose to cast their lot with the movement. The first organizers to come to Greenwood, near the heart of the Mississippi Delta, had to sleep catch-as catch can. Within a year, the level of movement activity was sufficient to bring the normal functioning of the city to a virtual standstill. Within two years, Black Greenwood was so much behind the movement that it could have slept a small army of civil rights workers (and did). It was one of the decade's earliest successful campaigns in the rural South.

In part, this book is an examination of that campaign. How was it possible, within a few years, to move large numbers of dependent and, to all appearances, apolitical people—none of them having any semblance of legal rights at the local level, all of them vulnerable to violence—how was it possible to move these people to a position of actively working to change the conditions of their own lives? What did the movement do to them and they to it? In the quotation that prefaces this Introduction, Du Bois reminds us that social history has tended to ignore or forget the record of ordinary people. A great deal has been written about the various national civil rights organizations and their leaders. The sheer volume of material written from a top-down perspective implies that the dynamism of the movement is to be understood in terms of these national leaders and national organizations. But the more closely one looks at the history, the less comfortable one becomes with reducing the tens of thousands of people across the South who participated in local movements to faceless masses, singing, praying, and marching in the background. Historian David Garrow contends that

> what the carefully-scrutinized historical record shows is that the actual human catalysts of the movement, the people who really gave direction to the movement's organizing work, the individuals whose records reflect the greatest substantive accomplishments, were not administrators or spokespersons, and were not those whom most scholarship on the movement identifies as the "leaders." Instead, in any list, long or short, of the activists who had the greatest personal impact upon the course of the southern movement, the vast majority of names will be ones that are unfamiliar to most readers.[3]

Many of the young leaders who spread across Mississippi in 1962 were carriers of a particular tradition of social struggle, and this book is also an examination of that tradition. Bob Moses, himself responsible for much of what made the Mississippi movement distinctive, even among SNCC projects, has written that the civil rights movement can be thought of as having two distinct traditions.[4] There was what he labels the community-mobilizing tradition, focused on large-scale, relatively short-term public events. This is the tradition of Birmingham, Selma, the March on Washington, the tradition best symbolized by the work of Martin Luther King. This is the movement of popular memory and the only part of the movement that has attracted sustained scholarly attention.

The Mississippi movement reflects another tradition of Black activism, one of community organizing, a tradition with a different sense of what freedom means and therefore a greater emphasis on the long-term development of leadership in ordinary men and women, a tradition best epitomized, Moses argues, by the teaching and example of Ella Baker—and, I would add, by that of Septima Clark. That tradition, and placing the history of Greenwood within it, is the second major theme of this book.

The book's structure is partly chronological and partly topical. Chapters 1 through 3 argue that in fact the initiative that made change possible was far more widely dispersed in Black communities than we ordinarily realize. The first chapter is partly a reminder of how utterly vicious the old system in Mississippi was and partly an outline of some of the systemic changes that made challenges to that system increasingly possible after 1940. The next two chapters are concerned with continuity; organizationally and intellectually, the well-known movement of the early sixties was predicated on the activism of an earlier, socially invisible generation. Chapters 4 through 9 examine the way the activists in the sixties built on and elaborated that legacy, concentrating on Greenwood between 1962 and 1964 and on the role that local people there played in the process. The period before mid–1964 is special because it marks a time when the Mississippi movement had only the most minimal resources. The federal government was still criminally lax about protecting the lives of civil rights workers, there were no large numbers of volunteers from outside the state, no consistent interest from the national media even when civil rights workers were killed, no particular reason to believe that the movement was ever going to achieve anything to justify the sacrifices it required. Those who became a part of the movement in that period really were trusting themselves to the air. The passage of the 1964 Civil Rights Act and the 1964 Freedom Summer Project signaled a shift to a different kind of movement. Chapter 10 discusses that shift. Chapters 11 and 12 look at Greenwood in the middle to late sixties, finding that the experience of the early years was sufficiently transformative—empowering, if you will—that local people who had become active in that period were able to create and sustain several movement-related institutions, even in the face of decreasing help from the outside organizers who had first brought many of them into political motion. Their very success contributed to the erosion of the climate of relationships that had helped energize the pre–1964 movement. The two final chapters deal with the decline of the organizing tradition and its relative invisibility in both activist communities and popular media. The bibliographic essay discusses the same issue as it applies to scholarship.

"I've got the light of Freedom" is a line from "This Little Light of Mine." A staple of Black church music, "This Little Light of Mine" is an appropriate symbol of the movement's rootedness in the cultural traditions of the rural Black South. Depending on tempo and emphasis, it can carry a variety of messages. In the small sanctified church in which I was raised, it was sung during collection, presumably signifying that whatever one had to give mattered to the Lord. In Mississippi particularly the song became an anthem of the movement and a special favorite of Fannie Lou Hamer's. One activist wrote: "It was sung in churches, in freedom schools, on marches, on picket lines, at jails and in Parchman [prison] where hundreds of demonstrators were jailed. The song became a force."[5] The idea that everyone had some part of freedom's light was close to the heart of the message that organizers both carried into the Delta and found there.

There are heroes and, emphatically, heroines enough in this history. Yielding to the temptation to focus on their courage, however, may miss the point. Part of the legacy of people like Ella Baker and Septima Clark is a faith that ordinary people who learn to believe in themselves are capable of extraordinary acts, or better, of acts that seem extraordinary to us precisely because we have such an impoverished sense of the capabilities of ordinary people. If we are surprised at what these people accomplished, our surprise may be a commentary on the angle of vision from which we view them. That same angle of vision may make it difficult to see that of the gifts they brought to the making of the movement, courage may have been the least.

Unreferenced quotations are from my own interviews with the person named. Several of the people interviewed have changed names since the sixties. I have followed a practice of using whatever name an individual was or is using at the time referred to. Idiosyncratic spelling and grammar in quotations have been retained except where they might interfere with clarity. Finally, within the movement, Ella Baker was always Miss Baker, Fannie Lou Hamer always Mrs. Hamer. Southern Blacks had to struggle for the use of "courtesy titles" and thus often had a different appreciation for them. More particularly, the use of titles was self-consciously a token of the respect and affection that women like Miss Baker and Mrs. Hamer commanded even from young men and women who were frequently contemptuous of social convention. I have followed their usage.

One

The show has been put on the road. . . . Three wars,
increased migration . . . radio and television have played their
parts in creating in [Mississippi] Negroes a dissatisfaction with the
status quo. The studied efforts to keep them poor and ignorant
have broken down under their own weight.

RUBY HURLEY
NAACP[1]

EVERYTHING THAT TOOK place in Mississippi during the 1960s took place against that state's long tradition of systematic racial terrorism. Without some minimal protection for the lives of potential activists, no real opposition to the system of white supremacy was possible. Lynching is only one form of racial terror and statistics on it virtually always underestimate the reality, but between the end of Reconstruction and the modern civil rights era, Mississippi lynched 539 Blacks, more than any other state. Between 1930 and 1950—during the two decades immediately preceding the modern phase of the civil rights movement—the state had at least 33 lynchings.[2]

The first victim was Dave Harris, shot to death in 1930 by a crowd of 250 white men who believed Harris had killed a young white man near Gunnison, Mississippi. The second and third victims were Pig Lockett and Holly Hite. Arrested for robbery, they were taken from the law enforcement officers by a mob, which hung them. In 1931, Steve Wiley was accused of attempting to assault the wife of a grocery-store owner while he was drunk. She shot him three times. A mob hung what was left of him from a railroad trestle. A week later, in Vicksburg, Eli Johnson, also accused of an attempted assault on a white woman, was lynched. In November of that year, the body of Coleman Franks was found hanging from a tree limb near Columbus. He had been charged with shooting and wounding a local white farmer. There were no lynchings in 1932, but two in 1933. In July an unnamed Negro man in Caledonia, Mississippi, was hung, accused of insulting a white woman. In Minter City that September, Richard Roscoe got into a fight with a white man. A mob shot him to death, tied his body to the rear of the sheriff's automobile, and paraded it through town before dumping it in front of his home.

Nineteen-thirty-four saw three killings. In Bolivar County, a mob overpowered sheriff's deputies and seized Isaac Thomas and Joe Love, who had been arrested for an alleged attack on a white woman. The men were hung from a railroad trestle. Less than two months later, in Pelahatchie, Mississippi, four white men beat seventy-year-old Henry Bedford to death. A tenant farmer, he was accused of having spoken disrespectfully to one of the whites in the course of a dispute about land rental. The sheriff arrested four whites—for which he suffered some criticism—but no indictments were ever handed down. About a month later, Robert Jones and Smith Houey were hung from a tree near Michigan City. They were accused of killing at least one white man.[3]

There were seven killings in 1935, three in the month of March alone. On March twelfth, Ab Young was hung from a tree in a school yard near Slayden. Young was wanted in connection with the shooting death of a white highway worker. When he was captured, the mob had an argument about whether to burn him or turn him over to the sheriff in Holly Springs. The brother of the murdered man had made a plea that Young not be mutilated. While the argument was still going on, a group of about fifty went off to hang him. He was allowed to sing a hymn, which he was able to do in a clear, unfaltering voice, apparently unnerving some of his captors. After he was dead, several in the crowd used his swinging body for target practice. When the lynchers got back to town the burn-him or give-him-to-the-sheriff argument was still going on.[4] Ten days later in Lawrence County, R. J. Tyronne was shot to death, apparently by neighbors who thought he had become too prosperous. On the thirtieth of the month, the body of Rev. T. A. Allen, weighted down with chain, was found in the Coldwater River. Allen had been involved in an attempt to organize sharecroppers. In June, R. D. McGee in Wiggins was both hung and shot for his alleged attack on an eleven-year-old white girl. In July, Bert Moore and Dooley Morton, both young farmers, were hung near Columbus, also for an alleged attack on a white woman. Bodie Bates was hung from a bridge in August for the same reason. In September, a mob in Oxford, site of the University of Mississippi, hung Ellwood Higginbotham, who was being tried for the murder of a white planter.

In 1936, J. B. Grant, seventeen years old, was shot over a hundred times by a mob, tied to an automobile, and dragged through the streets of Laurel before being hung from a railroad trestle. What he had done to deserve this is not known. It was a record fifteen months before the next killing, but that one proved particularly brutal: Roosevelt Townes and "Bootjack" McDaniel, both in their mid-twenties, were accused of murdering a white man and were taken from the sheriff by a mob. Three or four hundred people, including women and children, took them to a clearing in the woods near Duckhill, where they were chained to trees. According to one report, the mob turned on McDaniels first. A blowtorch was applied to his chest until he confessed, after which he was shot. The blowtorch was applied to Townes for as much as an hour; it was used to burn off his fingers and ears individually. While he was still alive, brush and wood were piled at his feet and fired with gasoline, finally burning him to death.[5]

During the first half of 1938, there were no lynchings anywhere in the South, perhaps in part because, in the wake of the Duckhill slayings, federal anti-lynching legislation was gaining new support. In the second half of the year, there were seven lynchings, four in Mississippi, in which the NAACP estimated a total of six hundred people took part. Only a few were involved in the murder of Wash Adams, who was beaten to death in Columbus for failing to pay the ten-dollar balance on his wife's funeral bill. In the Delta town of Rolling Fork, a blacksmith named Tom Green refused to do some work ordered by the plantation manager. Green was fired and then got into an argument with R. Purdy Flanagan, the plantation owner, about who owned which tools. Shooting started; Green was wounded but Flanagan was killed. Green holed up in his cabin where he was killed after a fifteen-minute gun battle with a mob of three hundred. His body was dragged by car to the place where he had killed Flanagan, doused with gasoline and burned, then dragged into town and burned again. That was near the beginning of July. Near the end of the month a mob in Canton shot and killed Claude Banks as he was driving home. In November, a mob of perhaps two hundred killed Wilder McGowan in Wiggins. McGowan was accused of assaulting a white woman.

Where we have more than fragmentary details about these cases, it is often because of the work of NAACP investigators, usually native white southerners. Their work repeatedly demonstrated that the underlying stories were much at variance with reported versions. Stories about sheriffs being "overpowered" by mobs often turned out to be cases of collusion between sheriffs and the mobs—although they also found cases where law-enforcement people did everything they could to protect their prisoners, sometimes successfully. Of course, investigators frequently found that the actual reasons victims were selected had no relationship to their alleged transgression. The crowd at Duck Hill may have seized Roosevelt Townes partly because he was a bootlegger in a part of the state where that occupation was thought a white man's prerogative.

Wilder McGowan was probably killed because he had trouble grasping the whole idea of white man's prerogative. On November 20, a Mrs. Murray reported that at about eight P.M. she had been attacked and robbed by a light-skinned colored man with straight hair. The seventy-four-year-old Mrs. Murray was a member of one of the area's prominent white families. A posse estimated at two hundred men descended upon the local Negro quarters and ordered that no one leave. One woman, thinking the order applied only to men, tried to leave for her job; she was hit on the head with a pistol butt and told to "git back." Bloodhounds led the posse through a rooming house. Learning that one resident, Wilder McGowan, age twenty-four, was not there, the mob became interested in him. When he returned home, he was taken into the nearby woods and hung.

In many respects, McGowan was an unlikely choice. Several witnesses could have accounted for his whereabouts during the time the crime was committed. He was dark-skinned, so he didn't fit Mrs. Murray's description. He was never taken before Mrs. Murray for identification. The NAACP investigator concluded that McGowan was selected because he had had several altercations with whites:

> On one occasion when he refused to run as other Negroes did when ordered to do so by some armed whites in an automobile, he was attacked but beat his assailants and took a revolver from one of them. Recently, he was suspected of having slashed with a knife one of a group of whites who visited a Negro dance hall "looking for some good-looking nigger women." It is known that he was one of two or three young Negro men who resented the slur on their women and had a fist fight with the whites. He called for the lights to be put out and in the darkness the whites were badly beaten and one cut on the arm.

"After they had Linched him," McGowan's uncle wrote the NAACP a year later, "they claim that they caught the right negroes But still Wilder is dead." In a larger sense, Wilder was the right Negro.[6]

The McGowan case was closer to the rule than to the exception. Southwide, allegations of rape were made in about one-sixth of all lynchings (but probably in one hundred percent of all southern speeches about lynching). Immediately after it was founded, the Association of Southern Women for the Prevention of Lynching (ASWPL) made an attempt to find out how many of the charges of rape had any validity:

> These investigations showed that white men, determined to get rid of a certain Negro, would accuse him of an attempted sex crime. They knew that officers would approve without question their action for this offense. . . . While in some instances the weight of the evidence supported the charge of attempted rape, investigations of many lynchings indicated so strongly that white women . . . were merely a front for lynchers that no report of a lynching for the

protection of a white woman could be accepted as true until it was verified.[7]

Of course, mobs had their own understanding of what constituted "assault"; looking a white woman in the eye could be enough.

Near the end of the thirties, Canton, Mississippi, had two killings, both of which, according to an NAACP investigator, reflected, in different ways, a trend toward "quieter" lynchings. In July of 1938, a white man named A. B. McAdam visited the city to see his daughter who was hospitalized there. After he left the hospital, he was, he claimed, attacked and robbed by a Black man. Law-enforcement officers and citizens decided to blockade the part of town where the incident was supposed to have taken place. At the same time, Claude Banks, twenty-two-year-old son of a prosperous Negro funeral home owner, was driving home from a party. As he drove by the blockade, members of the mob opened fire with pistols and shotguns, apparently making no effort to stop the car. Witnesses said that both deputies and police officers were among those doing the shooting. Banks was killed. His companion, Willie Jones, was arrested and roughed up before being released with the warning that if he ever said anything he would catch "sudden pneumonia"—that is, be killed. Canton's mayor did what he could to keep the story quiet, refusing to cooperate with a photographer who wanted to get a picture of the body—a departure from the older tradition in which murderers, smiling and grinning, posed with the bodies of their victims or pieces thereof, for photos that were sometimes turned into postcards. Claude Banks's father did what he could to keep the issue alive. He went to the mayor and requested the city render some form of compensation for his son's death and then asked a local judge if there were any legal avenues of redress. Both told him that nothing could be done.

Joe Rodgers was killed in Canton in 1939. Active in community affairs, a deacon and choir member at Mount Zion Baptist Church, Rodgers was employed at Dinkman Lumber Mill. He was asked to move into company-owned housing but refused, since that housing was more expensive than what he already had. On Saturday, May 6, there was an extra deduction from his pay. He was told that the deduction was for rent on a company house. The following Monday, Rodgers raised the issue with a foreman. Things ended with the foreman striking Rodgers with his fist and then grabbing a spade. Rodgers took the spade away and hit him with it before a friend of Rodgers's separated the two men. It is not known what happened immediately after that, but Joe Rodgers was never seen alive again. That Thursday, a constable found his body in the Pearl River, bound hand and foot and beaten to a pulp. He had been tortured with hot irons. The *Madison County Herald* never mentioned his death, and local residents were ordered not to discuss it.[8]

By the end of the thirties, NAACP officials and members of the ASWPL thought howling mobs were becoming passe. Small groups of men were doing quietly what large crowds used to do publicly. Kangaroo courts and charges of "killed while resisting arrest" were giving racial murder a quasi-legal air. Even when large groups were involved, there were more attempts to suppress news of murders—this in a state where lynchings had previously been announced in the newspapers a couple of days in advance in order to give the country people time to get to town.

World War II brought new possibilities of racial tension. On the one hand, whites worried that those Blacks who served in the armed forces would come back with "biggity" ideas. On the other hand, some whites felt that not enough Black men were going to war. Blacks were more likely to be excluded from service for reasons of health or illiteracy, leaving some whites feeling that there were too many Black men around. Nonetheless, the state's lynching rate did not change much during the war years; there were three in 1943, one more in 1944.

The 1943 killings were only a week apart, separated by only a few miles. The first involved two fourteen-year-old boys, Charlie Lang and Ernest Green, arrested for attempting to rape a thirteen-year-old white girl near the small town—population fourteen hundred—of Quitman. The sheriff claimed the boys had confessed. On October 12, a small group of men supposedly overpowered the constable at the jail and took the boys. They were found hanging from a beam of the bridge where the incident had taken place. The bridge was a traditional site for lynching in Clarke County. In 1918, four Negroes, two of them pregnant women, had been hung there for alleged complicity in the death of a local dentist.

Subsequent investigation of the 1943 killing by the NAACP again raised doubts about just what had happened. The girl and the two boys were friends, and they frequently played together, often around the bridge. On that day, according to the report of the NAACP's Madison Jones,

> they were running and jumping when the girl ran out from under the bridge and the boys behind her. A passing motorist saw them and the result you know. The boys were mutilated in the following fashion. Their reproductive organs were cut off. Pieces of flesh had been jerked away from their bodies with pliers and one boy had a screw driver rammed down his throat so that it protruded from his neck.[9]

The Quitman killings may have inspired the killers of Howard Wash, killed just five days later about thirty miles away. Wash had been tried and found guilty of murdering his employer, a local dairy farmer. He had pleaded self-defense, and the fact that the jury that convicted him refused to recommend the death penalty may indicate that some of its members found some validity in his claim. He was sentenced to life imprisonment, but a crowd broke into the jail and seized and hung him.

In 1944, the Reverend Isaac Simmons was farming 295 acres of land in Amite County. For a couple of years, a group of white men had been trying to get him to sell the land, but he had no interest in that. Simmons, sixty-six years of age, went to a lawyer to make certain that there would be no trouble about transferring the property to his children. Word of his visit to the lawyer got out. On the morning of March 26, six armed white men picked up Simmons and one of his sons and drove them to a thicketed area where Simmons was told to get out of the car. He tried to run, but two shotgun blasts caught him in the back. The killers then reloaded the shotgun, walked over to where he had fallen, and shot him a third time. His son, who had been forced to watch, was beaten and given ten days to get off the land. When the son returned with friends to reclaim his father's body, he found that all of his father's teeth had been knocked out with a club—presumably after he was already dead—and his arm broken and his tongue cut out.[10]

Such mutilations—parading dead bodies around the town, shooting or burning bodies already dead, severing body parts and using them for souvenirs, using corkscrews to pull spirals of flesh from living victims or roasting people over slow fires—were as much a part of the ritual of lynching as the actual act of killing. They sent a more powerful message than straightforward killing would have sent, graphically reinforcing the idea that Negroes were so far outside the human family that the most inhuman actions could be visited upon them.

There were two more killings after the war. In 1946, Leon McTate of West, Mississippi, was whipped to death by six white men who accused him of stealing a saddle. In July of 1949, Malcolm Wright was riding in his wagon with his wife and four children near Houston, Mississippi. Three white men in an automobile, angered because they could not pass the wagon on the narrow road, beat Wright to death while his family watched, the last Mississippi killing listed by the NAACP before the fifties.

The Wright killing, perhaps more eloquently than the more brutal slayings or the spectacle lynchings, underscores how tenuous Black life was. The point was that there did not have to be a point; Black life could be snuffed out on whim, you could be killed because some ignorant white man didn't like the color of your shirt or the way you drove a wagon. Mississippi Blacks had to understand that viscerally. Those who wanted to work for change had to understand that they were challenging a system that could and would take their lives casually.

THE STRUCTURAL BACKGROUND OF CHANGE

As terrible as the lynchings of the thirties and forties were, the system of racial violence was by then in decline, in part because the cotton-based political and economic system from which it had grown was declining. The increasing difficulty of maintaining a way of life in Mississippi based on cotton was a particularly important change for the Mississippi Delta.

Roughly the northwestern quarter of the state, bounded on the west by the Mississippi River, the Delta is flat and treeless, with soil so rich that it frequently produced a tenth of the nation's cotton crop, cotton of very high quality. In 1935, David Cohn, a Delta native and a firm believer in white supremacy, wrote "Cotton is more than a crop in the Delta, it is a form of mysticism. It is a religion and a way of life"—a way of life, as he noted elsewhere, dependent above all else upon Black labor.[11] Most Delta counties were three-quarters Black, and the Blacks were overwhelmingly agricultural laborers, tenant farmers, and domestics. They were a poor and suppressed population even as compared to Blacks in the rest of Mississippi. As Blacks from other states feared going to Mississippi, Blacks from the hill counties or piney woods of Mississippi were frequently reluctant to venture into the Delta. SNCC's Dorie Ladner, who had grown up in Hattiesburg, recalls being terrified on her first trip into the Delta and being amazed to learn that in 1962 there were still places where there were curfews for Negroes. It seemed to her that whatever was left over from slavery had been left in the Delta.

One of the most detailed portraits we have of traditional Delta life is that by the anthropologist Hortense Powdermaker. Her *After Freedom* is a study of the Delta town of Indianola in Sunflower County during the early 1930s. She describes a world structured around cotton production. Delta cotton production was organized around vast plantations rather than the smaller farms that dominated other parts of the state. The great majority of Delta Blacks were either sharecroppers or renters on a plantation. Individual landlords could be better or worse, but the system itself was profoundly corrupt, a form of life Blacks repeatedly said was only marginally better than slavery.[12]

Sharecroppers were vulnerable to all manner of exploitation. Powdermaker estimates that twenty-five or thirty percent of them may have gotten an honest settlement at the end of the year. Since sharecroppers and tenants were largely illiterate, without recourse to the law, and often unable even to move to a different plantation without the permission of their landlord, less scrupulous landowners were free to do as they chose. Indeed, it was for just this reason that Black tenants were preferred to white ones. Blacks could be more easily squeezed; poor whites were thought to be too "independent."[13] Even without the rapacity of landlords, cropping on shares barely allowed much more than a subsistence existence except in boom years. In 1932, Powdermaker's first year in the Delta, she estimates that seventeen or eighteen percent of those cropping on shares in Sunflower County made some profit, ranging from $30 to $150 for the year. The rest broke even or ended the year in debt. If the one study she cites is representative, half the Black families in the Delta could not afford a minimally decent diet.[14] Most could not even hope that their children, through education, could make a better life. The school calendar was built around the cotton season, which meant that most Black youngsters were in school only when they weren't needed in the fields. (Aaron Henry, who as an adult would be among the important most Black leaders in Mississippi, as a child asked his mother why he could only go to school for five months while the white kids went seven. She answered that it was because he was smarter than white kids; they needed extra time.)

Powdermaker did her work in the 1930s, the last decade in which she could have seen the cotton economy in relatively pure form. Change had been in motion at least since tractors first appeared in the Delta during the First World War. In the 1930s, flame cultivators were introduced that for thirty-five cents an acre cleared land that cost a dollar to clear by hand, even when hoe hands were only making a dollar a day. The 1940s saw the development of the first commercially viable cotton harvester, a machine capable of doing the work of forty or more pickers.[15]

While cotton production was being mechanized, competition from synthetics and cheap foreign cotton made cotton a less valuable crop. During the Depression, the bottom fell out of the cotton market. Across the South, the average price of a pound of cotton, which had been thirty-five cents in 1919, dropped to six cents in 1931. In Mississippi it fell to nine cents. Delta farmers began switching to other crops—corn, oats, soybeans—all requiring much less labor than cotton.[16] By the 1960s, modernized plantations found they needed barely a fifth of their former work force.

Suddenly most Blacks had no economic function. Schemes to reduce the size of the Black population became a popular subject of discussion. The Great Migration during World War I had generated near-panic among wealthier whites. Labor agents from the North were shot at, beaten, harassed with every legal device planters could think of. Blacks caught trying to leave might be jailed or even strung up as a lesson to others. By the 1950s, gubernatorial candidates were competing to see who could promise to drive the greatest number of Negroes from the state in the shortest period of time.

The separation of Negroes from the soil unraveled the balance of political and economic forces that had defined their place since shortly after the Civil War.[17] It meant, for example, increased out-migration of Blacks from the South to the North and West, a process accelerated by the northern demand for labor during World War II. During the 1940s, 1.6 million Blacks left the South, to be followed by almost 1.5 million during the 1950s. The North's new Black voters created a counterforce to the Dixiecrats who had previously enjoyed a virtual stranglehold on national policy concerning race. The new Black vote mattered enough that by 1940 the national Democratic platform spoke to the question of equal protection under the law for the first time. Referring to that period, historian David Lewis says, "Although isolation of any single election factor risks presenting a false picture, the reality that Afro-American votes were now determinative in 16 non-South states with 278 electoral votes escaped no serious political strategist."[18] In contrast, the white South controlled only 127 electoral votes.

Since the end of Reconstruction, the federal government had essentially taken a hands-off stance to the South's way of doing business. It amounted to tacit national support for southern racism. The withering of that support constituted a fundamental shift in the balance of forces. It meant, for example, that the South could be threatened with federal anti-lynching legislation. No such legislation ever passed, but the threat of it was salutary. Southwide, 1923 saw the sharpest one-year decrease in the number of lynchings in thirty-five years—from sixty-one the previous year to twenty-eight in 1923—a decrease attributed by the NAACP partly to the northward migration and partly to the first sustained agitation for a federal anti-lynching bill. By 1938, Senator Wagner of New York thought a clear pattern had been established: "Experiences in 1922, 1934 and 1935 demonstrated that the number of lynchings declined with significant regularity while anti-lynching legislation was pending in Congress, only to rise again when hope for passage of such legislation died." The pattern repeated itself in 1938, which saw a complete cessation of lynching across the South for the first six months of the year, while another bill was being discussed, only to have lynchings start up again almost as soon as Congress adjourned.[19]

Under the new political order, it became possible to have the FBI investigate racial murders. By the end of 1942, they had investigated at least five killings. Even though they took the position that there were grounds for federal involvement only in cases where state officials were involved in lynchings, their investigations did lead, directly or indirectly, to some people being indicted, including some in both the Howard Wash and the Isaac Simmons lynchings cited above. In Mississippi, of course, it was impossible to find a jury that would convict, but even the idea that lynchers could be indicted was a new thought for Mississippi, a clear reminder that the outside world was beginning to impinge in uncomfortable ways.[20]

An equally important factor in the gradual decline of racial terror may have been the collapse of the cotton economy, which led to less need to control Blacks, either through the near-peonage of sharecropping or through violence. Prior to the turn of the century racial lynchings across the South averaged around one hundred a year. Between 1900 and 1920, they fluctuated between fifty and seventy. By 1935, after the arrival of nickel-a-pound cotton, the number dropped to eighteen, and for the next twenty years it would not rise above eight in any one year.[21] There continued to be non-economic reasons for controlling Blacks, obviously, but economic changes removed one of the traditional pillars of the system.

In the early 1930s, according to Arthur Raper's classic study of lynching, Mississippi officials prevented fourteen lynchings, more than they allowed to take place. Hortense Powdermaker, conducting her study of Sunflower County at the same time, concluded that the fear of outside opinion was a potent factor in reducing community support for the mob. By the thirties, newspapers in larger Southern cities typically criticized lynchings, at least in principle. By the forties, their criticisms were clearly linked to fear of outside scrutiny. In 1943, for example, the Jackson *Clarion-Ledger* warned that the federal government was trying to find a way to bring lynching under federal jurisdiction, "a fact which all citizens, all law officers, and all court officials, should keep in mind constantly." The only absolutely certain way to block the menace of federal encroachment, they stressed, "is to prevent lynchings in the future, through education, through suasion, and by giving every prisoner or suspect full and adequate protection until the guilty are punished through due process of law."[22]

While political agitation was becoming more effective, the collapse of the cotton-based economy simultaneously removed the most fundamental reason for controlling Blacks. Lynching patterns had always been related in complicated ways to economic factors. In the Delta, the most common months for lynching were June and July, the months of the cotton season when cotton needs the least labor. Between the turn of the century and the Depression, there was a consistent relationship across the South between the price of cotton and the number of lynchings. In relatively prosperous times, lynchings were fewer. When whites were feeling more economic pressure, they were more likely to turn to rope and faggot.[23] In the midst of the Depression, with cotton at a nickel a pound, the correlation was broken. Instead of going up, as one would have predicted from past patterns, the number of lynchings went down. Economic insecurity during the Depression affected different classes of whites in different ways. Poor whites traditionally made up the majority of the mobs. Jessie Daniel Ames of the Association of Southern Women for the Prevention of Lynching pointed out that those poor whites reached by New Deal programs actually may have had more cash money in their pockets than they were accustomed to and thus had less need of "finding a Negro to lynch to prove their supremacy." For wealthier whites in the South, lynching was beginning to look counterproductive. In 1939,

Ames noted, "we have managed to reduce lynchings . . . not because we've grown more law-abiding or respectable but because lynchings became such bad advertising. The South is going after big industry at the moment and a lawless, lynch-mob population isn't going to attract very much outside capital."[24]

In the middle, shopkeepers in small towns, finding themselves hard-pressed to keep and find customers, began to relax some of the traditional rituals of degradation. In the Delta, according to Powdermaker:

> Under stress of hard times, the shopkeepers made an effort to attract Negro trade as they had never done before. Negro customers were no longer kept waiting indefinitely for attention. In many cases, they were permitted to try on garments rather than, as before, being required to buy shoes, gloves, hats, without first finding out whether they were the right size or shape. Once such concessions have been granted, they cannot easily be withdrawn.[25]

In small ways as well as large ones, careful observers during the Depression could see that the old system was eroding, creating opportunities for activism that had not existed before.

THE BLACK RESPONSE

Changes in the structural underpinnings of racism wouldn't have mattered if Black Mississippians weren't willing to challenge the system. There were always people who resisted, as witnessed by the slayings of Wilder McGowan and the Reverend T. A. Allen, killed in 1935 for organizing sharecroppers. In the 1940s, the pace of activism picked up, often in direct response to changes originating outside the state.

The generation of Black Mississippians coming to adulthood in the late 1940s had a stronger sense of entitlement than their parents. By 1947, the Delta's David Cohn could lament:

> The younger generation of Negroes is sharply at odds with their elders. If the latter suggest moderation in racial points of view, if they

say that the world cannot be changed in a day, younger Negroes are likely to dismiss them contemptuously as "handkerchief heads" or "Uncle Toms"—epithets taken from the Northern Negro press, whose often reckless and irresponsible outpourings they avidly read.[26]

It wouldn't take much for a man of Cohn's disposition to see a militant behind every other plow, but more judicious observers saw similar changes. Samuel Adams, studying one hundred sharecropper families in the Delta in the mid-1940s, found "evidence of a growing race consciousness" in their changing musical tastes. Increasingly, the songs that were popular were those that ridiculed whites, made subtle protests against segregation, or tried to stimulate racial pride.[27]

Hortense Powdermaker detected more aggressive attitudes emerging among Blacks in the early 1930s. While she found every possible shading of opinion among Blacks of every age and every status grouping, there were discernible patterns, with the most consistent patterns centering on age. The oldest generation, those over sixty at the time of the study, had been born either in slavery or just after the Civil War. They were the generation most prone to put their trust in "good" white people and most prone to believe that Blacks were indeed inferior to whites. Still, they resented the suffering the system imposed on them. Among this generation, both belief and behavior tended to acknowledge white superiority.

Their children, though, born just before the turn of the century, more typically continued to behave as if they accepted the superiority of whites but seldom really believed it. They grew up having less intimate contact with whites than had their parents, and many of them, with at least the rudiments of literacy and exposure to newspapers, movies, and the radio, were more aware of the world beyond the plantation. They held that Blacks were just as good as whites but recognized as a plain fact of life that such a belief could not be acted on publicly. In the presence of whites, they presented the countenance whites typically wanted to see—respectful, content, subservient.

Some derived a fleeting sense of superiority from their ability to deceive whites.

The children of that generation, people born in the early years of the century, exhibited a great deal more resentment at their station in life. They considered themselves entitled to equal treatment and were much less comfortable than their parents had been with the elaborate codes of ritual deference, a dilemma they resolved by trying to avoid contact with whites as much as possible. Similarly, the better-educated Blacks of whatever generation tended to be more visibly angry about the injustices and indignities of the system, and they, too, reacted by minimizing their contact with whites. For those who had too much pride to greet a white man with the traditional "Howdy, boss," or some equally humiliating variant, avoiding contact altogether was the next best thing.[28]

Powdermaker is careful to say that the more bitter, resentful attitudes characterized only a "dissenting minority," but "it is their attitude that is spreading and the more passive one that is on the wane as ... ideas of what is due the individual citizen penetrate ever more deeply into the Negro group."[29] While these attitudes in the 1930s seldom expressed themselves politically, that potential was clearly present. She reports that one young man, whom she presents as typical of the better-educated Negroes, "recognizes his inability to vote as the crucial point. For him the vote has become the symbol of the kernel of the inter-racial situation. He maintains that ... only a need for the votes of the Negroes will bring justice to them in work, in conditions of living, in the courts."[30]

By the 1940s, that attitude among Mississippi Blacks had begun to grow into various forms of political mobilization, much of it based in Jackson, the state's largest urban center. In the middle of the decade, T. B. Wilson, secretary of the Jackson NAACP ("Niggers, Apes, Alligators, Coons and Possums," according to the old racist joke), organized a chapter of the National Progressive Voters League. The *Jackson Advocate*, like many Black papers of the day, supported the drive vigorously. Response was slow at first but quickened with the 1944 Supreme Court decision outlawing the white primary. Before that decision, Wilson said, people were "indifferent, disinterested, but when we worked up this case of registering and voting them because the Supreme Court decision gave us to understand that we could vote, then they began to go register."[31]

The importance of the white-primary decision is still not widely appreciated. In much of the South, allowing only whites to vote in primary elections had been the most effective means of wholesale disenfranchisement. Once that became illegal, there was an almost immediate surge in Black registration, which historian David Garrow sees as the true beginning of Black political emergence in the South. In 1940, only three percent of Southern Blacks were registered, a figure that had not changed much since the turn of the century. By 1947, twelve percent were registered; by 1952, twenty percent.[32]

Negro veterans played an important role in the change. Like their predecessors from the First World War, some of them returned to the South with a new sense of the proper order of things. All across the South Negro veterans tried to register and protested attempts to keep them from doing so. In Birmingham in 1946, one hundred veterans marched to the courthouse to demand the right to vote. Mississippi had sent 83,000 Negroes into the segregated armed forces of World War II. In keeping with the southern patriotic tradition, some towns in Mississippi actually encouraged Black veterans to register (if not always to vote), but they were exceptional.[33]

Veterans became a factor in what was probably the most significant mobilization of Mississippi Blacks in the forties, the hearings on Senator Theodore Bilbo. For all of his long career, Bilbo had been a symbol of the most virulent sort of racism, best summarized by his famous admonition that the best way to keep a Negro from the polls on election day was to pay him a visit at home the evening before, a message he spread with increased vigor after the all-white primary was outlawed. Indeed, some observers thought many white Mississippians would have accepted the decision had not Bilbo and others whipped up a campaign against it.

After Bilbo's reelection in 1946, the national NAACP, in conjunction with organized labor and other groups Bilbo had offended, led a drive to convince the Senate to refuse to seat him, on the grounds that Bilbo had been a leader in the disenfranchisement of Blacks. At the hearing held in Jackson, Black veterans testified for three days. Moreover, Negroes packed the courtroom, perhaps the most significant act of public defiance from Negroes the state had seen in decades. County registrar after county registrar faced the national press and detailed with great honesty exactly how hard they worked to keep the voting rolls white, by advising Negroes not to try to register, by threatening those who didn't recognize good advice when they heard it, by employing a double standard on the literacy requirement.[34] Their candor was a gauge of how little some Mississippians of that period worried about the opinions of the outside world.

Bilbo died before the Senate reached a final decision on his seating, but he had served a purpose, providing Blacks with a symbol so universally hated that Mississippi Blacks with some help from out of state were able to mobilize publicly against it. In the context of this mobilization, Black voter registration rose steadily. There were an estimated two thousand registered Negroes in the state in 1940, twenty-five hundred in 1946, but five thousand in 1947, a one-hundred-percent increase in a year. (Even so, that amounted to about one percent of the eligible Negroes in the state, the lowest figure in the South. In 1946 in rural Leflore County, where Greenwood is located, twenty-six of the county's thirty-nine thousand Negroes were on the rolls, none of whom voted.) "Negro leaders in the state point out that perhaps the most crucial factor in this remarkable increase was the stimulation and courage" provided by the Bilbo hearing. The surge in Black registration started immediately after the war and continued for several years. There were seventeen thousand on the rolls by 1952, of whom perhaps fifty-six hundred were voting. The number of registrants peaked around 1954 or 1955, somewhere between twenty and twenty-five thousand, the highest figure in the twentieth century.[35]

Characteristically, Mississippi made less progress between the late forties and the early fifties than did nearby states. In that period, Mississippi saw a fourfold increase in Black registration. Both Alabama and Louisiana, the two states which, after Mississippi, were considered most determined to keep Blacks from the polls, changed more rapidly during the same years. In Louisiana, Black registration went from ten thousand to one hundred thousand. Even in Alabama, it went from six thousand to fifty thousand, an eightfold increase.[36]

The southern states as a whole, of course, had developed a long list of tactics to minimize Black voting. Among them were requiring one or more white character witnesses; requiring only Black applicants to show property tax receipts; strict enforcement of literacy tests against Negro applicants; rejecting Black applicants because of technical mistakes in filling out registration forms or requiring Black applicants to fill out their own forms while those of whites were filled out by registration officials; a variety of evasive tactics, such as claiming that registration cards had run out, that all members of the registration board had to be present, or that it was closing time; putting difficult questions about the Constitution to Negro applicants; holding registration in private homes, which Blacks were reluctant to enter.[37] Where other sections of the South relied primarily on a few such tactics, Mississippi, according to Margaret Price, appeared to use them all. As late as 1954, in the thirteen Mississippi counties that had majority Negro populations a *total* of fourteen votes were cast by Blacks in that year's elections.

The general pattern across the state obscured significant variations within the state. According to one 1951 NAACP report:

> In Jackson County there appear to be no voting restrictions. In George County Negroes are denied the right to vote; in Magee one Negro is encouraged to vote but the general Negro population is discouraged; in Washington County Negroes are invited to vote; in Sunflower County (Indianola) some Negroes are permitted, others are not. There are some counties in which Negroes are not permitted to pay their poll tax but are permitted to register; consequently they can't vote. In Jefferson Davis County there are different regulations in different towns. In Mt. Carmel, which is predominately, if not entirely Negro, ballot boxes are provided for the Negroes in the general election; they are manned by them, but no boxes are provided for the primary, which means in effect Negroes are denied the right to vote.[38]

The figure of twenty or twenty-five thousand registrants in Mississippi by the mid-fifties is hardly impressive in a state with an adult Negro population of nearly half a million. Still, it represents a tenfold increase in fifteen years, a rapid enough change to suggest some underlying qualitative shift in the political activity of Blacks. The same is suggested by the growing state NAACP membership. In 1949, the records of the national office listed twenty-three branches with a total of one thousand members. Southern branches were frequently short-lived. By 1951, there were only seventeen branches in the state, but they still claimed about one thousand members. In 1952, membership crept up to thirteen hundred; by the end of 1954, it reached twenty-seven hundred, still a small number but double the 1952 figure.[39]

The rising numbers of Black voters and NAACP members were not the only reasons in the early 1950s for thinking that the South, even Mississippi, had begun to turn away from the past. In Mississippi, median Negro family income was up, with almost all the increase associated with urban families. Racist violence across the South was less common than it had been. In Mississippi between 1946 and 1949, one observer found no evidence of significant Klan activity.[40] In 1952, for the first time in seventy years, Tuskegee Institute could not find an example of a lynching in the South. The more underground forms of racial killings continued, of course, and race-related bombings continued to occur, but observers thought even the latter might have their silver lining. A bombing may be the act of a lone individual or two and is a form of violence preferred by people who are afraid of being caught.[41]

In urban areas and the upper South, barriers to Negro registration were lowered, and Blacks even ran for office. In all areas of the South, even Mississippi, interracial groups such as the Southern Regional Conference had begun to work publicly for change. "Mississippi Negroes," said a Jackson newspaper in the mid-fifties, "have a gleam in their eyes and a feeling that they have a foot in the door." Another observer, sympathetic and well informed, said "It is to be hoped that the 1950s may be a decade of citizenship fully realized."[42]

Some very experienced Black activists were similarly optimistic. The NAACP's Ruby Hurley, in a memo written as late as 1955, noted an increase in the number of threats against NAACP officers in the state but also observed that people did not seem unduly worried by them. "Although our people are terribly annoyed, they are not frightened as they might have been a few years ago." She was meeting some determined Negroes, people who were telling her, "We just want our rights; we want to vote like the white folks do. . . . And they can pressure all they want, it won't make no difference. We ain't always eaten so high on the hog, we can eat poor again."

In his year-end report for 1954, E. J. Stringer, who had suffered various forms of harassment for serving as president of the NAACP State Conference of Branches, was full of optimism. In 1955, he thought, it should be possible to have at least one branch in each of the state's eighty-two counties; successful school integration was forthcoming. T. R. M. Howard, president of the Regional Council of Negro Leadership (RCNL), had also been harassed—at the age of 47, his draft board reclassified him 1-A—but still thought the future looked promising. In 1954, he noted that while three-fourths of Mississippi whites would take up arms to defend segregation, another year or so might change a great many attitudes.[43]

Partly because of economic change inside the state, partly because of Mississippi's increasing involvement with the social currents of the world outside the state, racial terror was no longer as common or as effective as it had been. If some observers were optimistic about the state's future, we may be sure that many others had to be uncertain. There was no way to tell how meaningful the apparent changes were until someone tested them.

Two

TESTING THE LIMITS

Black Activism in Postwar Mississippi

The Eldest have borne much. We who are younger will
neither see so much, nor live so long.

KING LEAR
Act III

WE DO NOT ORDINARILY REALIZE how much the well-publicized activism of the sixties depended upon the efforts of older activists who worked in obscurity throughout the 1940s and the 1950s. In Mississippi, Amzie Moore, Medgar Evers, and Aaron Henry were among those whose work connected most directly with the movement of the 1960s.

AMZIE MOORE: A SPIRIT BEYOND THE AVERAGE MAN

If asked to choose one person as the forerunner of the work they did in Mississippi in the 1960s and particularly of their work in the Delta, veteran SNCC workers would overwhelmingly choose Amzie Moore. Born in 1912, Moore grew up largely on the Wilkin plantation in Grenada County, just north of Greenwood. He was still a child when his parents separated and was only fourteen when his mother died. His father came back to take the two younger children but left Amzie pretty much on his own, floating from one relative to another for three years. Eventually, he went to Greenwood, where he lived catch-as-catch-can, often eating only because other kids were willing to buy him food. He finished tenth grade at Stone Street High School, which was as far as the school went.[1]

He has described himself at that period as embittered by the death of his mother and by the hard life he had to lead. Nonetheless, he was active in civic organizations while still fairly young. He moved to Bolivar County, bordering the Mississippi, because the schools were better there. In 1935, he got a job as post-office custodian, a high-status job for a Black man in the Delta. About the same time, he became involved with the Black and Tan Party, an organization of Negro Republicans that was still allowed to operate in a few areas of the state. He first registered to vote in 1936, although he wasn't able to vote in the all-important primaries. He helped start what may have been the first Negro Boy Scout troop in the Delta. His first knowledge of the Freedom Movement, as he termed it, came in 1940, when he attended a meeting of several thousand Delta Blacks concerning the modernization of life in the Delta, including the improvement of schools. Rather than challenging the separate-but-equal doctrine, Blacks were trying to get as much as possible under the doctrine.[2]

In 1942 he was drafted. "I really didn't know what segregation was like before I went into the Army."[3] Stateside, he was shipped from one racist post to another—Alabama, El Paso, Virginia. Overseas was hardly better; he got to Calcutta only to find that the enlisted-men's clubs were segregated even there. He didn't miss the contradiction: "Why were we fighting? Why were we there? If we were fighting for the four freedoms that Roosevelt and Churchill had talked about, then certainly we felt that the American soldier should be free first." To add to the indignity, the Japanese were using radio broadcasts to remind Black soldiers that there was going to be no freedom for them, even after the war was over. It became Corporal Moore's job to counter this propaganda by giving lectures to Negro troops on their stake in the war. It is not surprising that he returned home a little angry. "Here I'm being shipped overseas and I been segregated from this man whom I might have to save or he save my life. I didn't fail to tell it."[4]

Before he went into the service, he had trouble reconciling Christianity with the reality of Mississippi: "You're standing there and you hear the word, the message, and you believe in it but you're wondering about whether God believes in it." At one point in his life, he had concluded that the degradation of his people must have been divinely ordained. White people were special, and God must have wanted them to have everything. It took his military experience to divest him of the idea that white people were special. God had put him on a ship and sent him around the world so that he could see that people were pretty much the same all over. He lost his fear of white folks and joined the NAACP while still in the service.[5]

He returned home to Cleveland, Mississippi, in 1946 to find that local whites had organized a home guard to protect themselves against returning Negro veterans who were presumed to have acquired a taste for white women. A number of Blacks were killed, murders that Moore believed were intended to intimidate returning servicemen. After an FBI investigation, the murders stopped.[6]

He came home intending to put the poverty of his youth as far behind him as possible as quickly as possible. As he later remembered it, his outlook on life was modified by having the living conditions of Delta Negroes shoved in his face. He referred particularly to a visit to a family seven miles from his home where there were fourteen children, half-naked, without a bed in the house, with no food, burning cotton stalks to keep warm. The visit left him feeling that it was a sin to think about nothing but getting rich.[7]

Moore proceeded with his plans to acquire property, build a home, and start a combination service-station–restaurant, but he also continued to be involved in community affairs. In 1951 he helped start the Regional Council of Negro Leadership. Its founder and leading spirit was the prosperous, flamboyant and very popular surgeon, Dr. T. R. M. Howard, who saw RCNL as a parallel to the white Delta Council, an organization that allowed a variety of white economic interests to speak with one voice on matters of public policy. Based in the relatively safe, all-Black town of Mound Bayou, the Regional Council made an impact right away, attracting several thousand people to its first mass meetings to hear prominent speakers like Congressmen William Dawson and Charles Diggs and attorney Thurgood Marshall and getting the head of the state highway patrol to promise that Negro motorists would no longer be harassed and brutalized by his officers. A 1955 *Ebony* article has photographs of an RCNL meeting, where it estimated attendance at thirteen thousand. One photo shows Amzie Moore handing out voting instructions, the caption noting that he started a near-riot as people fought to get the handouts. The Council was composed of Black leaders from the full range of traditional organizations—ministers, heads of fraternal organizations, businesspeople, and NAACP officials. One of their first organizing efforts was a campaign that tried to get Negroes to stop buying gasoline at places where they couldn't use the restroom. They at least discussed using similar tactics within the Black community, by boycotting Uncle Toms. They also attempted to make segregation too expensive to maintain by insisting that the state live up to the "equal" part of the separate-but-equal doctrine.[8]

While its founders did not see it as a civil rights group as such, in practice the distinction got blurred. The RCNL began holding voter-registration classes and testimonial meetings at which people shared the difficulties they were having trying to register. Nearly all the leading figures in the RCNL were also in the NAACP, a group traditionally jealous of its position as *the* civil rights organization and ordinarily discouraging participation by its officers in competing groups. That Moore and other NAACP leaders felt a need for the RCNL suggests they found the program of the NAACP wanting in some respects. A part of the appeal of the Regional Council was its stress on economic issues, an area the NAACP was frequently criticized for underemphasizing. Some RCNL leaders also felt that a local organization could do things that an out-of-state organization could not. A significant number of southern leaders had become restive under the tight reins of the NAACP's national office. In Montgomery, for example, the initial decision to use the arrest of Rosa Parks as the focal point of a protest was made by E. D. Nixon, a longtime officer in both the local and state NAACP. Nixon initially wanted the boycott conducted under NAACP auspices, but when he contacted the local office, they said they would have to wait for approval from New York, whereupon Nixon decided to create a local organization to lead the boycott. This illustrates what many local leaders found frustrating about the national office. It was seen as being too committed to producing change through litigation to allow local leaders much initiative.[9] That Moore shared some of these feelings is suggested by the left-handed compliment he paid to the organization with which he worked much of his adult life. Speaking about the 1950s, he says:

> Mr. Roy Wilkins [from the national office], he's a fine man. He'd fly down here and hold our conferences and hold our annual "days" and raise our freedom money and be advised by different people outa the New York office. And that was it.[10]

Moore saw that style as a contrast to the more personal, direct involvement of the SNCC workers who came later. Although he never joined SNCC in any official capacity, by the early sixties he was spending so much time with them and so little with the NAACP as to create strain between himself and some of his NAACP comrades.

Still, NAACP organizing was the focus of his activism from the mid-1950s on. In 1955, at a meeting he did not attend, the Cleveland chapter surprised him by electing him president, perhaps because he had attracted attention for his refusal to put up "colored" and "white" signs over the restrooms at his service station.[11] Over the next year, a bad period for the NAACP statewide, he, with the help of Medgar Evers, built the chapter up to 439 members, making it the second largest branch in the state, and he became a vice-president of the state conference of NAACP branches. Herman Perry, a land-owning farmer who was one of the earliest members, thinks that the other person who deserves credit for the rapid growth of the Cleveland branch was a local barber with a gift for selling the NAACP while clipping hair. Still, it wasn't an easy sell for anyone. Perry helped "Brother Moore" start a Bolivar County Voters League in the mid-fifties precisely because they wanted to get away from the "controversial niggers" image of the NAACP.

Much of Moore's NAACP recruiting was done in area churches, taking advantage of the fact that he was a member of several different gospel-singing groups. The minister would give his group—precursors to the SNCC Freedom Singers—a few minutes to sing, after which he would go into his N-Double-A spiel and start passing out membership information. Allowed the time, he could give impromptu sermons relating contemporary social issues to biblical ones, quoting the Bible—he seldom went anywhere without one—at length and with great precision.[12] His main operational base was New Hope Baptist church, which received several threats because of Moore's activity. After one NAACP meeting there in May 1955, the church was burned to the ground.

In 1956, Moore and some of his colleagues decided to try again to get more people to vote. On primary day, fourteen Negroes, poll-tax receipts in hand, showed up to vote in East Cleveland. When they tried to put their ballots in the ballot box, a white man with a .38 on his hip prevented them from doing so, suggesting that they could put their ballots in a brown envelope lying nearby if they wanted to do that. After some argument, they did that, but Moore immediately went and called the Justice Department, which sent some agents from Memphis to investigate. Moore and his friends never heard anything more from the agents, but here, as in the case of the postwar murders in Cleveland, Moore, armed-forces veteran that he was, clearly saw the value of pitting the power of the federal government against that of white Mississippi.

In 1954, the Supreme Court handed down its ruling making *de jure* school segregation illegal, a ruling that represented the fruition of twenty years of NAACP efforts. The initial reaction from some southern leaders was rather mild. A grudging, reluctant acceptance looked entirely possible to some informed observers.[13] Even in Cleveland, Mississippi, according to Amzie Moore, the initial reaction from some whites was positive. They thought the change was overdue. It was politicians, he felt, who needed to whip up hatred so that poor whites could be played against poor Blacks. Within weeks moderation had been overwhelmed by more hysterical voices all across the South. The result would be a severe wave of repression.

In Mississippi, one of the most important reactions to the decision was the formation, in October 1954, of the White Citizens' Council (WCC), pursuing the agenda of the Klan with the demeanor of the

Rotary. Comprising professionals, businessmen, and planters, the Councils officially eschewed violence and other extralegal tactics, instead launching a wave of economic reprisals against anyone, Black or white, seen as a threat to the status quo. Its branch presidents were frequently the presidents of local banks. Most of its victims were associated with the NAACP, that "left-wing, power-mad organ of destruction that cares nothing about the Negro," as one Council document put it.[14] Despite the official disclaimers, violence frequently followed in the wake of Council intimidation campaigns. Nonetheless, the disclaimers show that by the 1950s white leadership thought it necessary to seek "respectable" methods of defending white supremacy. The Councils thought the best long-term solution to the race problem would be to drive half a million Black people out of the state. The organization was so deeply entrenched in state affairs as to have a quasi-official status; it even received funding from state revenues. Within a year of its founding it claimed twenty-five thousand members in the state; within two years, eighty thousand. The national office was located in Greenwood, and the early Council was probably more active in the Delta than anywhere else in the state.

Created in response to the school-desegregation issue, the Councils quickly became involved in a broader defense of white racism. It is largely to them that we owe the infamous law requiring that applicants for voting be able to interpret any clause in the state constitution to the satisfaction of the registrar. In the face of legal dodges like this, economic pressure, and outright violence, the numbers of Blacks on the voting rolls began to shrink. In the early 1950s, it had been at least twenty thousand by most estimates; by 1956 it was down around eight thousand.[15]

The shrinkage was a direct response to systematic repression. In 1955 alone, according to Amzie Moore, there were seven deaths. The number of leaders driven out of the state was certainly much larger. Bayard Rustin, visiting the state in the mid-fifties, chronicled several incidents around the little Delta town of Charleston: Robert Smith, local NAACP leader, simply disappeared, leaving a prosperous farm and a business. A few weeks later a Black laborer who had gotten into a fight with a white man was found dead in a creek. The Reverend L. Terry made some kind remarks to his congregation about Congressman Charles Diggs of Michigan, to Delta whites the personification of the uppity northern Negro. Six carloads of white men with shotguns told him that if he didn't leave town a lot of people were going to be hurt. He left, selling his farm for half its value to one of the whites who had threatened him.[16]

The events surrounding the murder of the Reverend George Lee and the shooting of his friend Gus Courts suggest how Mississippi's political situation was changing even as it seemed to turn back to its bloody past.[17] In 1953 and 1954, Lee and Courts had organized the Belzoni, Mississippi, branch of the NAACP, with Courts as president. Lee, a preacher who served four different congregations while running a prosperous printing business and a grocery store, was one of its most visible members and had been the first Negro in the county to get his name on the voting list.[18] One of his favorite sermons was about the day when the Black people of the Delta were going to elect somebody to the United States Congress. Doing their part to start the process, Lee and Courts had gotten about a hundred Blacks registered to vote in Humphreys County, where no Black person had voted since Reconstruction. Humphreys, a Delta county, at the time was almost two-thirds Black. The people who registered were nearly all laboring people, including some farm owners. When the local sheriff started refusing to accept poll-tax payments from Negroes, Lee and Courts filed suit against him. Courts, also a grocer, was the more vulnerable to economic reprisals, which caused him to resign the presidency in August 1954, though he took it on again in early 1955.

The threats and reprisals continued. A local bank refused to do business with him unless he turned over the records of the NAACP. His wholesaler refused to extend credit and then refused to take cash. Courts had to start getting supplies from Jackson or Memphis. A member of the Council told him that if he refused to take his name off the registration list—of the hundred Negroes once registered in the county, ninety had already yielded to the pressure to remove their names—he would lose his lease. He refused, saying that he had already paid his poll tax, and he wanted his money's worth. Three days later his landlord tripled his rent, and Courts had to move.

In April 1955 there were at least two incidents in which whites broke windshields in Negro-owned cars or broke windows in Black businesses, leaving a note in one case saying, "You niggers paying poll tax, this is just a token of what will happen to you." On April 19, there was a large RCNL meeting in Mound Bayou which Lee, an RCNL officer, apparently attended. The first Saturday evening in May, he and Courts met to talk about raising a fund to help Courts and about a written death threat that Lee had received. Telephone threats were common—e.g., "You're number one on a list of people we don't need around here anymore"—but this was the first written threat and it worried them. Courts left around 11 P.M., and even though it was late, the Reverend Lee went to the dry cleaners to pick up his "preaching suit." On his way home, a convertible pulled up behind him, and a shot was fired into his rear tire. As Lee slowed down, the other car pulled parallel and a second shot was fired, tearing away the lower left side of his face. He died on the way to the hospital. The investigating sheriff said that the whole thing had just been an automobile accident, and the lead pellets found in what was left of his jaw were probably dental fillings. No need for an autopsy. Shortly after this, the woman best positioned to see the assailants, a Negro woman, disappeared.

Ten years earlier, a killing of this sort might have been put down as a "traffic fatality," and no word of it would have crossed the county line. By 1955, Delta Blacks were better organized, better connected to concerned audiences outside the state. Negroes trying to use the phones the evening of the killing were told by the operators that all long-distance lines were tied up, so drivers were sent to officials of the NAACP and the RCNL across the state. When the news got to Mound Bayou, Dr. Howard called Congressman Diggs—who had headlined the RCNL rally a few weeks earlier—who called the White House. In Jackson, Medgar Evers, the newly hired state NAACP field secretary, who was to cut his teeth, as one writer put it, on the Lee killing, immediately began gathering material for the national press. When Evers and Ruby Hurley arrived in Belzoni, they found that many Negroes had been terrified by the shooting, but they also found that some were in a vengeful mood.[19] Before the funeral, Aaron Henry, president of the Clarksdale NAACP, was worried about the mood of white people; they typically got mean after a killing. He considered appealing for FBI protection:

> But for one of the first times, protection was not needed. There wasn't a white man on the streets the day of the service, except for members of the press. There was a great turnout of Negroes for the funeral, and this presence of Negroes and absence of whites marked a turning point.[20]

Among the thousand, perhaps two thousand, mourners there were some who felt frankly that it was all the Reverend Lee's fault for making the white folks angry. Most were in a militant mood, though. The size of the turnout forced the services to be held outdoors, where they were interrupted several times by shouts of "He was murdered!" The successful and militant RCNL rally that had been held just a few days before the killing probably helped to stimulate turnout at the funeral. Lee was killed at a moment when Black activists in the Delta were feeling their strength. Belzoni Blacks, to protest the killing, stopped spending money at white stores: "Instead of buying locally they sent orders to Memphis or elsewhere. Whites as well as blacks were beginning to be hurt in Belzoni and some of the loudest-talking Citizens' Council members were renewing their credit arrangements with Negroes—when nobody was looking."[21]

Gus Courts, then about sixty-five years of age, wouldn't back down. The day after Lee was killed, a Percy Ford of the Citizens' Council had warned Courts that he was to be next if he didn't get his name off the registration rolls. Instead, Courts led twenty-two Negroes to the courthouse to ask for ballots. The threats against him continued. When he found that no one would sell him gasoline locally, he got a group of Negroes to start pooling their money to purchase their own filling station. When wind of this got to the white community they started selling him gas again. He was summoned to the local bank and told that he was to be forced out of business. When his term as NAACP president ended, he stepped down and R. W. Reynolds took the job. The threats slowed down for a while, but after Reynolds was run out of town, Courts took the job again. That fall, another member of the Citizens' Council, in what may have been an act of friendship, warned Courts that, unless he was careful, he was going to be taken care of. At one point, Courts wrote the governor, asking for protection. Later, a member of the local Citizens' Council came in, waving the letter, saying, "You see what kind of protection you're going to get?"[22] On a Friday in late November, a car pulled up in front of his store, and he was shot twice, taking shotgun slugs in his left arm and stomach. Despite great loss of blood, Courts refused to be taken to the local hospital and was driven eighty miles to the Negro hospital in Mound Bayou.

The reaction of Mississippi officialdom, like the reaction of the local people in Belzoni, reflected the changing times. The Jackson *Clarion-Ledger* condemned the shooting. The Citizens' Council offered a $250 reward. The local sheriff swore that he was looking under every rock for the perpetrators (who were, he was sure, light-skinned Negroes). The pretense of concern with justice was due largely to fear of federal action: "If they can say that state law has broken down," said Governor Hugh White, "there's no telling how much federal interference might be forced on us."[23] A decade earlier at the Bilbo hearings, local political officials happily told a congressional investigating panel just how they cheated Blacks out of the ballot. They were then so confident that Mississippians ran Mississippi that there was no need for pretense. By the mid-fifties they at least felt a need to lie.

The governor was concerned with more than the Belzoni shootings. The Reverend Lee had been killed in May. In August, Lamar Smith, a sixty-year-old farmer, was killed. Less than two weeks earlier he had voted in a primary, and he had been trying to teach other Negroes how to use absentee ballots so they would not have to expose themselves to violence at the polls. He was shot at ten in the morning on the courthouse lawn in Brookhaven. In the same month, fourteen-year old Emmett Till was kidnapped and murdered. A month later, Elmer Kimbrell, a friend of one of Till's killers, killed Roy Melton, a Negro service station attendant in Glendora. Kimbrell claimed self-defense, but several white witnesses contradicted him.[24] Gus Courts was shot while the trial of the men accused of killing Till was getting worldwide publicity. The Till case attracted the most sustained notice outside the state—Lee's killing was not mentioned in the *New York Times* until two weeks after it happened—but the NAACP agitated in Washington and elsewhere about all the killings, publishing a booklet titled "M Is For Mississippi and for Murder."

The repression, violent and otherwise, was a substantial setback to the new, more aggressive leadership cadre that had developed among Mississippi Negroes in the postwar years. Courts recovered from the shooting, and his wife and Medgar Evers persuaded him to move to Chicago, where the NAACP helped set him up in business.[25] Dr. C. C. Battle, a friend of both Lee and Courts and an important figure in both the NAACP and the Regional Council, was driven out of the state. Even T. R. M. Howard, the main figure in the Regional Council and a man wealthy enough to have armed guards, left in the wake of the Courts shooting, fearing for the safety of his family after hearing that he was to be killed no later than January first. Courts, Howard, and Battle were all named in an August *Ebony* article as having been on a Klan death list along with the Reverend Lee. A. H. McCoy, also on that list, had his home attacked by gunfire. Of the eight men on the list, by the end of the year only E. J. Stringer, a Columbus dentist; Medgar Evers; and T. V. Johnson, a Belzoni undertaker, were still in the state and still relatively unscathed by the violence. In the previous year, NAACP membership statewide had gone up a staggering fifty percent; after the violence and economic intimidations of the fall, chapters all across the state started falling apart.

The decimation of the leadership is misleading, obscuring the fact that the return on racist violence was actually diminishing. It was no longer possible to kill or drive out every leader. And the people themselves had a different spirit, as shown by the reaction of Belzoni Blacks to the Lee killing—their willingness to show up at his funeral, their boycott of white businesses, the willingness of at least a few to continue pressing the voting issue. Two shootings were required to accomplish what a word from the sheriff would have gotten done in an earlier day. Blacks could still be intimidated but not as easily or as completely as had been the case.

This was true across the Delta in early 1955. The NAACP's Ruby Hurley noted in a report that "The White Citizens' Councils are finding themselves victims of their own plot, however. Merchants known or thought to be members are losing the business of Negroes who oftimes were their mainstay. Money is being withdrawn from banks. . . . The continued increase in NAACP memberships show that WCC does not generate the fear they might have developed a few years ago."[26]

Nor were whites quite as reckless in their use of violence as they might have been in years past. Their initial reliance on economic pressure reflects a desire to find some alternative to violence. They were denying credit and employment to men their fathers would have murdered out of hand. Black leaders forced whites to use violence by refusing to yield to anything less. Thus, the level of white violence is an ironic index of the forcefulness of Black activism. The Belzoni shootings were conducted in a manner that suggested that the perpetrators worried about being caught. The style of the Lamar Smith killing— in broad daylight in a public place, with plenty of witnesses about— is closer to the style of the old days, and that kind of attack had become less common by the mid-fifties. Part of the difference can probably be attributed to the fact that by the 1950s the dominant economic classes among whites were increasingly less dependent upon exploiting Black labor. Had that not been the case, even the specter of federal interference might not have prevented a greater bloodbath.

Rosebud Lee, the Reverend Lee's wife, refused to leave the state, despite the urgings of her friends. She refused to close her grocery store, and she refused to take her name off the registration list. Of her husband she said, "He had all the signs of being somebody, if he had a chance."[27]

The economic pressure that Gus Courts was subjected to was common across the state, much of it orchestrated by the Citizens' Councils. Farmers couldn't get their mortgages renewed. Servants and plantation workers were forced to go to white doctors if the Negro doctor in the area was an activist. White businessmen bought the negotiable paper of Negro leaders and made immediate demands for full payment. Poor people could be denied their surplus food from the federal government.[28]

E. J. Stringer, a veteran and a dentist from Columbus, was president of the state conference of NAACP branches in 1954. Under his energetic leadership membership had risen to twenty-seven hundred, a fifty-percent increase in a year. He paid for it. His liability insurance was canceled, leaving him without the use of a car. His wife, a school-teacher, was fired. Threatening phone calls were routine, as were cars driving slowly and repeatedly past his home at night. Like a number of other activists, he found himself audited by the IRS. (The Councils were consistently able to manipulate federal agencies in Mississippi, including military bases and the FHA.) The Stringers took to sleeping in the middle bedroom of their home, since that room would have been the most difficult to bomb. Stringer remained an NAACP officer, but he decided that one term as state president was enough. "Amid the cynicism of this century," the NAACP's Clarence Mitchell wrote after visiting the Stringers, "one feels humbly respectful in their presence."[29]

No Black person was too high and mighty to be touched by the Council. After visits from representatives of the Council, a prestigious group of Negroes—among them the president of the General Baptist Convention, the president of Mississippi Vocational College, the grand master of the Free Masons, even a vice-president of the Regional Council of Negro Leadership—all signed documents endorsing separate-but-equal education.[30]

Similar tactics were used to fight school desegregation. At the encouragement of NAACP leaders, particularly Medgar Evers, Black parents in at least five cities across the state submitted petitions to their local school boards requesting compliance with the Supreme Court decision. In Yazoo City, where the county annually spent $245 per child on the education of white children and $3 per child on Black children, the local Council, as a public service, ran a newspaper ad with the names, addresses, and telephone numbers of the fifty-three Negroes who had signed in that city. Signers and their spouses lost their jobs; banks and stores refused to deal with them. One man had a hearse sent to his home. Of the fifty-three, fifty-one removed their names from the petition; the other two left the county. Those who had removed their names still couldn't find work. NAACP membership fell from two hundred to sixty-five, and some bitterness against the local NAACP leadership developed within the Negro community. One of the leaders admitted himself that he hadn't known quite what he was getting into. "We expected pressure but not this much. We just weren't prepared for it."[31] It was a period during which each side seemed to catch the other a little off-guard.

College students were not exempt from repression. At Alcorn, a state-supported Black college, 489 of the 561 students walked out of their classes when a professor criticized the NAACP. The president of the college was fired for allowing the walkout, and the students were expelled.[32]

Sociologist Aldon Morris describes what was happening in the South in the late 1950s as a war against the NAACP, a war in which state governments participated along with semi-private groups like the Citizens Council. By the end of 1957, the organization had been legally put out of business in Alabama, the state from which its Deep South operations had been directed. Across the South, the NAACP was involved in twenty-five lawsuits that threatened the ability of the organization to function. Mississippi seems not to have pursued legal harassment as much as did some of the other states, perhaps a reflection of the stronger tradition in that state of more direct action. Between 1955 and 1958, the organization lost 246 southern branches and at least 48,000 members.[33]

Despite repression, Moore and Evers and Aaron Henry, among others, were able to continue functioning. After the 1957 passage of the law requiring that registration applicants interpret any section of the constitution to the satisfaction of the registrar, something that had frequently been required without sanction of law anyway, Moore and Henry, among others, tried to get the Eisenhower administration and various congressmen interested in doing something about disenfranchisement in the state, apparently without much success. At the local level, they mimeographed hundreds of copies of the constitution and set up a citizenship school at a Catholic church in Mound Bayou. (By this time, Moore's own church had been burned.) In that first year, they taught about a hundred and fifty people. Fewer than twenty passed the test, but that was an impressive number for the Delta.

Moore's survival strategies weren't limited to seeking federal intervention. Bayard Rustin, the veteran Black leftist who visited the Delta in the mid-fifties and thought Moore either very brave or very stupid, noted Moore's ability to play the Negro, to adopt the innocent, know-nothing, want-nothing demeanor that whites typically wanted to see in Blacks. At the other extreme, like most politically active Blacks in the Delta, Moore often carried a gun. His home was well armed, and at night the area around his house may have been the best-lit spot in Cleveland. (In 1954, the Mississippi legislature had discussed the alarming pattern of Blacks in the state acquiring guns and ammunition.) He made a point of taking circuitous routes wherever he was going and of not letting anyone know what those routes were going to be. He obviously felt the pressure, but Herman Perry, who worked closely with Moore for nearly thirty years, thought "he had a spirit beyond the average man. You couldn't hardly discourage him."[34]

Moore was also fortunate in that he had a federal job and even more fortunate that the local postmistress was an "extraordinarily good person." After the Emmett Till killing, Till's mother went on a speaking tour, with Cleveland, Tennessee, scheduled to be one stop. Somehow, whites in the Delta got the idea that she was coming to Cleveland, Mississippi, and assumed that nobody would have arranged that but Amzie Moore. According to Herman Perry, a white drugstore owner named Hamp Solomon, a man who "shot niggers like rabbits," came into the post office in a rage, called Amzie a communist, and pulled a gun. The postmistress interceded, yelling that they were on federal property and he couldn't shoot anybody there. Solomon calmed down enough to allow himself to be taken outside.[35]

Despite the relative security of the post office job, Moore could hardly avoid all forms of repression. By 1954, he and his wife Ruth had built a combination service station, beauty shop, and cafe; they also owned some rental property, and he was an agent for a funeral home. He had almost certainly overextended himself on credit. (He had built a brick home, which was considered way out of line for a Negro; he had to purchase the bricks out of town.) After refusing to put a "For Colored Only" sign on his building, he found that no local bank would advance him the credit he needed for operational costs. Suddenly, he could no longer get day-laborer jobs. After the postmistress left, his hours at the post office were reduced. Threats against his life were almost constant. As late as 1964, a reporter visiting Moore would record that Moore received three calls threatening his life in the course of an evening.[36] By that time, his marriage had fallen apart.

Mississippi activists were no longer as isolated as they would have been twenty years earlier. Moore had access to sources of assistance both inside and outside the state. *Jet* magazine and the *Pittsburgh Courier* ran stories soliciting aid for him. At one point, when the bank was about to foreclose on his home, Medgar Evers offered him a loan out of his rather meager salary, but that proved unnecessary when the national NAACP came up with a loan. At various times in the next few years, he was able to get financial assistance from the American Friends Service Committee, Tri-State Bank in Memphis, the National Sharecroppers Fund and a new group called In Friendship, a New York-based group especially concerned with offering financial support to Black activists facing reprisals, particularly in Mississippi and South Carolina. The veteran activist Ella Jo Baker was its executive secretary. In the early 1940s she had been with the NAACP, first as assistant field secretary and later as the national director of branches. In the mid-fifties, she, along with Bayard Rustin and Stanley Levison, both very experienced activists themselves, organized In Friendship. Its style—find someone who is already working and try to support that person—reflected a basic tenet in Ella Baker's politics.[37]

In Friendship was able to raise funds to help Amzie Moore out of the financial difficulties he had gotten himself into. The group also shipped clothing to Ruth and Amzie, which the Moores redistributed to poor families. In Friendship also arranged East Coast speaking engagements for Amzie and others, at which they tried to focus attention on disenfranchisement in the South and the federal role in the process. The relationship between the Moores and Ella Baker grew into a personal one. In a letter addressed to Ruth Moore, Miss Baker wrote:

> May I thank you for the very lovely stay in your home? It meant so much to me to be able to "rest" for a few days. I say rest advisedly because there is not too much difference between your home and

my office as far as the number of calls and requests for information and assistance are concerned.[38]

As it became clear that the Citizens' Councils were taking economic reprisals to a new level, the NAACP began making countermoves. When Medgar Evers came on board as state field secretary at the end of 1954, one of his first charges was to investigate the extent and nature of economic repression and make recommendations. By January 1955, the national office was able to announce the establishment of a war chest at the Black-owned Tri-State Bank in Memphis. With funds deposited by the NAACP and other groups, including organized labor, the bank was able to make loans to some Mississippi activists in danger of losing their homes, farms, or businesses. Within a few months the fund had grown to over a quarter-million dollars. When Mississippi banks saw that people were able to get loans out of state, some of them began making loans again.[39]

In one of her letters to Amzie Moore at the time In Friendship was trying to help him resolve his financial difficulties, Ella Baker notes that it is highly important to find a way to make it possible for him to remain in Mississippi. It is not difficult to follow her reasoning. By staying, he made the point that a Mississippi Negro could take a stand and not be run out of the state, financially ruined, or killed.[40] Moore was aware of the value of this sort of symbolism. When New Hope Baptist church in Cleveland was burned for supporting the movement, Moore immediately launched a fund-raising drive to put up a new structure; "This church," he said, "is a sort of symbol to the people in this region."[41]

In the same way, Moore himself was a symbol to people in the Delta. Every generation of Mississippi Blacks produced a nucleus of people willing to challenge white supremacy. As early as 1889, tenants in Leflore County, led by a man with the historically resonant name of Oliver Cromwell, created the Colored Farmers Alliance, a group willing to take up arms in defense of their rights. They were suppressed by three companies of state militia. Another attempt at organizing in the Delta, the Arkansas-based Progressive Farmers and

Household Union, was put down in 1919. In the late 1930s, the Southern Tenant Farmers Union had some short-lived success in five Black Belt counties, despite the murder of one of its organizers. By 1939 the union claimed three to five hundred members in Mississippi. Although the union tried to stay underground until it had built enough strength to bargain with landowners collectively, it was discovered and the leadership destroyed.[42]

What is different about the 1950s is not the presence of Blacks willing to resist but the fact that as the state became less isolated, politically and economically, as Black organizations like the NAACP and the RCNL became able to draw on a wider range of resources, it was possible for some of these leaders to survive long enough to begin making a difference.

MEDGAR EVERS: LOOKING FOR A WEAPON

If Amzie Moore was a living symbol of resistance to people in the Delta, Medgar Evers had the same meaning to Blacks across the state. Evers dropped out of high school in Decatur, Mississippi, a little sawmill town, to enlist for World War II, serving in France and England with the Red Ball Express. His time in the service made him less tolerant of Mississippi's way of life. He considered not returning to the state at all. He did return, though, and in 1946, at the urging of his brother Charles, also a vet, he helped convince four other young veterans to register, the first Negroes in Decatur to do so. In response, the parents of the Evers brothers were warned repeatedly, first by whites, then by their Negro messengers, that the boys should not try to actually vote. It appears that the boys did not find that out until much later. Come election day, Medgar and the five others held a solitary march to the courthouse. It was solitary because not another Negro in Decatur showed his or her face that morning. Entering the clerk's office, they found fifteen or twenty armed and angry white men, some of them men the Evers boys had grown up with, played ball with. The boys did not vote that day, after all.[43] That the Evers brothers would try to vote and that their parents would refuse to yield to threats is consistent with their family traditions. They were a farm family—poor but not destitute, Evers used to say—a very religious family, and a family that thought of itself as heirs to a fighting tradition. Medgar's great-grandfather had once killed two white men and left town before anything could be done about it. Medgar's father, who could neither read nor write, refused to participate in the local custom of stepping off the sidewalk when a white person approached. He once used a broken pop bottle to face down two white men over a disputed bill, an incident both Medgar and Charles witnessed. All of his life, Medgar seemed to be deeply frustrated by the inability of other Black men to be the man his father was. The timidity of Black people was as likely to send him into a towering rage as the viciousness of whites.

Decatur was no place for the timid. It was a popular Saturday evening sport for young white men to ride around looking for a Negro to run down with their cars. Evers was eleven or twelve when a close family friend was lynched, beaten to death at the local fairgrounds by a crowd of white men because he had sassed a white woman. His blood-stained clothes were left on a fence for over a year as a message to Negroes. Small wonder Evers considered staying out of Mississippi.

While in the service, a white lieutenant had encouraged him to think about college. The GI bill made it possible for Medgar to attend Alcorn College, where his charm made it possible for him to win the affection of Myrlie Beasley of Vicksburg, over the strenuous objections of her family. He was too old for her, they thought, and he was a veteran and veterans had a reputation for being wild. Actually, it would have been hard to find a more responsible young man. All of his life he would have a reputation for personal integrity. He neither drank nor smoked, rarely clowned around even with friends, and he was something of a cheapskate, at least on dates. He was a member of the debating team, the campus YMCA, the college choir, the football and track teams, was editor of the campus paper for two years and the yearbook for one, and was president of the junior class. By the time he was a senior, he was making honor-roll grades. It is a record that suggests an energetic person willing to assume leadership. He was also a person who felt very strongly about racial issues. In this period, as Myrlie remembers him, if whites were for it, he was against it.

For the first few years of the marriage, Myrlie was determined to leave the state. Now that he was back, though, Medgar loved it—the fishing and hunting, the friendliness. He saw it as it would be without segregation. In 1952, they moved to Mound Bayou, the all-Black Delta town, where Medgar made a bad living selling insurance for a company owned by the RCNL's T. R. M. Howard.

The work became an education for him. Although he had grown up in a poor family, he was from a hill county, where poverty is very different from the poverty of the Delta. He began returning home with stories "of children without shoes, without proper clothing; of adults with nothing to eat; of sanitary conditions no self-respecting farmer would permit in his pigpen . . . of shacks without windows and doors."[44] The anger that seems to have been a part of him all of his life had two edges—anger at the system for what it did to his people and anger at his people for taking it. He could not understand why sharecroppers could not do more to better their condition: "At least," he would say, "they could keep what they have clean. At least they could refuse to keep their children out of school to pick cotton. My parents never kept me out of school to work for any white man."[45]

He gradually increased his involvement with the NAACP and people in its network. He had never heard of the organization when he first tried to register in Decatur, but he was already a member when he started at Alcorn. In 1952, by the end of his first summer in Mound Bayou, he was organizing NAACP chapters among the small farmers and sharecroppers of the Delta, which eventually led to his helping Gus Courts and George Lee organize the Belzoni chapter.

He seems in this period to have been a man searching for a weapon. While working for the NAACP, he also worked with the Regional Council for Negro Leadership. He was also very impressed with the rebellions against African colonialism, especially that of the Mau-Mau in Kenya, enough so that he thought long and hard about the idea of Negroes engaging in guerrilla warfare in the Delta—not because he had any hope of winning, but because he thought such a campaign might focus the attention of the rest of the country on the injustice of Mississippi. Without that attention, he saw little possibility of change. Myrlie says that Jomo Kenyatta "dominated" his thinking in

1952. Eventually, he just dropped the idea, apparently because he couldn't reconcile it with his religious feelings. He was not, according to his wife, a deeply religious man in any formal sense—he had gotten enough church growing up in Decatur to last him a while—but there were some religious ideas he felt strongly about. Still, when their first child was born in the summer of 1953, Medgar and Myrlie named him Darrell Kenyatta Evers.

If he couldn't start a Mau-Mau rebellion, he could do other things. In late 1953, after hearing E. J. Stringer speak on the need to integrate the University of Mississippi, he decided that what the state really needed was a few more committed Black lawyers. At a point in his life when the family was just barely making it financially, with a new baby—another would be on the way soon—and political commitments that were already keeping him away from home enough to create substantial tension between himself and Myrlie, he decided that he should go to law school, and he decided further that the law school that would be best for him would be that of the University of Mississippi. In January 1954, over the protests of his wife and parents, all of whom thought he had finally lost his mind, he filed an application, helped by the NAACP's Thurgood Marshall.

While he was waiting for a response, his father was taken sick. While Medgar was with him in a hospital that used its basement as the Negro ward, a white mob gathered outside, trying to get at a Black youth who had been in a fight with a white man. His father was dying, and he had to listen to the howling of a lynch mob. He was so mad he cried. It proved, he said often, that a Negro in Mississippi could neither live nor die in peace as long as the situation remained as it was. He told this story to everybody who asked him why he worked for the NAACP.

After stalling for nine months, the state was able to reject Medgar's application to Ole Miss on technical grounds. University policy required two letters of recommendation from prominent citizens. Medgar's letters had come from Newton County, where he had grown up rather than from Bolivar County where he was living at the time. That would not do, decided the University, and for good measure, it announced that henceforth applicants would require five letters of recommendation from alumni. The suit had made him famous in the state and threats against his life were more or less constant from that point on.

Evers and the NAACP decided not to push the case further. Instead, in December 1954 he became the NAACP's first field secretary in Mississippi, a liaison between the national office and the state's local branches. Myrlie, who had once felt that she had to compete with the whole state for her husband's time and attention, had grown increasingly supportive of his political commitments. Together they opened an NAACP office in Jackson, the first ever in the state. Myrlie was the secretary. Medgar, who could be a wonderfully square man, insisted that in the office they call one another "Mr." and "Mrs." He started the job in late 1954, just in time for the violence of 1955.

His style was more aggressive than was customary for the NAACP. When Ruby Hurley and Medgar went to investigate the Reverend Lee's killing in May 1955, she noted that "Medgar was brand-new then and had some ideas we had to change." Part of the problem was that "he was anything but nonviolent." When she noticed an unmarked sheriff's car following them she didn't say anything to him, "because I was afraid he might stop and ask the man what he was following us for."[46]

It's actually misleading to say that he was not nonviolent. It is true that he seldom went anywhere without a rifle in the trunk of his car—CORE's Dave Dennis used to tease him, "If something happens, how are you going to get to the rifle in time?" It is true that he kept guns all over the house. Even Myrlie kept one by her bedside. If he was willing to defend himself, though, he could also have a patience with the worst racists that never failed to amaze his wife. She recalls that there were times when hate calls were so frequent that there was no point in hanging up on them. If you did, another call would come in a few minutes; it was better to just put the receiver down and let the callers spew their threats into the air. Once, though, she snapped and told the caller, a drunken woman full of talk about niggers and their low morals, to go to hell. Medgar, listening on an extension, told Myrlie to hang up and he then began a long, rambling conversation with the woman and eventually her husband about their racial attitudes.

Before it ended, they were almost cordial. He scolded Myrlie afterwards: "If you can't take it, just put the phone down. But don't curse at them. You can sometimes win them over if you are just patient enough." As Gandhi understood it, what underlies the nonviolent attitude is a confidence that your ugliest enemy can change, and that confidence Medgar had.[47]

He had his buttons, though. Myrlie recalls only twice seeing him in nearly uncontrollable rage, and both incidents say something about his sense of pride. The first involved nothing more than seeing a Black woman kissing a white man in a parked car. After he and Myrlie got home, Evers, who seldom cursed, cursed the woman, called her all kinds of slut, and muttered about getting a gun and blasting both of them. When Myrlie, puzzled and frightened by the strength of his reaction, tried to point out that what that woman did was none of his business, he responded that she was lowering herself to make love to a white man and was a traitor to her race. It was that lack of racial pride that he was reacting to. The other incident involved a young Black couple who came to the Jackson NAACP. The woman was a domestic in a white household; the man of the house had raped her that day. After he heard the story, Medgar wanted to go right down to the police station and file charges, but the young woman's husband refused, saying it was pointless. The police weren't going to do anything, he and his wife would both lose their jobs, and maybe worse. There was nothing to be done. That made absolutely no sense to Medgar. At the very least, he fumed, you can try to make the police do something, you can expose the man as a rapist. What you can't do is do nothing. In a cold rage, Evers told the youth he was less than a man, saying the words so that they had the ring of a curse.[48]

For a man who couldn't stand timidity, living among Jackson's Black middle class must have been a special torment. Schoolteachers, who had profited from the NAACP's push to equalize school expenditures, particularly irked him. In 1958, he told an interviewer:

> As much good as the NAACP has done to make the opportunities greater for teachers who once made $20 a month and are making up to $5,000 [a year] now, we don't get their cooperation. The pro-

fessionals are the same way. Only in isolated cases do they go all out to help us. Some ministers are almost in the same category. . . . [They] won't give us 50 cents for fear of losing face with the white man.

The same interviewer described Evers's working style:

On introduction, Evers may make "small talk" but before long, he inevitably swings into question and answer. Are you a registered voter, sir? Would you mind saying why you haven't registered? Do you feel you should take advantage of the ballot (in areas where there is no voting difficulty)? . . . Then, switching his theme, he will ask, bluntly, "Are you an NAACP member . . . familiar with the work of the organization . . . like to know more about it?" His personal contact is sometimes a slow process, but it gets results.[49]

Myrlie Evers writes that she remembers the fifties by the names of the victims—1956, Ed Duckworth shot to death, Milton Russell burned; 1957, Charles Brown killed in Yazoo City; 1958, George Love killed by a posse, Woodrow Wilson beaten to death by a sheriff; 1959, Jonas Causey killed in Clarksdale, William Roy Prather, a teenager, killed in a Halloween prank, Mack Charles Parker dragged from a jail cell and lynched, his body thrown into the Pearl River. Myrlie remembers seeing Medgar "sit and just pound the desk or the chair or whatever . . . in utter despair and grief and anger that these people's lives had been snuffed out like this."[50]

It was fortunate that he was a workaholic. He was responsible for getting victims and witnesses to testify and file suit; for getting them out of the state if necessary; finding them attorneys; getting out the publicity; pressuring federal agencies; documenting the poverty; finding clothing, shelter, and jobs for those who had been evicted or fired or for those who were just plain poor, heartening local leaders around the state and patching over the ongoing internal feuds among them; investigating all the cases of crimes against Negroes that the police and FBI were unwilling to investigate.[51]

One of his first cases attracted international attention. Emmett Till, a fourteen-year-old Negro from Chicago, was visiting his relatives in the Delta. On a dare from other youngsters, he went into a grocery store and smart-mouthed the white woman proprietor, saying something like "Bye, Baby" as he left.[52] Four nights later, with a boldness reminiscent of earlier years, two white men went to the home of his relatives, dragged Emmett outside, pistol-whipped him, shot him, and dumped the body into the Tallahatchie River. After two trials and two acquittals, the accused men gave *Look* magazine a detailed story on how they had done the killing. The killing and the trials aroused an unprecedented level of protests across the country; no lynching in history had received comparable publicity. Amzie Moore and Medgar Evers both searched for witnesses and took reporters around the Delta.

The Till case is interesting in at least two respects. First, the national reaction illustrates again that Mississippi was becoming less isolated, and the fact that Mississippi bothered with even a sham trial again suggests that whites in Mississippi were worried about the implications of the change. Amzie Moore said, "When a white man was openly tried for lynching a black boy, you know that hadn't happened in our memory."[53] Second, a number of observers, Moore among them, felt that the Till case represented a major turning point in Mississippi. Blacks in Mississippi reacted defiantly. Angry crowds of Negroes gathered at the trial, and some of them were carrying weapons. Amzie Moore always dated the beginning of the modern movement in Mississippi from that time, not from the 1954 Supreme Court decision. Ruby Hurley claimed that the Till killing led to an increase in regional NAACP membership.[54]

Joyce Ladner, a Mississippian who joined SNCC in the early 1960s, refers to herself and other young Black people in the state who came of age in the late 1950s as the Till generation. "I can name you ten SNCC workers who saw that picture [of Till's body] in *Jet* magazine, who remember it as the key thing about their youth that was emblazoned in their minds . . . One of them told me how they saw it and thought that one day they would avenge his death."

Twelve years old herself at the time of the killing, she daydreamed about growing up and having sons who would do something about the situation in Mississippi. "Back then little girls didn't dream of being doctors or lawyers or senators. I was going to have these kids, and my four sons were going to right all these wrongs."[55]

During the latter years of the decade, it looked as if the righting of wrongs was a long way off. One of the most frustrating cases Evers had to deal with was that of Clyde Kennard.[56] A paratrooper who served in Germany and Korea before studying at the University of Chicago, Kennard returned to his native Hattiesburg in 1955, when his stepfather became disabled. He wanted to finish college, but with his stepfather hurt and a chicken farm to run, he couldn't travel very far. The only local school was white Mississippi Southern College, and Kennard applied there. Although he had worked with the NAACP, Kennard did not see his application as some sort of crusade. He very pointedly rejected the help of the NAACP lawyers, thinking that if he made it clear that he was no militant, that he was willing to be patient and cooperative, the logic of his case would eventually win out. Instead, after a long period of negotiations with state officials, Kennard was accused of stealing $25 worth of chicken feed, for which he was sentenced to seven years in prison. Even some Mississippi newspapers commented on the harshness of the sentence. While NAACP lawyers appealed and Evers orchestrated a publicity campaign, Kennard was found to have cancer—but that did not excuse him from hard labor in the prison. In 1963, when Kennard had served about three years, Governor Ross Barnett, under mounting pressure, suspended his sentence. Kennard died shortly after his release.

Trying to tell Kennard's story at an NAACP banquet about a year after the sentencing, Evers broke down in tears three times before he could give his talk. This case was special because Evers knew and respected Kennard and because the case dragged on over so many years. Still, it was only one case among many.

In the second half of the decade, there seemed to be far more defeats than victories. As late as mid-1955 it was still possible to get Black parents to file local school-desegregation suits. Just a few months later, that was considered so futile that many NAACP officials decided to concentrate on voter-registration drives. Changes in state law, though, made registration more difficult as well. Many of the NAACP branches that had been organized in the first few years of the decade had fallen apart, and Evers had to set about the task of re-organizing them. From Evers's position, the future may not have seemed as bright from the vantage point of 1959 as it had in 1954 when he took the job.

AARON HENRY: THE SCIENCE OF WHITE FOLKS

Aaron Henry was another veteran of World War II who came home determined to do something. During the fifties, at least, Henry's activism had an almost charmed quality about it. Considering how much trouble he was making for white folks, he didn't suffer reprisals as severe as one might have expected, something he commented upon himself. Why this was so is not exactly clear, but it may have been connected to the fact that Henry was a particularly keen student of the Ways of White Folks. Any Black youngster growing up in the Delta of the thirties and forties was well advised to pay attention to the customs and foibles of whites but Henry seems to have made a science of it. He knew just how far he could push, when to back off, when to start pushing again.[57]

He grew up in a Delta sharecropping family, but his father learned cobbling, moved to town and did relatively well. "Town" meant Clarksdale, near the northern end of the Delta. Famous for the blues musicians it produced, Clarksdale was, by Delta standards, somewhat liberal. The Klan was not very active in the area. Along with Greenville, Vicksburg, and Jackson, it was one of the areas where there had been a history of Black and Tan Republicanism. Because of that history, a handful of Clarksdale Negroes were allowed to vote in national elections.

His relationships with whites ran the gamut. For a while, his best friend was a white boy, "Tut" Patterson. They remained friendly even after they passed the age when Black and white youth normally separated. In high school, Henry clerked in a motor inn, a job that allowed him to see the seamier side of life among the white and privileged. He was something of a pet of the inn's owner, who allowed him privileges Black boys didn't often get. In fact, he was so obviously favored by the owner that it often angered other whites, so Henry had to learn to be careful not to antagonize them further. The inn's owner encouraged Henry to go to college.

Growing up, Henry knew some very progressive Black adults. Clarksdale boasted one of the state's few high schools for Blacks, and many of the teachers were members of the NAACP—at-large members, since there was no nearby chapter. Henry cites one of them, Thelma Shelby, as the largest single influence pushing him toward civil rights. She was a young teacher—she could even jitterbug—devoted to her students, setting high academic standards for them, all the while introducing them to the NAACP line. In Henry's senior year, she got the whole senior class to join the NAACP.

After service, Henry returned to Clarksdale in 1946. While he had been gone, a Progressive Voters League had formed to work for the implementation of the 1944 Supreme Court decision overturning the all-white primary. As soon as he got home, he tried to register and to get other veterans to do so. Veterans were exempted from paying poll taxes. Three times, he tried to register, and three times the registrar told him he just didn't know anything about any such exemption. Henry was able to get a white veteran to come show his exemption certificate, after which the registrar gave up and let him register. He became the first Negro in Coahoma County to vote in a Democratic primary. Characteristically, Henry wrote the registrar a thank-you letter.

After attending pharmacy school in New Orleans, he returned to Clarksdale in 1950. About a year later, there was a racial incident that led to the formation of a local chapter of the NAACP. Two white men forced two Negro girls into a car at gunpoint, drove them to a deserted area just outside of town, and raped them. The white men were arrested but argued that the girls had consented. The justice of the peace believed them, and the men were acquitted. An angry meeting of the Voters League followed. Both of the victims and at least one of the fathers, who was fearful of losing his job at the cotton compress, wanted to just drop the matter. Henry and many others argued they couldn't ignore it, that they at least had to try for an indictment. They actually managed to find a local lawyer, one of the most liberal men in town, who would take the case, but he wanted the staggering sum of $2,000. They scraped the money together, and the lawyer actually managed to get an indictment. That was as far as they got, though; there was no conviction, and some Negroes were not sure their expensive lawyer argued the case very well. The incident made a number of people feel they needed the NAACP in town for the legal protection it offered. There were already several local members, including the high-school principal and most of the high-school teachers. Henry was elected president in 1954, and he quickly built one of the largest chapters in the state. One of the strongest members of the branch was Medgar Evers. The formation of the chapter drew very little white reaction, which Henry attributed to whites feeling that the system was so firmly entrenched that nothing could change it.

For the same reason, it was possible for Henry to have several close personal relationships with whites. He opened his own drugstore in partnership with a white man. It was a partnership that worked; his white partner never tried to take advantage on the basis of race and tried to speak up for Henry when Henry's NAACP work irritated other whites.

One such occasion involved Denzill Turner. Turner, a Black man in his twenties, was an epileptic. He was at the bus station with his father one day when he had a seizure. Several whites thought he was just drunk. After he recovered, confused, angry words were exchanged between Denzill and a white bus-station employee. The police were called. When Denzill tried to break away from them, they caught him, and while two officers were holding him a third officer put a bullet through his head. Aaron Henry protested to no effect. In a meeting with the mayor he argued so forcefully that someone decided he must be a communist, because only communists argued like that. Henry's business partner spoke up for him: "Hell, y'all are crazy. That boy ain't never seen a communist. He ain't never been North of Memphis."[58] The FBI were called in, and they too decided that Henry wasn't much of a communist threat.

Like Moore and Evers, Henry worked with the RCNL as well as the NAACP. Henry had become friends with T. R. M. Howard soon after returning to Clarksdale. Dr. Howard wrote many a prescription for Henry's store. At the first official RCNL meeting, Henry was elected secretary and Evers program director. Henry also headed the "separate but equal" committee, which among other things tried to make sure that Blacks got their fair share of every federal dollar coming into the state. As the RCNL became more active in voter-registration activities, white opposition was generally unorganized and ineffectual. In fact, the general white population often never knew that protests were going on. Newspapers and radio barely noticed them, even when there were rallies of thousands of people. Around Clarksdale in particular, white people were used to Negroes complaining. In areas where whites were complacent about it, RCNL made the most progress with registration. These tended to be the same areas of the state that had the strongest traditions of Black and Tan Republicans, so there was a pool of people who understood registration procedures and weren't afraid. In areas where there had been little previous protest or registration activity, RCNL caused quite a stir. In general, Henry felt that the result of the early-fifties work of the RCNL was that good areas got better but bad ones got worse.

After the Supreme Court's *Brown v. Board of Education* decision, Henry was among those who thought that since it was the law of the land, people would come around in time, if they weren't pressed too hard. This time, Henry had underestimated the opposition. In Clarksdale, he led an effort that got four hundred Negroes to request the desegregation of local schools. Having underestimated the opposition, they made the mistake of not using "hardened" names, people already conditioned to some level of threat. As elsewhere in the state, those who signed the petition were hit with reprisals they weren't ready for, and most wound up withdrawing their names.

After he came out in support of *Brown,* Henry found that he could no longer borrow money from his white friends. He also had some threats on his life, and there were times when his NAACP chapter thought it best to keep a system of rotating armed guards at his home. But on the whole, during the fifties he didn't suffer the level of threat and reprisals other leaders around the state were enduring. It's not likely that the relative liberalism of the Clarksdale area explains the difference. When Negroes got as far out of line as Henry had, Clarksdale was perfectly capable of responding with violence. There is no way to be certain, but Henry's ability to maintain very cordial personal relations with people who were his political enemies may have softened, temporarily, the response of white leadership to his defiance.

Henry's successful leadership of the Coahoma County NAACP branch made him an increasingly important figure statewide. By 1954, he was state NAACP secretary; by 1955, a state vice-president, and after the mid-fifties, he was becoming a player on the national scene, going to Washington, sometimes with Evers, to lobby for NAACP legislation. Henry's friendship with Evers was a part of what led him to run for the presidency of the state conference of NAACP branches. By 1957, Evers and state president C. R. Darden of Meridian were not getting along well. At a time when the organization was fighting to survive in Mississippi, their feuding was potentially destructive. Henry decided to run for the presidency, which he won in 1960. By the end of the decade, Henry was the closest thing there was to an official head of the resistance movement in Mississippi. Ironically, Robert Patterson, his white boyhood companion, had grown up to found the White Citizens Council, so the decade ended with the state's progressive and reactionary forces headed by two men who had once been as close as brothers, an apt symbol of the complexity of racial politics in Mississippi.[59]

In 1958, there was a slight increase in NAACP membership statewide and a decided one in those areas where the local branch was well-enough organized to have a membership drive. By 1959, Black registration in the state, which had sunk to 8,000 a few years earlier, had crept back up to 15,000. NAACP youth chapters were starting across the state, usually organized by Evers, himself only in his early thirties and particularly popular with young people. Several of the adult branches that had been put out of business had re-formed. Around Jackson, there had even been two cases in which Black voting strength had been sufficient to vote out two particularly vicious racists.[60] The indigenous movement had survived the decade. Merely by enduring the decade without retreating from their activism, continuing to test and probe, the leaders demonstrated that something had changed, encouraging others, especially young people, to think about themselves as possible agents of further change. One very important part of their legacy is that they were able to draw many such young people into leadership. Another is that through their efforts they had created networks among activists across the state, networks that could facilitate the work of another generation.

With some differences among them, Moore, Evers, and Henry were all open to working with organizations other than the NAACP, despite the clear disapproval of the national office. Evers, with his willingness to think seriously about guerrilla warfare, may have been the most eclectic, but all three of them played important roles in the Regional Council of Negro Leadership, an organization quite despised by the national NAACP. In 1957, he had been invited to attend one of the early meetings of the Southern Christian Leadership Conference (SCLC) and was elected assistant secretary of that organization, a post he resigned reluctantly when the national office of the NAACP indicated that they thought it raised conflict-of-interest problems. Later, he would become a critic of SCLC's style of work, thinking they put too much emphasis on mobilizing a community to precipitate a crisis and win concessions, and then moving on leaving the local organization to collapse. Nevertheless, when the pace of activity in Mississippi picked up in 1963 and Dr. King expressed an interest in coming into the state, but only if invited, Evers favored extending the invitation. The national office discouraged it, and he acquiesced.[61] Aaron Henry, however, did become an active member of the SCLC Board, and since he was not on the NAACP payroll there was not a great deal anyone could do about that.

The heightening of movement activity in the state after 1961 created a crisis of sorts for many of the older leaders. Evers initially turned a rather hostile face toward the outside organizations, but eventually, for a man who valued determination above all else, it was difficult not to admire some of the young people. According to Myrlie, "when the students came along with their spontaneity, with their willingness to be heard and to strike back if necessary, I think it was a kind of turning point for Medgar." He eventually came to think that maybe their methods made more sense than the old, gradual ones. When he asked the national office for permission to endorse sit-ins and demonstrations, he was turned down; as a result, Myrlie says:

Medgar had some difficult days trying to decide whether he should actually remain with the NAACP or not. The NAACP was more than an organization; it was a family, people who worked very closely together and loved each other. But he also realized that things were changing and the organization had to move along with it.[62]

At the same time, he faced the problem of SNCC and the Congress of Racial Equality (CORE) organizing a town by raiding the NAACP membership, probably while disparaging the timidity and rigidity of the NAACP.

One answer was a coalition. The basis for coalition had been laid earlier. In the summer of 1961, a number of Black groups had gotten together to seek a meeting with Governor Ross Barnett. In order to present a united front, they formed the Council of Federated Organizations (COFO). The organization was restarted in 1962, and SNCC and CORE were pulled into it. Evers, Moore, and Henry all played important roles in forming the coalition, and Henry became its president. SNCC was represented by Bob Moses, and CORE, which worked in the southeastern part of the state, by David Dennis. COFO became the organizational vehicle that allowed the younger activists to exploit the networks built at such cost by the older ones. Had the veteran Mississippi activists, with their credibility and contacts, taken the stance toward the other groups that the national organization consistently took, the movement of the sixties would have had more difficulty establishing itself. Instead, they chose to legitimate the outsiders.[63]

Early SNCC workers were well aware of their indebtedness to the older generation. Lawrence Guyot, a SNCC field secretary, says:

> We needed a person to provide contacts on a local basis, to provide an entree for us into the counties and that person was Amzie Moore. We met at his house, we stayed at his house. He had a hell of a network of individuals throughout the state and had had it for years. Whenever anyone was threatened, Amzie Moore was sort of an individual protection agency.

Similarly, Charles Cobb, another Mississippi field secretary says Amzie Moore "was central to SNCC's work in the Delta. . . . It was a place you could stay. It was a telephone number you could leave messages at in the Delta, and it was he who identified the people throughout the Delta who would be sympathetic."[64]

Sam Block, who in 1962 became the first SNCC organizer sent into Greenwood, commented on the relationship between Moore and Bob Moses, director of SNCC activities in the state:

> They understood each other. Their ideologies were the same. I think that Amzie served as a teacher to Bob. . . . [Amzie] was well traveled throughout the state of Mississippi because of his activities with the NAACP. He knew people in areas and could get Bob into doors that Bob could not have gotten into himself. Anytime he had a question that he couldn't deal with, he would call Amzie. Amzie Moore was really the father of the movement.

In her discussion of the 1960s resurgence of feminism, Jo Freeman places great emphasis on the role of existing communications networks, contending that the rapid spread of a movement is often possible only where such networks can be exploited.[65] Not all networks are equally valuable. They must be "cooptable" networks, she argues, composed of like-minded individuals predisposed by virtue of their background to being receptive to the ideas of a new movement.[66] Mississippi's older activists created such cooptable networks, and a younger generation found new uses for them.

The older leaders also helped to mold the next generation, self-consciously looking for and grooming younger people who might play leadership roles. SNCC's Sam Block, for example, grew up in Cleveland, not far from Amzie Moore's home. Block recalled that he used to like to go talk politics with Moore, "a man that I really respected because he was the only person in Cleveland who was really addressing the issues."[67] Thus, when SCLC and SNCC organizers started looking for young local people to work with them, Moore knew that Block would be a likely candidate.

This was a common pattern of recruitment into the movement. In the 1960s the Ladner sisters, Dorie and Joyce, were asked to leave Jackson State College because of their activism. They transferred to the more receptive atmosphere at Tougaloo. Subsequently, Dorie dropped out of school three times to work for SNCC, Joyce dropped out once, and both did movement work when they were in school. In the late 1950s, they were teenagers growing up in Hattiesburg, and they grew up surrounded by models of commitment. They were close to three men—Evers, Clyde Kennard, and Vernon Dahmer—who would be martyred by the late sixties.

Around 1958 an NAACP youth chapter formed in Hattiesburg with the assistance of Evers and Vernon Dahmer, a man who had been politically active at least since the early 1950s, when he had filed suit against the sheriff of Forrest County for preventing Negroes from registering. Dahmer's family was close to the Ladner family. He was a gregarious, outgoing man, so light-skinned he could have passed for white. Clyde Kennard, who also worked with the youth group, was just the opposite—he was always smiling but hardly ever said a word. When he did talk, people paid attention. Joyce had a schoolgirl's crush on him. Kennard and Dahmer used to take the girls to mass rallies in Jackson. Joyce remembers:

> I'd get to these mass meetings and say "God!! All these people!"
> From all over Mississippi, from Greenwood and Clarksdale, NAACP
> people. I used to wonder, "Do the police know that we're meeting?"
> . . . But it was just wonderful for a teenager to be able to go to
> these places, to be exposed to these people. Just an extraordinary experience.

Another friend of the family, Dr. McCloud, also an NAACP activist, used to come visit the family, bringing copies of *Jet, Ebony,* or the *Chicago Defender,* talking about their responsibility to carry on the race, uplift the race. People like McCloud and the people the girls met at mass meetings were quite a contrast to most of the adults the girls knew. Joyce described being "surrounded by a lot of mealy-mouthed people, teachers, principals who were scared of their shadow. And then there was this handful of others."

Her sister Dorie thinks those relationships with older activists were remarkable. "We were fifteen, sixteen, seventeen years old, and they were taking up time with us to try and teach us. . . . I wonder how they got the patience and the interest to work with young people. . . . I feel very good about those early people, all of whom were males . . . who took this interest and helped to develop my insight and gave me this guidance."

Sam Block wasn't the only young man living in Cleveland whose political growth was affected by Amzie Moore. Several young men who were politically active in the 1960s and 1970s—Beverly Perkins, Homer Crawford, B. L. Bell—attribute their political awakening to Moore. Bell, for example, cut grass for Amzie in the 1940s, and Amzie used to let him look at his World War II scrapbooks and talk about what he had learned during the war. Like other young people, he was struck by Moore's apparent fearlessness but was even more impressed by his moral standards. Moore didn't womanize, drink, or gamble, and he was an intellectual. Growing up, Bell knew lots of outwardly religious men, but Amzie Moore seemed more consistent about his faith than some. Some of the older activists were self-consciously trying to encourage youngsters to grow up thinking about their role in making change—a deliberate laying-on of hands.

Ruby Hurley's position as regional representative for the NAACP meant that she probably knew local leadership in the Deep South as well as anyone. Of the people she began working with in the early fifties, she said, "I would dare say that none of them thought of themselves as being brave."[68] She does not say that they were not brave, but rather that they didn't think of themselves that way, that their own bravery wasn't central to their definition of self. She saw their lives more fully than we can. Medgar Evers in college was a member of the debating team, the YMCA, the choir, the football and track teams, was editor of the campus paper and president of the junior class. Over the course of his life, Amzie Moore held important positions with more than a dozen organizations concerned directly with civil rights and poverty, but he was also always involved with gospel singing groups, helped start what he thought was the first Black Boy Scout troop in the Delta, and served for a long time on the board of the area's only Black hospital. Henry, in addition to his long list of civil rights memberships, was an Elk, a Mason, and a leader in the local PTA. A case could be made that these were men with an expansive sense of civic involvement and civic responsibility, whose civil rights activism was just one part of that. The courage that seems so central from our perspective may actually have been only peripheral to larger concerns for them.

In many respects, Moore and Evers and Henry typify a generation of leadership that historian John Dittmer describes as largely male, relatively well educated, frequently veterans, and ordinarily associated with the NAACP.[69] They and the others—C. C. Battle, T. R. M. Howard, Clyde Kennard, Vernon Dahmer, E. J. Stringer, W. A. Bender, Gus Courts, George Lee, Winnie Hudson, E. W. Steptoe, Herbert Lee, A. H. McCoy, C. C. Bryant, T. V. Johnson—most of whom came of age before or during the Second World War, took advantage of changing postwar economic and political conditions to increase, at least temporarily, the pace and intensity of Black activism. With racial terrorism somewhat more restrained than it had been, with a greater chance of drawing on political and economic resources from outside the state (the national press, In Friendship, the national NAACP, Tri-State Bank in Memphis, the Justice Department, for what it was worth) they were able to push white supremacy further than it had ever been pushed before, and when it pushed back they were able, as a leadership cadre, to survive. More, to an extent that they themselves probably did not realize in 1959, postwar activists had laid much of the groundwork for a rapid shift in momentum. Back in 1955, the worst year of the decade, one of the Belzoni NAACP members who had worked with Gus Courts and the Reverend Lee said, just after Courts was shot:

> Sure, things like this make folks more scared. But this is my home. I just don't feel like running. . . . The situation here is just like one of those big balloons. One sharp little something could prick it and Bam!![70]

Three

GIVE LIGHT AND THE PEOPLE
WILL FIND A WAY

The Roots of an Organizing Tradition

*I believe in the right of people to expect those who are older, those who
claim to have had more experience, to help them grow.*

ELLA BAKER

*We have plenty of men and women who can teach what they know; we
have very few who can teach their own capacity to learn.*

JOSEPH HART[1]

IF SOME BLACK ACTIVISTS working in the South prior to the 1960s
left an organizational heritage, others left a distinct philosophical heritage. Leadership among southern Blacks—in churches, on college
campuses, within families—has frequently leaned toward the authori-
tarian. Taken as a group, Mississippi's Black activists before the 1960s
reflected that traditional conception of leadership. They were shep-
herds; the people were to be cared for. Many of them liked being in
charge and did not easily share authority, which led to some intramu-
ral squabbling among them when they should have been fighting the
white folks.[2] At the same time, other activists across the South were
evolving a philosophy of collective leadership. More than any other
individual, Ella Jo Baker was responsible for transferring some of
those ideas to the young militants of SNCC, but a number of experi-

enced southern activists held ideas similar to hers, and some of them also influenced SNCC directly or indirectly. If people like Amzie Moore and Medgar Evers and Aaron Henry tested the limits of repression, people like Septima Clark and Ella Baker and Myles Horton tested another set of limits, the limits on the ability of the oppressed to participate in the reshaping of their own lives.

Generalizing about the beliefs of these people risks oversimplifying them.[3] The safest thing to say is that all of them had an expansive sense of the possibilities of democracy—an unrealistic sense of the possibilities, their critics would say. Highlander's statement of purpose, drafted by Mrs. Clark, speaks of "broadening the scope of democracy to include everyone and deepening the concept to include every relationship." Including everyone in democracy meant that the common assumption that poor people had to be led by their social betters was anathema. All three espoused a non-bureaucratic style of work, focused on local problems, sensitive to the social structure of local communities, appreciative of the culture of those communities. Above all else, perhaps, they stressed a developmental style of politics, one in which the important thing was the development of efficacy in those most affected by a problem. Over the long term, whether a community achieved this or that tactical objective was likely to matter less than whether the people in it came to see themselves as having the right and the capacity to have some say-so in their own lives. Getting people to feel that way requires participatory political and educational activities, in which the people themselves have a part in defining the problems—"Start where the people are"—and solving them. Not even organizations founded in the name of the poor can be relied upon. In the end, people have to learn to rely on themselves.

SEPTIMA CLARK AND MYLES HORTON:
DISCOVERING LOCAL LEADERSHIP

Septima Clark of South Carolina is best remembered for the Citizenship Schools she developed in conjunction with the Highlander Folk School. Born in 1898, her first name means "sufficient" in her mother's native Haiti.[4] She grew up in Charleston, where her mother was a washerwoman, her father a cook. In 1916, although she had only had the equivalent of two years of college—her parents could not afford more—she passed the teachers' examination. Since Black teachers could not teach in the public schools, she got a job on Johns Island, just off the coast from Charleston, where she and another teacher were responsible for 132 children of all ages. Johns is the largest of the Sea Islands, the coastal islands that traditionally have had Black-majority populations isolated from mainland culture. Most islanders lived a subsistence existence, even though many were landowners. Conditions on the island were primitive. There was little to do after work, so Septima started to spend part of her evenings teaching adults to read, just to occupy some time. She had few teaching materials and got into the habit of developing her own. In place of a blackboard, they used large drycleaner bags on which students wrote stories about their daily lives.

In 1918 someone came to the island talking about the NAACP, and she joined. In 1919 she returned to Charleston to teach in a private academy for Black children. With other NAACP members, she took part in a successful petition campaign to change the policy that prevented Black teachers from working in Charleston's public schools. Eventually hired by the Charleston schools herself, she continued working with the NAACP and a number of other civic groups including the YWCA. Working with these groups eventually brought her into contact with federal judge Waties Waring, arguably the most hated man in Charleston by the late 1940s. The product of eight generations of Charleston aristocracy, the son of a Confederate veteran, Waring had married an outspoken Yankee woman, had ruled that Black and white teachers had to receive the same pay, and in 1947 had ruled that Blacks could not be excluded from the Democratic primary. He let it be known that anyone trying to interfere with Black voters could expect to spend a long time in jail. On the day of the first election after his ruling he spent the day in court waiting, just in case anyone started trouble. After Mrs. Waring gave a speech at the Y in which she characterized anyone who supported white supremacy as mentally ill and morally defective, Mrs. Clark, who had been pressured to cancel the talk, became a friend of the Warings, a friendship that so frightened the other teachers at Clark's school that they devoted part of a faculty meeting to trying to convince her not to associate with the Warings.[5]

In 1953 a coworker at the Y, looking for someplace in the South where Blacks and whites could meet together, went to the Highlander Folk School in the Tennessee mountains and came back telling Septima that she had to go see the place herself. Highlander was indeed worth seeing. Highlander is what sociologist Aldon Morris calls a movement halfway house, his term for change-oriented institutions, lacking a mass base themselves, that bring together a range of key resources—skilled activists, tactical knowledge, training techniques, networks of valuable contacts.[6] It was not the communist training school the authorities assumed it to be, but it was a school for social activists.

Highlander was cofounded during the Depression by Myles Horton, who had grown up in a poor white sharecropping family in Tennessee. Horton saw Highlander as a school for the poor of Appalachia, "dedicated to developing its students' capacities for both individual and collective self-determination," a place where the "learned helplessness" of the poor would be replaced with a willingness to take more control over their own lives.[7] In the 1930s, it organized and taught coal miners, millhands, timber cutters, and small farmers. Later the school was heavily involved in training labor organizers, as CIO industrial unions penetrated the South (an often uneasy relationship, given the differences in values between Highlander and the CIO). In the 1950s it became a very important meeting place and training center for civil rights leaders at all levels. Almost from its beginning, defying state law saying that Blacks and whites could neither eat together nor sleep in the same building, Highlander's philosophy was interracial, a philosophy that frequently generated as much initial discomfort for Black visitors as for white ones. Many visitors testified that the experience of egalitarian living in an interracial situation had greater impact on them than the courses and workshops.

Highlander's work was guided by the belief that the oppressed themselves, collectively, already have much of the knowledge needed to produce change: "If they only knew how to analyze what their experiences were, what they know and generalize them . . . they would begin to draw on their own resources."[8] Thus, much of the burden of change is on the oppressed themselves.

Workshops at Highlander brought local leaders together to share experiences and to develop techniques that would, in the ideal cases, allow them to return home and develop the leadership potential of others. The emphasis on developing others was crucial to Highlander's conception of leadership. According to Horton: "We debunk the leadership role of going back and telling people and providing the thinking for them. We aren't into that. We're into people who can help other people develop and provide educational leadership and ideas, but at the same time, bring people along."[9]

Highlander was also committed to a vision of change that respected the culture of the people with whom they were working. People need something for the spirit and soul. Music and singing were an integral part of the Highlander experience. Horton's first wife, Zilphia, played a particularly important role in preserving the music of the people Highlander worked with and in providing the music that helped give Highlander workshops their emotional definition. In later years a similar role would be played by Guy and Candie Carawan. It is not accidental that "We Shall Overcome" was introduced to the modern civil rights movement at Highlander workshops.[10]

Many people who were to become well-known civil rights leaders—E. D. Nixon and Rosa Parks of Montgomery, James Bevel, Fred Shuttlesworth, C. T. Vivian, Bernard Lafayette, Bernard Lee, Dorothy Cotton, Andy Young, Hosea Williams of SCLC, John Lewis, Bob Zellner, Marion Barry, and Diane Nash of SNCC—attended Highlander workshops, and many of them attended regularly.[11] Mrs. Clark first visited Highlander in 1954, and she became a regular, carrying other people to workshops there and then directing workshops herself. Never a retiring woman, she said her visits to Highlander made her "more vociferous" and "more democratic." She first met Rosa Parks while directing a workshop on leadership. Mrs. Parks, quiet and soft-spoken, was quite a contrast to the more outgoing Mrs. Clark. Mrs. Parks had difficulty believing that she was in an interracial environment where she could safely say whatever she felt. She had been working with the NAACP Youth Council at home and had had some success with the group, enough so that she had begun to get threatening phone calls. She came to Highlander to get more ideas about what she could do with her young people. Highlander workshops often began by asking the participants what they wanted to learn and ended by asking them what they planned to do when they got home. Mrs. Parks wasn't optimistic about the latter. "Rosa answered that question by saying that Montgomery was the cradle of the Confederacy, that nothing would happen there because blacks wouldn't stick together. But she promised to work with those kids." Three months, later, of course, she sparked the Montgomery bus boycott.[12] Septima Clark remembered the 1955 workshop Mrs. Parks attended as a pivotal one. Previously, Negroes had made up only ten to fifteen percent of workshop participants and had tended not to be very outspoken. At this workshop, they were half the participants, and they lost much of their reluctance to speak out, setting two patterns that would continue.[13]

In 1955, the South Carolina legislature, reacting to *Brown,* decided that no city or state employee could belong to the NAACP. Refusing to resign her membership, Mrs. Clark lost her job. Being such a controversial figure—a friend of the despised Warings, an NAACP member, and someone who consorted with the subversives at Highlander—she could find no other work and suffered from the usual harassments and threats. Her sorority, AKA, was supportive enough to give her a testimonial in recognition of her courage, but her sorors took care not to be photographed with her. After failing in her attempts to organize other Black teachers to fight for their rights, she accepted a job at Highlander as director of workshops, starting in 1956. She was so emotionally drained from the experience of losing her job that it was three months before she could sleep well at nights.[14]

Highlander had tried with little success to get people from the Sea Islands to attend workshops. Islanders were not anxious for contact with outsiders. Mrs. Clark had the advantage of having taught on one of the islands, and she was able to get Esau Jenkins, whom she had taught on Johns Islands, to start coming to workshops. He came with a practical problem. By the middle 1950s, he had become a respected leader on the island.[15] He had run for school board on Johns Island

and had been defeated because so few Blacks were registered. A small farmer, Jenkins supplemented his income with a bus he used to carry tobacco workers and longshoremen to work in Charleston. One of the women who rode the bus, Mrs. Alice Wine, told him she had only been to the third grade, but she'd like to register if someone would teach her how to read and write. Jenkins's bus became a rolling school. He gave copies of the South Carolina laws on registering and voting to his passengers and went over them line by line. Mrs. Wine, who couldn't read but had a phenomenal memory, just memorized the section of the constitution that potential voters were tested on. She registered successfully, but she still wanted to learn to read and asked Jenkins what school she could go to. The local school principal and a minister that Jenkins approached were both afraid to get involved, and so he turned to Highlander.

With fifteen hundred dollars borrowed from Highlander, Jenkins's group bought and fixed up a run-down building. They called themselves the Progressive Club and had about twenty-six members. They set up the front part of the building like a grocery store, partly so that the white folks wouldn't learn that it was a school. The two back rooms were used for teaching. With the profits from the grocery store, they were able to pay back Highlander's loan. Mrs. Clark was too occupied at Highlander to be the teacher so she recruited her cousin, Bernice Robinson. Robinson was a beautician who had recently moved back to Charleston after living in the North and had worked with Esau Jenkins on a voter-registration campaign, which gave her a certain status on the island. "Esau could be trusted," wrote Mrs. Clark, "and because he could be trusted, he could introduce us to numbers of others who would trust us."[16]

For Mrs. Clark, the fact that the islanders did trust Mrs. Robinson and would not think her high-falutin' more than outweighed Robinson's lack of teaching experience. It was not that easy for an outsider to be trusted on the island. Septima Clark was very familiar with the patterns of class and color snobbery among Blacks in the area and the defensiveness these traditions engendered in the poor. Even though she was a teacher and had studied in the North, the light-skinned Negro upper class of Charleston would hardly have considered her a social equal. Similarly, people from the islands expected Blacks from the mainland to look down on them. That Bernice Robinson was socially accepted on the island was the important thing for Mrs. Clark, not her educational credentials.

Robinson didn't feel competent to be anybody's teacher, so Horton and Clark had to persuade her. Robinson quickly learned that grade-school material did not interest adults, so she worked directly from the voter-registration forms, going over and over short sections of the documents and teaching students to write their names in cursive. The teaching style developed by Robinson and Clark emphasized the direct experiences of the students. Students would talk about whatever they had done that day—started a vegetable plot, dug potatoes; their stories would be written down, becoming the text for the reading lesson. Discussion deliberately emphasized "big" ideas—citizenship, democracy, the powers of elected officials. The curriculum stressed what was interesting and familiar and important to students, and it changed in accordance with the desires of students. When students said they wanted to learn to write money orders, that was added; when some said they wanted to learn to use sewing machines, that was added. Eventually, Robinson began trying to teach skepticism as well, trying to get students to read newspaper stories critically and look cautiously at the promises of politicians.[17]

At first classes were held four hours a week for two months, January and February, the time of year when people didn't have much to do in the fields. The initial group brought others, and the following year class was held for three months, and another class was started on a nearby island. From the first class of fourteen people—three men and eleven women—eight were able to get registered.[18] It wasn't long before they had five schools going on various islands.

It took the local whites three years to figure out what was going on, although the increasing numbers of Blacks successfully registering caused a minor panic. Eventually, a white visitor to Johns Island found out about the original school and told the papers. By this time, Black islanders didn't care what white people knew.

By 1961, thirty-seven Citizenship Schools had been established in the islands and on the nearby mainland, and Black voting strength had increased significantly. The aim of the schools, though, was to create involved citizens, not just voters. Citizenship-School students helped start a credit union, a nursing home, a kindergarten, and a low-income housing project.[19]

Highlander was responsible for spreading the Citizenship Schools across the South. At first Mrs. Clark and Horton disagreed on some aspects of the program. He thought that registration campaigns could be conducted without so much emphasis on basic literacy. She disagreed, and they had several shouting matches over the issue, with Clark winning in the end. As the idea of the schools spread, she recruited and trained teachers. By the spring of 1961, she had trained eighty-one of them. About that time, the program was turned over to SCLC. At the time Highlander was afraid that it was about to be shut down by the state and, in any case, Highlander was more interested in starting programs than in administering them.[20] Although he was being lobbied by both Ella Baker and Septima Clark and the schools were registering voters across the South in far greater numbers than any SCLC program, Martin Luther King was reluctant to take the program over. Eventually, though, nearly ten thousand people would be trained as teachers, and as many as two hundred schools would be in operation at one time, "in people's kitchens, in beauty parlors, and under trees in the summertime."[21]

Under SCLC, Clark continued to treat literacy and registration as means to an end, not as ends in themselves. "The basic purpose of the Citizenship Schools is discovering local community leaders," she said. It was particularly important that the schools had "the ability to adapt at once to specific situations and stay in the local picture only long enough to help in the development of local leaders. . . . It is my belief that creative leadership is present in any community and only awaits discovery and development."[22] Her philosophy of recruiting teachers continued to reflect a concern for how they fit in with the local social structure:

> The teachers we need in a Citizenship School should be people
> who are respected by the members of the community, who can read
> well aloud, and who can write their names in cursive writing. These

are the ones that we looked for. . . . We were trying to make teachers out of these people who could barely read and write. But they could teach.[23]

Even so pre-eminently middle-class an activity as teaching the poor can and should provide a large share of the leadership. Similarly, Horton, in his work with miners, had learned that they learned best when taught by other miners. "Formally educated staff members, it turned out, were never as effective in teaching as the people themselves, once they saw themselves as teachers." Horton never tried to teach Citizenship classes himself and "discouraged other well-meaning whites from doing so, too."[24] With sclc, Mrs. Clark continued to exhibit a sensitivity to class privilege. She once chided Andrew Young for sitting down to breakfast at a time when there wasn't enough to share with the students. What he needed to do, she told him, was either find money to buy them breakfast or go hungry with them. She criticized Ralph Abernathy for his habit of being late for services at his own church in order "to flaunt his mastery over the common people." She spoke disdainfully of Negro women who came to civil rights meetings to play bourgeois games. "They were going to *be* there because they were going to show those beautiful clothes and those summer furs and the like, but they weren't listening."[25]

She was never entirely comfortable as a member of sclc's executive staff. sclc's conception of leadership was very different from her own. It bothered her that people all around the country would ask King to come lead marches, so "I sent a letter to Dr. King asking him not to lead all the marches himself, but instead to develop leaders who could lead their own marches. Dr. King read that letter before the staff. It just tickled them; they just laughed."[26]

Mrs. Clark idolized King, but she wasn't blind to his limitations, including his inability to treat women as equals. Women within sclc circles were expected to neither ask nor answer questions, and that expectation applied to the wives of the leadership as well as to staff. "Mrs. King and Mrs. Abernathy would come and they were just like chandeliers, shining lights, sitting up, saying nothing." She was unwilling to play chandelier herself, but it didn't make any difference. In executive staff meetings, "I was just a figurehead. . . . Whenever I had anything to say, I would put up my hand and say it. But I did know that they weren't paying any attention."[27]

Septima Clark's Citizenship Schools became an important organizing tool for younger activists in Mississippi and virtually everywhere else in the South. They were a relatively non-threatening way to get people involved in the broader movement. Once you bring people together to talk about literacy, you can get them to talk about a great many other things. Once the schools became funded, they became a source of income for people fired from their jobs because of activism. Highlander also continued to be an important source of support for SNCC. Indeed, before SNCC launched its first statewide registration campaign in Mississippi, Highlander conducted a week-long training workshop for them. Mrs. Clark and Highlander had evolved a distinctive way of thinking about the process of social change. Through long experience working with impoverished communities, they had developed a faith in the ability of communities of the poor to provide much of the leadership for their own struggle and concrete ideas about how that ability could be nurtured. That faith and those ideas were shared by Ella Baker.

ELLA BAKER: "STRONG PEOPLE DON'T NEED
STRONG LEADERS"

Writing about the students he knew at Howard University in 1962, SNCC's Cleveland Sellers says that when he tried to talk politics with the guys in his dorm, they would grunt and change the subject. "They were much more interested in cars, fraternities, clothes, parties and girls" and the high-paying jobs they expected to have after graduation.[28] Yet the turbulent sixties were born among just such students. In Greensboro, North Carolina, on February 1, 1960, four freshmen at North Carolina A & T College decided to go to the local Woolworth's and remain at the lunch counter until they were served. They were not served, although they stayed until closing time, but word of what they had done got back to campus before they did. The next day they were joined by twenty more students. Within a few days, even though sit-in demonstrations had spread to more stores, there were more students who wanted to sit in than there were places for them to sit. Within two weeks, sit-ins and the boycotts that frequently accompanied them had spread to fifteen cities in five states.[29]

By the end of March, students on at least twenty-one northern college campuses had become involved, usually by picketing or boycotting the northern outlets of some of the chains being hit in the South. Woolworth's and Kress were popular targets. Within the first year and a half, sit-ins had taken place in more than one hundred cities in twenty states, involving an estimated seventy thousand demonstrators and thirty-six hundred arrests.[30] Activity tended to be most intense in urban areas and in border states. Non-urban areas of Deep South states like Mississippi were not much affected.

The sit-ins had substantial impact. Some desegregation took place in at least one hundred cities. Although he did not support the sit-ins at first, Ralph McGill of the *Atlanta Constitution* eventually came to feel that "without question," the sit-ins were "productive of the most change. . . . No argument in a court of law could have dramatized the immorality and irrationality of such a custom as did the sit-ins."[31]

At the beginning some, probably most, of the young people involved thought that merely dramatizing injustice would be enough to produce change. It was seen as an aggressive form of moral suasion. However, the sit-ins, like the other forms of direct-action politics that were to develop around them, also meant directly interfering with the life of a community so that it had to respond. If the powers-that-be would not respond to moral suasion, they would have to do something about disruption.

Taking a view similar to that of Jo Freeman, Aldon Morris has explained that the rapid spread of the sit-ins was made possible by pre-existing movement networks. Starting in the early 1950s, what Morris calls local movement centers had begun developing in the South, most of them church-connected and largely church-financed. Montgomery, Alabama, was the most widely known, but there were also centers in Birmingham, Baton Rouge, Nashville, and Petersburg, Virginia, among other places. After 1957, many of these centers would be connected under the auspices of Martin Luther King's Southern Christian Leadership Conference. During the first few weeks of sit-in activity in early 1960, leaders from these centers helped spread the idea by contacting student leaders around the South, by providing bail funds, meeting places, and contacts with adults experienced in nonviolence as ideology and practice. The support of these older activists was important in part because the Black colleges themselves, frequently dependent on white economic or political support, were not always free to support the burgeoning movement. Protesting students were often suspended or expelled from publicly supported Black colleges. Dr. King was among the adults involved in furthering the spread of the movement, as were Fred Shuttlesworth of Birmingham, Wyatt Tee Walker of Petersburg, and Floyd McKissick of North Carolina. Another supportive adult was the omnipresent Ella Baker. After using her enormous contact network to encourage the spread of the movement, she went on to play a critical role in shaping and stabilizing this massive outpouring of activist energies, a role understandable in the context of her long activist history.

James Forman, the most important administrator in SNCC during its early years, has said that without Ella Baker, "there would be no story of the Student Nonviolent Coordinating Committee."[32] When she was asked to account for her lengthy activist career, Miss Baker often launched into a description of growing up in rural Virginia and North Carolina just after the turn of the century. Like Medgar Evers, she took considerable pride in being from a family with explicit traditions of defiance and race pride, but her reconstructions of her childhood also emphasize a family tradition of just being concerned about people, being involved in one's community.

She grew up hearing stories about slavery from her maternal grandmother, a light-skinned house slave, a daughter of the man who owned her. Miss Baker's grandmother had refused to marry the equally light-skinned man chosen for her by her mistress. For that, she was whipped and demoted to work in the fields, but she married the man she wanted to marry, a dark-skinned man, a slave on the same plantation, a man proud of being Black almost to the point of conceit. That kind of pride was not uncommon among the people who raised Ella Baker: "There was pride in Blackness. Even lighter skinned people wanted to be identified with being Black."[33] After the Civil War, her grandfather either bought or leased a large section of the plantation he had worked as a slave and tried to create a model Black community. He broke up the land into various-sized plots—twenty, thirty, forty acres—and settled members of the extended family on them. He was known to mortgage his own farm after the local rivers flooded, so that he could buy food for other families.

Ella Baker's mother was a good public speaker and an ardent church worker active in the efforts of local missionary societies. "I became active in things largely because my mother was active in the field of religion."[34] Her mother, like Clark's, was a strict disciplinarian who wasn't too concerned with listening to the opinions of children. Miss Baker had a more playful relationship with both her father and grandfather. Her grandfather, laconic with the rest of the world, liked to talk to her and listen to her. She was a baseball-playing tomboy, but her grandfather called her "Grand Lady" and took her on long horse-and-buggy rides, during which they discussed issues large and small. When he preached, he set up a big chair for her in front of the congregation, right next to his own seat. Her father was a waiter on the ferry that ran between Norfolk and Washington. With him, she could have a discussion, the kind of exchange of opinions that was seldom possible with her mother. Before she was out of grade school, she had acquired both a local reputation as an effective public speaker and a degree of skepticism about the real value of oratory. Her father, well aware of how highly Blacks valued good public speaking, used to speak derisively about preachers who were strong on style but, when you thought about what they said, there wasn't much substance.

She once described her childhood as a kind of family socialism.[35] Surrounded by kin, it was taken for granted that food, tools, homes, and responsibility for children would be shared.

> Where we lived there was no sense of social hierarchy in terms of those who have, having the right to look down upon, or to evaluate as a lesser breed, those who didn't have. Part of that could have re-

sulted . . . [from] the proximity of my maternal grandparents to slavery. They had known what it was to not have. Plus, . . . [we had] the "Christian" concept of sharing with others. . . . Your relationship to human beings was far more important than your relationship to the amount of money that you made.[36]

By her own interpretation, having been raised with an abiding sense of community was one of the motive forces behind her activism and

helped to strengthen my concept about the need for people to have a sense of their own value and *their* strengths and it became accentuated when I began to travel in the forties for the National Association of Colored People. . . . As people moved to towns and cities, the sense of community diminished.[37]

Her model of the Good Life was not derived from the lifestyle of middle-class whites, as it was for some of her NAACP colleagues, nor from any pre-cut ideological scheme, as it was for some of her Marxist acquaintances. During the decades when Blacks were fleeing the South, physically and often emotionally, she was trying to recreate the spirit of the self-sufficient, egalitarian people who raised her.[38] Like the people at Highlander, she found in folk culture sources of strength, not something to be ashamed of.

She attended both high school and college at Shaw University in Raleigh, finishing as valedictorian of the class of 1927, with nearly twice the number of credits needed to graduate. Scholarship aside, the administration was undoubtedly glad to see her leave; she had been protesting the school's restrictive dress code for students, its policy of having students sing Negro spirituals for white visitors, and its policy forbidding men and women students from walking across campus together.[39] She claimed to have left college with conventional notions of personal success, but that seems to have included a desire to be socially useful.[40] After graduation she wanted either to study sociology at the University of Chicago—sociology was still thought of as a helping occupation—or become a medical missionary. The family's financial situation would not allow her to do either, so in the summer of 1927, she migrated to New York, staying with a cousin her mother had raised. In New York, despite her record at Shaw, she could only find factory work and waitressing jobs. Her mother wanted her to go into teaching, but Miss Baker didn't want to do that, partly because a Black woman with a degree was expected to teach, partly because too many of the teachers she had known had been fearful people, afraid to have an opinion on anything or take a stand on anything lest they lose their jobs. She valued her opinion more than that.

Ideas were easier to find than jobs. The smorgasbord political environment of the city intrigued her:

> I went everywhere there was discussion. New York was not as hazardous as it now is. You could walk the streets at three in the morning. And so wherever there was a discussion, I'd go. . . . And maybe I was the only woman or the only black, it didn't matter. . . . You see, New York was the hotbed of—let's call it radical thinking. . . . Boy, it was *good,* stimulating![41]

Her community involvement started almost as soon as she got to New York. In 1928, she organized a Negro History Club at the 135th street YMCA in Harlem. Between 1929 and 1932, she was on the editorial staffs of at least two newspapers, the *American–West Indian News* and *Negro National News.*

Given her childhood, organizing economic cooperatives probably had a natural appeal. Around 1930 she was among several young Negroes who wrote responses to a column in one of the Negro newspapers urging Negroes to form cooperatives. The young people formed the Young Negroes' Cooperative League, which proceeded to establish stores, buying clubs, housing developments, coop restaurants and other cooperative economic ventures in Black neighborhoods up and down the East Coast, as far west as Omaha, as far south as New Orleans. For the first two years, she was the League's national director, and in one form or another she was involved with coops for at least a decade.

Largely forgotten now, there was vigorous interest among Blacks in cooperative ventures during the Depression. In a report written around 1941, she was still optimistic about their potential, noting that the mortality rate was high but those that survived were often valuable parts of their communities and sometimes forced other businesses to modify policies toward Black customers and employees. The high mortality rate she attributed partly to the fact that many groups, impatient to get started, launched their enterprises with insufficient capital, and partly to insufficient business expertise, problems compounded by the fact that initially, Negro wage earners of marginal economic status had been the most interested segment of the community.[42]

The Depression played an important part in her rejection of "the American illusion that anyone who is determined and persistent can get ahead."[43] She worked with a variety of labor organizations in Harlem, including the Women's Day Workers and Industrial League, which focused on the problems of domestic workers. At one point, Miss Baker pretended to be a domestic worker in order to investigate the employment conditions of Black domestics.[44] Her awareness of the problem of change-oriented organizations betraying their founding ideals may have stemmed from her work with labor organizations during this period. In the early days, she thought,

> basically, the labor movement was meeting the need of the non-powerful. . . . But I'm afraid it succumbed, to a large extent to the failures of what I call the American weakness of being recognized and of having arrived and taking on the characteristics and the values even, of the foe.[45]

In 1964, when Blacks in Mississippi were fighting to form their own political party, she warned an audience that "we must be careful lest we elect to represent us people who, for the first time, feel their sense of importance and will represent themselves before they represent you."[46] This woman who spent so much of her life working for and creating social change organizations had a generic distrust of organizations, especially large ones, and of those who led them.

By the Depression, she had a clear conception of what good political work meant that expressed itself even in relatively mundane projects. From 1934 to 1936 she was connected with the Adult Education Program of the Harlem library. A letter of recommendation written some years later by the librarian summarized her accomplishments:

> Her work was particularly good in organizing and acting as adviser to Young People's Forum. The group appealed to was from sixteen to twenty-six years of age, one not ordinarily touched by our education activities. Miss Baker successfully formed an active organization, which she brought into touch with other youth groups in the neighborhood and city. The public meetings included forums on social, economic, and cultural topics, literary and musical programs, debates and contests. Prominent speakers were brought into these meetings, but it was Miss Baker's plan always to place emphasis on increased participation by the members themselves. . . . Although Miss Baker left us for a better position, many of these people still show an active interest in the library's community program.[47]

Organizing means helping others develop their own potentials, and participatory social forms are a key part of that process. She was already a seasoned organizer. When she applied for an NAACP position, her application noted that she had been involved with the "Harlem Adult Education Committee, the Workers' Education Movement, the Consumer Movement, on both a national and local scale" and had maintained at least a speaking acquaintance with the leaders of "the articulate mass and semi-mass movements" in the area. Starting with the NAACP as an assistant field secretary in 1941, she found herself in a job that meant extensive travel through some quite dangerous parts of the South, raising funds, organizing new branches, and trying to make old ones more effective. She spent about half of each year on the road—especially in Florida, Alabama, Georgia, and Virginia. She organized at least three hundred membership drives and often traveled twelve thousand exhausting miles a year to do it. Returning to New York from one long trip, she wrote a friend:

I am too weary to think; and even if I could think, I could not write. This race saving business is. . . . But who am I to weary of the noble task of molding the destiny of 13,000,000?[48]

From the viewpoint of the national office, no part of her job was more important than conducting the membership campaigns upon which the organization's financial health depended. Some branches had the leadership to conduct effective campaigns. This was partly a matter of whether local leaders were willing to do the necessary "spadework," to use one of Miss Baker's favorite terms. In Birmingham, for example, "we have as chairman the Rev. J. W. Goodgame, Jr. . . . He is all preacher, but unlike most of them, he knows that it takes work to produce and he will work. We spent the morning visiting barber shops, filling stations, grocery stores and housewives, getting people to work."

Most branches were depressingly dependent on help from the national office: "What promised to be a well organized campaign here (Jacksonville, Florida) has turned out to be the usual thing of literally starting from scratch." Starting from scratch meant identifying a campaign chair, identifying workers and dividing them into competing teams, outlining a publicity plan, lining up speakers, doing advance canvassing of community groups, businesses, fraternal groups, churches, social clubs, unions, all while refereeing the personality conflicts that debilitated many branches.[49] It is hard to imagine a more effective practicum in the emerging social structure of Black communities. After being exposed to a broad spectrum of ideologies and change-oriented organizations as a young woman exploring New York, she now was making innumerable contacts and friends among southern leaders while being exposed to the widest possible variety of grassroots leadership styles and organizing tactics.

What she saw ran the gamut:

Rome [Georgia] manifests all the expected symptoms of a branch that has had the same president for 24 years; and a community that thinks nothing can be done in the South that would challenge the status quo; and hence makes of the NAACP meetings occasions for demonstrating literary, musical and oratorical abilities. However, I think our visit has served to "shock" them into greater action, as one "leader" put it.

Factionalization within branches required her to act as "Mother Confessor to the Little Folk":

> The outlook for this trip does not appear very rosy. . . . For instance, how can I create an alert and dynamic branch in West Point [Virginia] where the not-more-than three hundred colored residents are divided by one "fraction" after the other, when I am here but for a day and a night?

On another Virginia trip:

> All in all the branches visited were in a healthy state. Where they are engaged in securing school transportation, equal salaries for teachers or some local program . . . community response and support of the NAACP is no problem. The newer branches . . . exist largely on being new. Less active branches suffer from lack of functioning committees which places too much responsibility on the branch presidents or one or two officers and a lack of local programs which often springs from a lack of knowledge as to how to go about developing one.[50]

The problem was deeper than not knowing how to develop a program. Many local officers thought their entire reason for being was to support the national office; running a local program didn't occur to them as an option:

> As his answer to those who wish to know what the branch is doing locally Mr. Gilbert of Titusville [Florida] states that he hopes the time will never come when the branch will be *needed* locally (meaning, of course, that he hopes Brevard County will have no lynchings or race riots or the like).[51]

In an area where Blacks suffered every racial indignity—one nearby school had twenty-six classrooms for 1,876 students—local leadership saw no role for the branch in speaking to day-to-day injustices. It was a national problem, not just a southern one. While visiting the Albany, New York, branch, she repeatedly heard the opinion "that if cases were not brought to the branch, it could not be expected to seek them and that as long as it helped some unfortunate person in the South through its apportionment to the national office, the branch had fully justified itself."[52] She steered the conversation to local matters. It turned out that while the local schools were technically integrated, Black youngsters were almost automatically shunted into the dummy academic track. She began helping them map out a strategy for changing that. Every branch could find some local concern to work on. "Any branch which says it has nothing around which it can build a program is simply too lazy to concern itself with things on its own doorstep."[53] As soon as you can say you've done something, anything, people will respond, because they want action, not talk.

From her perspective, the national organization was victimized by its own success. It was successful enough with its program of attacking the legal base of racial oppression that its very success blinded the organization to its shortcomings. The legal strategy "had to be" directed by lawyers and other professionals, leaving most of the huge mass base of the NAACP—four hundred thousand members by 1944— little meaningful role in the development of policy and program except raising funds and cheering the victories as they came. Her criticisms were similar to those of many Deep South leaders. She thought the leadership was overly concerned with recognition from whites, a concern that helped prevent the organization from taking a confrontational stance even when such a stance would have made tactical sense. She thought the program was overly oriented to a middle-class agenda and not nearly strong enough on the kinds of economic issues that meant most to working-class Black people. The Second World War, she thought, had generated a more aggressive mood among Negroes, and the organization seemed unwilling or unable to capitalize on it. Perhaps above all she found the organization too centralized; too many decisions were being made in New York. "The work of the

National Office is one thing but the work of the branches is in the final analysis the life blood of the Association."[54]

She intended "to place the NAACP and its program on the lips of all the people . . . the uncouth MASSES included." She advocated regional offices so that local leaders would have a source of assistance nearer than New York. She suggested that at annual conferences, "instead of staff members making speeches, several delegates [from local branches] be designated to talk out of their branch experience." She argued that the overall structure of fieldwork in the Association made no sense. Three or four field workers were responsible for the whole country. They barely had time to organize membership campaigns, let alone help branches develop local programs. Getting the man or woman in the street need not be all that difficult if the organization made it a priority:

> We must have the "nerve" to take the Association to people wherever they are. As a case in point, the mass-supported beer gardens, night clubs, etc. in Baltimore were invaded on a small scale. We went in, addressed the crowds and secured memberships and campaign workers. With the results that were well summed up in a comment overheard in one club, "You certainly have some nerve coming in here, talking, but I'm going to join that doggone organization.[55]

Part of the problem, she maintained, was simple class snobbery. Like Septima Clark and Myles Horton, Miss Baker was sensitive to the way in which such class antagonisms, real or imagined, could undermine everything. An important part of the organizer's job was to get the matron in the fur coat to identify with the winehead and the prostitute, and vice versa. Significantly, she adds:

> And so you have to break that [inability to identify] down without alienating them at the same time. The gal who has been able to buy her minks and whose husband is a professional, they live well. You can't insult her, you never go and tell her she's a so-and-so for taking, for *not* identifying. You try to point where her interest lies in

identifying with that other one across the tracks who doesn't have minks.[56]

Everyone has a contribution to make. The organizer has to be aware of class exploitation, sensitive to class snobbery, without losing sight of the potential contribution to be made by those who do succumb to it. Just as one has to be able to look at a sharecropper and see a potential teacher, one must be able to look at a conservative lawyer and see a potential crusader for justice.

Given her populist stance, it is surprising that she became one of the Association's national officers. In April 1943, she was in Alabama when a letter from Walter White, national secretary of the Association, caught up with her, bringing the news that she had been appointed national director of branches. Despite her surprise ("Were I not more or less shock-proof," she wrote White, "I would now be suffering from a severe case of hypertension caused by your letter of the 15th"), she accepted the position and brought her agenda to it during the time when the Association was experiencing the most rapid growth it had known.[57]

From the director's chair, she was able to push regionalization and to reorganize membership campaigns in order to leave field workers more time for working with branch programs. Perhaps most characteristically, she was able to establish a training program for local leaders. Her superiors were skeptical about how much demand there would be for such programs, but by late 1944 she had won permission to do one training conference on an experimental basis. The theme for that first conference was "Give Light and the People Will Find a Way." Response was so good that the conferences became a permanent feature of the Association's program. She ran at least nine more of them in the next year and a half, usually holding them over a weekend and typically attracting a hundred or more delegates each time.[58]

Similar in structure and intent to Highlander workshops, the conferences (one of which was attended by Rosa Parks) were both skill-enhancing and consciousness-raising. Before they came, delegates were asked what issues they wanted addressed. What they asked for ranged from basic issues of organizational development (getting committees to function, holding on to members, mounting publicity campaigns) to more substantive requests for information on what to do about police brutality or employment discrimination or about reintegrating veterans into the community. The conferences then presented other local leaders who had successfully addressed the same kinds of dilemmas or national officers with some pertinent expertise. At the same time they tried to help local leaders find more effective ways to attack local problems the conferences also tried to help them see how local issues were, inevitably, expressions of broader social issues. While she was never satisfied with the thoroughness of the conferences, delegates themselves seemed well pleased, as with the 1945 Texas delegates who praised their conference for "a wonderful fellowship and [the] contacts . . . and the many and varied benefits resulting from the exchange of experiences and expert information."[59]

The conferences were a well-established feature of the Association's work when she resigned from the Association in May 1946. Her resignation letter gave three reasons for her leaving:

> I feel that the Association is falling far short of its present possibilities; that the full capacities of the staff have not been used in the past; and that there is little chance of mine being utilized in the immediate future.

The letter registered her complaint about the "inclination to disregard the individual's right to an opinion" as well as the "almost complete lack of appreciation for the collective thinking of the staff," the latter witnessed by the paucity of staff meetings during the "critical and portentous" war years. She was also disturbed by a demoralizing atmosphere among the staff occasioned by a supervisory style tantamount to espionage. Her public reasons for resigning reflected the criticisms she had long been making of the Association—lack of imagination in program, lack of democracy in operating style.[60]

She worked for a while as a fund-raiser for the National Urban League and continued to work with the NAACP at the local level. She became president of the New York City branch, which, in her phrase, she tried to "bring back to the people" by moving the office to a location more accessible to the Harlem community and by developing a program in which Black and Hispanic parents actively worked on issues involving school desegregation and the quality of education. For her, the point was that the parents worked on the issues themselves rather than having civil rights professionals work on their behalf.[61]

In the mid-1950s, with Bayard Rustin and Stanley Levison, she helped organize In Friendship to offer economic support for Blacks suffering reprisals for political activism in the South. Even before the Montgomery bus boycott, the group had been discussing ways to develop the idea of a mass-based southern organization as counterbalance to the NAACP. When the boycott came, they saw it as the potential base for developing something. From that idea, developed by several groups simultaneously, grew the Southern Christian Leadership Conference.

It is not clear whether without outside encouragement the local leadership in Montgomery would have sought to build something larger from the boycott. According to some observers, the momentum had stopped, and no plans were being made to carry on. When Baker asked Martin Luther King why he had let things wind down, she apparently offended him, not for the last time:

> I irritated [him] with the question. . . . His rationale was that after a big demonstration, there was a natural letdown and a need for people to sort of catch their breath. I didn't quite agree. . . . I don't think the leadership in Montgomery was prepared to capitalize [on what] . . . had come out of the Montgomery situation. Certainly they had not reached the point of developing an organizational format for the expansion of it.[62]

Levison and Rustin felt that the fledgling SCLC needed an experienced organizer and were able to talk a reluctant Ella Baker into taking the job.[63] Some of the ministers involved had substantial political experience before Montgomery—Martin Luther King was not among them, though—but none had the depth and breadth of political experience that Miss Baker could offer. In 1957, she went South intending only a six-week stay. She wound up staying two and a half years, becoming the first full-time executive director. At the beginning, she used to joke, SCLC's "office" was her purse and the nearest phone booth. She was responsible for organizing the voter-registration and citizenship-training drives that constituted the SCLC program during this period, which she did largely by exploiting the network of personal contacts she had developed while with the NAACP.[64]

As with the NAACP, she had trouble getting her own thinking built into the programs of SCLC. She wanted the organization to go into some of the hard-core counties where Blacks were not voting at all. Prophetically, she tried to get the organization to place more emphasis on women and young people, reflecting her sense of how southern Black organizations worked:

> All of the churches depended, in terms of things taking place, on women, not men. Men didn't do the things that had to be done and you had a large number of women who were involved in the bus boycott. They were the people who kept the spirit going [the women] and the young people.[65]

Being ignored was hardly a surprise to her:

> I had known . . . that there would never be any role for me in a leadership capacity with SCLC. Why? First, I'm a woman. Also, I'm not a minister. . . . The basic attitude of men and especially ministers, as to . . . the role of women in their church setups is that of taking orders, not providing leadership.[66]

Many SCLC preachers could go out and give stirring speeches about human equality and then come back and treat the office staff as if they were personal servants, never seeing the contradiction, although Miss Baker repeatedly pointed it out.

SCLC as it actually developed was a far cry from her sense of an effective social action organization. For all its faults, the NAACP had at least been a disciplined, tightly run ship, dependent on no one personality. SCLC's internal culture could be frustratingly disorganized, and its dependence on centralized, charismatic leadership was a leadership style of which she was most skeptical. She was certainly thinking of King, but not just King, when she said:

> I have always felt it was a handicap for oppressed people to depend so largely on a leader, because unfortunately in our culture, the charismatic leader usually becomes a leader because he has found a spot in the public limelight. It usually means that the media made him, and the media may undo him. There is also the danger in our culture that, because a person is called upon to give public statements and is acclaimed by the establishment, such a person gets to the point of believing that he *is* the movement. Such people get so involved with playing the game of being important that they exhaust themselves and their time and they don't do the work of actually organizing people.[67]

Under the best circumstances, traditional leadership creates a dependency relationship between the leaders and the led. Talk of *leading* people to freedom is almost a contradiction in terms. "Strong people," she said in one interview, "don't need strong leaders."[68]

> My basic sense of it has always been to get people to understand that in the long run they themselves are the only protection they have against violence or injustice. . . . People have to be made to understand that they cannot look for salvation anywhere but to themselves.[69]

Thus, leadership should be a form of teaching, where the leader's first responsibility is to develop the leadership potential in others: "I have always thought what is needed is the development of people who are interested not in being leaders as much as in developing leadership in others."[70] Just as she was out of step with SCLC on the nature of leadership, she held her own opinions about nonviolence: "I frankly could not have sat and let someone put a burning cigarette on the back of my neck as some young people did. . . . If necessary, if they hit me, I might hit them back."[71]

She was similarly skeptical about the long-term value of demonstrations, preferring to emphasize the development of stable, ongoing organizations at the local level. Nor was she particularly enamored of large organizations, with their tendency to make the individual irrelevant. She thought that one of the most sensible structures for change-oriented organizations would have small groups of people maintaining effective working relationships among themselves but also retaining contact in some form with other such cells, so that coordinated action would be possible whenever large numbers really were necessary. For this reason, she admired the cell structure of the Communist Party: "I don't think we had any more effective demonstration of organizing people for whatever purpose."[72]

It is impossible to say how deeply she was disturbed by being marginalized inside the organizations she worked for. She said many times that being shoved to the side and ignored did not necessarily bother her because her ego wasn't involved in that way. Such statements should probably be taken as reflecting more her ideals than her actual feelings. By this time, she had worked with any number of leaders and would-be leaders whose effectiveness was undercut by their egos, and it was only natural that she try to distance herself from them.

Her thinking was so fundamentally different from that of the men who ran SCLC that it is hardly surprising that few of her ideas were implemented. One of her suggestions did bear fruit. She tried to convince SCLC to build a program around the citizenship training schools that had been developed by Septima Clark and the Highlander Center. She was, again, unable to get this idea adopted while she was with SCLC, but after her departure in the summer of 1960, SCLC did take over the citizenship schools.

A memo she wrote in the fall of 1959 conveys some sense of her thinking just before the sit-ins began and just before she left SCLC. Addressed to SCLC's Committee on Administration, the memo tries to expand on the idea of SCLC as a "Crusade for Citizenship." To her, she says, the word *crusade* denotes "a vigorous movement, with high purpose and involving masses of people."[73] To be effective, she continues, such a movement must provide a sense of achievement and recognition for many people, particularly local leadership. The memo outlines four concrete steps by which such a crusade might be realized. SCLC, she suggests, could start searching out and sponsoring indigenous leadership, especially in the hard-core states. The examples she gives are all of people working on voter registration in Mississippi, people whose work, she feels, could be strengthened with some of the resources SCLC could draw on. It sounds very much like an elaboration of the In Friendship idea—find someone who is already working and support that person.

The second idea calls for recruiting one thousand ministers to participate in house-to-house canvassing for voter registration. Each would be asked to give only eight hours a month and if each worked for ten months, she estimates, three hundred thousand persons could be contacted personally. The same emphasis on working directly with people is reflected in the third idea, a campaign to reduce illiteracy. She thinks SCLC could coordinate women's groups, church groups, and sororities in a campaign using the Laubach literacy method. The Laubach program asks that each person who learns teaches someone else, a feature she must have found appealing. She sees the idea as an investment in developing people: "The real value to s.c.l.c. would be that more people would be equipped with the basic tools (reading and writing) and would then be ready for effective social action." As with most of the other ideas, she mentions several people or groups who might be helpful, another reflection of her extensive contacts within politically active groups.

She notes that the literacy project could provide a "respectable" channel for helping the cause for those who would be uncomfortable being identified with the more militant aspects of the struggle—again, there is work for the matron in the fur coat. The final idea calls for training teams in techniques of nonviolent resistance, with the teams to be composed of persons committed to doing spadework in their local communities. She may not have been personally committed to nonviolence, but she was willing to use it. None of the ideas reserved a central place for Dr. King.

The memo was dated late October 1959. The sit-ins would start in February 1960, less than four months later. With Ella Baker's help the sit-ins would develop into an organization that would lead a more "vigorous" movement, involving masses of people; that would share her skepticism about the long-term value of centralized leadership; would stress the development of indigenous leadership and would work directly with the people; would go into the hard-core areas of the rural South that other organizations had shunned and that would, far more than previous organizations, make it possible for women and young people to take leadership roles. The young people who formed SNCC were the product of a number of political influences, but Ella Baker's was among the most significant. In its organizational structure, its program, its ideology, early SNCC would be almost exactly the kind of organization Ella Baker had been trying to create for almost three decades.

The actual formation of SNCC took place in April of 1960. Soon after the sit-ins started, Ella Baker decided that they needed some coordination. With eight hundred dollars appropriated by SCLC, she arranged a conference of sit-in activists at Shaw University, her alma mater, where she was still in friendly contact with one of the deans. More than two hundred delegates attended the meeting, twice the number she had hoped for. The Reverend King spoke, as did the Reverend James Lawson, who had been working with a group of activist young people in Nashville. The fiery Lawson, the young people's Martin Luther King, as some called him, received a standing ovation from the students.[74] Miss Baker's own speech, titled "More Than a Hamburger" got a more polite reception. She tried to get them to see sit-ins as a wedge into a broader array of social problems affecting Blacks. She also warned the students against letting themselves be coopted by older groups. According to Julian Bond, students at that point just weren't ready to see past hamburgers: "To our mind, lunch-counter segregation was the greatest evil facing black people in the country."[75]

Helping people see the connection between personal troubles and larger social issues was a central concern of Miss Baker's. It is also typical of her, though, that, having made the point, she apparently did nothing to push it, perhaps as a result of her feeling that it was important for young people to learn to think things through for themselves and decide things for themselves. Within a few years, the young people of SNCC had learned on their own to see more clearly the connections she was pointing them toward. A number of descriptions of her emphasize her willingness to let people think through issues on their own.

SNCC's Courtland Cox said:

The most vivid memory I have of Ella Baker is of her sitting in on these SNCC meetings that ran for days—you didn't measure them in hours, they ran days—with a smoke mask over her nose, listening patiently to words and discussions she must have heard a thousand times.

Much of her interaction with students took the form of her asking questions, sometimes quite aggressively, rather than telling them what they had to do. Still, she could get her points across, and one of her frequently stressed points was a warning against dogmatism. Mary King, who worked closely with Ella Baker, claims that:

> At a very important period in my life, Miss Baker tempered my natural tenacity and determination with flexibility and made me suspicious of dogmatism. . . . She taught me one of the most important lessons I have learned in life: There are many legitimate and effective avenues for social change and there is no single right way. She helped me see that the profound changes we were seeking in the social order could not be won without multiple strategies. She encouraged me to avoid being doctrinaire. "Ask questions, Mary," she would say.

Similarly, Tim Jenkins notes that SNCC's original approach was just to attack all the ministers as Uncle Tom sell-outs. "One of the major contributions she made," he says, "was to help us see them in some way that was positive and [see] some way we could coordinate our efforts [with them] and be non-threatening to them."[76] Another of her contributions was the style of interpersonal interaction she modeled for the young people. One of the reasons Bob Moses wound up working for SNCC rather than SCLC was his feeling that Ella Baker cared about him as a person in a way that Martin Luther King did not. Diane Nash said, "When I left her I always felt that she'd picked me up and brushed me off emotionally." According to Moses, partly because of Miss Baker SNCC evolved an operating style with certain characteristics:

Whenever you want to really do something with somebody else then the first thing you have to do is make this personal connection, you have to find out who it is you're really working with. You really have to be interested in that person to work with them. . . . You saw that all across the South in the grassroots and rural people. That was their style and Ella carried that style into this other level. . . . She's sort of shepherding the SNCC people through this maze and in doing that part of the initial steps is always making these personal connections with all of them as they come through.[77]

The Raleigh meeting reflected her distinctive style. She kept the press out of policy sessions. She was aware of the advantages of publicity, but she was aware of its drawbacks as well. She was also at pains to see that the representatives of northern colleges met separately from those of southern colleges. The students from the North were better educated, more articulate in terms of political and social philosophies. The southern students, in contrast, came with what she saw as "a rather simple philosophical orientation, namely of the Christian, non-violent approach,"[78] but they had been the ones actually involved, demonstrating their capacity for suffering and confrontation in ways that the northern students had not. They were the ones who suffered from the problem and it was important to her that they be allowed to determine the shape and substance of the response to it. The southern character of the movement had to be preserved.

If her attempts to get students to think in terms of a whole social structure that needed changing did not go very far, Miss Baker was more immediately successful in her attempt to keep one of the established civil rights groups from absorbing the new student movement. The established groups were very interested in doing so. CORE, which had never established an organizational base in the South, saw the student movement as the solution to that problem. The NAACP, which had been less than enthusiastic about the sit-ins at first, was interested in the fund-raising and public-relations advantages of being associated with the most interesting thing going on in the South. Many of the sit-inners had been NAACP youth chapter members. SCLC was also interested and appeared to have the inside track. King was widely known and respected; SCLC had bankrolled the conference, it had been organized by one of their staff, and many SCLC leaders knew the student leaders and had worked with them over a period of time.

Miss Baker was adamantly opposed. She walked out of an SCLC staff meeting where strategies to bring the kids on board were being discussed. At the Raleigh meeting, her position prevailed, partly because some of the young people were skeptical of older leaders, even Dr. King, and partly because King, perhaps not wishing to look like he was trying to empire-build, did not push the issue as hard as he might have.[79] All this aside, Julian Bond is likely quite right when he says that the students were just excited about the possibility of running things themselves.

> You were running your own little group. You had your own office. You may have had your own bank account. *You* made decisions. You sat down with whoever was the biggest nigger in town before you came along. You spoke with white folks, made them tremble with fear. It was very heady stuff.[80]

It was also very idealistic stuff. The statement of purpose adopted a month later reflected southern Christian ideals, leavened with this new nonviolence:

> We affirm the philosophical or religious ideal of nonviolence as the foundation of our purpose, the presupposition of our faith, and the manner of our action. Nonviolence as it grows from the Judaeo-Christian tradition seeks a social order of justice permeated by love. . . . Through nonviolence, courage displaces fear; love transforms hate. Acceptance dissipates prejudice; hope ends despair. Peace dominates war; faith reconciles doubt. Mutual regard cancels enmity. Justice for all overcomes injustice. The redemptive community supersedes systems of gross social immorality.
>   Love is the central motif of nonviolence. Love is the force by which God binds man to himself and man to man. Such love goes to the extreme; it remains loving and forgiving even in the midst of

hostility. It matches the capacity of evil to inflict suffering with an even more enduring capacity to absorb evil, all the while persisting in love.[81]

SNCC would never become a very large organization and would seldom receive as much publicity as some of the other civil rights organizations did. Nonetheless, it is not too much to say that it did a great deal to invent the sixties. Bernice Reagon calls the civil rights movement the "borning struggle" of the decade, in that it was the movement that stimulated and informed those that followed it. In the same sense, SNCC may have the firmest claim to being called the borning organization. SNCC initiated the mass-based, disruptive political style we associate with the sixties, and it provided philosophical and organizational models and hands-on training for people who would become leaders in the student power movement, the anti-war movement, and the feminist movement.[82] SNCC forced the civil rights movement to enter the most dangerous areas of the South. It pioneered the idea of young people "dropping out" for a year or two to work for social change. It pushed the proposition that merely bettering the living conditions of the oppressed was insufficient; that has to be done in conjunction with giving those people a voice in the decisions that shape their lives. As SNCC learned to see beyond the lunch counter, the increasingly radical philosophies that emerged within the organization directly and indirectly encouraged a generation of scholars and activists to reconsider the ways social inequality is generated and sustained. SNCC's entry, along with the expanded visibility of the similarly aggressive CORE, pressured older civil rights organizations into a reconsideration of tactics. It put the NAACP in a position where it was forced to support some direct-action projects, even though that ran counter to the organization's essential style. Similarly, it is likely that SCLC's return to direct action in 1962 has to be understood in the context of SNCC and CORE having stolen the initiative in 1960 and 1961. SNCC strengthened the negotiating position of the older organizations. In 1962 or 1963, even King was considered too radical by many of the powers-that-be. The development of a left wing in the movement, essentially SNCC and CORE, made centrist organizations like SCLC more acceptable. Given a choice between the relatively reasonable ministers of SCLC or the sometimes brash, frequently uncompromising young people of SNCC, business and political leaders were likely to choose SCLC. It very soon became impossible to think of the NAACP as "radical" at all.[83]

SNCC is so different from the better-known civil rights organizations that it is easy to see it as a sharp break with the past. In fact, while SNCC was primarily an organization of young people, it was an organization that owed a great deal to a much older generation of activists. Philosophically, the distinctive style of work SNCC would carry into the hard-core South drew directly and indirectly from the congealed experience of people like Ella Baker, Septima Clark, and Myles Horton, experience acquired in exactly the kinds of communities the SNCC kids would work in.

The three of them took remarkably similar lessons from their experiences. They were all radical democrats, insistent on the right of people to have a voice in the decisions affecting their lives, confident in the potential of ordinary men and women to develop the capacity to do that effectively, skeptical of top-down organizations, the people who led them, and the egotism that leadership frequently engendered. Therefore, they were committed to participatory political forms because people develop by participating, not by being lectured to or told what to do. They might all be called localists in terms of how they thought programs should be developed but they were hardly parochial. They all thought that if one worked on "local" problems with an open mind, one was likely to learn that the roots of those problems lay elsewhere. They all liked to think of themselves as non-dogmatic, able to hold strong beliefs while remaining open to learning from new experiences. All of them found in southern folk culture, Black or white, a set of values more sustaining than those of bourgeois culture and a code of conduct for governing interpersonal relationships. What Bob Moses said about Ella Baker could have been said about all of them: they were taking the style and substance of the rural South and elevating it to another level. If many of Mississippi's early Black leaders seemed to have an expansive sense of citizenship, these three had an equally broad sense of community, intolerant of invidious distinctions among people and concerned with the well-being of individuals as such.

The SNCC organizers who started working in the most feared counties in the Deep South in 1961 and 1962 had to learn a great deal quickly but they were not starting from scratch. They were heirs to a complex intellectual legacy shaped by older people whose thinking had been informed by lifetimes of practical experience, a legacy reaching at least as far back as Miss Baker's grandfather's farm.

Four

***

MOVING ON MISSISSIPPI

We tried to warn SNCC. *We were all Southerners and we
knew the depth of the depravity of southern racism. We knew better
than to try to take on Mississippi.*

ANDY YOUNG
SCLC

*[*SNCC*] exercised the independence that only young people or
unattached people, those who are not caught up in a framework of
thought, can exercise. They were open to ideas that would not have been
cherished or . . . tolerated by either the* N.A.A.C.P. *or* S.C.L.C. *As a
chief example, the moving into Mississippi. When they decided they
called it "Move On Mississippi" and they called it "MOM."*

ELLA BAKER

Would to God there were *communists in Snick. . . .
They would be a moderating influence.*

CHARLES MORGAN
ACLU

Snick people would argue with a signpost.

JOYCE LADNER[1]

IF THE YOUNG MILITANTS of the sixties didn't bring the movement to Mississippi, they brought it new forms of organization, new tactics, and new energy. Looking back at the NAACP mass meetings of the early 1950s Amzie Moore said: "We had a nice crowd, but we didn't know about methods and procedures for demanding things."[2] The young people in SNCC brought a greater sophistication about creative ways to make demands on the out-of-state institutions that determined the balance of power within Mississippi.

SNCC established its national office—at first a corner in a room rented by SCLC—in Atlanta. By the summer of 1960, it had already begun to take tentative steps toward working in Mississippi. One of the persons who would define that effort was Bob Moses. Raised in a closely knit working class family in Harlem, Moses went to Hamilton College on scholarship and then took a master's in philosophy at Harvard in 1957.[3] Among philosophers, he was particularly drawn to Albert Camus, who, in the words of Clayborne Carson, "combined an individualistic moral code with a humanistic approach to social change. According to Moses, his principal lesson from Camus was the need to cease being 'a victim' while at the same time not becoming 'an executioner.'"[4] The death of his mother, only forty-three years old, and the poor health of his father led to his leaving graduate school, and for two years he taught math at a New York City high school. In 1959, he helped Bayard Rustin (the veteran activist who had worked with Ella Baker on In Friendship and had played an important role in SCLC's early development) organize a Youth March for Integrated Schools. A few months later, the sit-ins broke out, and he wanted to go South to have a first-hand look. During spring break that year, he went to visit an uncle in Hampton, Virginia, where he encountered students picketing and conducting sit-ins. He joined in and experienced "a feeling of release" from having to accommodate himself to racial affronts.[5] Moses returned to New York, talked with Rustin, and then went South to work with SCLC for the summer.[6] SCLC really had very little for him to do, and he gravitated toward the SNCC kids, even though some of them found the well-educated, older New Yorker a little strange. Julian Bond recalls, "We thought he was a Communist because he was from New York and wore glasses and was smarter than we were."

We were immensely suspicious of him. . . . He had a much broader view of social problems and social concerns than we did. We had tunnel vision. . . . Bob Moses, on the other hand, had already begun to project a systematic analysis; not just of the South, but of the country, the world. He didn't try to impress it on us. He didn't say, "Here's what's right, you've been doing this wrong."[7]

That he would not try to force his viewpoint on others is, according to all reports, typical of Bob Moses. In this respect, his working style was similar to Ella Baker's, and like her, he thought it was important for the movement to try the hard-core rural areas, partly, according to Cleveland Sellers, because the concentration of organizations in the cities led to interorganizational turf battles, partly because the people who most needed help were the rural people.[8] It was decided that Moses would make a trip to Mississippi, using his own money, trying to interest people in a conference SNCC was planning for that October. Ella Baker suggested he contact Amzie Moore, because Moore, by this time the vice-president of the state's conference of NAACP branches, knew the state and could give Bob entree.

During that summer of 1960, preceded by a letter from Miss Baker, Bob Moses did meet Moore. In the course of that meeting, Moses later recalled,

Amzie laid out what was to become the voter registration project of the Delta of Mississippi. He wanted SNCC to come and do it. In fact, he was the only person in the leadership of the NAACP I met at that time that was willing to welcome SNCC. I think he saw in the students what had been lacking—that is, some kind of deep commitment that no matter what the cost, people were going to get this done. . . . He didn't want the legal procedures that he had been going through for years.

It is not accidental that Ella Baker sent Moses to someone who would be receptive to new ways of doing things. She had also sent him to someone who was focused firmly on the right to vote. Bob Moses said:

I keep coming back to . . . his insight into Mississippi, into the consciousness and the mentality of white people who lived in Mississippi, and what it was that would be the key to unlocking the situation in Mississippi. He wasn't distracted by school integration. He was for it but it didn't distract him from the centrality of the right to vote. He wasn't distracted about the integration of public facilities. It was a good thing, but it was not going straight to the heart of what was the trouble in Mississippi. Somehow, in following his guidance there, we stumbled on the key—the right to vote and the political action that ensued.

For his part, Moore was struck by the absence of class snobbery in a man who had been to Harvard and taught in New York. "I felt like if a man was educated, there wasn't very much you could tell him. I didn't think you could give him any advice. . . . Bob was altogether different."[9] The two of them had a lot of time to just talk at first, and Moore gave Moses an oral history of the state and a political map, "analyzing and laying out this whole cast of characters across the state, bringing me in on who were the players, how to work with them, what to expect from this one, what this one's orientation was." He started introducing Moses to his extensive network, much of which would have been invisible to white people.[10] On these trips, Moses noted, Amzie would ordinarily not confide the destination until they were on the way. That became a part of Moses's style as well; one protected oneself by keeping information about one's movements as close as possible.

At the same time Moore was schooling Moses, he was doing a reading on him. In order to survive Mississippi, Moses feels, people like Moore had to become astute judges of character. As he initiated Moses into the Mississippi realities, Moore was also assessing Moses's character. Was this someone who could be relied upon? Someone who could stick it out?

Amzie Moore did attend the meeting in Atlanta that fall where he invited SNCC to come to Mississippi. Moses, in the meantime, had gone back to his teaching job in New York, promising to return to Mississippi the following summer. The broad outlines of the Mississippi movement of the sixties had been laid out, primarily between an older warrior with little formal education but years of experience fighting Mississippi and a younger man with sense enough to listen, Harvard notwithstanding.

ELITE PARTICIPATION IN VOTING RIGHTS

During the time Bob Moses was making his first contact with Mississippi, events were taking place within SNCC and across the South that would help shape events in Mississippi. During 1960, the sit-ins captured the attention of the nation. During 1961, it was to be the Freedom Rides initiated by CORE. Formed in Chicago in the early 1940s as a vehicle for exploring the relevance of Gandhi's techniques to American racial inequality, CORE had conducted successful nonviolent campaigns in a number of northern cities during the 1950s. Spurred by a 1961 Supreme Court decision outlawing segregation in interstate bus terminals, CORE decided to test the law by sending integrated teams of riders into the Deep South, a technique it had used years earlier.

Like the sit-ins, the Freedom Rides encountered enormous levels of white violence. The first ride, in May 1961, was planned to go from Washington to New Orleans. It got as far as Birmingham before it was stopped. The first bus was burned by a mob before it got to Birmingham. A mob in Birmingham wrecked the replacement bus and gave the riders a brutal beating. No bus driver could be found to take them further. (As one said, "I have only one life to give and I'm not going to give it to NAACP or CORE.")[11] Although SNCC had not initiated the rides, it chose to become more involved at this point. After asking the Justice Department for protection for the riders and getting the usual promise to investigate, members of SNCC, including Diane Nash of Nashville and John Lewis—Lewis had gone on the original bus—decided the rides had to continue; otherwise, racists would think that violence could stop protest. As soon as they boarded a bus in Birmingham, they were arrested, put under protective custody, and later transported by police to the state line. Within two days they had made their way back to Birmingham, where there was still no bus driver willing to carry them. Finally, with some reluctant behind-the-scenes pressure from the Kennedy administration, a bus was found. The riders got as far as Montgomery before they encountered another mob and another vicious beating. This time the Kennedy administration sent in federal marshals and encouraged the governor to call up the National Guard. Strengthened by new riders from CORE and escorted by the National Guard, the riders were able to get as far as Jackson, Mississippi, where the state authorities had promised the Kennedy administration there would be no public violence.

The Freedom Rides were to continue throughout the summer of 1961, placing the Kennedy administration in an awkward position. On the one hand, the federal government could not allow southern racists to flout the law with the world watching. On the other hand, interceding on behalf of civil rights workers put the Kennedys into a confrontational situation with southern political leaders at a time John Kennedy needed the support of southern congressmen for his domestic and foreign policy. The Kennedys issued a little-heeded call for a "cooling-off" period. They also tried to resolve the dilemma by encouraging the civil rights organizations, CORE and SNCC in particular, to spend more of their efforts on voter-registration work and less on the more dramatic and confrontational direct-action projects. They expected voter-registration work to generate a less violent response, a profound misreading of the situation.

A series of meetings took place that spring and summer among administration officials, foundation representatives close to the administration, and civil rights groups, leading by early 1962 to the formation of the Voter Education Project (VEP). Ostensibly charged with researching the causes and remedies of low voter registration in the South, it was a way by which foundation money could be channeled to civil rights groups.[12] Most of its "research" would take the form of demonstrating just how hard it was to register Blacks in much of the South. Endorsed by both national political parties, VEP received most of its funding from foundations closely allied with the Kennedy administration, particularly the Field Foundation, the Taconic Fund, and the Stern Family Fund. Over its first two-and-a-half years, VEP expended a little more than $870,000, not a great deal of money spread over that period of time and across the whole South but enough to allow the organizations to sustain a more intense level of activity. The first director of VEP was Wiley Branton of Arkansas, a tough-minded Black attorney who had been counsel to the youngsters who desegregated Central High in Little Rock in 1957.

In the discussions that led to VEP, the students were at odds with the others right from the beginning. Some of them thought the entire discussion amounted to the Kennedys trying to buy off the movement. According to James Farmer, Bobby Kennedy and the SNCC representative almost came to blows in one meeting.[13] Then again, if the students were going to do voter registration, they were going to do it in the hard-core counties, notwithstanding the united advice of their more experienced elders to concentrate on the urbanized areas. At one meeting, "King, Wilkins, Whitney Young of the Urban League, [Harold] Fleming [of the Southern Regional Council] and [Burke] Marshall [of the Justice Department] all argued that going into the cities would not only get more votes but would be much safer."[14]

The movement people who participated in the meetings left with the impression that the federal government was committed to aggressively protecting civil rights workers and Blacks attempting to register. Tim Jenkins of SNCC says:

> And I recall very vividly one of the representations—I believe it was made by Harris Wofford, who was then principal assistant to the President—that if necessary in the course of protecting people's rights to vote, that the Kennedy Administration would fill every jail in the South.

Similarly, Lonnie King, who had helped start the sit-ins in Atlanta and who attended some of the meetings with the administration even though he opposed the idea of diluting the direct-action campaign with voter-registration work, recalls that at another meeting "Bobby pledged marshals and what have you to help us out." Before he returned to southwest Mississippi, Bob Moses asked what the Justice Department would do in response to lawlessness: "The Justice Department's response was rapid and emphatic: The government would 'vigorously enforce' federal statutes forbidding the use of intimidation, threats and coercion against voter aspirants."[15]

Some administration officials have maintained that they made it clear they could offer only limited protection. There were several meetings, and it is likely that slightly different things were said at different times or that the same things were differently interpreted. When Robert Kennedy said the government would do everything it could to support voter-registration workers his language may have meant one thing to Kennedy and another to the activists.[16] Whatever was said or intended, SNCC activists initially went into Mississippi thinking they carried the weight of Washington with them.

The proposal to engage in voter registration came close to splitting SNCC in two. To some within the organization, the whole idea sounded like cooptation, which of course was fairly close to the truth. They were reluctant to see organizational resources directed away from the spiritually empowering nonviolent direct-action tactics, which, they had already shown, forced the powers-that-be to respond and to respond quickly. By comparison, voter registration seemed a long, slow road, a narrower form of politics. This debate overlapped with another debate that had been going on in SNCC since its inception, the question of whether nonviolence was merely a technique to be used when appropriate or a way of life. For those holding the latter position, moving away from nonviolence risked all that was good and valuable in the movement. According to Chuck McDew, the arguments also had a territorial base, with the Atlanta kids being more political and secular in orientation and the Nashville kids more religious and moral. At a meeting held at Highlander in August 1961, the two sides were so far apart that splitting the organization seemed the only solution. More lay between them than the issues being discussed, according to Ella Baker. The advocates of voter registration had more fully developed plans and rationales, which, she says, led to "the old business of groups that are better prepared to advocate their position sometimes engendering a defensiveness on the part of those who are less prepared,"[17] a situation in which the group on the defensive may try to resolve the conflict by leaving the organization.

Ella Baker was ordinarily reluctant to intercede too directly in the affairs of the students, preferring to exert influence largely by asking the right questions. When it appeared that SNCC was going to break up over the direct action–voter registration issue, Miss Baker took a more direct stand, making a plea against splitting, pointing out how destructive that kind of thing had been in the history of Black organizations. She argued that nonviolent direct action and voter registration would in fact complement one another. Attempting to register people was sure to produce the same sort of violent reaction direct action was producing, providing plenty of opportunity for a nonviolent response.

The compromise solution agreed to at Miss Baker's urging was to have two wings inside of SNCC, one for voter-registration work and one for direct action. She predicted that once they got into Mississippi, debates about the relative merits of direct action as against voter registration would quickly become academic.

Students of social movements have an ongoing debate about whether the involvement of social elites in non-elite movements ordinarily reduces the militancy of a movement. In this case, that is very much the intention of the administration, but elites may not understand the consequences of their own actions. Trying to contain the energy of the students, the administration wound up encouraging voter-registration efforts that became at least as problematic for the administration as the direct-action campaigns had been.

FINDING FAMILY IN MCCOMB

While some SNCC workers were debating the worth of voter registration, the actual work had already begun. In July 1961, Bob Moses kept his promise about returning to Mississippi. The original plan had been to start in Amzie Moore's hometown of Cleveland, but when Moses got there, he found that it was going to be hard getting started in Cleveland. There was no place to meet, no equipment, and no funds.[18] Meanwhile, some activists in southwest Mississippi read a *Jet* magazine story about the plans Moore and Moses were making. One of them, C. C. Bryant of Pike County, invited Moses to start work there. After consulting with Moore and visiting Bryant, Moses agreed to start the work in the Southwest.

The counties in the southwestern part of the state—including Pike, Amite, and Walthall—were vicious. Working there instead of in the Delta meant exchanging the Citizens' Councils for the Klan. Pike County had eight thousand adult Blacks, of whom two hundred were registered; in Amite, it was one out of five thousand; in Walthall, none out of three thousand. What journalist Jack Newfield said of Amite County could have been said of the whole area: "It has not only missed the civil-rights movement, but the Industrial Revolution as well."[19]

The counties of the Southwest are hill counties rather than Delta counties, which characteristically means much smaller Black populations, less emphasis on cotton, and more subsistence farming, dairy farming, and lumbering. The land and the people, regardless of race, were poorer in the hills. When land was selling for fifteen dollars an acre in the hills it was one hundred dollars an acre in the Delta, where an acre easily produced twice as much cotton. The Delta was dominated by enormous plantations, the hills by small farms. Culturally, the rednecks of the hills were more fundamentalist religiously, more staunchly behind Prohibition. Much of the state's political history revolved around the mutual antipathy between Delta planters and hill rednecks, particularly the usually successful struggle of planters to control the more numerous rednecks in state politics.[20]

Race relations differed in the two contexts. In the hills, Blacks and whites were more likely to find themselves in economic competition, and among hill country whites there was little of the Delta's pretense about an aristocratic tradition of race relations. Hill counties were plain mean, and they didn't try to dress it up. Rabid racists like Bilbo tended to be champions of the hills; their crudity was considered an embarrassment in the Delta. The Klan was typically stronger in the hills. Where the racial rules were relatively less absolute, where individual Blacks weren't so completely dependent on individual whites, someone was occasionally likely to bend the rules too far. In the Delta, as in many Black Belt counties, social distance between Blacks and whites was so great that no one ever needed to be reminded of it, rendering the Klan less necessary and lynchings less common.[21]

Members of the national NAACP staff were hard to impress, but as far back as the 1940s some of them regarded the small towns of southwest Mississippi as remarkably hateful. One report refers to Tylertown in that area as having one of the most flagrantly abusive police systems NAACP lawyers had encountered, a place where police officers just went out and systematically whipped on a large number of Negroes every Saturday night, where there was a designated "Beating Ground" not far from the city.[22]

If the Southwest was Klan country, it was also NAACP country. The chapters of the Southwest were permanently established earlier than those in many other parts of the state, and while they too suffered ups and downs during the fifties, they generally seem to have weathered the repression better than branches in other "easier" parts of the state. The Walthall branch had been the first in the state to file a school desegregation suit. In 1957, when chapters across the state were struggling, the McComb branch claimed to be having larger meetings than it had ever had. Members of the Pike County branch had gone to Washington to testify for the 1957 Civil Rights Act, and the branch was holding regular Wednesday-night voter-education meetings before Moses came. With Medgar Evers's help, Bryant had started a youth group that concerned itself mostly with police-brutality cases and with sharing Black literature.

Pike County's chapter was led by C. C. Bryant, a voter since 1948 and branch president since 1954, who had a job on the railroad, which made him relatively independent of local whites. He also ran a barber shop *cum* library in his front yard, the place to go for "radical" literature—Black newspapers and magazines, NAACP material, political broadsides, and the like. Bryant began plugging Moses into the activist community.[23]

E. W. Steptoe, the head of the Amite branch, was one of the first people Bryant took Moses to meet. Steptoe was a landowner, a dairy farmer. His father had been a landowner before him, and E. W. had grown up relatively protected from white racism and unafraid of it. He learned about the NAACP during a trip to New Orleans and came back and started the Amite County branch in 1953. The branch was almost entirely male at first. Eventually, a group of forceful women, afraid that Steptoe was running himself ragged trying to keep the organization going, joined the organization and took more of the day-to-day burden off him. At first, he said later, it was easy to get people to come to any kind of meeting; that was before the post-*Brown* repression. He had gotten local membership up to about two hundred until one evening in 1954, when E. L. Caston, the sheriff, walked into a meeting and walked out with the membership lists and records. Steptoe contacted the FBI, which was enough to make Caston return the books, but people had gotten the message. One of Steptoe's uncles hid himself in the woods for a week and then left the state. Shortly thereafter, one of the chapter members was charged with murder, apparently in retaliation for NAACP activities. Participation fell off sharply for a while, although Steptoe was able to keep the branch technically alive by buying some memberships himself. The branch was also able to start its own newsletter, *The Informer*.[24]

Steptoe, of course, was a marked man. He started going about very heavily armed. It became a family ritual for his wife, Sing, who disapproved of his carrying guns, to pat him down as he was leaving the house, but he invariably got something by her, if only his derringer. By the early sixties, he was having trouble selling his milk or getting a loan anywhere in the area. In November 1960, he wrote Roy Wilkins asking for help in obtaining "a federal loan are eny [i.e., or any] kin of a Loan except in the State of Mississippi for I am being pressed here in Mississippi Because of my [being] Active."[25]

Steptoe was one of Moses's important early contacts; Webb Owens was another. A retired railroad porter and the membership chair of the Pike County NAACP, everybody in town knew Webb Owens. He was a cigar-smoking dandy, super cool, invariably sharply dressed, friendly and outgoing, the kind of man people trusted with their money because he had enough of his own not to be bothered with pilfering anybody else's. In fact, he supplemented his income by lending money out. For two weeks in July, Bryant and Owens took Moses around McComb and its environs, introducing him to their friends, explaining that they needed to supply room, board, and transportation expenses for student workers to conduct a registration campaign. They got enough pledges to support ten students, to begin early in August. The intention was that the students would only stay for that month. As soon as the students got there, according to Bob Moses, Owens took them by Miss Quinn's cafe—Miss Quinn herself had started going down to register in 1955—and told her "Whenever any of them came by you feed 'em, you feed 'em whether they got money or not."[26]

Webb Owens also sent Moses to a group of honor students from the local high schools, kids who had known Owens all their lives. Five or six of them agreed to canvass for a month, which was how lots of people found out about the movement. The kids had little luck with their own parents, which was frustrating for them. Owens did what he could to keep them motivated, taking them to lunch, treating them to ice cream sodas.

The first two weeks of August were given over to house-to-house canvassing. Moses was especially concerned that the civil rights workers impress local people as serious and responsible. He learned that for him the most effective way to canvass was to introduce himself to people and show them a registration form, asking if they had ever tried to fill one out. Then he could ask them if they would like to try it right there in their own homes. There was psychological value in just getting people to imagine themselves at the registrar's office.[27]

During the first week of August, they were able to open their first voter-registration school. The school was necessary, not only because so many Blacks in the area were semi-literate but because registering to vote in Mississippi required answering a twenty-one-question form and then interpreting any section of the state constitution to the satisfaction of the registrar. The Mississippi constitution at the time had 285 sections.

Under the circumstances, the initial response seems quite good. Fairly soon after the school opened, sixteen people went to take the test, and six passed. Farmers from neighboring Amite and Walthall counties requested schools of their own. At that point, SNCC was not necessarily ready to take on two more tough counties, but they couldn't very well say no, either. As local authorities came to understand that something was going on more systematic than a few individuals trying to register, things got tougher. On the 15th of August, three Negroes from Amite—one elderly farmer and two middle-aged women—went to Liberty, the county seat, to register, accompanied by Bob Moses. All three were people who had tried unsuccessfully to register before. There was some harassment—the registrar made them wait nearly six hours, and a crowd of city-hall employees gathered to watch them, staring and muttering. Still, they were able to fill out the form, which was more than had happened before.

A highway patrolman followed them out of town and eventually stopped them. Moses was arrested and charged with interfering with an officer. Before the trial, Moses placed a collect call to John Doar at the Justice Department, deliberately speaking loudly enough to be overheard. Before going to Mississippi, he had gotten letters from the Justice Department outlining the sections of the 1957 and 1960 civil rights acts guaranteeing protection to people trying to register and to anyone trying to help people do that. Hearing Moses talk to the Justice Department seemed to unnerve the local authorities. Moses was given an amazingly light sentence: a ninety-day suspended sentence and a five-dollar fine for court costs. Nonetheless, he refused to pay any fine and was jailed. The NAACP had him bonded out, and he spent most of the last two weeks of August setting up a registration school on Steptoe's farm in Amite, where again, people came in small but steady numbers.

On the 22nd, another group in Liberty tried to fill out the forms, and they were allowed to do so without any difficulty. Everyone was encouraged, falsely as it turned out. On the 29th, after accompanying two more people, the Reverend Knox and Curtis Dawson, to Liberty, Moses was attacked on the street by Billy Jack Caston, a cousin of the sheriff and a son-in-law of a state representative. Caston knocked Moses down with a punch to the temple and then hit him repeatedly with the butt end of a knife. Moses

> just sat in the street trying to protect himself as best he could in the traditional nonviolent position, his head between his knees and his arms shielding his face. The Reverend Knox tried to pull Caston off his victim, but white bystanders ordered him not to intervene.[28]

Mr. Dawson was eventually able to pull Caston away from Moses. Afraid he'd frighten people if he went into town in his bloodied condition, Moses went to Steptoe's farm, where even Steptoe didn't recognize him at first. The next day, continuing to defy the area's racial mores, Moses filed suit against Caston, who was quickly acquitted in a courthouse filled with angry, armed white farmers. "At the trial," Mr. Dawson recalled," the High Sheriff was scareder than I was." The sheriff and deputy followed them out of Amite after the trial to make sure nothing happened.[29]

Not all the action revolved around registration work. In mid-August, when some of the Freedom Riders were released from jail, they gravitated to the McComb area. These included Travis Britt, Reggie Robinson, MacArthur Cotton, and John Hardy. Some of the leaders of the newly formed direct action wing of SNCC also came, including Marion Barry. There was still some lingering sense of competition between voter-registration people and direct-action people. The latter started holding workshops on nonviolent direct action. On the same day Moses was assaulted, two eighteen-year-old local residents who had been attending the workshops, Curtis Hayes and Hollis Watkins, sat in at the local Woolworth's, the first such action in the area. That night, two hundred Negroes attended a mass meeting, and plans were made for more sit-ins and more voter registration work. The SNCC workers wanted to make it plain the beating hadn't frightened them, and they wanted to step up the pace of things before the whites could rally their forces.[30]

During the month of August, white repression seems to have been disorganized and ineffective. The authorities seemed fearful about following through on the arrest of Bob Moses. His beating seems to have been the act of a lone lunatic. There did not seem to be any clear sense among local whites of how to crush the incipient rebellion. For the first month, at least, both violence and legal repression seem timid, judged against the standards of Mississippi. Very probably, as suggested by the reaction of officials to Bob Moses calling the Justice Department, this timidity was partly a result of local whites looking over their shoulder. At this point in the process, they could not have had a clear idea of what a voter-registration drive was, nor of how forces outside of Mississippi, the federal government in particular, might react to unrestrained violence against one.

At the same time, local Negroes seem to have been almost immediately responsive. Fear notwithstanding, the organizers had people trying to register almost immediately, they were invited into neighboring counties, and they were getting good turnouts for at least some mass meetings. Even in one of the worst sections of Mississippi, there was a constituency for SNCC right away, a reflection in part of the earlier organizing done in the 1950s.

DEVELOPING ORGANIZERS WHERE YOU FIND THEM

Part of what made the McComb movement possible was the ability of SNCC to plug into work that an older generation of activists had begun. What made a more sustained, statewide movement possible was the fact that SNCC in its early years found, in virtually every town, a few young people who got so caught up in the movement as to become full-time workers. In Mississippi, one of the first of these was Hollis Watkins, who had grown up on a farm near the line between Lincoln and Pike counties. When he was growing up southwest Mississippi was a very different place from the Delta. He thought race relations were more relaxed; whites and Blacks had more contact. He saw white kids working in the fields just like Black kids. Blacks living in the Southwest worked hard, but they seldom had to work the way people in the Delta worked. Even during the busy season, people in Southwest didn't have to work on Sundays.

Watkins's mother had a sixth-grade education; his father had only a couple of years of schooling. Hollis himself started working in the fields before he started school. Like many farm wives, his mother, who had twelve children to look after, worked a fourteen- or fifteen-hour day. On days when they were working away from the house, she got up and cooked two hundred biscuits—breakfast and lunch—and then went to the fields herself. During slack times, his father worked in New Orleans or in the Delta and, by the time Hollis was seven, had earned enough to buy a small farm.

Hollis graduated high school in 1960 and went to California—he had relatives there—hoping that he could put on some weight and join the police force. That didn't pan out, and he started watching the Freedom Rides on television, which made him wonder what was going on in the South. He returned home, trying to decide whether to try to get the money to go to Tougaloo College. One day, a "friend-girl" told him that Martin Luther King was in town with a lot of other important people. He and a friend, Curtis Hayes, went into McComb, where they found that it wasn't Dr. King who was around but Bob Moses. Moses explained the registration project to them and went over the Mississippi constitution. It didn't seem difficult to Hollis, and he said he could teach it to other people. The next day he started canvassing door-to-door.

Soon after, Marion Barry came to town and explained SNCC's direct action component to Hollis and others, which led to the Pike County Nonviolent Movement. Hollis didn't particularly believe in nonviolence but was willing to go along with the program. About fifteen or twenty young people decided to sit in at Woolworth's lunch counter. Come the appointed day, only he and Curtis Hayes showed up, and to make matters worse, when they got to Woolworth's, all the stools were occupied. They had to pretend to be shopping. Finally, two people got up at the same time, and they rushed for the seats. The waitress just ignored them. A cop came, promising they wouldn't be arrested if they left right away. They refused, and pandemonium broke out. They wound up doing thirty-four days in jail for bringing the sit-in movement to Mississippi. Subsequently, Hayes and Watkins, along with Emma Bell, Bobby Talbert, and Ike Lewis, three more local young people, became full-time organizers, work they would continue as long as SNCC existed and beyond.

McComb is always remembered as a defeat for SNCC, which is true in a narrow sense, but it overlooks the fact that SNCC learned in McComb that merely the process of trying to organize a town would attract young people, a few of whom were willing to identify completely with the organization's work. The Mississippi movement would be built largely around these home-grown organizers.

The surprisingly good progress the Movement seemed to be making in McComb in August came to a disappointing end. Shortly after the first sit-ins, Brenda Travis, a fifteen-year-old who had grown frustrated with what seemed to her the slow response of adults to the movement, told SNCC workers she was eighteen years old and led five other high-school students in a sit-in. She was arrested, expelled from high school, and sentenced to a year in a school for delinquents. The Black community was incensed that a fifteen-year-old child was in jail, and many blamed SNCC. Whites were angry that SNCC had stooped to using children. Angry meetings, white and Black, were held all over town.

In early September, about a week after Brenda Travis had been arrested, an older white man described by Moses as "tall, reedy and thin, very mean with a lot of hatred" attacked SNCC's Travis Britt, as he and Bob Moses were taking some people to register in Liberty. Britt recalled that

> he was holding me so tight around the collar, I put my hands on my collar to ease the choking. This set off a reaction of punches from this fellow they called Bryant; I counted fifteen; he just kept hitting and shouting, "Why don't you hit me, nigger?" I was beaten into a semi-conscious state. My vison was blurred by the punch to the eye. I heard Bob yell to cover my head.[31]

Two days after that, John Hardy, a SNCC worker who had been running a voter-registration school in Walthall, took a group to register. The registrar pulled a gun and hit Hardy with the butt of it. Hardy staggered outside, where he was arrested for disturbing the peace. (The Justice Department later blocked the prosecution of Hardy, saying it constituted intimidation of voters under the 1957 Civil Rights Act. In the following months, as activity across the South became more intense, the Justice Department would time and again deny it had the legal authority to do what it had already done in McComb.)

The jailing of Brenda Travis and the other youngsters and the beating of Britt just about brought the movement to a standstill. The farmers in Walthall and Amite were no longer willing to try to register. Everyone in Pike County was upset over the jailing of the youngsters who were under five-thousand-dollar bonds. SNCC thought it would raise the bond money and start all over. Instead, things got worse. In the beginning, the presence of SNCC workers had given local people some sense of protection. Moses recalled:

> I think they felt some sense of security, and clearly we were acting as a kind of buffer, because the initial physical violence was always directed at the voter registration workers. That was the first stage. Now, when that didn't work, you began to get violence directed at the local people who were involved. The first being Herbert Lee.

A boyhood friend of Steptoe's, Lee had joined the Amite County NAACP when it was founded in 1953 and had remained an open member through the persecution of the mid-fifties. In 1961, when many of those who had initially been interested in the movement in McComb were frightened off by the repression, Lee continued to support the movement, frequently providing transportation for the students.[32]

Lee has been described as the kind of man who was content to stay in the background. A dairy farmer and the father of nine children, he could neither read nor write, but he had some self-pride. He traded across the state line in Louisiana, because he knew the local stores were going to cheat him. He would have sent his children to school in Louisiana if that had been possible. He was strict about not allowing his kids to work anyplace but on his own farm. When he went anyplace with his family, he would drive far out of his way to avoid gas stations and stores where they might receive racial slights. Some of this impressed some of his neighbors negatively. It seemed to them he was putting on airs. What made his kids so much better than anybody else's?

Around mid-September, the Justice Department sent a team of lawyers led by John Doar to investigate the situation. For two weeks, they went around interviewing people, which helped to raise spirits. When they interviewed Steptoe, whose name they had gotten from Medgar Evers, he told them that a man named E. H. Hurst had threatened the lives of several people—Steptoe himself, a Mr. George Reese, and Herbert Lee. Steptoe also told them that whites were coming to meetings, taking down the license numbers of the Black people there. Steptoe hadn't actually seen this happening but thought Herbert Lee had. Doar went looking for Lee but couldn't find him before he had to leave for Washington. When he got back to Washington the next night, the 25th of September, there was a note on his desk—Herbert Lee had been shot dead.[33]

For several nights after the killing, SNCC workers searched for witnesses, blundering around the countryside in the dark, pulling up into the driveways and yards of people they could only hope wouldn't be white. They were able to find three farmers who told the same story: Lee had pulled into the local cotton gin, followed by Hurst, who left his pickup and went up to Lee, saying something like "I'm not fooling around this time. I really mean business." Lee said, "Put the gun down. I'm not going to talk to you until you put the gun down." Hurst put the gun back under his coat, but as Lee got out of the passenger side of his pickup—presumably to avoid Hurst—Hurst ran around the front of the truck, pulled the gun, and shot Lee. Perhaps a dozen people, white and Black, had seen the whole thing. Shot just above the ear, Lee's body lay on the ground for two hours; nobody wanted to come near it.

The Black witnesses had been pressured by the sheriff and others to testify that Lee (about five feet four and 150 pounds) had tried to hit Hurst (six three and about 200 pounds) with a tire tool. They testified as ordered. Hurst was acquitted by a coroner's jury, the same day as the killing, never spending a night in jail.

Hurst was a prominent citizen, a member of the state legislature. He was also the father-in-law of Billy Jack Caston, the man who had beaten Moses, and his farm sat right across the road from Steptoe's. There was some surprise in the Black community that the killer should be Hurst; he was a man with whom many Blacks in the area interacted every day. One neighbor said:

> We knew E. H. Hurst. . . . He was a deceiving kind of person, if
> that was put into his mind but I don't think anyone would come
> out and say he was such a terrible type of person, 'cause he lived
> among the Blacks and nothing he did didn't ever show that he was

that kind of person. I know when my daddy passed, he would come down and ask my mother what could he do. . . . It was a disbelief to everyone who knew him [that Hurst should be the killer].[34]

Hurst, Steptoe, and Lee had all grown up together and had been boyhood friends. According to Roosevelt Steptoe, E. W.'s son, the relationship began to go sour when Lee and Steptoe prospered more than Hurst thought appropriate for Black men and then became openly involved in civil rights agitation. From that time on, Hurst became a bitter enemy of both Lee and Steptoe.

One of the Black witnesses that SNCC workers turned up was Louis Allen. At the coroner's trial, Allen had said exactly what the sheriff told him to say, but afterwards he told SNCC workers he would be willing to tell the truth at the impending federal grand-jury hearing, provided he could get some kind of protection. Contacted by SNCC on Allen's behalf, the Justice Department claimed that it couldn't provide him with any protection, and in any case, Hurst couldn't be indicted in Mississippi. Six months later, a local deputy sheriff would tell Allen that he knew Allen had tried to get FBI help. The deputy then broke Allen's jaw with a flashlight. SNCC people felt only someone inside the Justice Department could have told the local officials what Allen had wanted to do. Incidents of that sort encouraged the belief in SNCC that local law-enforcement people and local representatives of the Justice Department were in collusion.

The pattern that the Justice Department set in McComb was a pattern consistent only in its inconsistencies. On the one hand, they might accept a collect call from a jailed civil rights worker and they might file suit on behalf of one who had been beaten. (The policy of accepting calls from civil rights workers had been one outcome of the meetings between the Kennedy administration and the civil rights organizations. It was stopped when southern congressmen got wind of it.)[35] On the other hand, they might ignore the situation of a man willing to risk his life to see justice done; they might even make that man a target for reprisals. Nonetheless, from the viewpoint of local law-enforcement people, the mere possibility of federal intervention was probably enough to put some limits, however slight, on violence and blatant illegalities.

SNCC activists were beginning to develop a very different view of the federal government from that held by many local Black Mississippians. For SNCC, the Kennedy administration increasingly came to symbolize a callous and cynical preference for political expediency over law and common decency. At Herbert Lee's funeral, his wife came up to Bob Moses and Chuck McDew and shouted at them, "You killed my husband! You killed my husband!" She was saying what they already felt. The lives the government couldn't find legal grounds for protecting—not in the Constitution, not in the Fourteenth Amendment, not in the Civil Rights Acts of 1957 or 1960—were lives SNCC workers felt personally, individually, responsible for. It is not surprising that by the time of the 1963 March on Washington, the talk SNCC's John Lewis wanted to give was titled "Which Side is the Federal Government On?" Local Blacks, on the other hand, were likely to be grateful for whatever federal help they got. Any help at all was a good deal more than they were used to. They were comparing the Kennedys to Mississippi whites, and the Kennedys came off well.

After the Herbert Lee murder, it was almost impossible to gain further ground with voter registration. The young people of McComb, though, were still not intimidated. By early October, the students arrested in August were out of jail. At an assembly at school, someone from the Pike County Nonviolent Movement asked the principal whether Brenda Travis was going to be readmitted to school. His hedging was taken to mean that she wouldn't be reinstated, and over a hundred students walked out and held an impromptu march to the movement headquarters. There they decided, against the advice of SNCC staff, to march over to city hall and pray in support of their classmate and in protest of the Herbert Lee murder.

Once the kids decided that they were going to go anyway, SNCC workers felt they had no choice but to go with them. The only white person on the march was SNCC's Bob Zellner. A mob gathered, and the sight of a white person marching with the Blacks threw them into a frenzy. The mob's vanguard, ten or twelve white men, began beating on him. They would take a swing at him, and then look to see how the nearby cops reacted. The cops didn't do anything until other SNCC workers, including Moses and Chuck McDew, came and tried to shield Zellner with their bodies. Thereupon the cops sprang into action, giving Moses and McDew a thorough beating. Zellner could hear the sounds of the blackjacks bouncing off their heads. The mob tried to drag Zellner away from everyone else, but he grabbed the railings on the city-hall steps and held on for all he was worth, while they continued to beat him with chains, pipes, and fists. One guy kept getting his fingers in Zellner's eye socket, trying to pry his eyeball out. (Zellner: "I remember being amazed that it would stretch that far.") Throughout the beating, FBI agents were standing by, taking notes. Eventually, the police did intercede and pulled Zellner away from the mob. The SNCC workers and 119 students were arrested.[36]

Hollis Watkins was among the arrested. While he was being questioned, he decided not to say "sir." His obstinance was clearly making the roomful of white men nervous, and he was frightened himself. He tried to answer everything in full sentences so that there would be no need for a "sir." He was taken to a room and left there. Two white men walked in with a hangman's noose, threatening him. While he sat there smiling at them, trying to decide which window to go through, they turned and left.

The arrestees were out on bond within a few days. When the principal of the local Negro high school demanded that students sign a pledge promising not to demonstrate any more, over a hundred of them stayed out of school. Many parents supported their children. Every day the kids would go to school, refuse to sign, and march away. The principal issued an ultimatum: return to school by 3 P.M. on October 16 or be expelled. At quarter to three on the 16th, 103 students returned to the school, handed in their books, and walked out. SNCC opened Nonviolent High in Pike County, with 50 to 75 kids in one large room, offering algebra, English, physics, geometry, and French, although the students seemed to like the singing best. The school remained open a couple of weeks before Campbell College in Jackson made space for them.[37]

By late October, most of the SNCC staff was jailed again. The bonds totalled $14,000, far more than SNCC could raise—indeed, it was roughly the same as SNCC's national budget for the year—so they spent several weeks in jail. The violence continued while they were off the street. In October, two people visiting the McComb project, Paul Potter of the National Student Association and Tom Hayden of the then-young Students for a Democratic Society, were dragged from a car and beaten. In November, four CORE workers were beaten by a mob when they tried to eat at the lunch counter in the local bus station. FBI officials again watched and took notes. In November, a shotgun was fired into a home where two SNCC workers were staying. In December, four whites attacked three out-of-town newspapermen, and three more CORE people were attacked at the bus station.[38]

Those arrested did thirty-nine days in jail this time, most of November and into the early part of December. Their morale wasn't necessarily low. Some local people continued to be supportive, bringing food, smuggling letters in and out. One of the notes Bob Moses smuggled out came to be much quoted:

> We are smuggling this note from the drunk tank of the county jail in Magnolia, Mississippi. Twelve of us are here, sprawled along the concrete bunker; Curtis Hayes, Hollis Watkins, Ike Lewis, and Robert Talbert, four veterans of the bunker, are sitting up talking— mostly about girls; Charles McDew ("Tell the Story") is curled into the concrete and the wall; Harold Robinson, Stephen Ashley, James Wells, Lee Chester Vick, Leotus Eubanks and Ivory Diggs lay cramped on the cold bunker. . . . Myrtis Bennett and Janie Campbell are across the way wedded to a different icy cubicle. . . . This is Mississippi, the middle of the iceberg. Hollis is leading off with his tenor, "Michael, row the boat ashore, Alleluia; Christian brothers don't be slow, Alleluia; Mississippi's next to go, Alleluia." This is a tremor in the middle of the iceberg—from a stone that the builders rejected.[39]

Going into McComb, there was no way that SNCC could have much sense of what it took to sustain an organizing drive in the hard-core

South. It was virgin territory. They learned from the older activists, of course, but it is worth noting that this was a period in the organization's history when it was particularly open to learning; it was a flexible, relatively non-dogmatic moment, notwithstanding the fight over voter registration as opposed to direct action. They seemed to be saying, "Let's try something and see what happens." There was no assumption that they had the answers. In another context, Bob Moses would comment that the problems to be attacked by the movement were so intertwined that all you could do was break off a piece of it, work on that and see where it led.[40] He once quoted approvingly a SNCC member who wrote this description of the attitude of SNCC workers toward finding truth:

> Here I am, looking at the world and at the situation I am in and we are in, and from the position I hold in the universal scheme of things, I have reached this conclusion. And this conclusion is no more or less valid than yours, no more or less important, so let us all consider what I see and what you see and from it all we can ultimately find the Truth.[41]

Similarly, commenting on the McComb period, Jim Forman noted that "Rather than set up rigid definitions of goals and tactics, it seemed best then to experiment and learn and experiment some more and draw conclusions from this process."[42] This openness to experience can be contrasted with the rigidity of the NAACP at the national level, with its firmly fixed methodology. It is also to be contrasted to SNCC in its later years, when the pattern would seem to involve much more dogmatic answers to the important questions, answers that were not always directly informed by their practice.

In interviews some years later, Bob Moses summarized the lessons learned from the five months in southwest Mississippi. They had learned that it did make sense for a person like himself, an outsider, to come into a town, live there, and start voter-registration work. It was possible to get a critical mass of local people to respond, young people certainly and some older people as well, particularly small, independent farmers, who like the young people were relatively free of the economic control of whites. Businessmen and ministers were more likely to vacillate, although there was some under-the-cover economic support from businessmen even after things got rough. They had also learned not to count on their friends in Washington. For Moses, perhaps nothing was more important than the fact that they did find family:

> One of the things that we learned out here [in Amite] was that we could find family in Mississippi. We could go anyplace in Mississippi before we were through and we knew that somewhere down some road there was family. And we could show up there unannounced with no money or no anything and there were people there ready to take care of us. That's what we had here in Amite. One of the things that happened in the movement was that there was a joining of a young generation of people with an older generation that nurtured and sustained them. . . . It was an amazing experience. I've never before or since had that experience where it's almost literally like you're throwing yourself on the people and they have actually picked you up and gone on to carry you so you don't really need money, you don't really need transportation. . . . They're going to see that you eat. It's a liberating kind of experience.[43]

Similarly, SNCC's Jean Wheeler Smith thought of local movement supporters as the soil, the substratum that allowed the younger activists to grow and flourish.

Released from jail in December, some of the SNCC staff went north to Jackson, where they spent part of early 1962 working on the congressional campaign of R. L. Smith, a friend of Medgar Evers and the first Black to run for that office since Reconstruction. Curtis Hayes and Hollis Watkins decided to put off their own plans for a year or so, as they thought, and went to Hattiesburg to help Vernon Dahmer put together a registration campaign there. It was Dahmer who had had such an effect on the Ladner sisters when they were growing up. Dahmer was a prosperous man, making a hundred bales of cotton a year and operating his own sawmill. The boys lived with him and worked on the farm to pay their keep. This was fortunate, since SNCC, with characteristic generosity, had given them $50 to run a three-month campaign. Dahmer gave them all the support they needed; they had the run of his place and took his pickup any time they wanted, and he told them whom to contact.

Early 1962 was also spent mapping the plans for a wider program of voter registration. A series of meetings was held, involving Bob Moses from SNCC, Tom Gaither and Dave Dennis from CORE, and Medgar Evers, Amzie Moore, and Aaron Henry of the NAACP, among others. A memo written in January of 1962 by Moses and Gaither reflects the state of their thinking at the time.[44] They thought it was important to have coordinated efforts among the several organizations to avoid duplication, confusion, and general lack of direction. The basic goals are identified as developing effective leadership at the county level, the fundamental political unit in Mississippi, and as linking together leaders in a given area. The work was to be concentrated in those areas of the state where the Black population was heaviest, 45 percent of the population or more. Cities where Blacks could vote without as much fear of physical or economic reprisals—Greenville, Clarksdale, Jackson, Vicksburg, and Natchez—were to be targeted with special programs to address the ignorance and apathy of the Black population. It was hoped that Black schoolteachers could eventually take over the leadership roles in some areas, but in the rural areas the expectation was that the leadership would have to come largely from the church and individuals relatively protected from economic reprisals.

Wherever possible, the plan calls for workers to live with people in the community they are trying to organize, "so that a real relationship between all concerned may be realized." In the smallest communities, it may be advisable to stay only a week or two at a time. Organizers are to be cautioned to give "considerable weight" to the opinions of local residents as to which approach should be taken in their communities. Students are envisioned as the main workers in rural areas and in towns where adult leadership was minimal, but students would only be used as auxiliary help when adults were willing to lead. It was hoped that thirty-five students from Mississippi could be trained during the spring semester and that a high-caliber student could be attracted to the work. The work in the rural areas was expected to be largely door-to-door. Where possible, it was advised that several contiguous counties be organized at once, so that it would be more difficult to concentrate reprisals on a few people. If possible, schools were to be set up to teach basic skills as a supplement to the voter-registration work.

The document suggests that another of the lessons taken from McComb was an awareness of the dangers of working in isolated areas, like the Southwest. It also reflects the consistent concern with developing indigenous leadership; Ella Baker or Septima Clark could have written it. It is proposing in effect that civil rights workers exert as much leadership as necessary, but only that much. Local people are being asked to do as much for themselves as they can, and the document specifically hopes to recruit students from Mississippi, students who would be more likely to stay around after the movement ended and continue to contribute a degree of leadership. The thinking embedded in the document is focused much more around developing leadership than around getting large numbers of people registered to vote. For many in SNCC, registration was a tactic, a means to the more important end of getting people involved politically.

The document mentions the need for some coordinating council of civil rights groups. The response to that was the February 1962 reorganization of the Council of Federated Organizations (COFO), which put all the civil rights groups in the state under one umbrella, with Aaron Henry as titular head and SNCC supplying most of the personnel, except in the southeastern part of the state, where CORE was strong.[45] SNCC seldom let the absence of money bother it. Projects like McComb were "funded" largely by willingness—the willingness of SNCC workers to work for little or nothing and by the willingness of local Blacks to provide food and shelter. The latter kind of contribution has been largely overlooked, but for the work that SNCC was doing, it was of pivotal importance. Still, as the inability to raise bail money in McComb suggests, more money would have made a more efficient operation possible. By mid-1962, COFO was receiving enough outside funding from the Voter Education Project to make possible an expansion of their work.

By the spring of 1962, SNCC had a little more money than it was used to, in COFO it had an organizational structure from which to work, and from the months in Southwest it had taken some hard lessons in the theory and practice of community organizing. The young people were ready to start applying what they had learned to the rest of the state, Greenwood included, where they would, again, find family.

Five

Building on the Past

*Our adherence to the organizing principle that you
find people who are already working and build on what they
are doing was the basis of our strength.*

JEAN WHEELER SMITH
SNCC[1]

COFO REGARDED GREENWOOD as a place of particular strategic importance. By 1960, its population of twenty-two thousand made it one of
the largest cities between Memphis to the north and Jackson to the
south. A movement beachhead in Greenwood would allow penetration into the surrounding Delta counties with their enormous Black
populations. Moreover, it was one of the tough areas of the state,
home to the Citizens' Council, and the movement had to demonstrate, sooner or later, that it could survive in such places.

Between the spring of 1962 and the spring of 1963, Black Greenwood did in fact become an organized town. It required a remarkable
transformation. Most Black adults and a great majority of the traditional leadership initially wanted nothing to do with "dat mess." By
the following spring, the movement had developed enough momentum that even some of the town's more conservative Black leaders felt
constrained to offer at least the appearance of support.

How were a few organizers able to accomplish as much as they did
in so short a time? As in McComb, younger activists were able to ar-

ticulate their work with the work of older, local activists. The younger activists were able to draw resources from all levels of the Black social system but, while there were middle-class individuals who played vital roles, Greenwood's Black middle class as a class decided to wait for another day. During that first year, the viability of the movement hinged largely on the ability of young organizers to win the confidence of yardmen and maids, cab drivers, beauticians and barbers, custodians and field hands.

LEFLORE COUNTY

The town of Greenwood and the county of Leflore both take their name from an eccentric nineteenth-century Native American chieftain. At the Treaty of Dancing Rabbit Creek in 1830, Greenwood Leflore, part Choctaw, part French, ceded to the American government all that remained of the Choctaw lands in Mississippi, amounting to about a third of the present-day state. He earned the name of traitor from the Choctaws and a large estate from the government. Leflore remained loyal to Washington to the end of his days, supported the Union during the Civil War, and insisted that he be laid to his final rest wrapped in the Stars and Stripes.[2]

Over the next century, Greenwood became an important Delta town, especially known for its long-staple cotton market. By 1960, over 600,000 people, thirty percent of the state's population, lived within sixty miles of Greenwood. The county population of about 47,000 was almost two-thirds Black and very poor. Median family income for the county in 1960 was just about $2,300 compared to $5,660 for the nation as a whole. Median income for white families was $5,200; for Blacks, $1,400. Only eleven percent of Black families earned more than $3,000. The disparity in education was similar. Among adults over twenty-five years of age, median years of schooling was 5.1 for Blacks compared to 11.2 for whites. Sixty-three percent of employed Blacks were either private household workers or laborers of some kind, usually farm laborers. Eighty-two percent of Negro housing in the county was substandard, which in the Delta could mean sub-any-human-standard. Nevertheless, Negroes living in tar-paper shacks with one or two light bulbs would regularly receive higher utility bills than white families in modern homes.[3]

In 1960 agriculture was still the center of the economy, if not as dominant as it had been two decades earlier. Of the forty million dollars earned by county residents in 1959, twenty-three million had been earned in agricultural production. Farm land, of course, was controlled by whites. Ninety percent of the farm land in the county was owned by 551 white farmers; 1,162 Black farmers owned the other ten percent, and they were rapidly losing that.

The county actively courted industrial development. By 1963, perhaps twelve percent of those employed were working in some form of manufacturing, producing pianos, electronic components, farm machinery, and clothing. Some of these companies were from out of state, another indication of the Delta's lessening isolation from the outside world.

Blacks were becoming increasingly irrelevant to the local economy. Each year, cotton production was more mechanized. Small farm owners, largely Black, found it increasingly hard to make a go of it. Between 1954 and 1959, fully two-thirds of the farms in the county went out of business, many of them swallowed up by the larger landowners. In the same period, Negro-owned acreage dropped from 71,000 acres to just 24,000. Of those Blacks who were unemployed in 1960, forty percent had been agricultural workers.[4]

If Blacks were being marginalized, so were the big planters. Even the fact that by 1960 the county was courting industry was a token of how much influence planters had lost. Fearful of having to share their labor supply with factories, Delta planters had for decades opposed industrialization. After the surplus-labor conditions of the 1950s, planters across the Delta held to their anti-industry prejudices, but local businessmen, a social class in the ascendancy, were much less likely to go along.[5] The same erosion of planter status was evident on other questions. Prior to World War II, elite Delta planters had pretty much called the tune politically. They had great economic leverage against businessmen, and by a variety of strategies managed to disenfranchise enough poor whites to render them largely irrelevant as a political class. By the end of the 1950s, it was no longer possible for the elite planters to decide things among themselves and then have that translated into public policy. Still, in Greenwood, they were able to elect their candidate, Charles Sampson, to the mayor's office in 1957, thus assuring that the town would be led through the civil rights era by an advocate of the hard-line white-supremacist position of the planter class.

LOCAL POLITICAL ACTIVITY BEFORE THE SIXTIES

Twentieth-century attempts to register by Leflore County Blacks date at least as far back as the Depression and the formation of a small Voter's League. There may have been three dozen Blacks on the voting rolls by the time of the Second World War. Getting registered ordinarily required some form of white patronage, which meant convincing some white man that you were really a good nigger without a political thought in the world. For some, the desire to be registered really was apolitical, a mark of personal distinction, a way of proclaiming their superiority to common Negroes. Others were explicitly concerned with the vote as a collective weapon and were willing to engage in as much bowing-and-scraping as necessary to get it. It was a most circumspect way to make change, but it was enough to get the white folks mad from time to time. When the numbers of Blacks inquiring about registration got too high, there might be a rash of cross-burnings or threats against individuals suspected of stirring up their neighbors. Plenty of people in Black Greenwood were thought to be willing to win the favor of some powerful white man by reporting—perhaps accurately, perhaps not—the names of people "trying to start trouble." As a result, a form of canvassing went on but within very limited circles. One talked about voting only to those whose trustworthiness had been clearly established. Talking about it in a public meeting was seen as the equivalent of just turning your name into city hall. Whether there really were as many tale-carrying spies as the folklore of the Black South suggests is always an open question, but the belief that they were ubiquitous shaped everyone's behavior, and, in fact, local authorities certainly had some informants reporting on incipient activism.

The younger people playing leadership roles after the war represent a bridging generation, more aggressive than the strictly accommodationist leadership of previous decades, less caught up in the patronage system, a foreshadowing of the still more aggressive local leadership to come. John Dittmer's characterization of Black leadership across the state in the 1950s—predominately male, including a number of World War II veterans, relatively well educated and relatively free of white economic control—fits, with minor adjustments, many of the people who were active in Greenwood at the time.

Richard West, eighty-six years of age when I interviewed him, is not an educated man, a fact for which he kept apologizing. Growing up in a large plantation family before World War I, he had gotten less than a grade-school education. His real education began when he migrated to Chicago after the war. He had worked in a tannery, been a chauffeur, shined shoes, run a concession stand at an El stop, and been a Pullman porter traveling throughout the South and the West. He loved the railroad, if only because it put him into contact with people of every type and station, always giving him something to think about. In the 1930s, on his railroad trips through the Delta, he told people the mechanical cotton picker was coming. He had seen the machines being built at International Harvester in Chicago. People thought he was crazy.

He moved to Greenwood in 1948 and opened a service station shortly after that. At some point in the early 1950s he needed an operation for varicose veins. He went to Dr. T. R. M. Howard in Mound Bayou, the founder of the Regional Council of Negro Leadership. In the course of conversation with Howard and later with Amzie Moore, West got sold on the RCNL program and soon became a very active member. By the mid-fifties, West had managed, apparently without white sponsorship, to get himself registered after several unsuccessful attempts. (The first time he went, the registrar told him he had to know how many seeds were in a watermelon and how many bubbles in a bar of soap, questions of the sort that registrars often asked as a form of teasing Black applicants.) After he was registered, he led a campaign in Greenwood to get Negroes to pay their poll tax. One of the people who worked with him on that campaign was Louie Redd.

Redd spent World War II in the Navy and like West was a much-traveled man. After the war, Redd had been among the veterans testifying at the hearing on Theodore Bilbo in Jackson. Before the war, he had been a professional baseball player with the Memphis Redstockings of the old Negro Professional Leagues. The team occasionally played in Greenwood, and since the Greenwood women wouldn't leave him alone he decided he might as well settle down there, later becoming a man of the cloth. Leflore County allowed Black veterans to register, but most were uninterested or afraid. J. D. Collins, a minister and an important community leader, bet Redd that he wouldn't try to register, so he did, and no one gave him any trouble about it.

Redd and West organized the first Black Boy Scout troop in Greenwood. The Black churches were reluctant to support even that; they just weren't civic-minded, according to Redd. Sometimes it was easier to get support from white people. Once, when they needed a truck to take the boys camping, a white car dealer filled a truck with gas and gave it to them for a week. Eventually, Redd and West managed to get into even worse trouble with the churches. Greenwood's annual Christmas parade had always been all-white. One Christmas in the early fifties, Redd and West had their Boy Scouts jump into the line of march with everyone else, which created a small furor. Black ministers were furious, but this early application of direct action shows that West and Redd were a different breed from the prewar leaders.

Redd was among the original members of the Greenwood NAACP after it was organized in 1952. Aaron Henry had come down from Clarksdale to help them get started. Many of the leading members had a degree of financial independence and more education than was average. W. J. Bishop—"Foots" Bishop when he was a halfback at Alcorn State College—was a bartender and a property owner who held a variety of jobs on the side. Charles Golden, the NAACP secretary and one of those who worked hardest to start the chapter, was a barber. Ed Cochrane, the first president, owned a great deal of rental property as well as some small businesses and was considered the most prosperous Black man in the county. It may only be apocryphal, but some people claimed that some early meetings were held in darkened rooms using flashlights. It is true that all NAACP mail went to Golden,

Bishop, or Cochrane and was then redistributed, so that the authorities wouldn't know who was taking part. At times, mail for the Greenwood NAACP was sent first to Jackson and then hand-carried to Greenwood. Once established, the organization quietly encouraged people to register and to keep their poll taxes paid. They also regularly brought speakers to town, something almost impossible to keep from the authorities and thus the subject of some controversy.

Most of the members of the NAACP were also members of the Elks, one of the most prestigious social groups in town. Some of the Elks, though, were far from supportive of the NAACP. Schoolteachers and principals in particular were aghast at virtually any form of open activism. The small businesspersons—barbers, carpenters, housepainters, beauticians, shopkeepers—were split. A person like Ed Cochrane, with ties to both sides, was pressured from both sides. Whenever the NAACP or RCNL brought a controversial speaker to town, there was likely to be a fight over it among the Elks, especially if Elks Hall was going to be used for the talk. One school principal apparently once kept Ralph Abernathy of SCLC from appearing at the hall. On other occasions, after the activists had brought in a speaker, the schoolteachers would invite the mayor to speak, so that he would know they weren't a part of that foolishness.

Richard West joined the Greenwood NAACP shortly after it was formed. Ruby Hurley from the regional NAACP office had heard of him because of his RCNL activity. She came by the garage one day while he was working under a car and asked him if he were afraid to join the NAACP. Annoyed by the way she put it, which was probably her intent, he fished out the two-dollar membership fee and threw it to her.

The Greenwood NAACP could hardly have been formed at a less auspicious time. In general, 1952, by Mississippi standards was a relatively peaceful year in terms of race relations. The Supreme Court school integration decision of 1954, however, initiated a wave of repression across the state, and some of Greenwood's activists were caught up in it. Both West and Redd had been involved in voter-registration activities around the Belzoni area. When George Lee was killed in Belzoni in 1955, West attended the funeral. He was carrying a .38, his wife had a .32, and his mother had a switchblade knife. After the funeral, Redd was invited back to Belzoni to conduct registration classes, and he accepted. The murder of Emmett Till, also in 1955, had a special impact in Leflore County. Before the body was found, Richard West put on dungarees, grabbed a cotton sack, and went out in the fields to see what people had heard. Till's body was brought to a funeral home in Greenwood, and the local NAACP chapter was expected to offer support to staff members coming in from the national office. There is some controversy about how well that was done. Some survivors contend that some of the local chapter officials were too frightened to offer the national office much support, so much so that the national office threatened to revoke the charter. Others denied that anything of the sort happened.[6] Whatever happened, it is clear that the local chapter fell on hard times after the Till murder. It had started with a membership of fifty-three, with hopes of doubling that in a year. Within two years, active membership had fallen off so much that the chapter became inactive.

Even people like West and Redd, initially defiant in the face of the new wave of violence, felt the pressure eventually. West had often been afraid for himself and his wife, and he had often thought about getting out, but every time he thought about that, something would happen to make him mad all over again. Like Evers, he toyed with the idea of more drastic action. He had learned to make pipe bombs in Chicago, and he dreamed about giving whites a taste of their own, not that he thought it would really do any good. His name was circulated on a list of people who were to be killed; the Reverend Lee's name had been on the same list.[7] West was very disturbed when T. R. M. Howard, also on the list, decided he had to leave the state. Howard had all the advantages of money and contacts, he lived in an all-Black town, and he had guards with him all the time. West had none of these advantages. After a cross was burned outside his home, West decided to leave the state, moving to California. He tried without success to get Medgar Evers, named on the same death list, to do the same.

People like West and Redd pushed the system harder than had earlier leadership, but the 1955–1956 wave of repression put many activists temporarily out of business. The late fifties was a period of slow recovery. In 1957 or 1958 a Citizen's League was founded in Greenwood, to pursue much the same agenda as the NAACP but with even more focus on voting rights. The founders thought that if they did not use the hated NAACP name, they might encounter less opposition. Its membership, all registered, was pretty much the same as that of the defunct NAACP, with the addition of the Reverend Aaron Johnson, a young minister who was particularly involved with the town's young people. The NAACP itself was reorganized in 1956, only to have its charter revoked for a lack of membership; it sputtered briefly to life in 1958, partly because of the prodding of Medgar Evers, partly because some of the local people thought that not having a chapter was a badge of civic backwardness. Again, it went defunct, probably within a year.[8] One of the most outspoken members of the Citizen's League was Cleveland Jordan, an older man and a plantation laborer most of his life, who made people nervous by raising, with commanding eloquence, the issue of disenfranchisement at any meeting he happened to attend, no matter how inappropriate it might be to the subject at hand. He also sold the *Eagle Eye,* a radical and somewhat eccentric one-sheet broadside from Jackson. A deacon at Zion Baptist Church, he had a formidable knowledge of the Bible, notwithstanding his fourth-grade education. "He could break your spirit with the Bible," one of his sons recalled. "Whatever your issue was, he could take that Bible and whip you to death with it." He had little use for local ministers unwilling to take a stand—"grip toters and chicken eaters," he called them. He found ministers more to his liking at national church gatherings. From the 1940s on, his neighbors took up an annual collection to send him to the National Baptist Convention. In the postwar years the convention was going through an internal struggle between the conservatives who had long dominated it and a younger, better-educated, and politically more aggressive wing. Jordan found himself in sympathy with the younger wing, ministers such as Fred Shuttlesworth of Birmingham, William Holmes Borders, Martin Luther King, and Mordecai Johnson. Within the state, he aligned himself with people like Medgar Evers, Aaron Henry, Amzie Moore, and the Reverend Lee of Belzoni, the more radical leaders.

By the fifties, leadership in Black Greenwood, as in other Delta communities, had changed significantly. During the Depression community leaders had tended to be small landowners with important positions in the church, usually ministers. Landowning had become less significant by the late fifties; leaders still tended to have church positions, but more of the leadership was secular, especially the more aggressive leaders—West, Cochrane, and Bishop, for example—and they tended to have some measure of financial independence. Although there were women who had influence inside the NAACP, leaders still tended to be men, many of whom had spent significant periods of time outside the southern racial system and its parochialism, in the form of military service or extensive travel or involvement in activities like national church organizations. As was true across the state in the fifties, a number of the Greenwood leaders—for example, West and Redd with their Boy Scout troop—seemed to have a sense of civic involvement that went beyond any narrow conception of civil rights.

By the end of the fifties, the organizations created by local activists could point to no dramatic accomplishments, but they were what Jo Freeman calls cooptable networks—like-minded individuals in communication with one another, with some resources, material and otherwise, under their command. When younger activists entered the county in 1962, they would find elements from this network supportive at crucial moments, if a little inconsistent about it.

WYATT EARP AND THE SUMMER OF 1962

With Kennedy administration blessing, the Voter Education Project had been established. In June of 1962, SNCC received five thousand dollars of VEP funds, and with that they went ahead with their plans for an enlarged voter registration drive in six counties—Washington, Coahoma, Sunflower, Bolivar, Marshall, and Leflore. Bob Moses was the statewide director of the project. They sent one young man to Greenwood, Sam Block, twenty-three years old at the time.

Block, from nearby Cleveland, had been identified by Amzie Moore as a likely recruit for the movement. Block's mother cooked, kept house, and cared for the children of a local judge. His father did construction work and worked at a local cotton compress until an accident at work rendered him unemployable. After graduating from high school, he attended a teachers' college in St. Louis prior to a stint in the Air Force that was cut short by his asthma. By this time, the Freedom Rides had started, and he wanted to be back in the South anyway.[9]

When he did get back to Cleveland around October 1961, the Freedom Riders had passed on to other things, jail mostly. He took a job at his uncle's gas station and started taking classes at Mississippi Vocational College in Itta Bena, seven miles from Greenwood, which meant that he started meeting young people from Greenwood.

Amzie Moore, who owned the other Black service station in Cleveland, was an old friend of the Blocks and lived down the street from them. Sam talked with Moore frequently. Block, a teenager at the time of Emmett Till's murder, was very much affected by it and by the way Amzie Moore spoke up about the killing. When Block lost his service-station job for arguing with a white customer, he told Amzie Moore that he wanted to "do something." Moore, the Reverend James Bevel of SCLC, and Bob Moses invited him to work with SCLC setting up citizenship classes. In 1961, Septima Clark's citizenship program had been transferred from Highlander to SCLC, and they entered Mississippi the same year, starting in Clarksdale, where Aaron Henry, a member of the SCLC board, was a natural link. SCLC's James Bevel, a native of Itta Bena just outside of Greenwood, lived with Amzie Moore, starting citizenship classes in several small Delta towns. Block spent much of early 1962 doing the same work.

As a part of their preparation for expanded voter-registration efforts, SNCC held a workshop on registration at the Highlander Center, then in Knoxville, in June of 1962. Block attended, as did Curtis Hayes and Hollis Watkins. The workshop, following a format frequently used at Highlander, brought experienced activists from across the South to talk with the young people who had been recruited by SNCC.[10] Together, they studied state registration laws, discussed strategies of persuasion to be used in canvassing and strategies for penetrating a community. They engaged in role-playing exercises modeled around the kinds of dilemmas the new recruits could expect to encounter in the field.

They got plenty of advice. Esau Jenkins, whose problems had stimulated the development of the Citizenship Schools, was there from South Carolina to testify to the importance of the vote. Since his group had gotten started, four thousand Black people had been added to the rolls. The kids on the islands now had a high school for the first time. They had bus transportation. Police were learning to keep their nightsticks to themselves. If you were taken before a magistrate, you had a chance of fair treatment.

One man advised them to sell voting as a Christian thing to do. Another, almost describing what would become SNCC's style of organizing, advised organizers to "go to their homes, eat with them, talk the language that they talk, associate with them on a personal level. Then go into your talk about the vote."[11]

Bernice Robinson, from John's Island, who a few years earlier had not thought herself competent to run a single citizenship class, was also prophetic, noting that around Knoxville people acted like women couldn't do anything. She was there to testify to the contrary. People, she said, ignore the fact that women do the hardest work. She illustrated with the story of a male minister who agreed to head up a registration campaign and failed to follow through. She had to finish the work for him, but, of course, he got all the credit.

Another woman warned against adopting the local class snobberies. Don't ignore the bootlegger. He talks to a lot of people. Put him on your committee. A man from a rural area questioned the need for developing a personal relationship with the people you were trying to reach. Rural people get very few letters so they take those they do get very seriously. He had always gotten a good response by organizing his campaigns around written appeals.

The young people were admonished against bickering with other organizations. Push your program, not your organization, and one way to do that is to give as much responsibility as possible to local people. They were warned that preachers could be a problem, but that alienating them wasn't going to help anything. They were warned against assuming that they knew what the local problems were. They would have to learn to listen to the people who lived with the problems. They were reminded that everything they did reflected on their movement. If they got caught drunk, that reflected on the movement. If they failed to go to church, that reflected on the movement. Myles Horton ended one session by pointing out that the Delta farmer, who had lived through things the young people had only read about, had very real reasons for his fear but that didn't mean that a person, no matter how old, could not be challenged, so long as you respected the basis for those fears.

The advice the young people received from the older organizers was often divergent, even contradictory, but from Highlander's viewpoint that was not a problem. The intent was to expose the kids to as rich a body of concrete experience, to as wide a variety of perspectives as possible. In the field, the recruits would have to cut and tailor what they had learned to fit their particular situations and their particular talents. It was traditional at Highlander to end workshops by asking "And what are you going to do when you get back home?" Near the end of the week, the recruits were asked to draft a written plan of attack for whatever community they were going into. Thus, the young recruits went into the field armed with as much vicarious experience as the older activists and Highlander could make available to them.

Block returned from the workshop with Moses, Hollis Watkins, and Curtis Hayes in Amzie Moore's 1949 Packard, singing freedom songs as they made their way back to Mississippi. Watkins and Hayes went back to Hattiesburg, and Bob Moses took Sam Block to Greenwood. Block had asked to be assigned to Greenwood in part because it had been a part of the Till killing. Moses warned him about the possibility of being killed there himself.

SNCC's initial entry into many towns is reminiscent of the Old West, with one or two marshals coming to clean up Dodge City. Arriving just after mid-June, Block was to be a one-man movement for much of the summer. Left on his own resources, he was able to contact some of the students he had met at Mississippi Vocational; they put him in touch with Mrs. McNease, principal of the elementary school. Innocent of Block's intentions, she rented him a room.

As she would go to school in the morning, I would go canvassing, just talking to people in the community about voter education and registration, sort of testing the pulse of the people. Hanging out in the pool halls, wherever people were, the laundromat, run around the grocery stores, meeting people. I was always introduced as a student at Mississippi Vocational College. I found that there were a lot of angry people in Greenwood. . . . I found that the people who were most receptive to me were the older people. Mr. Cleveland Jordan sat me down and gave me a whole history of what had been going on in Leflore County. He told me about how he had decided to start a voter education movement in the early 50s. He gave me the names of those persons who were involved in that and the names of those who he felt also were still interested in getting a voter education movement started. Finally, we were able to get our first meeting of about 15 or 20 people together and we met at the Elks Hall. Mr. Jordan was an Elk. And we began to set up some sort of an organizational structure, gave people responsibilities, let them know what I would be doing, to sort of watch out for me—they knew the history of Greenwood—and I asked them for suggestions of things that they felt I should do, places that they thought I should go to, and people whom they thought I should talk to.[12]

Mr. Jordan had been a member of the Citizen's League in the 1950s and had worked with the NAACP, although he had not been a member himself. At the second meeting held at Elks Hall, Block began teaching the freedom songs, after which the Elks asked him to leave, claiming they didn't like all that singing. In fact, they had been pressured by the mayor.[13] Having lost his meeting place, he then lost his living quarters. Mrs. McNease, his landlady, began receiving threatening calls, and he had to move.

Block slept in an abandoned car for a week before Robert Burns, a friend of Mrs. McNease, took Block in and was very supportive of the work Block was doing. But the police arrested Burns on dubious charges, and Block had to move again. For a while, he and the other SNCC workers who were in and out of town had to stay in Cleveland and commute to Greenwood. Because the Freedom Rides had generated so much excitement in Mississippi the year before, people associated Block with that. "People would just get afraid of me. . . . They said, He's a Freedom Rider. . . . I was just there to stir up trouble."[14] Even young people crossed the street when they saw him coming. The idea that they were just going to start trouble and then move on, leaving local people to suffer the consequences was something that SNCC and COFO workers heard all the time, and with some justification. It looked to many as if that had happened in McComb. Nevertheless, Block was able to find some people right away who were receptive to his message, at least in part because he had people like Mr. Jordan steering him. VEP records for July and August show that he was taking people down to the registrar's office at least a couple of times a week, usually just four or five people a day but sometimes twice that. They weren't getting registered, but they were going down. By the end of July, he was also able to get two of the churches in town to let him use their buildings sporadically. One of those churches was Wesley Methodist Chapel, which had a history of political activity. Indeed, in April, just before Block came, the Regional Council on Negro Leadership had met there.

Before taking his first group down to register, Block told Bob Moses that he didn't know what might happen and needed reinforcements. Moses promised to send Luvaughn Brown and Lawrence Guyot soon. Before they got there, Greenwood had its first mass meeting, publicized by word of mouth only and held at the Reverend Aaron Johnson's First Christian Church. Sam taught the freedom songs, and Mr. Jordon endorsed him, saying, as Block recollects it, something like:

> Well, we got somebody now that is going to help us do something. We have been wanting somebody, now here he is. I want you all to give him all the support that you can. Don't be scared of him. Treat him like he is one of us because he is.[15]

The next day on the street he got a different kind of reception. People were asking him when they were going to have another meeting and when were they going to learn some more of those songs.

And I began to see the music itself as an important organizing tool to really bring people together—not only to bring them together but also as the organizational glue to hold them together. I started to give people the responsibility of thinking about a song that they would want to sing that night and of changing that song, you know, from a gospel song.[16]

After a second mass meeting, Block decided to take the first group, a group of about twenty-one people, down to the courthouse. They were older people, anywhere from forty years of age to seventy or eighty. At the courthouse, the group was first stonewalled by Martha Lamb, the registrar, and then confronted by the sheriff, who wanted to know where Block was from, since he, the sheriff, knew "every nigger and his mammy" around Greenwood. According to a much-told story in the movement, Block asked if he knew any colored people, at which the sheriff spat in his face and told him to get out of town. Block's reply was "If you don't want to see me here, I think the best thing for you to do is pack your clothes and leave, get out of town, cause I'm here to stay."[17] Public defiance of the "laws" was an important element in the style of many of the workers in the Delta, and it was certainly a part of Block's style.

As Block took his people home, the law-enforcement officers followed, taking down names and addresses, but some people refused to act intimidated, shouting back "You don't scare me no more. You don't scare me no more."

Block endeared himself to the authorities by bringing a police-brutality charge against them. On the 28th of July, fourteen-year-old Welton McSwine was arrested and charged with having peeped into a white woman's window. Even though he claimed to have been at work at the time of the incident, McSwine was kicked and beaten with nightsticks, a blackjack, and a bullwhip until his father came for him. His father's boss had to call to ask that the boy be released. Block took affidavits on the case and had Robert Burns, who was a photographer on the side, photograph the welts on the boy's body. The material was sent to what Howard Zinn calls "the bottomless, bucketless well of the Justice Department." Police took to following Block home from the registrar or having a police cruiser stay with him all day when he was canvassing door-to-door.

Through all of this, he continued to make slow progress, as suggested by some of the reports he filed that summer. On July 26, he wrote:

> Sorry I am late with my report, but in making an excuse it only satisfies the person that makes it, so I will try to do better next time. O.K.
>
> Gee! May I say that I am glad that things have begun to come my way at last. Wait! I am not excited—just glad *now*.
>
> Today, Mr. Jerry T. Chestnut, a leading citizen of Greenwood, was in the office. He made himself known. He is a leading salesman for some big insurance company, a registered voter, a member of the Leflore County Voters League, a well-known person. He wants to offer his support financially and bodily. In addition to that, he is going to be responsible for contacting some of the big men and women that he knows will give their support in both ways. . . .
>
> I am waiting on one of my fellows to come back from Mt. Beulah's work shop. His name is Dewey Greene, a student at Mississippi Vocational College, an ex-navyman. He is pretty well ready to work. We are planning some direct action here Monday morning at 9. The people that are going to participate have been pretty well disposed to what's happening.
>
> By the way, I cannot send a budget for this week because I did not have any money to spend anyway. My fund raising campaign has been rather slow. For this two weeks, I was donated $10 by one of the young fellows that runs a pool hall on Broad Street. He said that he is going to support us from now on, regardless of what happens. . . .
>
> I have been speaking so enthusiastically to the people around here until they would be less than human if they didn't do something to help.

On the 12th of August, he wrote:

> There's plenty going on here, and right now I am kept busy trying to keep up with the people I have working. It has taken a long time

to get them to do anything at all, so I can't afford to lose them now. . . .

Mrs. Corine Gay was told if she knew the constitution she had to write a poem about it. She couldn't write the poem, so she couldn't take the test.

The FBI is here. They seem to have every white person in Greenwood upset. They are wondering how the FBI got all of the information that they have about Greenwood.

I don't have anything to say about money, because there is none here, as a matter of fact there hasn't been any for a month now so why worry: I mean here.

His temporary access to the Elks Club and his reference to getting an offer of help from one of the leading businessmen are interesting. It is usually held that in small towns the top and the bottom of the social order were the most difficult to organize. This is true but with significant exceptions, frequently involving people who had been active in NAACP networks in the 1950s. Among the more socially prominent of Block's early supporters were Ed Cochrane and W. J. Bishop.[18] Both were members of the Elks and had been instrumental in getting Block access to their building. Both were good about bailing people out of jail. When the movement became more established, Cochrane frequently loaned his car to movement workers (who smashed it up at least once). Bishop also became increasingly active, as COFO made progress in Greenwood. At one point, his employer, Mr. Malouf, was pressured to do something about Bishop. Malouf (one of the wealthiest men in the county but a man socially ostracized by the county's big families because of his Arab background) let it be known that what Bishop did away from work was Bishop's damn business.

August was a month of small victories and dramatic defeats. On the first of the month, Block was told by a policeman that if he didn't learn to "sir" a white man, he could expect to find his teeth on the sidewalk. The next day, police walked in on a mass meeting where Block was teaching people how to register. On a Friday afternoon early in the month, Block accompanied a group of people to the office of Martha Lamb, county registrar. The deputy registrar, clearly hostile, greeted him with "What's for you, boy?" His tone frightened the applicants, but Block gave as good as he got. The deputy registrar said they would have to come back when Mrs. Lamb could see them. Block asked her what her job was and why she couldn't register them and how many Negroes were registered to vote at her office anyway? All that, she told him, was none of his business, but she did decide to give the applicants the test, a small victory but one we can be certain was talked up in the Black neighborhoods that evening.[19]

On the 13th of August, Block was walking home when a red and white Ford made a U-turn and pulled to the curb alongside him. Three white men jumped out, pulled Block into a nearby vacant lot, and gave him a good going over. When he struggled home, he found that his landlord, Robert Burns, who had been very supportive, had been arrested. A few days later Burns was charged with bigamy.[20]

On the 16th, the day before Burns was arrested, two additional SNCC workers, Luvaughn Brown and Lawrence Guyot, had come to lend a hand for a while. That evening they held a meeting with the local volunteers, all teenagers apparently, to plan for the next day's canvassing. Brown, only eighteen years old at the time, noted in a report that there was "a tremendous amount of fear among the workers that night."[21] Nonetheless, seven volunteers showed up the next morning for canvassing. By noon, they had contacted a hundred people—it is likely that some of them were people who had been contacted before—and ten people agreed to go register. Two of the volunteer workers, though, had been harassed by the police, and when the others heard that, they decided they had had enough canvassing for one day. Of the ten residents who had agreed to go register, three showed up. Brown and Guyot went back to talk with the other seven, to no avail. After a quick lesson on the Constitution and the literacy test, Guyot took the three women who had shown up down to the courthouse. The police chief was there, and after he cursed them all, the three would-be registrants were afraid to even go into the courthouse. That evening there was another meeting with the volunteers. Apparently, the police intimidation frightened them but not enough to keep them away. After the volunteers left, the three SNCC workers stayed late to talk about the problem of fear.

As the number of registration attempts increased, the Greenwood *Daily Commonwealth* began to take more notice, publishing the address of the COFO office. Standard operating procedure required Block to call Bob Moses daily. On August 16, a day after there had been a particularly large group trying to register, Moses, at Amzie Moore's in Cleveland, received an emergency call from Block around midnight. Block, Guyot, and Brown were still in the Greenwood office. It was a second-floor office. In the street below, Block reported, there were several police cars and several carloads of white men. Moses called the Justice Department. Block called back a while later. The police had gone, and the whites had formed a milling crowd in front of the building, brandishing guns and chains. Moses, along with Willie Peacock, decided to drive over, arriving in Greenwood around 3 or 4 A.M. (Peacock: "I don't know what we were supposed to do when we got there.") They found the office door knocked down and the office deserted and the records missing. Block and the others showed up in the morning. When the armed mob started coming up the back stairs the previous evening, the workers decided not to wait and see what they wanted. They had gone out the window, across the roof of the building next door and down a television antenna.[22] They made it to the home of Cleve Jordan's son. Before they were run out of the office, Block had called the Justice Department, which told him they couldn't do anything until a crime had been committed but advised him to call the local FBI agent. (An agent had been stationed in Greenwood since the Emmett Till murder.) He showed up the next day, apologizing for being late.

Two days later the office was broken into again. In addition, Mr. Burns, their landlord, was still being harassed by the police and had to ask them to leave. The group had a meeting in a cafe near what had been their office. There was some thought that Block should get himself out of town before he got himself killed. If he stayed, he certainly ought not to have to stay alone. After the group mulled it over for an hour, Willie Peacock, who had previously been critical of SNCC for not sticking it out when things got tough, decided to "get patriotic. I said, 'Well, I'll stay' and no one challenged me. Well, so there I was." There they were without even a place to stay, so he and Block stayed in Cleveland for a while, spending a couple of nights in Greenwood sleeping in abandoned cars. When they did find another place to stay in Greenwood, they tried not to let themselves be seen coming or going, and for several months they had to work without a real office, though the Reverend Redd gave them desk space in the barbershop.

Despite the repression, things were getting done. Peacock had chosen to stay, and by the end of the summer Hollis Watkins came from Hattiesburg to join them. Peacock was another product of Amzie Moore's contact network. That spring he had graduated from Rust College in Holly Springs, where he had been doing some movement work. He returned to his home in Sunflower County, planning just to pick up his things before moving to Detroit, where he wanted to make some money before enrolling in Meharry Medical School. He hadn't unpacked before Amzie Moore and Bob Moses showed up. One of Moore's contacts told Moore that Peacock was home. He and Moses then recruited him to work in the Delta, after which Amzie rode him around Tallahatchie County. Peacock, who had grown up in the county, was surprised at how many people were trying to get a movement afoot.

In addition to Peacock and Watkins, Lawrence Guyot, Luvaughn Brown, and Moses were in and out of town. Block had built up a stable core of at least six or seven local volunteers to help with canvassing. He had so much confidence in them that in early August he had planned to leave town for a week-long conference. He wasn't worried about losing momentum because "Dewey Greene and the boys," as he put it, could keep things going till he got back. They had access to at least one church, the Reverend Aaron Johnson's, on a regular basis. The SNCC workers had developed some form of relationship with the town's traditional Black leadership. Although it wasn't always dependable, the help of older activists meant the younger activists were immediately able to find people willing to cast their fortunes with the movement. They had done more in a few months than most of Black Greenwood would have thought possible.

THE FALL OF 1962: DIGGING IN

John Doar, frequently the Justice Department's man on the scene all over the South, believes that there had been a more or less tacit understanding in Mississippi that public officials would do all in their power to stop integration. In effect they were saying to the public, "Y'all let us handle this." During the fall of 1962, the federal "invasion" of Ole Miss in support of James Meredith's admission to the school, along with SNCC's initial penetration into the Delta, must have suggested to some that the state's politicians were no longer able to "handle it." As that became clearer, some elements of the white community became increasingly likely to take matters into their own hands. According to SNCC's Charlie Cobb, "If it's possible to feel violence and tension in the air, you could certainly feel it in the Delta of Mississippi in the late summer and fall of 1962."[23] Perhaps the most significant achievement of SNCC workers in the Delta during that period was that, in contrast to McComb, they were able to demonstrate to local people that they could outlast the repression, and the longer they lasted, the deeper the relationships they could build.

Another important target for COFO in the Delta was Sunflower County, immediately west of Leflore County, where, according to Fannie Lou Hamer, every white man who could afford a gun and a dog was a police officer. Sunflower was an inviting target partly because it was there that Senator James Eastland, then the ranking Democrat in the Senate, owned a fifty-four-hundred-acre plantation. (He was, at the time, getting about $100,000 a year in federal agricultural subsidies, which didn't stop him from railing against government handouts to the shiftless poor.)[24] One focus of activity in the county was Ruleville, a town of about eleven hundred. Around 1960, Amzie Moore accompanied a local group to the courthouse to register, but they were turned away by the highway patrol. Sometime in early 1962, a local resident, Mrs. Celeste Davis, had started citizenship classes under the auspices of SCLC.[25] Moore and Bob Moses started visiting her in August. On the 14th, five went down to register; on the 16th, four more.

The mayor of Ruleville was a Mr. Charles Dorrough. He was mayor and justice of the peace, owned the largest store in town, and was a newscaster for the local radio station. On the 17th, he paid a visit to Mrs. Davis's father-in-law, a worker in the city sanitation department, to tell him that anybody attending those classes was going to get a one-way ticket out of town. He also suggested that Mr. Davis's city job was in jeopardy.

On the 19th, three student workers arrived. Charles McLaurin and Landy McNair were both Mississippians. Charlie Cobb was a Howard University student who had been in Mississippi all of three days. Two days after they arrived, McLaurin and McNair were arrested and then released without being charged.

As in Leflore County, some residents were drawn to the movement despite—sometimes because of—the repression. In Sunflower County one of the most notable of these was Mrs. Fannie Lou Hamer. For the previous eighteen years, Mrs. Hamer had worked and lived on the Marlowe Plantation outside of Ruleville. She had been a sharecropper for much of that time, and in 1962 she was the plantation time-keeper. She had, as she phrased it, something of a reputation for not having good sense, which meant that she complained about conditions more than was thought advisable. On a Sunday in late August, her pastor announced a mass meeting to discuss registration. She had never heard of voter registration and had no idea what a "mass meeting" might be, but she went, partly out of curiosity and partly because a friend asked her to go. SCLC's eloquent and fiery James Bevel was the main speaker. As soon as she heard people explaining what voting meant, "I could just see myself votin' people outa office that I know was wrong."[26]

Although she frequently cited that mass meeting as a turning point, she was politically active before that. In one interview she mentions selling NAACP memberships, and while she is vague about the time, she appears to mean the 1950s. In the fifties she did regularly attend the annual Mound Bayou Days organized by T. R. M. Howard, which would have brought her into contact with the NAACP and RCNL networks. Hollis Watkins remembers that when Amzie Moore took him on a tour of the Delta in early 1962—several months before the Bevel meeting—one of the people he met was Mrs. Hamer, implying that she was already on Moore's key contact list. Like so many of the others, it wasn't so much that she was found by the movement as that she had been searching for it.[27]

She first attempted to register on the 31st of August. As soon as she got back to the plantation, she was informed that her boss was looking for her. She was frightened, but when her boss came and told her to either go withdraw her application or get off the plantation, she wouldn't back down. ("Mr. Dee, I didn't go down there to register for you. I went down there to register for myself.") She left the plantation that night, moving in with Mrs. Tucker, a friend of hers in Ruleville. In early September, her husband Pap went into the maintenance shop on the plantation and saw buckshot shells lying out, which was puzzling. There is no form of hunting that requires buckshot in September. On the tenth of September, nightriders fired into Mrs. Tucker's home and also into the home of the McDonald family, who had taken in some of the SNCC workers. Two young women were injured. Charlie Cobb of SNCC was arrested and charged with the shooting. He was released the next day, but the shooting and his arrest terrorized the town.

Mrs. Hamer fled to the home of a niece in nearby Tallahatchie County, where she stayed through November. In December, she was able to find a house she could rent in Ruleville. Neither she nor Pap could get work. Their house rented for $18 a month, and they had a hard time making that. In early December, she took the registration test again. She also deepened her involvement with the movement by starting to teach citizenship classes for SCLC, then becoming the county supervisor for citizenship training and later a field secretary for SNCC.

The shootings in early September had essentially brought voter-registration efforts in Sunflower to a halt. According to Cobb, it was months after the shooting before anyone else could be convinced to try to register. Even so, SNCC workers decided to stay on in the county, just to show that if they couldn't offer people protection they weren't going to run either. "And that's basically what we did for months, just were there talking on porches, holding some meetings, small, in the one church that would let us meet."[28] People didn't want to be seen with SNCC workers or even have them send mail to their homes. According to Charles McLaurin, the workers responded by trying to get involved with people's everyday problems, carrying people to the store, helping to pick cotton and chop wood, and gradually, very gradually, winning back the town's confidence.[29]

The same process was going on in Greenwood. After the mob attack in August, it was hard for the movement to gain much momentum. VEP records for September and October show a steady stream of people trying to register, but usually not more than a couple of dozen a week, often the same faithful few. The weekly mass meetings, according to Hollis Watkins, were drawing between thirty and fifty people. Having established a beachhead in town, the movement was having trouble building on it. That period from August through the first of the year, according to Peacock, is when he learned the difference between mobilizing and real organizing. He, Block, and Watkins penetrated the community that fall, spending a lot of time just getting to know people and letting people get to know them. In the process they were locating more of the community's human and organizational resources.

They were able to re-establish stable residence. The woman who ran the cafe next to the Burns place had two sons who had become involved with the registration drive. A while after the SNCC workers were put out of the Burns place, she sent them word of a friend of hers who wouldn't be afraid to put them up. The friend, Miss Hattie Miller, a beautician, kept them through the fall, the boys leaving before dawn and returning late at night. Peacock remembers it as a lot of fun: "Cops be trying to keep up with us. We'd be ducking and dodging." By the fall, they had enough support around town that they didn't have to return to Miss Hattie's every night; various families around town would let them stay for a night or two, making it more difficult for the police to trace them. This, according to Peacock, "is where we have to give Sam credit for a lot of energy, going door-to-door, talking to people, finding out from this one who was sympathetic. . . . 'How much can you help? How much can you afford to do?' . . . It was to the point that there was not a block in the Black community where you couldn't find refuge somewhere."[30]

They also got to know many of the members of the Citizen's League, the group of about twenty members that had quietly tried to stimulate registration before SNCC came. Around October, the boys presented the League with a proposal that listed ways the League could help without its members being too visibly involved. Because of that proposal, the League rented an office in its name and turned it over to SNCC. The landlord was Mr. Campbell, an older man whose father had been white and who owned a cleaners and some other property. He had a grandson involved with the movement and he wasn't worried about reprisals. He gave them three rooms on the first floor of one of his buildings.[31] The League also agreed to raise five hundred dollars as a down payment on a car so the boys could get around. (The money was eventually used as a down payment on one car for Greenwood and another for Frank Smith up in Holly Springs.)[32] With the new office open in January, more college students from nearby Mississippi Valley, mostly women at first, started coming in to help with the clerical work and the canvassing. The SNCC workers made up a packet of materials about registration for them and helped them work up a standard spiel.

In January, when the police did find out where they were staying, Miss Hattie shrugged and said she didn't care anymore what the police knew. From that point on, they were able to operate completely in the open again. By early 1963, the Greenwood organizers were, relative to the situation when they began, into the tall cotton. They had a place to stay, a real office, and transportation—the latter making them the envy of foot-weary COFO organizers across the state. They could eat on credit at a number of little cafes, especially "Blood" Bullins's place. They were getting free haircuts from the Reverend Louie Redd and from Charles Golden, both among the town's original NAACP members. Some young men who lived largely on the wrong side of the law were making occasional cash contributions. They were growing a reliable corps of young volunteers, and they had won the admiration of growing numbers of older people who were helping them stay a step ahead of the law. They were webbed into the community, making it and themselves stronger.

The Greenwood movement was given a boost by a miscalculation of the local power structure. In October, the Leflore County Board of Supervisors voted to halt most distribution of surplus commodities from the federal government. The commodities—usually meal, rice, flour, and sugar—were free but the supervisors explained that it was getting too expensive to distribute them. For 27,000 people in the county, most of them Black, those commodities had been the main source of sustenance during the winter months. Few doubted that the move was in retaliation for the continuing voter-registration drive.

It was an awkward reprisal in several ways. It was non-selective, punishing the innocent as well as the guilty. It put some people in a position where they no longer had anything to lose by trying to register. It made plain a point COFO workers always wanted to put across, that there was a connection between exclusion from the political process and poverty. It also gave COFO a chance to show that they were more than the bunch of rag-tail kids they might appear to be.

In response to the food cut-off, the Atlanta office and Friends of SNCC chapters in the North put out a nationwide call for food for the Delta. Responses came from churches, Black and white, from college campuses and liberal political groups. Ivanhoe Donaldson and Ben Taylor, students at Michigan State, became famous for their truck runs into the Delta, at least twelve that winter, carrying food, clothing, and medical supplies. Medgar Evers also contributed. According to June Johnson, "Medgar put a lot of time in Greenwood . . . saw a lot of people. He raised food and money and helped different families [who had been evicted] get reestablished on the plantations." Dick Gregory, then near the pinnacle of his career as a comedian, was heavily involved. In November 1962, Medgar Evers had asked Gregory to speak in Jackson. He found himself on a program with an old man "the kind of big-lipped, kinky-haired, black-faced verb-buster every other Negro in America looks down on." The old man had just been released from jail. He had been leading a registration campaign, someone had been sent to burn down his home, and the old man had killed him. While he was in jail, his wife died. Clyde Kennard's mother was also on the program. Evers had to explain to Gregory who Kennard was. Gregory was moved by the whole experience, and when he got back to Chicago, he joined the campaign for Kennard's release from jail. When he heard about the food cut-off in Leflore, he immediately helped collect 14,000 pounds of food and started making trips to the Delta, lending his visibility to the effort.[33]

Substantial quantities of foodstuffs got to Leflore, but never enough. The cotton crop had been very good that year, but Blacks got even less than usual out of it. More of the picking had been done with machines, leaving many families destitute.[34] It was also a bitter winter, one of the coldest in many years. In January, the temperature went below zero several times. At least two Blacks in the county froze to death.[35] In January, Block and Peacock sent a report to the Atlanta office in which they mentioned the Meeks family, which had eleven children, none of whom were in school because they had "no money, no food, no clothes, and no wood to keep warm by, and now they want to go register. The house they are living in has no paper or nothing on the walls and you can look at the ground through the floor." In the same month, Block reported a day when he visited ten families who lived

> up in little nasty alleys, it was cold, cold outside, and some of them were sitting beside the fireplace with a small amount of wood burning trying to keep warm. They had little children that had no shoes to put on their feet in that cold, cold house. . . . We found out that the people . . . had to tell their kids that Santa Claus was sick and that he would be able to see them when he gets well.

Bob Moses wrote a supporter in Michigan:

> We *do* need the actual food. . . . Just this afternoon, I was sitting reading, having finished a bowl of stew, and a silent hand reached

over from behind, its owner mumbling some words of apology and stumbling up with a neckbone from the plate under the bowl, one which I had discarded, which had some meat on it. The hand was back again, five seconds later, groping for the potato I had left in the bowl. I never saw the face. I didn't look. The hand was dark, dry and wind-cracked, a man's hand, from the cotton chopping and cotton picking. Lafayette and I got up and walked out. What the hell are you going to do when a man has to pick up a left-over potato from a bowl of stew?[36]

Willie Peacock chaired the food relief committee. By February, he had at least nine hundred applicants, far more than they could serve, even though many of the people signing up clearly didn't believe anything would ever come of it. On the 13th, 400 boxes of food were handed out; on the 20th, another 561, but each time hundreds were standing in line when the food ran out. Nevertheless, several reports commented on how cooperative the disappointed were: "The people were very nice and attentive when we told them we just couldn't get to them." The distribution stimulated voter registration since COFO announced that first priority would go to people suffering reprisals for trying to register, a position some staff weren't comfortable with and didn't always enforce. They also weren't comfortable with having to make decisions about who was most needy, but given the movement's limited resources they had to, so they began visiting homes to evaluate the conditions. They did find some people who didn't seem to need the food, but they found more living under conditions that broke their hearts.[37]

The distribution attracted people who weren't necessarily attracted to civil rights as such, some of whom found themselves drawn into the larger movement without ever having made an explicit decision to join. One thing just led to another. On February 12, 1963, Monetta Hancock

saw a crowd of people standing in front of Campbell's Cleaners which aroused my curiosity. I found out that these people were signing up for food and clothes which was to be given away to needy families. After seeing this, I was asked by someone on the inside of the building to come in and help. After this, I was carried over to Redd's Barber Shop to sign people up over in that area.

The next day she went to Wesley Chapel, where the food was being distributed. "I continued to help out and I really became interested in the movement." For the rest of that week, she attended nightly meetings to discuss the future of the program. At the beginning of the week she was just curious; at the end she had a voice in policy decisions. In between, it is a good bet that she met some people she liked, found some intellectual stimulation, and found other people reacting to her differently because she was identified as a movement person.[38]

The local newspaper had virtually ignored the existence of the movement through the fall. When it did begin covering the movement, it could see no more than outside agitators and communists. It lost no opportunity to say that true Delta Negroes rejected the movement and its claims. In early February, it prominently ran a story about an unnamed "concerned Negro citizen" who deplored the bad publicity the city was getting about the so-called food crisis. The food wasn't really needed; nobody in the area was destitute. The paper pronounced itself satisfied that the nameless citizen spoke for a substantial group of county Negroes.[39]

The paper took the same unbelieving stance toward violent reprisals even while the pace and severity of such incidents increased between mid-February and late March. On the morning of February 20, the same day as the food distribution, Mrs. Nancy Brand in the SNCC office received an anonymous call. She was told that she wouldn't have to worry about going to the SNCC office any more because the office was going to be taken care of. That evening four Negro businesses a block from the office were burned: Jackson's Garage, Porter's Pressing Shop, George's Cafe, and the Esquire Club. Sam Block told UPI that it was a bungled attempt to get at SNCC. Two days later, Block was charged with making statements calculated to breach the peace, fined $500, and given six months in jail.

This was Block's seventh arrest since the summer, and this time he reaped the benefits of having dug himself into the community. Over a hundred protesting Negroes attended Block's trial, overflowing city hall and shocking the city. Many of these were new people, people Peacock didn't know. At the trial, according to Peacock,

> people from these plantations, from all over, they were there, just like that. Say "That little boy, he ain't done nothing to nobody." This really shocked the city officials. They looked and saw all these people packed in the hallway. They were drinking out of the [white] water fountain. They really had their chests stuck out. They came to get Sam out of jail.[40]

Under the circumstances, the city may not have wanted to make Block a martyr. When he was released on bail, people took it to be a personal victory. That night's mass meeting was the largest ever, and the numbers of people trying to register jumped sharply.

On the 25th and the 26th, 150 Negroes tried to register, believed to be the largest groups of people to try to register at one time anywhere in the Black Belt South.[41] The police tried to intimidate the crowd in the usual ways, but the people simply ignored them. Medgar Evers drove up from Jackson to see it. The Atlanta office of SNCC didn't believe the report when it came in. The Jackson COFO office was skeptical. On the 28th of February, Bob Moses decided to drive up along with Jimmy Travis, a Tougaloo student and a former Freedom Rider, and Randolph Blackwell, a field director of the Voter Education Project on a tour of VEP projects. After seeing Greenwood with his own eyes, Moses wrote, "This is a new dimension. . . . Negroes have never stood en masse in protest at the seat of power in the iceberg of Mississippi politics. . . . We don't know this plateau at all."[42]

Twenty-eight people tried to register that day. That afternoon, Blackwell noticed a 1962 white Buick parked near the SNCC office with three white men in it. The car had no license plates, always a sign of potential trouble. The car sat in front of the office all afternoon and into the evening. Police drove by but took no notice of it, despite the absence of tags. Around nine that evening, either Blackwell or another staff member left the office and drove around the block, returning to the SNCC office. The Buick followed him. The workers in the office were warned to be careful. Willie Peacock thought that wasn't enough. He argued that a planned trip to Amzie Moore's should be put off until the next day. Nonetheless, Blackwell set out for Greenville, along with Moses and Jimmy Travis. Travis was driving. The Buick tailed them. Travis pulled into a service station and killed his lights, hoping to lose the Buick. Almost as soon as he had gotten back on the highway, the Buick found them again. About seven miles outside the city, the Buick sped up, pulled parallel and fired several shots, one of which passed through Travis's shoulder and lodged behind his spine. Thirteen bullet holes were later counted in the car.[43]

In the wake of the Travis shooting, COFO felt it had to make the point that violence would lead to more civil rights activity, not less. Angry, the VEP's Wiley Branton announced that organizers from across the South were going to congregate in Greenwood for a concerted push. To Bob Moses,

> it seemed to be the only way to answer this kind of violence: instead of letting up, to pour it on; instead of backing out, to move more people in; instead of giving any signs of fear, to show them that for once the Negro was not going to turn around and it was not possible to shoot them out, and that if anything was going to happen at all, there was going to be increased activity.[44]

Although often reluctant to leave their own projects—and Greenwood organizers were somewhat reluctant to have them come—at least fifty organizers came into Leflore by mid-March, many of them staying until mid-April.

In early March, the homes of two liberal whites, a Mrs. Wheatley and the Reverend Archie Meadows of First Methodist, were fired on.[45] On March 6, Block and Peacock, along with two local residents, Peggy Mary and Essie Broome, left an evening meeting at Wesley Methodist Church where the food and clothing drive had been discussed. As they arrived at the SNCC office, a 1958 Dodge station wagon pulled up and fired a load of buckshot. No one was seriously injured, perhaps because the shooter was so close the buckshot hadn't had a chance to disperse, but they were all cut by flying glass. Willie Peacock, for a moment too angry to be frightened, got out of the car and chased the station wagon up the street, throwing bricks at it. Not to be outdone in point of absurdity, the police said the SNCC workers had staged the shooting for publicity. About a week after that, a group of white men fired into a group of Negroes who were coming out of the movies.[46]

The violence—at least four shootings in about two weeks—frightened people, but the overall story of March is one of gathering momentum, some of which can almost certainly be attributed to the presence of so many organizers and a parade of prominent speakers, conveying the message that local people weren't going to have to stand the storm alone.

Medgar Evers and Aaron Henry were scheduled to speak at a March 4 mass meeting at Locust Grove Baptist Church. When people showed up there, its officials had changed their minds and they locked the meeting out. The meeting was moved to the Reverend Johnson's First Christian, the usual meeting place. The Reverend Johnson's sister reported to him that she had heard that he was to be killed that night. Near the end of a particularly emotional and fear-filled meeting, people were asked who wanted to register and dozens of hands went up. The SNCC workers spent the night in the office. The next morning they were awakened by people from the meeting knocking on the door, ready to go register.[47]

It was a spirit the COFO workers hadn't seen before, and it sustained itself despite the fear. At the mass meeting on the 11th, Block and Aaron Henry spoke, along with Merrill Lindsey, an outspoken minister who had left Greenwood but was still much respected there. At that meeting, they had people recounting their experiences while trying to register. The next day's turnout for registration was again larger than usual. A week later, AME Bishop Charles Golden spoke at Wesley Chapel. SNCC workers had invited Golden as a way of putting pressure on Methodist pastors, and it seemed to do some good.

The excitement in the Black community didn't necessarily arouse much reaction among the general white citizenry. Jack Minnis, a white VEP staff member, visiting during the third week of March, tried to get a rise out of whites at the courthouse and couldn't. He asked one white citizen why there was such a crowd of Negroes—maybe thirty-five that day—around the circuit clerk's office.

> He said he didn't know, but he suggested that they might be registering. I said "You reckon?" He said he didn't really know, but he thought "Ross" [Barnett] had said the other day they weren't going to let anymore Negroes register. I asked him if he thought Ross ought to do this. He said he had never given that much thought. I concluded from the conversation with these courthouse hangers-on, that they were not aware of any particular insurrectionary activity among the Negroes and they were not at all excited about the state of race relations in Leflore County. . . . The Negroes, however, seemed rather uniformly apprehensive as they looked at the whites who passed. I thought it significant that, despite their apprehension, the Negroes remained in the line as it very slowly delivered them to the tender mercies of the Circuit Clerk.[48]

During the last week of March, VEP's Randolph Blackwell was back in town, to find an office buzzing like an army headquarters. Twenty people were working in the three-room office, most of them under twenty-five years of age. He wrote a status report on each of the five components the movement had evolved—canvassing and registration, clothing and food distribution, the youth program, mass meetings, and citizenship schools.

There were at least twenty regular canvassers by this point, going out twice a day, morning and evening, holding debriefing meetings before and after each canvass. Canvassers solicited basic information about attitudes toward registering and then took whatever action seemed appropriate. If people weren't ready to register, maybe they could just come down to the COFO office and try their hand at filling out a registration form, or maybe they wanted to sign up for the citizenship classes that were about to start, or maybe they needed to be referred to the food committee. In the first three weeks of March, canvassers had contacted over 850 people, and more than 250 had gone down to register.

The youth committee was led by Al Garner, a high-school senior who already had experience from his work with the NAACP youth group. The committee had thirty or forty regular members who distributed handbills, canvassed, helped communicate with the churches, and helped take care of the office, at least on paper. Blackwell attended one meeting where sixty-eight people showed up for a frank and spirited discussion of nonviolence.

Attendance at the regular Monday-night mass meeting was increasing weekly. The meetings were attracting more people from the city of Greenwood itself who, Blackwell thought, had been among the most intimidated up to this point. In order to reach people who wouldn't come to meetings, there was a program of Sunday speakers, people who would visit those churches where they were allowed, giving brief talks about the movement.

Blackwell was especially impressed by the thoughtful quality of work being done by the citizenship schools. Highlander had sent Bernice Robinson, and at James Bevel's request, SCLC had sent Annell Ponder, a field supervisor for the schools much in the mold of Septima Clark, focused on developing leadership in others and capable of seeing potential where it wasn't obvious. Bob Moses remembers her as having great depth of spirit and a stubborn, disciplined persistence in her work. In Greenwood, she was quickly able to find twelve people to undergo teacher training, which they completed during the week Blackwell was in town. The classes had not changed much since their early development by Septima Clark and Bernice Robinson. Classes met twice a week for three months, concentrating on literacy, the state constitution, and local and state government, but supplementing that with Negro history and community problem-solving, by which they meant boycotts, demonstrations, and the like. The first fifteen classes started that spring, all taught by women, enrolled close to two hundred students, mostly older people, in their middle forties or older. Septima Clark, who believed firmly that social status has nothing to do with leadership ability, would have been delighted to know that the first class to get started, and the largest, was taught by Ida "Cat" Holland, a former prostitute who had become interested in the movement.[49]

The food and clothing distribution had become a mammoth undertaking, contacting 1,349 people in the first three weeks of March. There was still not enough to meet the need, and there were touches of ugliness that weren't reflected in the reports from February, including accusations that COFO workers were taking the best items for themselves. Frank Smith, who had come down from Holly Springs and been assigned to food distribution, found it to be

> a hectic job that tore away at your emotions. People lied to you about their incomes and family sizes and various other things. You see yourself becoming more and more inhuman and strict each day. . . . You work eighteen hours per day, without food or drink in many cases. . . . On one occasion where a lady had been there three times to receive food, I compared notes. She had twelve kids the first time, fourteen kids the second time and here she sat now telling you she had sixteen kids. When you were all finished with your sermon and was ready to send her home for lying and deny her food, Lawrence [Guyot] came to you and protested. You turned the case over to him. . . . There were occasions when persons would dress raggedy and came to you with sad stories that didn't check out. It was amazing, where you had to say "no" to a person. It seemed as though they could not conceive of one Negro saying "no" to another. In some instances the persons would want to resort to violence.[50]

He, Emma Bell, Guyot, and John O'Neal often wound up contributing their $15 weekly salary to the emergency cases. When he went to jail near the end of the month, he was thankful for the rest.

Blackwell saw a number of problems. Bob Moses was doing too much; housing conditions were poor, with as many as ten workers living in one room; nobody was taking time to keep decent financial records. (Emma Bell, who had joined the McComb movement, was eventually drafted to take care of the latter.) On the whole, though, Greenwood at the end of March struck him as a model of what a concerted campaign could be.[51]

A number of college students spent their spring breaks in Greenwood that year, among them Joyce Ladner, who had been drawn into the movement while still a high school student in Hattiesburg and was now a student at Tougaloo. Her report on the last week of March gives a sense of the quickening pace of events.[52] She arrived on Saturday the 23rd; that Sunday she left the COFO office around eight in the evening. The next morning she learned that the office had been burned around midnight. Neighbors reported seeing two white men fleeing down the alley. Most of the voter registration records were saved, but all the office equipment was ruined. Wesley Chapel offered temporary office space, and she spent Monday morning trying to salvage what she could of the office records, after which she cut stencils for that night's mass meeting and then typed reports for staff members. John Morsell, Roy Wilkins's assistant, was the main speaker, and she thought he was inspiring.

Tuesday, she again did general office work. That evening, the home of Dewey Greene, Sr., was shotgunned. Greene had been an early member of the local NAACP, his son George was active in the local NAACP youth chapter, his son Dewey had applied to Ole Miss, and both boys and their sister Freddie were among SNCC's earliest and most reliable local volunteers. The Greenes were a respected and well-liked family. Jim Forman says Freddie Greene was called the "nicest girl in Greenwood." George Greene was just coming home from a mass meeting when the shots were fired, one hitting the front door and the other a bedroom window. His father let it be known that anyone else who came shooting around his home could expect to get shot himself.[53]

Joyce overslept the next morning and missed Greenwood's first protest march, a reaction to the shooting. Fifteen to twenty people gathered at one of the churches and started singing freedom songs. The songs attracted more people. Someone suggested marching to the mayor's office and protesting the lack of police protection. When unlicensed cars could drive around town and shoot into Black homes, the organizers argued, the police were at least implicitly involved. After Mr. Jordan led a prayer, about a hundred of them set out for city hall, where the mayor told them to either break it up or he was going to have the police dog brought out. They decided to move on to the courthouse, but they were intercepted before they got there by police who sicced a dog on SNCC's Matt Hughes and Bob Moses. According to Peacock, "Bob had a phobia about dogs. But that day he stood there, he let that dog do whatever he wanted. The dog just ripped his pants leg up." Eight workers were arrested: Moses, Jim Forman, James Jones, Curtis Hayes, Charles McLaurin, Frank Smith, Bobby Talbert, Willie Peacock, and Lafayette Surney. Forman had snapped some pictures of the dog attacking Matt Hughes, and before he was hauled off he managed to toss the camera to another SNCC worker. Wire services around the country picked up the photos. There was another large mass meeting that night, at which it was decided to have meetings nightly for a week. The Reverend Tucker spoke at that meeting expressing a desire to become a leader in the movement and volunteering to lead people to the courthouse the next day.[54]

On Thursday the 28th, Joyce helped move the temporary headquarters to First Christian, took several people down to register, taught a citizenship class for Annell Ponder, and helped organize the mass meeting for that night. Forty people were taken to the courthouse that day and were again attacked by the police. The group had left the courthouse just before noon, with the usual reminders about walking two abreast so as to leave room on the sidewalk for others, obeying traffic signals, not making any noise and so forth. The Reverend Tucker and Ida Holland, a member of his church, were in the lead. Two blocks from the courthouse, a policeman with a police dog came out, cursed them, and, goaded on by white on-lookers, put his dog on them. The dog bit Tucker, who fell to the ground. Ida Holland tried to reach him, but the cop turned the dog on her. "The dog and I stared at each other, he bared his lips, and I saw all those horrible teeth in his mouth, it was like a nightmare." SNCC's Landy McNair and Cleve Jordan got the Reverend Tucker to his feet and hustled him into Aaron Henry's car, which happened to be passing by, while Ida Holland got the crowd back together and led them back to First Christian.[55] This was only three days after she and the other citizenship-school teachers had received their certification in front of a cheering mass meeting.

That night's mass meeting was memorable. CORE's James Farmer was in town, and he spoke, as did Aaron Henry. The Reverend Tucker gave a dramatic recounting of that afternoon's attack. Against all that oratorical competition, VEP's Wiley Branton, so light-skinned he could have passed for white, brought the house down answering the charge that all the trouble in Greenwood was being caused by outside agitators. He took particular umbrage at being called an outsider. True, he was from Arkansas, but his family had moved there from Leflore; true, he was a Negro, but he had some white blood; in fact it just so happened that he was the great-grandson of Greenwood Leflore, namesake of both the city and the county. He hoped to see his father's side of the family and his mother's side of the family walk down to the courthouse to register in peace.

The next day, Friday, Joyce helped set up headquarters at Friendship Baptist Church, taught a citizenship class of about thirty students, and then followed a group going down to register. The police ordered them to break up into smaller groups of five and arrested a SNCC worker from Georgia when he questioned their right to do so. The mass meeting that night was at First Christian, with Chuck McDew, SNCC's national chair, as featured speaker. "The spirit was with us and I firmly believe that before very long Greenwood will be a better place in which to live."

Saturday was her last day. She typed stencils, passed out copies of the *Mississippi Free Press*, "walked about a thousand miles" canvassing, and convinced—she thought—a few people to go down to register.

In concentrated form, Ladner's report captures both the mundane and the dramatic sides of the movement at that point. In the course of one week, she had met three national officers of civil rights groups, had met organizers from across the South, had been exposed to one burning, one shooting, and numberless acts of police violence and intimidation, in between typing a lot of stencils and stuffing a lot of envelopes. She was also seeing a Black community responding to more repression with more activism—with more mass meetings, with daily marches. People were calling the SNCC office to say that they were willing to register, if they could be assured that food and clothing would be available if they lost their jobs. Bob Moses commented several times on the new spirit of defiance:

> If you can imagine it, people were standing in line in front of the church waiting for food while their plantation owner was riding by in the street, calling out their names and telling them to leave and go back to the plantations; and they [the plantation workers] were telling them that they were going to stand there and get their food because their children were hungry.[56]

When Joyce Ladner left town, the eight workers who had been arrested that Wednesday were still in jail. Overall, they were treated decently by the jail staff, probably a result of the fact that both police-commissioner Buff Hammond and police-chief Curtis Lary were at some pains to restrain the more abusive of their employees. Local people were sending them food, a local Black doctor was allowed in several times to treat Forman's ulcers. They were a more erudite group of prisoners than the jail was used to holding. In order to make use of the time, Moses lectured on math, Forman on writing, and Guyot on biology. They had discussions on Thoreau and Kwame Nkrumah, though not all their discussions were so high-minded. Some of the younger workers spent a lot of time talking about women in ways that Forman, at least, seems to have found chauvinistic.[57]

By the end of March, Black Greenwood was acting, and white officialdom was reacting. Greenwood had put police officers on twelve-hour shifts with no days off, brought in law enforcement officers from surrounding counties, and mobilized civil-defense volunteers. There had been so much negative reaction to their use of police dogs that they had stopped doing it. SNCC workers believed the Citizens' Council was meeting nightly. The local paper was filled with editorials expressing a fear of federal intervention, a fear made palpable by the considerable number of Justice Department personnel drawn to the city by the violence. Some of Greenwood's tactical adjustments were fairly petty. During one march in early April, Wiley Branton realized that officials were trying to figure out which way marchers were heading; then, a police car or fire truck would be placed in their path and photographed in such a way as to make it appear that the marchers were blocking traffic.[58] In the midst of their larger problems, Dick Gregory was a special trial for local officials. He was in town a great deal that spring, speaking at mass meetings and leading marches. Recordings from the mass meetings suggest that "Mr. Gregory" was very much respected by local Blacks. He got quite a bit of respect from white officials as well. Gregory was as acid-tongued with them as he was in his nightclub act. If a cop called him a nigger, he was likely to reply that the cop's momma was a nigger, or he might say:

> Come here, boy, let me tell you something. I could take you back to Chicago today and let you walk through my home, then come back here and walk through your home, and out of the two of us you'd know which one was the nigger.[59]

Wary of more negative publicity, Greenwood officials went out of their way to avoid arresting him, leaving him free to act as a model of defiance on the streets.

The excitement of the spring led to the rejuvenation of the NAACP. As excited as he may have been about what the COFO coalition was doing in Greenwood, Medgar Evers hadn't forgotten his responsibility to the NAACP. During one of his mid-April visits, he encouraged the Reverend Tucker and Andrew Jordan, Cleve Jordan's son, to re-start the NAACP chapter. A meeting was held for that purpose on April 18, and Tucker was elected president.[60]

By April the city jail was filled, and prisoners had to be sent to the county jail. Local Blacks were sponsoring two marches some days, one in the morning and one in the evening. Bob Moses said that by April, perhaps five hundred or six hundred people were openly supporting the movement. VEP records indicate that between late February and the end of April, 513 tried to register, and hundreds more were taking registration classes, an improvement over the 40 or so who had tried to register in the previous seven years.[61] Indeed, even with the influx of organizers, the movement was not able to keep up with the demand for classes, leading to a shift in policy. They adopted the stance that illiterate Blacks should be registered, just like illiterate whites. Overall, it seems safe to conclude that by late spring of 1963, not less than a thousand local people were involved in the movement in some form, a far cry from the situation Block had encountered eleven months earlier.

What had not changed over those months was the unpredictability of the Justice Department, which eventually undercut much of the building momentum. On the last of March, Justice filed for a temporary restraining order that could have been drafted by SNCC, requesting the release of the eight civil rights workers who had been jailed on the 27th—but more importantly, it requested that the city be required to cease interfering with the registration campaign and allow Negroes to exercise their right to assemble for peaceful protest. The government was finally addressing constitutional issues head-on. After two years of struggle and fear, it seemed a real victory was impending. Instead, within a week, Justice shifted gears, agreeing on April 4 to a deal that gave the movement a victory, but a minor one.

The Department agreed to drop its request for a temporary injunction. In return, the city agreed to release eight people who had no business being in jail in the first place, promised that "legitimate applicants" would not be interfered with, and agreed to provide a bus to carry people to the courthouse. The county board of supervisors also announced the resumption of the commodities program, explaining that they were afraid that federal troops and marshals would be sent in otherwise. (Actually, the Agriculture Department had only said that they would take over the program if local officials refused to act.) No one, including Washington, believed that Blacks were actually going to be allowed to register. City officials had successfully fended off Washington with what amounted to a promise to be nicer in the ways they disenfranchised Negroes.

Why the administration backed down is not clear. They were certainly worried about the possibility of white violence. According to John Doar, they felt that pushing the constitutional issues in Greenwood would have drawn it into playing policeman across the South. Wiley Branton believed that Mississippi Senator James Eastland had prevailed upon the administration. Historian John Dittmer suspects that the Kennedys had never been serious about following through with the injunction. Its threat won enough token concessions to defuse the situation.[62]

A year and a half earlier, SNCC workers had been bitterly disappointed at the failure of Washington to move assertively on behalf of the courageous people of the Southwest. In Greenwood, after having their hopes built up again, they felt completely betrayed again. Historians Pat Watters and Reese Cleghorn see the timidity of the Justice Department as pivotal, since "Greenwood was the only place where the Justice Department moved at all to protect constitutional rights as such . . . in the whole movement history from 1960 to 1966." Had it stuck to its position there, "solution of the basic, bedrock issues of voting and the administration of justice might have begun two years sooner than it did," which might have meant that the disillusionment that took root among Black activists in those two years would at least have been delayed.[63] Instead, COFO workers were given vivid evidence that when matters came to it, the liberal government could not be relied upon, no matter how clear—from SNCC's point of view—the moral and legal issues. It was becoming increasingly difficult for them to think of themselves as being in partnership with the government or the society it represented.

By mid-April, most of the celebrities and out-of-town organizers had left, many going to a SNCC staff meeting in Atlanta before returning to their own projects; national attention switched to SCLC's pivotal campaign in Birmingham. It is common for scholars to drop the Greenwood story at this point, referring to its "collapse" or "demise."[64] How true that is depends on what we take the movement to be. If we understand it as being fundamentally an attempt to focus national attention, those characterizations can at least be defended. If we understand it as Myles Horton or Ella Baker or Septima Clark would—Are people learning to stand up and fight their own battles?—they are way off the mark.

Highlander's Guy Carawan taped some Greenwood youngsters talking about their movement experience, probably during the last week of May 1963. June Johnson was there, and Mary Lane, Susie

Taylor, Mary Boothe, and several others. About a week earlier, Milton Hancock, a cab driver and movement stalwart, had been badly beaten by the cops. The youngsters, without any input from SNCC so far as I know, sent a delegation to protest to the police chief and another to protest to the mayor. Chief Lary impressed several of the youngsters as being confused, scared, trying to be on both sides of the issue at once. Mayor Sampson—member of the Citizens Council and a man who said repeatedly he would never meet with a nigger while he was in office—was evasive and swore he wasn't going to have any brutality in his town. Susie Taylor (who worked in a laundry that got bloody sheets from the city jail every Monday from the cells of Negroes who had been beaten over the weekend) thought that the nervousness of the mayor and police chief wasn't unusual; she thought whites as a whole were scared and trying to hide it. The city officials seemed more funny than fearsome to the kids. The concessions the movement won that spring may have been trivial by the standards of the world beyond the Delta, but they were still concessions. By May, harassment at the voter-registration office was much reduced. It was even possible to keep a movement worker there all day—usually Mary Boothe—to help people with the forms, and city officials were trying to placate Black youngsters. Black people by the hundreds had gotten in the streets and fought for themselves, they had withstood a wave of re-pression as severe as anything the Delta had seen in at least a decade, and they had set the white folk back on their heels for awhile. For young people long disgusted with what looked like the cowardice of the older generations, for older activists who had been working for years with little to show for it, there was some triumph mixed in with the disappointment. The movement hardly collapsed. Indeed, more people were arrested for activism in June than in March, and they were local people. After most of the outsiders had left, local organizers and local people went right back to the slow process of building a solid movement, with more confidence than ever.

The food drive gave SNCC-COFO an opportunity to show that Greenwood Blacks were not as alone and isolated as they had thought. It would be an error, though, to put too much emphasis on that. The first factor in the transformation of Black Greenwood has to be the sheer courage and persistence of the young organizers, awakening a like response in some local residents, the more so as the organizers became deeply rooted into the Black community. The Sam Block the police roughed up in July 1962 was, in most eyes, at best a foolhardy young stranger. The Sam Block they arrested in February 1963 was someone who had patiently earned the respect and admiration of a great many people.

All the courage in the world would not have mattered had there not been a small core of people willing to cast their lot with the movement right away, people with a lot to contribute. People like Amzie Moore and Cleve Jordan had been accumulating political capital for a decade, in the form of contact networks, knowledge of resources, and personal credibility, capital they were able to transfer to the younger activists, a pattern repeated across the state. In the counties along the Mississippi River, the key person was Henry Sias, a patriarch in his seventies. (Charlie Cobb: "Once Henry Sias said it was ok, then everybody in the county was willing to deal with us.") In Canton, C. O. Chinn was among the staunchest early supporters. (CORE's Matt Suarez: "Every white person knew C. O. Chinn and every white person in that town knew that you did not fuck with C. O. Chinn because he would kick your natural ass.") The indomitable Chinn paid for his movement involvement by losing nearly all his property and serving a term on the chain gang, but he never stopped agitating. In Ruleville, there were Joe and Rebecca McDonald; in Panola County, when people understood what Frank Smith was trying to do they sent him to Robert Miles. In Hattiesburg, there was Vernon Dahmer, a man who could have retreated behind his wealth but who instead went to his deathbed insisting that Negroes without sense enough to register and vote were dregs on society.[65] The organizers of the sixties were able to do so much so quickly against such odds because part of the work had been done before them.

Part of the contribution of the younger activists is their willingness to work with nearly all of the community. It would have been understandable had they written off nearly all of the old leadership as hopeless, but they did not do that. They persisted in trying to build relationships with people who initially either rejected them or were inconsistent, and some of those relationships eventually paid off. Within a few years, SNCC organizers would be less flexible, but at this point they seemed to have operated, often with gritted teeth, in accord with Ella Baker's admonition to remember that even the frivolous matron in the fur coat has something to contribute.

Some of the factors that predisposed people to participation are reasonably clear. Knowledge of the wider world, such as comes from service in the armed forces or travel, is one such factor; a degree of economic independence is another. Aaron Johnson, the most reliable minister in this period, was a barber and was also able to get some financial help from his church headquarters. The first people to provide living space or office space for SNCC workers—Mr. Burns, Mrs. Miller, Mr. Campbell, Mr. Sanders—were all less economically vulnerable than most Blacks in Greenwood.

Middle-class individuals made significant contributions. Businesspeople, no matter which side of the law they operated on, seem especially likely to have made under-the-table contributions, so as not to draw the attention of the authorities. The two Black doctors in town were both supportive. Dr. Cornwall secretly let the organizers stay with him for a while; Dr. Mable Garner used her position as a physician to bring food to people in jail when no one else could get in.

On the whole, though, middle-class status militated against participation in the early years, especially for ministers and schoolteachers, the heart of the middle class.[66] During the first year after COFO came to Greenwood, it appears that only one teacher—Cleve Jordan's son—was openly active, though at least two or three others at the high school were sympathetic. Teachers had such high status in these communities that their visible participation would certainly have swayed others. By the same token, the very fact that they had such high status gave them and ministers a kind of stake in the existing system. Not only did they fail to participate in the early movement, but to the extent that there was vocal opposition to the movement, teachers and preachers were most likely to be leading it.

That many young people eagerly joined the movement is not surprising. What is less easily explained is the subset of older people who were also critical to the early movement. SNCC workers seem convinced that it was more than the fact that there were so many elderly people left in the Delta in the wake of outmigrations. According to SNCC's Charlie Cobb, "It was always the older people, contrary to popular opinion. . . . In the rural areas it was primarily the older people [who were] instrumental to SNCC." Sam Block said that the Greenwood movement "was built with older people who were angry, who were looking for somebody who could give form and expression to ideas and thoughts that they had in mind for years, that they wanted to do and just couldn't bring together."[67]

SNCC workers and younger Greenwood residents remember many of the older people as saying they were just too old to be afraid of anything. They had led their lives, raised their families, and the white folks could do what they wanted now.

Both Cobb and SNCC's MacArthur Cotton suggested another possibility, that some of the older people had a tradition of resistance built into their collective memories. At a 1965 hearing in Jackson of the U.S. Commission on Civil Rights, one of the commissioners noted, "We southerners are strong on tradition. We have had Negro witnesses here who remember things that occurred 80 years before, incidents of violence."[68] Cobb recalls that the first time he entered Carroll County with Amzie Moore, Moore, in the course of teasing Cobb, went into hair-raising detail about a massacre that had occurred in Carrollton when a group of Black farmers had attended a trial after being warned not to. The massacre he was talking about had taken place in 1886, but Moore painted so vivid a picture that Cobb thought he was talking about something contemporary. Black Mississippians born in the first two decades of the century learned about slavery and Reconstruction from people who had lived through them. Both Cobb and Cotton suggested that their familiarity with a period when Blacks aggressively resisted white supremacy may have been a part of what spurred some of the older people on.

What happened in Greenwood should be placed in the context of the broader movement. The sit-ins and Freedom Rides of the previous two years, the national attention given to Ole Miss and James Meredith in the fall of 1962, had to affect the way local residents received the young organizers, had to make some people in Black Greenwood think differently about the possibilities for change.

Background changes made a difference, but the story of Greenwood in 1962–63 is fundamentally about a young activist tradition building upon an older one. Together, local people and the younger COFO activists made a way where there had appeared to be no way.

Six

IF YOU DON'T GO, DON'T HINDER ME

The Redefinition of Leadership

There go my people. I must hurry and catch up
to them for I am their leader.

ATTRIBUTED TO GANDHI

The leadership is there. If you go out and work with
your people, then the leadership will emerge. . . . We don't know
who they are now; we don't need to know. But the leadership
will emerge from the movement that emerges.

BOB MOSES[1]

BEING A LOCAL ACTIVIST in Greenwood in 1962 or 1963 called for substantial independence of spirit. It meant refusal to conform not just to the expectations of white supremacy but to the fears and pleadings of one's own community as well. The first part of this chapter looks more closely at some of those who "led out" in Greenwood, in order to convey a sense of what they were like as individuals. The second part looks at some of the ways the collective behavior of these people affected their traditional leaders, the SNCC-COFO workers, and the more rabidly racist of the local whites. They forced traditional leaders to become more radical, while teaching already militant COFO workers to show a little restraint and teaching white people caution. The earliest local movement supporters collectively reshaped the definition and price of leadership in both the white and Black communities.

Among the individuals who clearly stood out in the early period were Robert Burns, the first knowingly to give COFO workers a place to stay and office space; Al Garner, who headed the NAACP Youth Council; the Reverend Aaron Johnson, the first minister to open the doors of his church; and Lou Emma Allen, one of the early adult volunteers.

ROBERT BURNS

Until he got involved with Sam Block, Robert Burns had never done much that one would think of as "political." He joined no groups, held no offices. An army staff sergeant in World War II, a farm-equipment operator before and after the war, he had come to Greenwood near the end of 1947, where he found work in the post office.

Many of the activists of the 1940s or 1950s—Amzie Moore, Louis Redd, Henry Sias, C. C. Bryant, Richard West, Cleve Jordan among them—were working-class intellectuals, active seekers after ideas and information, usually through some combination of travel and self-study. Robert Burns was a seeker in this sense, and for him as for many of the others, military service first started him thinking and listening. The army barracks had been a kind of school for him. Guys would just sit around and talk:

> You know, 75 or 100 men and just sit down and talk about what happened in their home and this one talk about what happened in my home and this one lives in Chicago and that one lives in the south part of Mississippi, that one lives in Georgia, one lives in California, and you get all that together, you stop to think. You know when you're in your own little group you only know what's around you but when . . . you had people from every state . . . so everybody could laugh and talk about what went on, and how it went on, and what did they do about it and all this kind of stuff. So you'd just stop and think, it gave you something to think and study about.

Mr. Burns tended not to take a very active part in these discussions. He had only a third-grade education and worried about embarrassing himself, so he just listened and thought. He continued to think and study after his discharge. He sold the *Chicago Defender* for a while in the late 1940s, a paper he liked reading because it gave him new ideas. He stopped when some of his Black customers got nervous about it, though the whites who knew about it actually didn't seem to mind. He first registered to vote around 1951. He had learned that votes controlled the law, and he wanted to be a part of that. He didn't actually vote, though, until ten or twelve years later, but he kept his poll tax paid all that time.

One evening in July 1962, he got a phone call from a friend of his, Mrs. McNease, a school principal. Because she had rented a room to Sam Block, "they" were threatening to burn her house down. Over the objections of family and friends, Robert Burns decided to offer Sam Block a place to stay, a place he could use as both residence and office.

What did Mr. Burns see in Block? After he worried about his ability to make himself clear—"I might not can explain myself as well as I can think inside of myself about it"—he said:

> Well I thought he was a child, a young man that was trying to do a good part, and [I] had good thoughts about it and I felt like in his position that he needed some help, he needed all our support, which he didn't get. They tried to set all kinds of traps to get him killed. . . . I felt like all blacks were standing in the mud hole especially [in] the South, I felt like they should be pulled out on dry land. You can get no hold in mud.

Burns saw "power," as he put it, in SNCC partly because he wanted to. He had been looking for something that might make a difference, and when Sam came along, he looked like he might be it.

> Well, I looked at it like this—what with my ups and downs that I had came through with, with the white man from the time that I've been in the world—well, I felt like it should be something or some kind of laws some day to change this. I know that me alone by myself wouldn't be a drop in the bucket but I just always went along every day [thinking] to myself and I felt like it could be a change.

White man talked to you any way they wanted to here in the South—"Don't talk to me, nigger," and all that kind of stuff. . . . Well, just, you'll go along sometime by yourself and go over things in your mind and you say to yourself—"Something can be done, who can do it?" But I always had this in mind with anything, anything set up by man can be tore down by man. Now you're going to have to find the right man that knows how to get into it and tear it down and reset it. So that is my idea. . . . Oh yeah, yeah. And when I met Sam Block it was a thrill, it was a thrill to me. And then when they commenced to explain to me about Martin Luther King and I commenced to read the pamphlets and literature . . . because it was things I had thought over years and years but I just didn't have the education and the know-how to make the speeches, to get it across, there was nothing I could do. See I only made it to third grade.

Burns saw a version of himself in Sam Block, himself as he might have been with a little more education, a little more exposure to the world. He was perfectly aware that the young people did have a wild and rambunctious side—Dewey Greene, Jr., once ran up a seventy-dollar bill on Burns's phone. He certainly did not believe each and every thing Sam said. Sam apparently tried to give the impression that he had some awfully powerful friends up north, and Mr. Burns thought that maybe he was stretching some of that. Nonetheless, on balance, Mr. Burns saw a lot of himself in those young people.

Mr. Burns lost more than a few friends. People stopped him on the street to tell him what a fool he was: white folks had always done what they wanted to, and that was that. ("That's true," he said, "but it's a bad road that don't have an ending. It's a rough road that don't have an ending.") It seemed to Burns that there had already been some changes, and some of them had benefited Negroes. If people wanted more changes, they were going to have to do something. "You're not going to have Sandy Claus come and drop the pattern in your lap all the time."

The friends who just criticized what he was doing hurt him less than those who felt a need to tell the white people who was going in and out of his place, what kind of "radical" literature was being passed around there, and so forth. "We had so many Blacks that were sneaky and shiftless. . . . I had a white lawyer tell me that he couldn't even eat his supper in peace for someone always calling to tell him what that Robert Burns is doing."

The postmaster was pressured to fire him but refused to do so. Willie Peacock thinks that it was partly because he was relatively secure financially that Burns felt he could stick his neck out. Burns was also fortunate in that his wife wasn't afraid. He and his family were threatened repeatedly over the phone, and cars of white men took to driving slowly around his home in the evenings. On one occasion, a group of white kids—Burns was sure they had been hired or encouraged by the police—broke out all the windows in his new station wagon. After that, he spent several nights sitting up in a tree in his yard with a rifle. Some of his neighbors had agreed to help him stand watch, but they never showed up.

The authorities found a way to get him. Ten years before, he had separated from his first wife without legally divorcing her, a common practice among poor people in the area. The two of them maintained cordial relations even after he remarried. After he took Sam Block in, city officials convinced his first wife to sign a document she had been led to believe would keep him out of legal trouble. In fact, the papers were a demand for his arrest on a charge of bigamy. After a few days in jail, he was released on ten thousand dollars' bail, a ridiculously large sum. His first wife protested to no avail. His landlady and his brother-in-law had to put up their property to cover it.

There is some ambiguity about how much support Robert Burns got from SNCC after his arrest. Burns still has great affection and respect for "his boys," but he is not sure they did everything they could have done to help him. They did get him a lawyer, and they were able to get the Justice Department's ubiquitous John Doar to talk with him. SNCC files suggest they were quite active in seeking sources of help for Burns. Still, he feels that after those initial efforts, they did not follow through. That may or may not be a fair assessment of this particular case, but it is important to note, given the furious pace of activity and the limited resources that SNCC-COFO commanded, that it was quite likely there would be times when people like Burns simply got lost in the shuffle, best intentions in the world notwithstanding.

Despite—perhaps because of—his lack of formal education, Robert Burns is a learner. In his time, he has made a living picking cotton, painting, repairing farm equipment, working in a motor pool, breaking in farm animals, repairing air conditioners, refrigerators, and washing machines, making cabinets, running a snack bar, and doing photography. Perhaps the fact that he is a man of so many crafts is connected to his movement involvement. Being able to do so many things is empowering; one is always learning that the physical world yields to patient effort. Maybe that carries over in some way to how one sees the social world. Anything made by people can be torn down by people.

Mr. Burns's story suggests something of the price Black communities pay for class snobbery. Here is a thoughtful, talented man who clearly had a contribution to make, yet he led a relatively withdrawn life because of his embarrassment about a lack of formal schooling— and there were in fact places in Black Greenwood where he would not have been welcomed. Social groups like the Elks certainly would not have wanted him, and even the Greenwood NAACP in the fifties would have been doubtful. SNCC will always be remembered for its militance, but an even more important key to its legacy is the respect it had for people regardless of their status and the ways in which that respect empowered those people to make the contributions they had in them.

Years later, after the various poverty programs started coming in, Burns mentioned to one of the Black women working at the Head Start Center that he had suffered some to see people like her get those jobs. "She turned around and looked at me and turned up her nose and said, 'That was going to happen even if there had never been no you. President Kennedy had that all laid out.'"

ALBERT GARNER

Had Medgar Evers done nothing else, SNCC workers would have been deeply in his debt for all the time in the late fifties and early sixties he spent organizing NAACP youth chapters. It meant that when SNCC arrived in a town, they would frequently inherit semi-organized groups of youngsters looking for something to do that felt real. Prodded by Evers, some Greenwood youngsters started a chapter around 1961. They may have been responding as much to his prodding as to their own interests. They weren't the most energetic social activists at first. "Many of us," recalls Al Garner, "would go to sleep in the room while he was trying to organize us."

Garner, along with his friend John Hodges, helped found the chapter and became its first president. As he reconstructs the history of the youth chapter, he wraps it around social-class dynamics. He had grown up in the part of Greenwood called Buckeye Quarters, an area dominated by a mill that processed cotton seeds. Viewed from one angle, what is remarkable about the Black South is the degree of solidarity it achieved. From another, it is the problem of divisiveness, of "fractions," as Miss Baker put it, expressed in part in a tendency to make distinctions of status on the basis of the most trivial differences—the texture of one's hair, one's complexion, the size of the plantation one got exploited on, the kind of southern accent one spoke with, and so on. As poor as Black Greenwood was, they had the nerve to look down their noses at the Buckeye. Children from there or from the nearby plantations bore some stigma when they went to Greenwood schools.

Perhaps as a result, some Buckeye children adopted what seems like an immigrant attitude toward school. They were serious about their work; Greenwood children seemed frivolous in comparison. John Hodges, who grew up on the Whitington Plantation next to the Buckeye, remembers children making up quizzes and drills while they were working in the fields. He and Garner both started school in the Buckeye, where Miss Ollie B. Simms—a name people pronounce with a certain resonance—usually taught all the grades at once, teaching the day's lesson to the older children first and then having them teach it to the younger ones. She was an effective taskmaster, and kids from the Buckeye got a good foundation from her.

Neither Garner's parents nor Hodges's had much education, but they insisted that their children were going to get one. Garner's mother was the PTA president, and he was expected to read, to be involved with books. Before he started high school he had read about the NAACP and Little Rock, and he had read Walter White's book on lynching, *Rope and Faggot*. Hodges's stepfather argued with the plantation owner about whether the boy was going to be kept out of school to go to the fields, ending the discussion by promising that he would work harder to make up for the boy's being in school. Children used to have to demonstrate their lessons in Sunday School, and Hodges got so much praise for how well he did his that it started him thinking that he was smart.

When they formed the youth chapter, they used to meet at one of the Methodist churches or at Aaron Johnson's church or Edward Cochrane's hotel. According to Garner, the group was basically formed among working-class youngsters. The Greenes—George, Freddie, and Cookie—were the only early members who might be considered middle class, in that they owned their own home and Mr. Greene had had some college. Others, like Cody Sanders and the Reverend Johnson's daughter, had parents who had been involved with the adult branch. There were more boys in the branch than girls. The youth group cooperated with the adult branch, even though some of them suspected one or two of the adults of being spies for the power structure.

Ever since the Freedom Rides in 1961, the chapter members had been looking for a way to get involved in them. When Garner met Sam Block while Block was canvassing, he saw Block as the opportunity they had been looking for—and they, of course, were a godsend for him. By the spring of 1963, youth-chapter activity had been largely folded into the larger COFO structure, with both Hodges and Garner added to the paid staff, with Garner responsible for running the youth program. Randolph Blackwell's report on Greenwood that spring expressed enthusiasm about the large, spirited youth group.[2] Some of the group's energy that spring went into a running battle with Mr. Threadgill, the principal who had forbidden COFO workers from school grounds and promised to suspend anyone caught demonstrating.

The two boys from the wrong side of the track graduated in June 1963, with Hodges as valedictorian and president of the state association of student councils and Garner as class president. Hodges left that fall for Morehouse. Garner went on to Tougaloo and after graduation worked with the poverty program in Mississippi and with the Lawyers Committee for Civil Rights under Law. He left the state in 1970 and wound up in Chicago organizing in housing projects, precisely the kind of activist career SNCC was hoping to initiate. Any who knew Albert Garner when he was, say, fourteen years old, could have seen that he was going to be a leader of some kind. That his talents were devoted to social action for so long, though, is probably a result of his encounter with SNCC.

THE REVEREND AARON JOHNSON

By the end of the summer of 1962, a few local churches, usually Methodist, had shown interest in the movement, but the most reliable was First Christian Church, pastored by the Reverend Aaron Johnson.

The Reverend Johnson grew up in a sharecropping family, and he has bitter memories of what that life was like. Farm work itself he liked, and even today he talks about going back to it at some point, but only as an independent landowner. He remembers that when he was a child the landlord once took the family's last cow, nailed the corn crib shut, and took the hog while his mother stood at the door crying. Some years the family barely had food to eat. His parents would let the children eat first, and then they would eat whatever was left. When there wasn't enough work on the farm, his father walked into town to work at a service station. On cold days, he would get home with his hands and feet aching and half-frozen. By the time he was warm, it was time to go back again. Year after year, he watched the family get cheated out of its labor. One year, when the family got a government allotment check, he convinced his father not to turn it over to the landlord, which led to the family being evicted.

The Reverend Johnson, another army veteran, offers no explanation for why he was willing to get involved with SNCC. Actually, he had been doing similar kinds of things for some time. In the middle 1950s, he worked with the on-again, off-again Greenwood NAACP, and in the later fifties with the Citizen's League, a local group dedicated to increasing the numbers of Blacks who were registered and voting. The NAACP youth chapter was a turning point for him. He had always run a youth-oriented ministry, and when the young people were meeting at Ed Cochrane's hotel, he started thinking a church would be a better environment for them to meet in. Later, after SNCC-COFO came, and his young people were attracted to it, he felt he had to support them and so offered his church as a meeting place for them as well. He bailed them out of jail, hid workers from the police, and became a regular on the picket line and at the mass meetings. Over the next few years, he became a founding member of the NAACP when it started up again in 1963, a founding member of the local chapter of the Freedom Democratic Party (FDP), and a member of the executive committee of the group that led the boycotts that eventually forced downtown merchants to desegregate. His children were among those who integrated Greenwood High. There were few who stayed the course that long, and none I know of who came through it all with as widespread a reputation for trustworthiness as the Reverend Johnson.

He got pressured as soon as he opened his church to SNCC. White employers threatened his congregants, including one of his deacons. Attendance fell off drastically. If he got twenty people for a Sunday service, it was a good Sunday. The sheriff, the local police, and the highway patrol took to driving slowly around his church on Sunday morning, adding to the fear. People called to tell him privately that they were sorry, they wanted to come, but they just couldn't. His salary went down to $17 a week, too little to support his family, even with what he made barbering on the side. At the mass meetings, people would say "We're behind you, Rev." He used to wonder how far behind they were.

He was able to survive financially because his church headquarters in Indianapolis supported him. They sent him thirteen hundred dollars and then started sending fifty dollars a week. Without that, he would have had to leave town. He sees this support as the key difference between himself and some of the other ministers. He thinks that they were concerned, but many of them, especially the Baptists, had no such hierarchy to call on for help. All of the pressure fell on the individual minister and congregation.

Even with the support from his headquarters the pressure was substantial, and it took its toll. He was followed wherever he went, sometimes by police, sometimes by unidentified white men. The family received threatening calls. His home was located near the highway, and he worried about someone shooting into the house. As the pace of movement activity picked up, he found himself going to his barbershop at seven in the morning, working half a day, going to the picket lines or the demonstrations in the afternoon, to mass meetings in the evening, getting home at midnight or later, and starting it all over the next morning. His weight fell off. He just lost the desire to eat. His church hierarchy, which was integrated and included, according to the Reverend Johnson, some decent people and some not so decent, offered to move him to another town, build him a new church and help him go to college. They were more concerned with getting him out of the movement than with his welfare, and he turned them down.

Like the SNCC workers, he did receive some under-the-table support that seems to have meant a great deal to him. He remembers a Mr. Moore, a well-to-do brickmason who worked for wealthy whites all over the state. Because of the kind of work he did, he didn't want to be publicly involved, but he would help any way he could, including providing funds. He was a man you didn't have to worry about; he was going to do exactly what he said he was going to do. This was true of a number of the older people drawn into the movement. Once they decided to join, you could count on them absolutely:

> We had some old folks that was ready. We had enough old folks that you just didn't believe they had the nerve that they had. They would stand out there with you. Like Mr. Jordan . . . Miss Pinkie Pilcher, Dave Sanders, James Campbell. . . . And when those people told you that they meant it, they meant it and they would just stay on it.

By way of contrast, he tells the story of a time when things in town got so hot that it was thought necessary to have round-the-clock guards, younger adults, posted at the church. As it turned out, they fell asleep, and Mr. and Mrs. Johnson had to stay awake all night.

By late spring of 1963, more churches had begun supporting the movement, or at least claimed to. Methodist churches tended to come around sooner than Baptist, although even Methodist ministers sometimes needed a little prodding. There were occasions on which they agreed to help and subsequently tried to renege. The SNCC organizers pressured one Methodist minister to open his building to the movement. When that didn't work, Peacock, who had grown up in the AME church, contacted the area bishop and got him, somewhat reluctantly, to come and lead a mass meeting at the church, something the local minister could hardly refuse. Baptist ministers were generally less educated than their Methodist counterparts and more likely, according to the Reverend Johnson to have financial dependency on whites. On the plantations, some planters subsidized Baptist churches directly; in other cases, Baptist preachers expected a sizeable year-end bonus from nearby landlords for keeping their flocks happy.

As more churches came into the movement, the Reverend Johnson found himself mediating disputes among his brother clergy—between the activist and non-activist churches, between Baptists and Methodists, the latter as difficult and as frustrating as trying to work with the white folks.

The church has gotten more credit for generating the leadership of the movement than it deserves, probably a matter of people looking at the movement's national leaders, many of whom were ministers, and assuming they were all the leadership that mattered. In fact, the local situation could be very different. In the urban South, where churches were larger and better financed, where ministers were not so subject to reprisal, churches could afford to play a more active role in the early stages of the movement. Even so, SCLC's Wyatt Walker noted that during the Birmingham campaign no more than ten percent of the Black ministers were actively supportive.[3] In much of the rural South, the church as an institution became involved even more gradually, and only after much effort by organizers. Individuals like the

Reverend Johnson "led out," but they did so as individuals and at substantial cost to themselves.

For many people, one of the permanent memories of the Greenwood Movement is the sound of Lou Emma Allen's voice leading the singing at mass meetings.[4] Asked to generalize about the kinds of people who became leaders in the Delta, Charlie Cobb noted that they were often better educated than their neighbors, which could just mean being literate. They were also approachable people, people to whom others felt comfortable coming for help. Lou Emma Allen fits that mold.

She was born in 1913 in Carroll County, Mississippi, and started school there. At fifteen, she moved to Memphis and finished the seventh and eighth grades there, a better education than many Delta Blacks were getting at the time, and she also had the cultural advantages of living in Memphis. She moved to Greenwood with her husband, a Baptist minister. When he died in 1944, she married another minister.

They lived on an alley in Greenwood, and while the movement had yet to invent the idea of block captain, that describes the role Mrs. Allen played in the alley. People came to her to read and answer their mail. She was the town crier, reading newspapers from out of town and telling her neighbors what they said. As Cobb implies, when a neighborhood picks a person to play that kind of role, they are ordinarily going to pick a certain kind of person—someone seen as trustworthy, as discreet about other people's business, as having good judgment and the ability to do a favor without being condescending.

Her son Thomas says "Thou shalt read" was treated like another commandment in his home. His mother read Black magazines and Black history all the time and insisted that he read them, too, as well as Shakespeare, an idea she got from some of the white homes she worked in and from which she sometimes brought him books.

She first heard of the NAACP when Emmett Till was killed, and she and her husband met the NAACP's Ruby Hurley when she came to investigate. She joined the NAACP sometime after that, thinking that if she ever needed help she would be able to get it. In the early 1960s her oldest son, Thomas, was going to Campbell College in Jackson. AME-supported, Campbell could afford to be more supportive of the movement than the state's public colleges—this was the school that took in the McComb students who had been put out of school. Thomas got caught up in movement activity and began bringing home information about it. She remembers particularly a speech he brought home by Martin Luther King. She grew more interested, enough so to go to a mass meeting. She can't remember the church or the speakers, but she is sure the first song she sang was "Take Your Burdens to the Lord and Leave Them There." The songs hooked her, and she became deeply involved, helping to start virtually every new movement initiative over at least the next five years.

She lost a couple of jobs and caused one of her employers to lose his. When her movement involvement first came to public notice, she was cleaning for the family of a white minister, the Reverend Anderson. They thought that what she was doing was right and was in any case her own business. His congregation kept pressuring him to fire her and he kept refusing, so they ran him out of town. Subsequently, she quit one job when the lady she was cleaning for asked her if it was true she was taking part in those marches. Then she was cleaning up at a white prep school, and they told her she was going to have to stop being in the movement, so she quit that.

She was always amazed that white folks kept assuming she couldn't think for herself. In the late 1960s when the push started to integrate the public school, she was cleaning at previously all-white Davis school, which had decided they simply weren't going to let any Black children or parents in the door. She was responsible for opening the building, and she was told to open for white parents and children only. She said to herself "'I guess they think I'm crazy.' I went and unlocked the door and I went and got way back on the stage behind the curtains; they didn't know where I was. All of 'em come in."

Obviously, no one person typifies the early movement's core, but Mrs. Allen comes close. She was a working woman of moderate education but large aspirations for her children, initially anointed for leadership by neighbors who depended on her in a movement that came to be dominated by such women. Like so many of the women at the movement's core, she came to regard civil rights workers as family, which had a great deal to do with establishing the emotional tone of the early movement. For all her cheerful, motherly bearing, she would not hesitate, according to Hollis Watkins, to call a fool a fool to his face—which captures another theme that runs through descriptions of the local women in the movement—Mrs. Hamer, say, or Victoria Gray or Annie Devine, to mention the women best known at the state level. They were loving and open, but they were also intellectually tough-minded, quite capable of doing their own thinking.

Although she holds no formal office in any political organization, well into the 1990s politicians in the Delta, at least Black ones, were trying to enlist Mrs. Allen's support. They still respect her ability to influence her neighbors.

Even under the repressive circumstances of the 1940s and 1950s Delta leadership potential could be stimulated in a variety of ways—a stint in the armed forces, a desire to prove oneself to town kids, a little more education than most people had, the desire to be a Christian neighbor, getting the right teacher at the right point in one's life, or having parents who took leadership in directing their children's lives. Many of the people with whom SNCC worked were leaders in their own sphere, formal or informal, before SNCC ever came. SNCC was so deeply rooted in its communities that they were in position to see and groom leadership where others might have overlooked it. Asked how good a job SNCC had done of developing local leadership, MacArthur Cotton responded that in many cases, SNCC did not so much develop leadership as remove barriers, so that leadership that was already there might emerge. That might mean helping people get over the class and gender snobbery that restricts leadership roles to certain people; it might mean attacking the fear that had immobilized many people, or showing people how they might bring resources to bear from outside the state. In a great many cases, it just meant creating motion that then drew out people who were looking for something. As local leadership did get drawn in, it necessarily changed the character of the movement.

An image that captures much of the contribution that local people made to the early-sixties movement would picture a movement supporter—a maid or a small farmer or a beautician, perhaps. With one hand, they would be shoving the reluctant—preachers and teachers particularly—forward. With the other hand, the movement supporter should be holding back a group of COFO kids, hellbent on having revolution yesterday. And the local supporter should be speaking to the COFO organizers: "No reason in this worl' your revolution can't wait till after church." Older local activists played a mediating role. They pushed conservative traditional leaders into a more militant posture while keeping the young people from taking militance too far too fast.

From at least the early 1970s, Mississippi Blacks aspiring to leadership positions have almost invariably wrapped themselves in the mantle of the civil rights movement, to use John Dittmer's phrase. Lawyers presented themselves as civil rights lawyers, ministers implied that they had always run movement churches, Black college presidents implied that their campus had been solidly behind the movement. Many such claims, of course, were entirely specious. That people felt constrained to make them reflects how much community norms had changed in a decade. By the 1970s, claims to leadership in Black communities had to be legitimated by associating oneself with what had been a pariah movement ten years earlier.

The pressure that changed what it meant to be a leader was bottom-up pressure, and it was felt across the South. SNCC's Lonnie King says that the greatest speech he ever heard Martin Luther King give was a speech in defense of Daddy King. In 1960 Atlanta college students had organized boycotts, sit-ins, and demonstrations trying to force downtown businesses to desegregate. By the Christmas shopping season, business leaders had reluctantly offered concessions to integrate lunch counters, but not until the following September. Daddy King was among a group of older local leaders who persuaded the student negotiators to accept the offered compromise despite the delay. When the decision was presented to a mass meeting, the crowd was furious.

There were accusations that the negotiators had been misled by Uncle Toms. Daddy King rose to defend himself. According to SNCC's Lonnie King:

> [He] said that he had been working in this town for thirty years, and before he could say the rest of it, somebody up in the balcony jumped up and said, "That's what's wrong. . . ." And that crushed that man. Okay? And it crushed Martin, seeing his daddy booed down. They all booed him and there was hissing.

Martin, Jr., defended his father and the generation of leadership his father represented. "He gave," Lonnie King says, "the best speech I've ever heard him make, off the cuff, in defense of his father but at the same time trying to march with the hounds who were chasing him." The younger King was trying to keep faith with his father's leadership while making clear that his own was of a different, more militant order. Obviously, leaders who wanted to remain leaders had to align themselves with a growing mood of aggressiveness.[5]

In local communities across the South, ministers and other traditional leaders, people far more conservative than King, felt the same push from their constituencies. To SNCC members, the contemporary tendency to assume that movement leadership was basically ministerial is laughable. Deacons, though, were another matter. It was often they who opened churches to the movement. In Bolivar County during the fifties one of the churches Amzie Moore had access to was a small holiness church in Shaw. His friend Herman Perry was chairman of the Deacon Board:

> I used to say, "Reverend Robb, you preaching holiness, you say God can do everything. Now don't come back off your profession. If God can do everything and we done dedicated and give this church to God and if God can't take care of his own house, it's got to go, 'cause we gonna have the meetings."
>   . . . . All these preachers, Baptists, Methodists, claim like they had so much God but they didn't believe the God they served could

keep this white man off him. I used to tell them that white man was their God. If you gon' trust God, trust Him for everything.

In Holly Springs, Frank Smith found that "the image of students knocking on doors, the fact of their speaking at churches on Sundays, and the threat of demonstration have served to build respect for them and has challenged the local ministers no end. They see this and are beginning to work to try to build their images and redeem themselves."[6]

At a meeting at Greenwood's Wesley Chapel in April of 1963, the Reverend Donald Tucker, who while leading a demonstration the previous week had been attacked by a police dog, began by criticizing some of his fellow clergy for misplaced priorities, for being more concerned with their own material well-being than with the welfare of their people. If the other ministers had been at that demonstration, the police would have kept that dog off him. He asked that all ministers in the building meet with him after the meeting, but those who were still kindergarten children, those who were afraid, those who couldn't act on their faith could leave with the crowd. Time had come to pronounce the benediction on the afraid. Every time he laid another lick on his brother clergy, the crowd roared approval.[7]

The Reverend B. T. McSwine was in the audience. A Baptist, he was already annoyed at the invidious comparisons people were making between Baptist and Methodist activism. Seventy or eighty of his congregants were there. The Reverend McSwine rose to speak, and booing started. Cleve Jordan shouted the whole house down: "Let him speak! Let him speak!" McSwine announced that he was a Baptist, not a shamed Baptist, and Union Grove Baptist was open to the movement right away, and so was Friendship Baptist, and others could be expected to follow. The spirit was catching. James Bevel noted in a report that the Reverend Hayes at Jennings Temple CME "was really frightened but he polled his members and most people were in agreement with letting the church be used."[8]

Sharp-tongued Dick Gregory ("The only thing a white man has to identify with is a drinking fountain, a toilet and the right to call me a nigger") reserved some of his harshest remarks for people who claimed to be leaders. At a meeting taped during the first week of April 1963 he termed it

> disgraceful that in this area, the Negro religious leaders haven't played their part. [*Loud applause.*] I'm a Baptist by choice, but if I had to spend much time in this area, they'd have to force me to be a Baptist because even little kids are in the struggle and not one Baptist church has opened up its doors in this area. [*Loud and sustained applause.*]
>
> In college, I almost decided to be a schoolteacher but when I see how far behind schoolteachers in this area are dragging their feet, I'm glad I didn't decide it. [*Loud applause.*] And your principal you have here [*Loud and very sustained applause, shouting*], this guy . . . or whatever his name is. [*Loud applause.*] When this man would ask Negro kids to stop fighting for their rights, he is lower than the lowest Negro, lower than the lowest animal that walks the face of the earth. [*Very sustained applause.*] . . . These handkerchief heads don't realize this area is going to break. It's going to learn to obey the Constitution. And these teachers will be the first to go. . . . Any good Baptists in the house? [*People murmur assent.*] When you go to church Sunday [*pause*], look him in the face [*pause*], then pray for him [*long pause*], then walk out!! [*The house comes down with applause and laughter.*] If you won't even try to get some dignity, God can't use you. They so worried about their church, give 'em their church! Give it to 'em empty! If you have to pray in the street, it's better than worshipping with a man who is less than a man! [*The clapping, laughing, and footstomping continue for a long time.*][9]

Pillars of the community were being denounced by name, ridiculed as cowards and hypocrites before God, and audiences of four or five hundred people were cheering and stomping. Deacons and church mothers sat in those audiences and laughed along with everyone else.

Not long after Gregory's speech, thirty-one local ministers affixed their signatures to the following:

We the undersigned Pastors and Ministers of the city of Greenwood and Leflore County do hereby endorse the Freedom Movement one-hundred percent and urge our members and friends of Leflore County and the state of Mississippi to register and become first-class citizens.

The announcement was a forward step, but organizers did not take it at face value. Probably a good majority of those who signed did so with significant reservations. In the weeks after they signed, Bob Moses noted in several reports sent to VEP that one of the biggest problems in Greenwood was the lack of real support from the ministerial or professional communities.[10] Nonetheless, it is clear that many ministers felt sufficiently pressured from below to pretend at least to align themselves with the movement. The people were radicalizing the clergy.

If some people needed to be pushed into activism, others needed to be restrained. The organizing cadre were young, often very angry and emotionally intense. Patience was not their distinguishing virtue. They were capable of a certain rashness of behavior, a pattern that might have gotten out of hand had they not been under the restraining influence of local communities. At the initial training session at Highlander, the first group of organizers had been warned that ministers might be conservative but one should still try to work with them. Early SNCC members remember Ella Baker conveying the same message: Don't write conservative leaders off as Uncle Toms. Everyone has a contribution to make, and it is the job of an organizer to figure out how.

Local people in the South often took the same position. In Canton, Mississippi, one of the most important local people was Mrs. Annie Devine. Matt Suarez of CORE says of the organizers in Canton, "We were young and full of energy. We were trying to bust down brick walls by running our heads through them." Mrs. Devine, though,

> knew what we could get away with and what we could not, who to talk to, who to trust. Too often we tried to intimidate people into

becoming involved. She agreed with our goals, but she believed in approaching people with more subtlety and sensitivity, and she was more successful.

Bob Moses noted:

> What happens with the students in our movement is that they are identifying with these people—people who come off the land— they're unsophisticated and they simply voice, time and time again, the simple truths you can't ignore because they speak from their own lives. It's this the students are rooted in and this is what keeps them from going off at some tangent . . . and as long as the students are tied in with these, their revolt is well-based.[11]

So long as organizers were living in daily contact with local people, they were forced to confront the complexities and contradictions of flesh-and-blood people. On the one hand, it was becoming clearer to some of the young organizers that the objective conditions of the lives of these people could not be altered by anything less than radical change in social structures, changes few traditional leaders could even envision. On the other hand, local people were in many respects culturally conservative, deeply religious, patriotic Americans, who were often bound by strong personal ties to some of the traditional leaders in whom SNCC-COFO workers had little faith.

Even a supportive businessman like Ed Cochrane might have been too conservative for some of the SNCC-COFO workers, but Cochrane and Belle Johnson, a local woman whose family took the movement to heart early, were quite fond of one another. If movement workers didn't want to lose people like her, they had to try to work with people like him. The Reverend Tucker, who got attacked by the dog, seems to have been interested in the movement very early, but Willie Peacock and others went through all kinds of machinations to get him involved. Their willingness to be patient with him is probably partly attributable to the fact that people like Susie Morgan and Ida Holland, strong supporters of the movement, worshipped with Tucker and thought well of him. Once he did get involved, he was deeply involved.

In its later years, I think, as the organization drifted away from grassroots organizing, many SNCC workers would have written off a man like Tucker from the start, losing an opportunity to involve a man with a contribution to make. So long as their organizing styles required them to work with the Belle Johnsons and Susie Morgans, they couldn't just label people like Tucker Uncle Toms and walk away from them. Being forced to deal with the complex potential of real individuals is, as Bob Moses said, one way to keep from going off on tangents, ideological or otherwise. One could get as angry as one liked; working with local people requires a semblance of balance.

It could be argued that attitudes toward whites in the movement represent another area where the attitudes of local people restrained those of SNCC workers. By the winter of 1963–1964 the possibility of bringing in large numbers of white volunteers for the summer was under discussion. (See Chapter 10.) For a variety of reasons, most of the Mississippi SNCC staff were against it. For some of the younger people, there was often an edge of personal bitterness in their reluctance to have too many whites around. Local adults active in COFO overwhelmingly felt that, whatever problems they might bring, the movement needed help, and white students represented help. It was clear, Bob Moses thought, that if the matter were put to a vote, local adults were going to vote the project in.[12] It seems likely that their support of the project helped ensure that it would happen, despite the feelings of the staff.

THE TIMIDITY OF VIOLENT REPRESSION

While local movement supporters were changing what it meant to be a leader at the local level, some of them were also changing the cost of being racist. Violence had always been the ultimate answer to attempts at Black self-assertion. Destructive and terrifying as it was, white violence of the early sixties often seems confused, ill-timed, sometimes even timid when compared to the violence of the past. In Greenwood in the spring of 1963, those whites most desperately opposed to the movement were slow to understand that the calculus of repression had changed. They had now entered a situation in which a significant number of Greenwood Blacks, no longer feeling so alone and in some cases no longer fearing that there was much more that could be done to them anyway, reacted to each additional act of intimidation by becoming more aggressive themselves.

As terrorists, the perpetrators of white violence in Greenwood in the early sixties fall far short of their racist forefathers. Except for the summer and the early fall—the beatings of Sam Block and the mob that ran the SNCC staff out of the office—there are relatively few cases where perpetrators of violence operate openly. Most trouble took place at night. Most of the people involved took care not to be seen. They often used cars with no license plates. Bombings and drive-by shootings, increasingly the repressive tactics of choice in the early sixties, were not a traditional form of racist violence in Mississippi. They represent tactical adjustments to a new situation, and at least in the case of drive-by shootings, an adjustment not as likely to be effective as the old methods, which partly accounts for why more people weren't killed.

The days were past when whites would, in broad daylight, boldly stride into the home of any Black who had offended custom and drag that person out. In the 1920s, newspapers used to advertise lynchings a day or two in advance to give the country people time to get to town. Even in the mid-fifties, the killers of Emmett Till had felt little need to hide their identities and treated their trial as the joke it was.

The changing patterns of violence are partly a reflection of the structural changes that had taken place in the South's relationship with the rest of the nation. There was no way to be sure that violence wouldn't stir up a reaction from Washington. A common theme in editorials in the *Greenwood Commonwealth* in the spring of 1963 was that the quickest way to get a civil rights bill passed was to kill a few civil rights workers. (It was also illegal, the editorials would note, almost parenthetically.) The local Citizens Council, or at least the dominant faction within it, seems to have taken the same stance. In any case, it several times tried to prevent mobs of white teenagers from forming at demonstrations, fearful that the teenagers couldn't be restrained. Federal troops had "invaded" Little Rock in 1957 and Ole Miss in the fall of 1962. If most FBI agents in the state were good ole boys, Justice Department people often had a different agenda, and they were enough of a presence by 1963 that local authorities and vigilantes had to take them into account. White leaders found themselves in a tough situation tactically. When the movement came into a new area, it was probably vulnerable to immediate, unrestrained violence, but probably only to lethal violence. Violent attacks on civil rights workers started right away, but they were not lethal attacks, and in general white reaction seemed initially uncertain. A period of uncertainty was probably almost guaranteed by the fact that not all whites were in agreement. In McComb, those disagreements didn't stop Herbert Lee from getting killed less than two months after the local movement began. In Greenwood, as in many other places in the state, white violence was frequent during that summer and fall, but it was also episodic, and it was short—though just barely—of lethal. The movement was able to root itself in that period.

Almost certainly, the increasingly marginal position of Blacks in the economy was another factor shaping white strategy. The large planters who had always dominated the Delta politically were losing ground to the new middle classes of professionals and businessmen. In Greenwood the 1957 election of Charles Sampson as mayor was seen as the last hurrah of the planter class. The election was hard fought, and even though the planter candidate won, it was clear planters could no longer call the shots. By the 1960s, then, there was no politically meaningful class of whites for whom suppression of Blacks was the kind of economic necessity it had been in years past. As terrible as it was for its victims, the level of violence is not what one would expect from people defending a vital class interest. White Mississippians still believed passionately in the old order, but far fewer of them owed their economic existence to it, which probably reduced the numbers of people willing to use any means to defend it.

Nonetheless, the arson attempts, shootings, and bombings mean that there were still numerous whites who believed that violence was the way to stop the movement. Why weren't they more successful? Part of the answer may have to do with the more aggressive behavior of Black people. Compared to the number of shootings in Mississippi, the number of people actually shot is fairly small. One reason for that may be that night-time marauders had learned to keep a more respectful distance from their targets because the targets were increasingly prone to shoot back.

In rural areas particularly, self-defense was just not an issue among Blacks. If attacked, people were going to shoot back. Farmers living on their own lands were especially likely to do so, particularly when there were whole communities of them. The Mileston area a little south of Greenwood was a community of land-owning farmers who became active in the movement in the spring of 1963, and it was well-known that it could be dangerous to come on their land unexpectedly. Indeed, Blacks in that county still believe that Hartman Turnbow killed one of the white men who attacked his home, and whites covered it up by saying the man had a heart attack.[13] In Greenwood, Dewey Greene was not the only person who responded to an attack on his home by telling local officials that the next people to try it were going to get killed. Just outside of Greenwood, Laura McGhee made the same announcement about anyone coming on her farm, and at least once she thought one of her boys hit the car of the men who had exploded something in her mailbox. There were jokes in the movement about farmers carrying their nonviolent Winchesters to meetings. Volunteers who came for the summer of 1964 were warned that there were areas where you couldn't approach Black homes at night unless you were expected. Whatever they felt about nonviolence personally, SNCC workers seem to have almost never tried to talk local people into putting down their guns. Mary King quotes Bob Moses as saying

> I don't know if anyone in Mississippi preached to local Negroes that they shouldn't defend themselves. . . . Probably the closest is when I asked Mr. E. W. Steptoe not to carry guns when we go together at night. So, instead, he just hides his gun and then I find out later. . . . Self-defense is so deeply engrained in rural southern America that we as a small group can't affect it. It's not contradictory for a farmer to say he's nonviolent and also to pledge to shoot a marauder's head off.[14]

The farmers may have done more to change the behavior of SNCC workers in this respect than vice versa. When Hollis Watkins found that the farmers in Holmes County had a system of posting armed guards around their community center, he took a turn too. Many SNCC people who personally believed in nonviolence found themselves in similar situations, and many responded the way Watkins did.

Mississippi has a long tradition of Blacks taking up arms to defend themselves or their communities. What happened in the early sixties seems to be a good deal more systematic. Very little attention has been paid to the possibility that the success of the movement in the rural South owes something to the attitude of local people toward self-defense. Testimony from the most important source, those whites who engaged in violence or wanted to, is not available. We can only make inferences from their behavior. We know that whoever shot Jimmy Travis, whoever shot at the workers in front of the SNCC office in March of 1963, whoever shot at George Greene that same month, whoever shot Silas McGhee in the head in the summer of 1964, were unwilling to stick around long enough to make sure they had done a thorough job. In each case, they fired quickly and got away quickly. What were they afraid of? The local police? That seems farfetched. It also seems likely that the social element most worried about the federal government would have been the white middle class, not the social element that had traditionally produced the bulk of racial terrorists. Indeed, if members of that element were studying the signs in mid-1963, say, they should have found them favorable. In the case of the Travis shooting in February, there were indictments, but they came to nothing. When Medgar Evers was killed in June, it was clear that there was not going to be a conviction. The objective evidence still said that a white man couldn't be brought to justice for killing a Black person in Mississippi. Their new-found caution is probably best explained by their new appreciation of the probability of getting shot themselves. At the least, that gave them an additional factor to mull over, a factor their fathers had not had to worry about to the same extent. It should have encouraged nearly all of them to be more careful and some to go looking for safer sport.

The cost of being racist was being recalculated. For a hundred years white supremacists had been declaiming their willingness to give their lives in defense of the Southern Way of Life, should matters come to that. Now matters had indeed come to that. Continuing the old tradition of racist violence was coming to mean that you really could lose your life or your liberty. A part of the calculus of change was that by the early sixties, there were more Black people willing to defend themselves at all costs than there were white people willing to live up to all the Confederate bluster. SNCC-COFO workers had something of the best of both worlds. They could maintain the high moral ground of nonviolence while enjoying at least a measure of protection, provided by rural Blacks who had a more practical understanding of what nonviolence meant.

The local people at the movement's core gave the movement certain parameters to which others had to adjust. Their vocal impatience with leaders perceived to be Uncle Toms meant that traditional community leaders had to learn to mouth, at least, the new rhetoric of militance, in effect redefining leadership. The young COFO organizers had to learn to move at a pace local people dictated and to respect the mores and beliefs of local communities. White racists of the more violent sort had to adjust to the possibility of dying for their cause. The stance of local people gave the movement both balance and breathing room.

Seven

THEY KEPT THE STORY BEFORE ME

Families and Traditions

> *The values of any new generation do not spring*
> *full blown from their head; they are already there, inherent*
> *if not clearly articulated in the older generation.*

ERIK ERIKSON[1]

IN HIS INTERVIEW WITH me, the Reverend Aaron Johnson speculated about where some of the older people in the movement got their strength:

> I think somehow you've always had families that were not afraid, but they had sense enough to hold their cool and they just talked to their immediate family and let them know, you know, "You're somebody. You're somebody. You can't express it right now but you keep this in mind. You're just as much as anybody, you keep it in mind." And then when the time for this came, we produced. And I think this has just been handed down.

Many of the people who played particularly important roles in the first year or two of the Greenwood movement, younger people as well as older ones, seem to have come from families like those described by the Reverend Johnson. I began this study with the unconscious assumption that I would be studying individuals, some in the movement, some not. In many ways, the more appropriate starting point is the distinction between movement families and non-movement families. Much of what drew individuals into the movement and kept them there is explicable only in the light of the nature and the history of the particular families they came from. Put differently, the more intense movement of the 1960s was built on earlier work, not only in the sense that it was able to draw resources and inspiration from older organizations and activists but also in the sense that it was able to draw some of its most important members from families that had, if you will, been grooming its members for such roles. This chapter will examine four such families—the Johnsons (not related to the Reverend Johnson), the McGhees, the Morgans, and the Greenes.

THE MCGHEES: IF YOU DON'T FIGHT FOR IT, YOU DON'T NEED IT

Mrs. Laura McGhee was seventy-three years of age at the time I interviewed her. Her appearance belied her reputation. One would not think that this small and soft-spoken woman punched out a police officer in the police station and snatched the nightstick away from another officer in the middle of a demonstration, or that she raised three sons who in their willingness to court danger out-SNCCed SNCC. SNCC's Bob Zellner thought

> that pound for pound and person for person, the McGhees—and I include Silas and Jake and Mrs. McGhee and Clarence—were the bravest people I ever met in my life. They simply just didn't take no shit. Not only didn't they take no shit, they gave shit out—in massive doses. They were going to do their thing no matter what happened. . . . You can't even shoot 'em in the head and do anything with them.

Mrs. McGhee dates her political involvement, or at least her concern with politics, from the shooting of her brother, Gus Courts, a victim of the wave of reprisals that swept the South in the wake of the Supreme Court's *Brown* decision. An officer in the Belzoni NAACP, Courts was shot by assailants unknown in 1955 (see Chapter 2). Seriously wounded, he subsequently left the state. When SNCC first came to Greenwood some years later, Mrs. McGhee, a widow who owned a small farm just outside of Greenwood, was among the first to respond. She first tried to register in 1962 and encouraged her friends and neighbors to do the same. She worked closely with the Reverend Tucker, one of the first ministers to become involved. She taught citizenship classes, and her home was available for meetings and her land for rallies. When farm workers were kicked off the plantations for civil rights activity, her farm was one of the places they could go until they could find a place of their own. She used her farm as security to bail people out of jail. Indeed, she did this so frequently, often signing for twenty-five or thirty people at a time, that the authorities eventually refused to let her guarantee bonds.

Mrs. McGhee carried a reputation for personal fearlessness. During one of the early demonstrations, police gave an order to disperse. She ignored it, and an officer came over and shoved her with his nightstick. She knocked the nightstick down, and the officer drew it back as if to hit her, so she grabbed the officer and his nightstick. Dick Gregory and several others had to pull her off him. On another occasion, when her farm was being used for a rally, the high sheriff came to give her a warning. She gave him to understand that *he* was on *her* property, that *he* was trespassing, and that if he couldn't offer her protection from the nightriders who kept shooting in her home, she didn't need his advice now. He left, which actually seems to have surprised her. She did a fairly good job of protecting herself against the nightriders. During the particularly bad periods, she slept during the day and sat up on the porch at night with her Winchester. One night a car drove by and somebody threw something in her mailbox—the FBI later said it was a cherry bomb—which caused it to explode. Her dog chased the car, and they shot the dog. Two of her sons fired at the car, hit it, it weaved and then pulled away. The FBI and the sheriff came the next day to warn her against letting her boys shoot back. She said that was okay; she'd do all the rest of the shooting herself. They were not bothered by nightriders for a while after that. At one point, her home had been fired on so many times that Zellner and some other SNCC workers built a fence of bridge timbers in front of her house to make it harder for nightriders to see what they were shooting at.[2]

Her three sons were especially active during the summer of 1964. The year before, Silas and Jake had gone to Washington for the famous march. The following spring, while the 1964 Civil Rights Act was nearing passage in Congress, Silas was a high-school senior. He had a number of discussions about the bill with his civics teacher, who used to loan his car to Silas during class time so that he could go downtown and watch the demonstrations. The civil rights bill itself struck Silas as a sham, offering only rights that were already guaranteed in the Constitution and the Bill of Rights. Still, without consulting his family or SNCC or anyone else, he made up his mind that he was going to test that bill as soon as it was passed.

Lyndon Johnson signed the bill into law on July 2. A few days later, Silas walked into Greenwood, a four- or five-mile walk, where he planned to integrate the Crystal Club, one of white Greenwood's most popular restaurants. When he got there in the late afternoon, the restaurant was already closed. Rather than walk all that way back home with nothing to show for it, he decided he might as well integrate one of the white movie theaters. He was only in the Leflore Theater a few minutes when an employee came to ask him what he was doing there. "Watching the movie," Silas replied. Well, why couldn't he watch a movie at the Black theater? Didn't want to see that movie. Attempts to persuade him to leave became threats. Finally, he went to the lobby and called the police, who picked him up and took him home. During the ride back, he had to listen to a speech about how shocked the police were that he'd get involved in something like this. They had always thought he was a good boy from a good family. Despite his denials, the police clearly thought that SNCC or somebody had put him up to it.

Silas and his brother Jake ordinarily did things together. Jake was the older and thought of himself as Silas's protector. When they were both tackles on the high-school football team, if Silas was having trouble handling the man assigned to him, Jake would leave his man alone and go beat up on Silas's. When Silas told his family about his trip to the movies, Jake was more than a little miffed at having been left out.

They agreed they would go to the movies together the following Wednesday.

As it happened, though, Aaron Henry asked Silas to come to Clarksdale that Wednesday to talk to a mass meeting about his adventure. Jake just decided he would go to the movies by himself. The whites were not caught so off guard this time, and Jake had to fight his way through a mob to get out. Undaunted, Jake, Silas, and three of their friends decided they would go again that Friday. As they walked into town the other three boys remembered other pressing obligations, and Jake and Silas found themselves alone. After an hour or so inside the movie, they found that there was a mob outside, and this time they called a cab. The crowd threw things at them and followed the cab all the way to the Black section of town, but no harm was done.

Going to the movies became a regular event, and so did reprisals. On the 16th, Silas was walking home from a demonstration in Greenwood when three white men with a gun forced him into their truck and drove him to a deserted shack, where they intended to teach him a lesson. Inside the shack, they laid down the gun and proceeded to pick up pipes and sticks. In the ensuing melee, Silas was able to pick up a spade, with which he cleared enough space to enable him to duck out the door. Once he was out, "they couldn't have caught me if they had a pick-up." He was able to get back to the FBI office in Greenwood before he passed out from his injuries. (The incident led to the first arrests under the 1964 Civil Rights Act.) On the 25th, the McGhee home was shot at; on the 26th, the boys were back at the movies, and this time Silas was carrying a small .22-caliber pistol. After they had gotten in, some white adults, including a police officer, tried to push them out into the hands of the mob. No cab was willing to come this time, so they contacted the SNCC office. The office sent over two white volunteers who intended to pretend to be members of the mob until they saw a chance to spirit Jake and Silas away. They were recognized, though, and run off. Silas tried to talk the police officer into arresting him and Jake, but without success. As he was considering telling the officer about the gun in his pocket, Jake got the SNCC office on the phone again, and they promised to send a car.

They sent two cars, the first to decoy the crowd, but the brothers hadn't understood that and tried to fight their way through the crowd as soon as they saw the first car. They were pummeled, with Jake taking the worst of it. After they made it to the car, something was thrown through the windshield, and Silas got cut by flying glass and had to be taken to the hospital. While he was there, his mother came, accompanied by Clarence, the oldest brother, a soldier home on leave from Korea, who had joined his brothers on some of their theater excursions. Another mob formed outside the hospital, and the family was unable to leave, the sheriff saying there was nothing he could do about it. He insisted that they had to leave the hospital, and they insisted that they weren't going to do that. Clarence called his commanding officer, and the SNCC office called someone from the Justice Department who promised to intercede. Around one or two in the morning, a phalanx of state troopers and local police materialized and escorted them home.

On the afternoon of August 15, Silas got into an argument with a police officer over an illegally parked car. Incensed over Silas's refusal to show proper respect, the officer called him several kinds of sons of bitches and said that he ought to blow Silas's brains out, unholstering his gun for emphasis. He was still cursing when Silas drove off. Later that evening, Silas was ferrying people between the SNCC office and a going-away party for some of the summer volunteers. He pulled over to wait out a rainstorm and dozed off. He awoke to the sight of a man in a nearby car pointing a gun at him. The man shot before Silas could move. He was hit in the head with a .38 slug, which broke his jaw and went down his throat. Still conscious, he could hear a woman's voice over his car's short-wave radio: "They got the nigger! They got him!" By the time Bob Zellner had gotten outside, Silas had managed to get the car door open and was falling out. Certain that Silas was done for, Zellner took off his shirt and wrapped it around the wound.

By the time they got Silas to the hospital, a crowd of cops was there, crowing about how that goddammed Silas had finally gotten his. Zellner remembers being surprised that no one brought a stretcher. Finally, he went into the building, got a rolling stretcher, and wheeled Silas inside, where he was just ignored. No one made any effort to help him. "It was like that wasn't a question," says Zellner, who was threatened with arrest for indecent exposure; his shirt was still wrapped around Silas's head. Finally, a Black doctor showed up and began treatment. Silas spent about ten days in the hospital in Jackson, surviving in part because the slug that hit him had not broken up into fragments. His mother, whose brother had almost been killed by buckshot, kept the bullet they took out of her son.

During this period, all of the McGhee boys got arrested regularly. Between June and December of 1964, Silas and Jake were arrested at least seven times between them.[3] Clarence was arrested the day of Silas's shooting and was still in jail when he learned about it. Three days after Silas's shooting, Jake got arrested. Mrs. McGhee went to check on him, accompanied by Zellner, a volunteer lawyer who had only been in town a short while, and a couple of other SNCC workers. On the way to the jail, Zellner tried to explain the situation to the non-southerners. Once they got to the jail, the chief was going to want to talk with the lawyer, not Mrs. McGhee, he explained, but Mrs. McGhee was a proud woman and would want to speak for herself. Sure enough, when they got to the station, the chief ushered the lawyer off into a side office. When Mrs. McGhee tried to go in a cop slammed the door and stood in front of it, telling her she couldn't go in there. According to Zellner:

> She says, "The hell I can't. I come down here to get my son, Jake." He says "You can't go in there" and she says "Boppp!" hit him right in the eye, right in the eye as hard as I've ever seen anybody hit in my life. I remember it just like a movie. . . . I remember his eye swelling up and I remember thinking to myself "God, I didn't know you could *see* something swell up. . . ." And he's losing consciousness, sliding down the door. Meanwhile, Mrs. McGhee is following him on the way down. She's not missing a lick—boom, boom, boom!—and every time she hits him, his head hits the door. Meantime . . . he's going for his gun reflexively, but the man is practically knocked out. . . . [B]y the second or third time she hit him, they're trying to get from inside the office. The chief is going, "What the hell's going on? Let us out. By this time, the cop is slumped down on the floor. When he started going for his gun I sensed a clear and present danger, so I pounced on him, simply holding his gun hand. . . . In the meantime, I'm saying to Mrs.

McGhee [*softly*], "Mrs. McGhee, I think you've got him enough now," 'cause she was trying to get around me to give him another pop. Meantime . . . every time the chief would try to open the door it would hit the man—whomp—in the head again. I said, "Chief, Ralph is trying to shoot Mrs. McGhee."

Mrs. McGhee was arrested but apparently never tried, perhaps because Zellner convinced the chief that it wouldn't do to have the story get out. It was, Zellner thought, a valuable lesson in race relations. "A new day is coming when a Black woman can just whip the yard-dog shit out of a white cop and not have to account for it."[4]

A few weeks later, Silas and Jake were going to the movies again. Because the Leflore Theater continued to sell them tickets, whites started a boycott of it, which led to its going out of business. The McGhees transferred their patronage to the Paramount, the only other white theater in town.

The courage of the McGhees eventually had some effect on other local people. Although Silas generally minimizes the results of what he did, he does believe that large numbers of young people were drawn to the movement by his example. Bob Zellner agreed. Indeed, the pure direct-action style of the McGhees so captured the imagination of the youth that some of them started saying, in effect, that voter-registration campaigns and demonstrations were too tame. They wanted the more direct confrontation with evil in which the McGhees specialized. (Zellner, laughing: "The kids were saying SNCC was becoming conservative. We were fighting off an attack from the Left.")

When the theaters near her home finally did desegregate, people from Browning, the area outside Greenwood where the McGhees lived, didn't want to go unless Mrs. McGhee went with them. As late as 1965, when federal registrars fanned out across the South, many people from Browning wouldn't go to register unless Mrs. McGhee went with them. She rode down with each carload, standing across the street while they registered. In the eyes of their neighbors the McGhees had earned a form of charisma.

Asked what kept himself and his brothers going, Silas McGhee mentioned two factors. He and Jake, he says, thought the whole thing was comical in some senses. They just never believed they were going to get seriously hurt, even after it started to happen. "Maybe I was foolish at that particular time," Silas says now. The other factor he mentioned, of course, is the support within the family itself. When Silas talks about incidents in which he himself was involved, he jokes and kids, but when he talks about his mother it is with a note of unmistakable pride. He tells, for example, of an altercation she had with one of her white neighbors in the 1950s. Because they were farm owners, the McGhees frequently had trouble with neighbors who wanted their land. (The problem continued into the sixties. A month or two before his death, Medgar Evers had promised to find a way to stop the harassment.) Livestock got stolen or killed, their fences got ignored or taken down. She looked up from her kitchen window one morning to see one of her white neighbors cutting a ditch inside the boundaries of her land. "She didn't take nothing but her bare hands, and she went down there, climbed up on that bulldozer and pulled that man off. She pulled that man out of there and shook him so." When the sheriff arrived, she told him they had ten minutes to get that bulldozer off her land before she burned it. Silas says:

> She is the type of person that would do anything she could for you, anything, irregardless of what it is. If she can do it, she'll do it, but, on the other hand, if you try to mess over her, you got trouble. . . . My mother would always tell me, "I don't care what you do as long as you be within the law. You stay within the law and you can do anything you want to."

If Mrs. McGhee managed to convey a sense of entitlement to her children, she also conveyed a sense of responsibility. "She had this feeling that if it's worthwhile, it's worth fighting for," Silas says, "and if you don't want to fight for it, you don't need it."

Mrs. McGhee herself attributes what she calls her temper to her upbringing. Her parents separated while she was still young. Her mother had a place of her own in the hill country, where she encountered all sorts of harassment from whites, but she was afraid that complaining was only going to make things worse. Her father, with whom she stayed for a couple of years in the Delta, was just the opposite sort. He stood up for himself and would go after a white man as quick as he would a Black one. He was the only colored worker on his plantation to get paid cash; everybody else got paid in "furnish." It is from him, Mrs. McGhee says, that she gets her temper. When she was a teenager, she went to stay in Dallas, where she learned that little children in school knew more than she did. Looking like the mother of everyone else in her class was embarrassing, so she quit and went to work, later returning to Mississippi to marry a man much like her father in his racial attitudes. Although Silas's father died while Silas was very young, the stories that Silas heard about him while growing up depicted an independent man, a man who didn't particularly like white people—he didn't hate them (Silas: "You know, you don't have to hate a person to watch them"), but he didn't trust many of them either. With the exception of two businessmen who weren't "really white"—one was a Jew, the other an Arab—he took care that his business dealings with whites were on a cash basis.

It is not surprising that quite apart from the movement, the McGhee children tended to stand up for themselves. While still in high school, Silas drove a school bus. Farm children learn to drive very young, of course. As was customary in a great many places, younger drivers were paid less than adult drivers. This struck Silas as unfair, so he led a protest, earning himself the lasting enmity of the school principal but also eventually earning a raise for the younger drivers.

Mrs. McGhee was a model for her boys as well as an ongoing source of support. During his movie-going adventures, Silas says, he always felt that he had all the support in the world at home. For her part, Mrs. McGhee was often very frightened for her boys, but she was very proud of them. She can't remember ever wanting to discourage them from doing what they thought necessary. The ability of COFO workers to challenge and survive white violence was an important element in making Black Greenwood understand that the old order might be passing. That may be even more the case when local people like the McGhees are involved. The message conveyed is not merely that white violence can't stop the somewhat mysterious SNCC workers, but that it can no longer even stop people we've known all our lives, people just like us. Violence is further stripped of its mystique.

The McGhees represent a tradition of defiance, but it is important to note that not all of it is what we would call political defiance. The involvement of Mrs. McGhee's brother in the NAACP or her own early decision to join SNCC are overtly political, of course. From what Silas says about them, though, it seems probable that he and his brothers were very much influenced by more general attitudes of their parents—their outspokenness, their willingness to defend what was theirs, their assumption that they did not have to accept any and every damn thing that whites wanted to do. The McGhees continued to take part in the movement as long as there was anything to take part in. After their home burned down, they moved into a trailer on their land. (There had been several unsuccessful firebombings; the actual burning of the house may have been an accident.) Silas became a member of SNCC's national executive committee, probably the youngest person to serve on it. While Silas was in the service, Jake was an officer in the NAACP and the newly formed Freedom Democratic Party. When boycotts became the main movement tactic in the late sixties, Jake was one of the boycott leaders. (In 1968, another boycott leader told an interviewer that the movement was under injunction, but one person continued to defy it, picketing when and where he liked: Jake McGhee.[5]) Mrs. McGhee says that she never seriously considered getting out, even though she had her disappointments. When she was being harassed financially, various organizations raised money in her name, and she is quite sure that she never saw all of that money. She never thought the movement or the people in it were perfect, but once she was in it, she was in it.

Silas's skeptical attitude toward the 1964 Civil Rights Act is worth noting. He felt that there had been laws before, there had been court decisions before, and they had not necessarily meant anything. Legislation serves our need to render history understandable by giving us convenient benchmarks, and we may therefore be tempted to exaggerate its significance. The bill is taken to be a great watershed. The bill in itself, though, may have been less important than the willingness of people like the McGhees to insist that it be enforced. That insistence, I would argue, is the crucial break with the past, not the legislation itself. There is nothing about the record of the postwar federal government, the Kennedy administration not excepted, to suggest that Washington was going to enforce any more Black rights than it had to enforce.

THE GREENES: KEEPING THE STORY BEFORE ME

Dewey Greene, Senior, died in March 1980 at the age of eighty, after he and his wife had raised three boys and four girls. His sons Dewey, Jr., and George were among SNCC's first local canvassers in Greenwood. During the Greenwood movement's initial and most dangerous year, two of the Greene daughters, Freddie and Alma, were at least as active as their brothers.

When Dewey Greene's children talk about how they were raised, they leave little doubt that they were raised to think in a certain way about racial issues and about their place in the southern system. The family had its own party line on these issues. Thus, their mother never worked outside her own home. "Working out" would have meant domestic work in some white woman's kitchen, with its attendant humiliations. Like the children in many southern Black families, the Greene children were told repeatedly that they were just as good as anybody else, but it went further than that. Certain stories were also repeated. According to Alma Greene Henderson, "My mama always kept the story before me" about a man who was burned at the stake in nearby Moorhead during the 1920s and also repeated another story, apparently from the same period, involving a Black woman whose family was brutalized. Afterward, the men who had done it tried to purchase sex from the woman.

Other things, the children were able to witness for themselves. Three of the Greene boys used to play with a white boy named Charlie. They had a falling out over something, which resulted in Charlie standing in front of their house calling them niggers. Mr. Greene, tall and heavy, walked over to him and "slapped him so hard and spun him right around like a spinning top and he left his handprint on his face." Mrs. Greene thought her husband was going to be lynched, but he refused to run, and nothing came of the incident.

Once, at the carnival, young Freddie started to fall off the merry-go-round. Her father jumped on it to catch her. The white man running the ride hadn't seen the child falling and thought Mr. Greene was trying to steal a free ride. He cursed Mr. Greene, who called him a redneck. The two men squared off, the white man brandishing a large wrench, Mr. Greene inviting him to come on and do something with it. The white man declined to do that, and no one called the police, so the incident ended there. One story that Mr. Greene kept before the children captured some of racism's irony. He was going into the paint store when he noticed that no one seemed to be around. He went in anyway, to find that the lady in charge had fallen and broken her hip. He had to have a debate with himself. If discovered there, he could be accused of having hurt a white woman. On the other hand, she was a human being. He went for help. He repeated the story to his children to convey a double message, a way of pointing out that things "are so bad that a black man couldn't go anywhere without being accused of stealing or hurting somebody, but regardless of the color of a person, you do what you could for him." It is because of that kind of double message, Alma thinks, that none of the Greene children grew up hating white folks. They may be careful with them, but they don't hate.

The Greenes were a high-status family within Black Greenwood. Mr. Greene's job was a relatively prestigious one, and he had gone to college for three years. Indeed, one of his sons attributes Mr. Greene's activism to the fact that his education and his reading a great deal made him more aware of things than most people in the community. The fact that many of the family were light-complexioned also helped place them in the upper levels of the community. George Greene thinks that he and his siblings got away with some things at school that would have gotten darker-skinned children punished.

While George was still in high school, he was among the young people, who, prodded by Medgar Evers, established a chapter of the NAACP Youth Councils. George's father approved of his involvement, but took some pains to be sure that George understood the possible repercussions. His mother, a very quiet woman, did not try to discourage him. The chapter did not, in George's estimation, have a great deal of direction, but it was his feeling at the time that any form of involvement was a step. If all a person did was give one dollar a year to the organization, then maybe that person would pay a little more attention to what the organization did.

During the first fall that SNCC was in Greenwood, the attention of the state and much of the country was turned to the campus of the University of Mississippi at Oxford, where James Meredith's enrollment would eventually lead to several days of rioting and at least two deaths. Only federal troops made it possible for him to stay there.

Dewey, Jr., a young navy veteran, decided that he, too, wanted to go to Ole Miss. Apparently, he got some white friends to get an application for him. By late 1962 or early 1963, the application was public knowledge, and the family began receiving threatening phone calls.[6] Dewey, Sr., who had always made a decent living as a housepainter and paperhanger, suddenly could find no work at all. The one white family brave enough to hire him awoke one morning to find that his work had been spoiled by a broad, black ring painted all the way around the building. Mr. Greene was especially galled with the local Black principal, who told him that Dewey, Jr., wasn't the kind of person who needed to go to Ole Miss. The mayor called Mr. Greene downtown for a meeting. Mr. Greene sent word that he'd be there when he could fit it in. When he did go, he was asked to make his son withdraw his application, to which he replied that when his boy had applied to the navy, no one asked him to withdraw from that.

That was the end of that discussion, though not of the harassment of the family. Even without work, though, the Greenes were in a better position than most to withstand harassment. Mr. Greene was able to retire on Social Security. They owned their own home. This seems to be one of the cases in which repression had the opposite effect from that intended. Mr. Greene had been the sort of man who took all the work he could find. Now, with all this time on his hands, he was able to throw himself into the movement full time. He soon found himself traveling all over the state for COFO.

Physical reprisals were still possible. One night during the turbulent spring of 1963, George Greene was coming home from a mass meeting. Almost as soon as he had gotten into the house, a shotgun blast shattered the window he had just passed in front of. Another blast shattered the window of the bedroom where his niece was sleeping. The next day there was a large protest march, the first ever in Greenwood. There had been several other shootings or similar incidents in the previous two months, but they had mostly involved COFO staff, not local people. George thinks that part of the reason the town responded so vigorously to the attack on his home was that people could identify with an old Greenwood family in a way they could not with outsiders. George's father reacted by calling the police and telling them that he had a gun, too, and if anybody else came shooting at his house, the police could just come and collect their bodies.[7] The home received police protection for a period after that. Shortly after the shooting, Mr. Greene was finally allowed to register.[8]

The large march the day after the shooting reflected the movement's growing support, but there were still many who were frightened by it. For the Greenes, according to Alma, "it was just like we had leprosy. . . . They didn't want to be seen talking to us. They just didn't have anything to do with us." The family attended Wesley United Methodist Church, one of the first to be open to the movement, but even most of that congregation avoided them, though they received some support from the Reverend Rucker. Ironically, their isolation within the Black community had the effect of pushing them even more firmly into the Movement. Alma says, "See, we didn't have anybody to deal with but the people in the movement—Sam and Peacock and Robert Moses and all those people."

Mr. Greene's increasing involvement led to his selection as a delegate to the 1964 Democratic National Convention for the Freedom Democratic Party and to his becoming NAACP president in the same year. By the time he took it over, the Greenwood NAACP was in need of a rescue operation. Greene had been one of the founding members in 1952–53 and had taken part in each of its periodic revivals, including the 1963 re-organization of the branch. By the spring of 1964, the branch was again in trouble. The Reverend Tucker, the president, moved from town and in June, so did the branch secretary. The secretary had been put under enormous financial pressure because of his activism and when he left town he apparently took the contents of the NAACP treasury with him, including the fees from about a hundred memberships. People weren't clear on whether they should be mad at him in particular or the NAACP in general, so a great many people compromised by being angry at both. In the middle of this mess, Dewey Greene was elected president with an explicit mission of restoring the branch's credibility.[9]

Some of the children expanded their involvement as much as did their father. In George's case, that led to several run-ins with the law. He was once arrested fifteen minutes after he crossed the Alabama state line. George attributes his penchant for getting arrested while minding his own business to some flaw in his looks; other people think it may have had something to do with his flair for mouthing off at cops. George to an Alabama deputy: "You didn't invite me here, so I guess you can't invite me to leave." To an Alabama state trooper: "I haven't done anything. You don't even think I've done anything, so why are we having this conversation?" The bravado does not indicate an absence of fear. George admits readily that he was frightened much of the time, but for him and many of the other workers, trying to intimidate police officers was a matter of policy.

His first arrest was right at home in Greenwood. Picked up along with several others during a demonstration, he got six months at hard labor and a $500 fine. At the Leflore County Penal Farm, he refused to do any work since he didn't see that he had done anything wrong. The captain at the farm—that is, the warden—tried at first to be accommodating. The warden knew George's father and had known George from a child. As far as he was concerned, George was a good boy who had been led into something he couldn't understand. But George managed to get himself on the warden's bad side pretty quickly. During their first weekend in jail, he convinced the others arrested with him to refuse to work and to start a hunger strike. That was enough to get the lot of them transferred to Parchman, the state's largest prison, a place legendary for brutality and degradation. At Parchman, their clothes were taken from them and they slept on steel cots in unheated cells.

George got in further trouble over his refusal to "sir" the guards. This got him thrown into what was inappropriately called the "hot box," along with SNCC's MacArthur Cotton. It was a tiny, ice-cold cell, with no source of light and barely enough space for one person. They had to sleep sitting against the wall since there wasn't room enough to stretch out. A hole in the floor served for sanitary facilities. After ten days in there, during which he refused to eat, they were both sent back to the regular cells, just in time for the Fourth of July barbecue. George did a total of sixty-seven days and contracted an intestinal virus before his father got him out.

For the next few years, George became a full-time organizer, working in some of the most dangerous parts of the South—southwest Mississippi, Natchez, Lowndes County and Greene County in Alabama. One journalist wrote dramatically that George Greene had "more bullet holes in his shroud than any man in Mississippi."[10] There could be lots of claimants for that title, but George was certainly involved in more than his fair share of incidents. In February 1964, he was shot by police during a Jackson demonstration but was not seriously injured. A few months later, he, along with his sister Freddie and Curtis Hayes, was in the Freedom House in McComb when it was bombed. He had done some auto racing in high school, acquiring skills that were much appreciated within the movement. In one incident in November 1963 he was doing voter-registration work near Natchez. On November 2, he was leaving Natchez with volunteer Bruce Payne when he realized that they were being followed by two of the men who had given Payne a beating the day before and had warned him to stay out of town. George could neither evade the vehicle nor outrun it, even at 105 miles per hour. He was forced off the road near a bridge, where one of the pursuers got out of his car and with drawn pistol told Greene to get out of his car. George, who had never shut his motor off, had a better idea. He swerved back onto the highway and took off. The man with the gun fired three times, hitting one of the tires. With a leaking tire, George managed to turn off unseen onto a side road where they could change the tire.[11]

George's father had come from a background relatively free of economic dependence on whites. Dewey, Senior's parents had owned their own farm, and his father was the janitor at the local post office. It was fortunate that they were fairly independent, since Dewey had the kind of temper that could have gotten them all in trouble otherwise. His mother looked up the road one day, and who should be trudging home but Dewey, who was supposed to be in school at Alcorn College. He had been put out for fighting, which didn't surprise his mother much at all.

He had a temper, but he was far from being a rabble-rouser. In fact, in most situations he seems to have been a quiet man. If there were a way to get something done without upsetting everyone, he'd prefer that, more so, say, than Cleve Jordan or David Sanders. The Reverend Redd, a member of the NAACP, describes him as staunch, but not outspoken. He wasn't even fond of leading prayer at church. Still, if there was work that needed doing, he'd see that it got done. He may have been quiet in some contexts but he loved to argue. He sat around the barbershop for hours arguing with his friends about everything. He probably appreciated the company of the SNCC workers partly because they were good people to talk politics with. He certainly admired their courage and their willingness to help people who sometimes acted like they didn't want to help themselves. He was especially close to Bob Moses, Sam Block, Willie Peacock, and Stokely Carmichael. Carmichael called him "Big Daddy," which is what his own children and the children in the neighborhood called him.

So friendly and outgoing a man must have been very hurt when most of his buddies decided they didn't want anything to do with him. If so, he seems not to have held any grudges about it. After the movement in Greenwood was effectively over, many old friendships started up again, and he even became close again to some of those who had fought him most bitterly during the movement years, including the principal who had said that Dewey, Junior, didn't deserve to go to Ole Miss. The principal was well along in years now, and Mr. Greene spent part of every day visiting the sick and the elderly. He visited the retired principal almost every day, and if he missed a day the principal called to see what had gone wrong.

It is not surprising that the Greene children feel they got much of their resolve from their father's example. George, whom the other family members describe as being particularly like his father, attributes to his father his own temper, his willingness to go to any lengths to back up his convictions, a sense of his own worth as well as of the worth of others. Similarly, his sister Alma explains her decision to go attempt to register by herself at a time when most people wanted to go in the safety of a group by saying, "I had that much Dewey Greene in me, I guess." Phrasing it so, she places her own behavior within a tradition that both strengthens and obligates.

By all accounts, Dewey Greene was as devoted to his family as to his community. As he felt death approaching in early 1980, his chief worry was whether his grandson Buster would be able to make it home from Korea in time. He died before the boy was able to get there. Considering what he had contributed to his community, his daughter Alma feels, the Black community did not have much reaction to his passing. Some of the leading lights in the community didn't so much as trouble themselves to say "I'm sorry." The NAACP had a meeting scheduled for the day of his funeral and didn't see any reason to cancel it.

THE JOHNSONS

In families like the McGhees and the Greenes, the activism of the younger generation is clearly a response, in part, to the activism of their parents. Of course, that was not a one-way process. The older generation both influenced the younger and was influenced by it. With or without adult encouragement, hard-headed youngsters might get involved, pulling their reluctant elders into the movement after them, and those elders might then become more deeply involved than their children. The involvement of both Lula Belle Johnson's family and Susie Morgan's family fits this pattern.

The involvement of the Johnsons started with Waite Johnson, one of the twelve children. In high school at the time, he was "hypnotized," as he puts it, by Sam Block and Willie Peacock, becoming one of their first regular canvassers. He did so against his mother's wishes. His grandmother, though, Mrs. Emily Holt, was interested from the very beginning. We noted earlier that there are numerous cases where the broadening experience of military service or travel seems to be a part of what politicized some men. In Mrs. Holt's case the analog seems to be her experience as a migrant laborer. She traveled all across the South, following the crops as far away as Florida. It was a hard life, but she preferred it to work in some white woman's kitchen. Mrs. Holt is a feisty woman; one would not want to be on her bad side. According to one of her granddaughters, "It's nothing for her to tell anybody—I don't care what color you are or who you are—where to get off."[12] She always argued that none of the girls in the family—there were seven girls and five boys—should be allowed to do domestic work for whites, no matter how badly they might need the money. Belle Johnson, though, did not take such a hard stance on the issue, and the older girls were allowed to work in white homes.

While his mother was telling Waite not to go to SNCC meetings, his grandmother was encouraging him to go and to report back to her on whatever was happening. June, his younger sister, went with him whenever she could.

Mrs. Johnson was a strict mother. She frequently worked part-time as a restaurant cook which sometimes meant she didn't get home until three in the morning. Even at that hour, if she got home and found the kids had gone to bed without finishing their chores, it was nothing for her to turn everybody out of bed, whip every behind in sight, and set them to mopping, sweeping, and washing. She and June had more than their share of run-ins. June, fourteen years old when the movement came to Greenwood, was somewhat outspoken. What she thought of as questioning things, her mother thought of as talking back, and when June wasn't being whipped for that she was being whipped for fighting in school or sneaking off to SNCC meetings with Waite.

For most of the first year the movement was in Greenwood, June's interest in the movement was a source of friction between her and her mother. Mrs. Johnson didn't like Waite's involvement, but he was older and a boy. It was harder for June to get permission to take part in movement activities. She hung around the SNCC office more than her mother knew, and she went to her first mass meeting—at the Reverend Johnson's church—without permission. She was sometimes able to go canvassing on the sly.

Belle Johnson was skeptical of the movement, but she liked and trusted some of the movement workers that she met through her children. Sam Block and Bob Moses were among her favorites, along with Annell Ponder of SCLC. By the spring of 1963, June could usually get permission to go to meetings so long as Bob or Annell was around. This was a very common pattern. Adults who were skeptical about the movement itself were often impressed with the character of the people who represented it.

June's involvement was eventually to trigger her mother's. When school was out for the summer of 1963, June, after much pleading, including a special plea from Bob Moses, was able to get permission to go on a COFO trip to South Carolina. Euvester Simpson, a young woman from nearby Itta Bena, also went. The trip involved a meeting with Septima Clark. Annell Ponder was on the trip, and it was very clear that she was to keep close watch on June. In Atlanta, when everyone else stayed at a dormitory, June stayed at Ms. Ponder's apartment. Aside from the bus breaking down about every two miles, the trip went well until the return. The bus stopped in Winona, Mississippi, not very far from Greenwood. Some of the COFO group went into the white restroom and got arrested for it.

Their reception in the Winona jail was brutal. Annell Ponder apparently was the first to be beaten. Mrs. Hamer later remembered:

> And I could hear somebody when they say, "Cain't you say yessir, nigger? Cain't you say yessir, bitch?" And I could understand Miss Ponder's voice. She said, "Yes, I can say yessir." He said, "Well, say it." She said, "I don't know you well enough." She never would say yessir and I could hear when she would hit the flo', and then I could hear them licks just soundin'. . . . But anyway, she kept screamin' and they kept beatin' on her and finally she started prayin' for 'em, and she asked God to have mercy on 'em, because they didn't know what they were doing.
>
> And after then . . . I heard some real *keen* screams, and that's

when they passed my cell with a girl, she was fifteen years old, Miss Johnson, June Johnson. They passed my cell and the blood was runnin' down in her face.[13]

Guards had taken turns beating June with nightsticks and a leather strap. She lost consciousness twice and had to be carried back to her cell. When Mrs. Hamer's turn came, the guards, perhaps tired by this time, had her lie face down on a bunk and ordered two Black prisoners to beat her with a studded leather strap until she couldn't get up.

When the travelers did not show up in Greenwood at the expected time, Hollis Watkins started calling all the jails in the area. He told each one that he knew they had arrested the group, and he wanted to know what the charges were. SNCC had done this before when people disappeared. The intent was to make local law-enforcement officials think they were being watched. Eventually, they learned that the group was in Winona, and Guyot went over to inquire after them. He was arrested himself, and a group of cops took turns beating him off and on for four hours (see Chapter 10).[14]

So far as I have been able to learn, Belle Johnson never expressed her feelings about what had happened to June to any of her children, but from that point on Belle Johnson was a full-time activist and so were virtually all of her children. She quit her job and opened her home to the movement. There were often more COFO workers in the house than family members. By October of 1963, she was on the COFO payroll, earning ten dollars a week. She was an indefatigable canvasser, and she influenced a number of older women to join the movement, an important plateau in the movement's development. Women like Belle Johnson could go into homes where COFO workers were not welcome. Ed Cochrane, probably the wealthiest Black man in town, was very fond of her. He would do things for her that he might have been reluctant to do for SNCC alone. At the same time, she could go into the beer gardens and the pool halls and be listened to by the young boys there. When she wasn't canvassing or attending meetings or going to a march, she was likely to be raising money for displaced families or finding housing for out-of-town volunteers. The entire family got into the act. Her daughter Barbara became a volunteer office worker for SNCC, Dorothea worked with the food and clothing drive, and she, Waite, and June continued to be all-around volunteers. Even Jeffrey, her eight-year-old nephew, went around telling everybody that he was going to grow up to be a "Snick."

The Johnsons are remembered by every SNCC worker with whom I have spoken. SNCC's Jean Wheeler Smith writes of returning to the SNCC office in Greenwood years after the movement ended and walking through the kitchen

> where Miss Johnson, our mother-in-Greenwood performed feats of magic to provide us with beans and greens and cornbread and sometimes even a sweet potato pie. There would also be a plate on the back of the stove for those who couldn't get back before she went home to cook for her own family.[15]

Her involvement led to some friction with their church, Strangers Home Baptist. Church had always been very important to her. Indeed, one of her daughters resented the way her mother had always tried to be accepted at church. Strangers Home was quite uninvolved in the movement, although the Reverend Matthews once bailed her daughter Barbara out of jail. As their involvement with the movement increased, the family felt increasingly estranged from their church community.

Despite that, once in motion, Belle Johnson continued to be politically active, even after most of the COFO workers had left the Delta. She became an officer in the Freedom Democratic Party, after it was organized in 1964. Before her death in 1966, she was instrumental in bringing what would become the Head Start program to Leflore, over the objections of local politicians. In many ways her case, like that of Mrs. Morgan, represents the ideal type of what SNCC was trying to do in the Delta—create a new leadership cadre that would be independent of both the traditional leadership and of SNCC itself.

There is a southern phrase for people like Mrs. Susie Morgan: "She covers all the ground she stands on." Mrs. Morgan is a staunch woman, strong in her opinions, some of which involve white people. She has known some good ones, including some in the movement, but by and large, she doesn't have too much use for them. Whites have always been scheming, she says, to keep Black people down. Peckerwoods manage to stick together in that, even when they can't agree on anything else. They'll lie in a minute to get what they want. If anything, she has even less use for "whitemouthed" Negroes, the ones who have to tell a white man everything they know.

According to her daughter Arance, Mrs. Morgan had a standing rule that white salesmen were not to come to her home, because she knew she would not be welcome in theirs. When the police once brought her son Paul home—they wanted him to inform on some other boys—she read them the riot act, making it clear that they were never to put her child in a police car again without talking to her first. When she had trouble with her white neighbors, she gave as good as she got. Her children felt that as long as they had not done anything wrong, their mother would back them against anyone, Black or white. Arance remembers that when the movement started she was surprised at how frightened Black people were; she had just assumed that everyone was like her mother.

The involvement of the Morgans is tied to that of the Johnsons. Belle Johnson and Susie Morgan were friends, and so were their children. Arance, a high school student, was walking home sometime in the fall of 1962 when some SNCC workers gave her some leaflets and asked her to stop by the Freedom Office sometime. When she did, she was impressed by Block, Peacock, and Watkins. She went to her first mass meeting with Dot Johnson, and the girls gradually became more involved.

Before the movement came to Greenwood, Mrs. Morgan had tried several times to register on her own, but she did not think much of the movement at first. Arance was able to get her mother's grudging permission to take part in SNCC activities so long as her mother always knew where she was and so long as she got herself home before dark. Mrs. Morgan gradually got to know some of the SNCC workers individually, especially Sam Block, who, Mrs. Morgan says, "called himself courting one of my girls." When Mrs. Morgan learned that Sam and the other young men were civil rights workers, she told the girls she didn't think it was such a good idea to have them around the house, but she stopped short of forbidding it. The year before, she had paid close attention as the Freedom Riders moved across the South, eventually getting as close as Jackson. "I know they ain't coming here," she said to herself at the time. Come to look up, and there they were in her living room.

Arance describes her mother as being a difficult woman to impress. She gave the movement a good hard look. Her girls told her about the meetings they attended, including one where Medgar Evers gave a hundred dollars to someone who had been kicked off a plantation, and eventually they were able to get her to a meeting or two; Mrs. Morgan was impressed by the idea that people were being given concrete help. She also found the young men from SNCC appealing, precisely because they were her idea of men; they were doing something, and they were not afraid. Again, she was responding first to their character, more than to their program. It still took her a while to come around. She studied over it and prayed over it. Then one Sunday morning while she was sitting on her porch, "Something hit me like a new religion." She made up her mind she was going to be involved, no matter the consequences.

As with June and Lula Belle Johnson, Arance's first arrest caused Mrs. Morgan to become more heavily involved. Arance smart-mouthed a cop at a demonstration. Her younger sister Rebecca came over to defend her, and they were both arrested. At the jail, the girls were recognized by a lawyer who socialized with Mr. Brewer, the attorney for whom Mrs. Morgan had worked for almost eight years. Mr. Morgan had died while the children were young, and Mrs. Morgan supported the family by herself. Mr. Brewer informed Mrs. Morgan that her services would no longer be needed, a blessing in disguise, according to Arance, since it was the last time her mother ever worked in a white man's kitchen.

From that point on, Mrs. Morgan became virtually a full-time movement worker. The Voter Education Project was eventually able to put her on its payroll at twenty-five dollars a week. She remembers the movement work as the hardest work she has ever done, chopping cotton not excluded. She would come home exhausted at the end of the day and just flop across the bed. Like Lula Belle Johnson, she was an especially effective canvasser, according to the SNCC workers, and she and Belle frequently worked together. She recalled one campaign where they were trying to get people to sign a petition requesting federal protection for people trying to register. She and Mrs. Johnson would go into homes and say, "You know I'm black and poor, just like you are. You know I wouldn't tell you nothing wrong." Older people warned them that she was going to get herself in trouble because Negroes couldn't be trusted. Sometimes people got mean with them, but Mrs. Morgan remembers people telling her to go away, they didn't want to sign, and before she could get out of their yard, they'd change their minds and call her back—which, Mrs. Morgan says, teaches you something about the power of prayer. She had known all along that God was in the plan.

Her home was small, but she housed civil rights people whenever she could. One minister from Baltimore tried to get her to move up there for her own safety. Her relations with local ministers deteriorated. She was angry that so few of them took part in the movement, and she told her friends that if they would all stop putting money in the collection plate on Sunday, they could make the ministers come around. But nobody wanted to listen to that.

Her own minister, though, was the Reverend Tucker, one of those who had supported the movement fairly early. In 1963, he became the NAACP president, and she worked on the membership committee. Tucker got a great deal of harassment, which she saw firsthand. Their homes were close together, and she could see the police circling the block, keeping a watch on his house. When there were a lot of them, she would call him and warn him to be careful. Once, she was sitting on her porch watching the cops when a bomb went off near Reverend Tucker's house. She was sure nobody had done it but the police. In those days, she says, she didn't worry much about her own safety, trusting that the Lord would take care of that, but she did worry about her children and her friends. It was only in later years that she thought very much about what might have happened to her. She joined the Freedom Democratic Party when it was formed in 1964, helped organize boycotts, and helped to bring the Child Development Group of Mississippi, the precursor of Head Start, to Greenwood. In fact, the night before Belle Johnson died, she and Mrs. Morgan were at the Elks Hall trying to raise funds for a trip to Washington to lobby for CDGM. Mr. Brewer, the man who had fired her, tried several times to hire her back, but she always refused. After the movement in Greenwood was effectively over, she worked at various jobs for a while and went back to picking cotton in the fall. Later, she was able to get a maintenance position with the Board of Education, which she quit in 1980.

Ella Baker saw her own activism as part of a tradition of social involvement in her family that went back to slavery.[16] James Meredith, who integrated the University of Mississippi, says that he was taught growing up that the worst thing a Meredith could do was work in white folks' kitchens or take care of white folks' children. Medgar Evers's standard of manhood was set largely by his father's refusal to kowtow to whites. Fannie Lou Hamer says that her mother, a sharecropper known to carry a pistol to the fields in her lunch basket if trouble was brewing, taught her to stand up for herself no matter what the odds.[17] Septima Clark attributed her lack of fear to her mother, raised in Haiti and very outspoken on racial matters; she liked to boast that she "never gave a white woman a drink of water." Visiting Amite County in 1965, reporter Jack Newfield found that one of the young people working with the movement was fifteen-year-old Herbert Lee, Jr., whose father had been murdered in 1961.[18] Among SNCC members, John Watkins, Hollis's father had to leave home while still a boy because he fired a shotgun at a white man who was cursing his mother in their front yard. As a grown man, John Watkins had to move again when he got into a fight with a white man with whom he was stacking cross ties. Martha Prescod Norman's parents sent her to a school where they knew she would encounter racial hostility, because they wanted her to be tough enough to take it. Ivanhoe Donaldson's father supported the tenets of Garveyism.

Bob Moses thinks the reason he was so susceptible to Ella Baker's way of thinking was his father. His father modeled a certain acceptance of other people:

> He had this great capacity to deal with the person that's presented and to sort out the various stereotypes so he's always dealing with the actual person. And then within that, he also has this capacity to look for and respond to human qualities of that person so he's not predisposed to try to put that person down.

Bob used to go with his father on his father's regular rounds of his friends and acquaintances in Harlem, stopping at each place to argue the social and political issues of the day, not just in terms of their personal consequences but in terms of their larger ramifications as well. Whatever the issue, "he was always asking, Well, what does this mean for the little guy? How does this translate out?" After each conversation, his father would do a social mapping of it with Bob, a who-said-what-and-why analysis. In Ella Baker and then in Amzie Moore, Bob found more sophisticated versions of what he admired in his father—a sense of the importance of the individual embedded in a broader social analysis.

The people who formed much of the core of the movement in Greenwood in 1962 and 1963 frequently came from families with similar traditions of social involvement or defiance, subtle or overt. These were the people who joined earliest and often the people who worked hardest. In cases like the Greenes, defiance takes the form of explicit political involvement pre-dating SNCC's entry into the Delta. In other cases, it takes the form of self-conscious attempts to shape the way in which children thought about race and in ways that go beyond the familiar custom of telling children that they were just as good as whites. People like the Greenes and Mrs. Holt refused to allow women in their families to do domestic work; the McGhees wouldn't accept credit from whites; the Greenes tried to give their children a sense of racial history; Mrs. McGhee told her boys that they could do anything that was legal; the Morgans wouldn't let white salesmen come to the house.

The common thread is a refusal to see oneself as merely acted upon, as merely victim. These are families in which children were encouraged to believe that even within an oppressive social structure one retains some control over one's life. It is as if they were saying with e. e. cummings that there is *some* shit we will not eat.

Oddly, the children of these families, so nearly as I can tell, are not now being raised in the traditions their parents were raised in. The parents I spoke to in the 1980s and 1990s do not talk to their children about the movement and apparently don't talk to them much about racial issues at all. Children of the families in Greenwood that were most active in the early sixties ordinarily have no idea of what their parents or grandparents did. Why this should be so is not clear. Perhaps it is a side effect of the movement's success itself. Perhaps the civil rights movement so changed the world that, to the older generation, "keeping the story before" their children no longer seems relevant. In any case, the kinds of family traditions that we have been examining, traditions which informed the activism of the sixties, appear to have ended with the sixties.

SNCC preached a gospel of individual efficacy. What you do matters. In order to move politically, people had to believe that. In Greenwood the movement was able to exploit communal and familial traditions that encouraged people to believe in their own light.

Eight

SLOW AND RESPECTFUL WORK

Organizers and Organizing

Bob and a band of ten or so organizers, all under 20, could go into a community in the morning . . . find their contacts, establish sleeping quarters and some means to eat, get a church and turn out the community for a mass meeting that same night.

JEAN WHEELER SMITH

Anytime a man come in my community and took the hardships that he took, if he was wrong, I better join with him anyway. He's ready to take a beating, [get] jailed, being bombed and get back on two feet. . . . I'm ready to join that fellow, wherever he is, right or wrong.

PERCY LARRY
McComb

I hope this [newsletter] will give you some idea of one phase of the activity in Amite County. It is less spectacular than marches and such, but, I feel, much more meaningful. Marches help to remove some of the external barriers to the Negro people's freedom. They do little to emancipate people from within. . . . It is by talking and acting together—on their own initiative and their own decision— that some of these bonds begin to be loosed.

MARSHALL GANZ
SNCC

What we did in essence was to try to do for the community people that we were working with what Ella had already done for us.

BOB MOSES[1]

MORE HAS BEEN WRITTEN about the role of oratory in the movement than about the role of organizing. Historian David Garrow contends that the real emergence of a sustained, widespread movement in the South can be traced in many respects to SNCC's decision in the summer of 1961 to create a cadre of locally based, full-time, grass-roots organizers, marking the first time that indigenous activists had such day-to-day assistance available to them. "It was the firsthand experience of working with people, day in, day out, that educated both local activists and field secretaries to the item-by-item, conversation-by-conversation reality of what 'leadership' really amounted to in the civil rights movement."[2] We have overlooked the crucial level of leadership provided by the Sam Blocks, the Willie Peacocks, and the Hollis Watkins's of the South.

Howard Zinn has given us a portrait of the Mississippi field staff as it existed near the end of 1963.[3] The forty-one workers comprised about one-third of the total SNCC staff in the Deep South. Thirty-five of them were Black. Two of the six whites and twenty-five of the Blacks came from the Deep South. The white youngsters and most of the northern Blacks came from middle-class homes; their fathers were ministers or teachers or civil-service workers. All of the southern workers came from homes where the mothers had been maids or domestic workers, and most of the fathers had been farmers, factory workers, truck drivers, and construction workers. The ages ran from fifteen to over fifty, but most were in their late teens or early twenties. The staff, then, was mostly Black, mostly southern, mostly from working-class backgrounds. The common image of SNCC as being an organization of middle-class college kids is misleading as applied to the Mississippi staff. It is true that many of them either were in college or were planning to go until the movement got in the way, but most of those represented the first generation in their families to attend college. They were an upwardly mobile group, but few were products of the traditional southern Black middle class. None of the early Greenwood organizers came from the most oppressed strata of Mississippi Blacks, but none of them came from backgrounds that could reasonably be called middle-class. Indeed, they came from backgrounds very much like those of the people they were trying to organize.

In Florida during the 1940s there was a school principal and NAACP officer named Harry T. Moore, who helped lead the fight to get equal pay for Black teachers in his area. He was fired and then, on Christmas Eve 1951, his home was bombed and he and his wife killed. Black people in the area did not soon forget the work he had done. According to Ella Baker:

> You could go into that area of Florida, and you could talk about the virtue of the NAACP, because they knew Harry T. Moore. They hadn't discussed a whole lot of theory. But there was a *man* who served *their* interests and who *identified* with them.[4]

In the same way, for many people in Mississippi, attachment to the movement meant attachment to the particular individuals who represented it rather than to particular organizations or political strategies. Percy Larry, a McComb resident who supported SNCC's early initiatives in that town, said "I don't understand the position of some of the people that came here. I've never understood their position. But I would go along with them."[5] You don't, he explained, have to understand everything about a man's politics to appreciate the "fullness" of a man. Waite Johnson and George Greene made the same comment about people in Greenwood; not everyone understood all the political ramifications of what they were being asked to do—although they understood perfectly well what it would cost them—but they came to appreciate the people doing the asking. CORE's Matt Suarez, who worked in and around Canton, Mississippi, commented that country folk

> deal more with the character of an individual rather than what he's saying. . . . When you met him, whatever way he was when you met, when you saw him ten years later . . . he would still be that same way, ten years down the road. And they had much more of a perception about the real character of a man. They didn't get caught up in images. . . . A lot of people who came into Canton, [the local people] didn't respond to and it was simply because they

could see a lot of stuff that we couldn't see about an individual. They knew who was strong and who was for real and who wasn't. . . . We would get caught up in words and logic. That didn't mean nothing to them. They were dealing with motives and intent. Skip all the words and everything else. They brushed that aside and got right to what the individual was about.[6]

Organizers were in a situation in which their character was being continually assessed. Once they were judged to be worthwhile people, they and local people often entered into relationships in which each side called forth and reinforced the best in the other. Amzie Moore spoke with evident sincerity about how much he admired the courage of the youngsters:

But when an individual stood at a courthouse like the courthouse in Greenwood and in Greenville and watch tiny figures [of the SNCC workers] standing against a huge column . . . [against white] triggermen and drivers and lookout men riding in automobiles with automatic guns . . . *how they stood* . . . how gladly they got in the front of that line, those leaders, and went to jail. It didn't seem to bother 'em. It was an awakening for me.[7]

In turn, virtually every early COFO worker in the Delta has commented on how inspiring Amzie Moore's courage was. It was hardly possible for idealistic young people to spend time with a Mrs. Hamer or a Mrs. McGhee and not feel some stiffening of their own spines. Bob Zellner, commenting on the courage of Moore and the McGhees, added "We breathed people like that. . . . There was nothing I could refuse them." It wasn't just courage. Martha Prescod Norman has pointed out that people referring to SNCC as non-elitist often forget that SNCC had no choice in the matter. If you wanted to be around people like Amzie Moore or Mrs. Hamer, you had to be non-elitist, and you had to listen. Mrs. Annie Devine played a crucial role in the movement in Canton, Mississippi. CORE's Rudy Lombard speaks of a meeting where "She looked me in the eye and said 'Rudy, I *know* you won't deny us your talents in Canton this summer. I'm depending on you.' I knew I was trapped. No way I could turn that woman down."[8] The organizers and the local people who took to them were in a positive feedback loop, in which the courage and humanistic values of one side encouraged a like response from the other. "They were gentlemen," said Mr. Larry of the McComb organizers, "and around them we were gentle." That would be even more true in reverse.

In Greenwood, the praise of local people for the organizers is effusive and is only partly about their courage. Dewey Greene thought the world of the SNCC kids. He couldn't say enough about them. Silas McGhee was especially impressed by Stokely Carmichael and his strong beliefs. "He was highly educated. He was very intelligent, and he knew how to communicate with a person." Waite Johnson thought even the worst Tom in Greenwood couldn't find anything negative to say about Block and Peacock. Bob Moses, he thought, seemed to have what Waite called a special charisma with the old folks. They just seemed to trust him. Alberta Barnet admired Block and Peacock for their nerve but also for their intelligence. Indeed, people refer to the intelligence of SNCC workers, to their ability to make other people understand, just about as often as they refer to their courage. Mary Lane remembers Bob Moses as

> someone you could sit down and talk with. And really, after talking to him, you would really understand. . . . You'll be a little broader than you were at first. And he was a person that could come to you, ask you to do a thing and you were willing to do it. Whatever it might have been. He had this thing about him like if it was Bob who said it, you know it had to be done.

Mary Boothe remembers Bob as a "straight cat," the person who showed her how to be Black without being ashamed, as a person who didn't care for publicity. "I doubt if ten local people would know him." Will Henry Rogers remembers Guyot as being respected in Greenwood because people could see he "was about something and he wasn't about no bullshit." Similarly, he attributes Willie Peacock's influence to the way he "carried himself" around people; people knew he was serious.⁹ Phrases attesting to the character of organizers are recurrent—he was straight, he was about something, he carried himself well, he had this thing about him. Local people were duly impressed with the courage of the organizers, but it seems to have been important to them that it was courage embedded in character.

Guyot has commented that "the SNCC workers were no saints," and local people knew that, and it is not true that all the criticisms came from Toms. Those who kept themselves outside the movement, of course, had an investment in believing that the organizers were only in it for the glory, but those in the movement had some misgivings as well. The skirt-chasing of some of the organizers offended some of the older people, and they knew more about some of what was going on than some SNCC workers wanted them to. The SNCC workers and the local young people partied hard when the opportunity arose, and that was offensive to the moral codes of some local people. A number of people didn't like the way they dressed; anybody wearing old work clothes all the time couldn't be about very much. It was disrespectful. Some of the SNCC workers had reputations for being a little pushy, not giving other people time to make up their own minds. If they impressed some people as smart, they impressed others as smart-assed. The very idea of young people coming into a town and trying to tell grownups how to run their business struck some as presumptuous. Keeping one's word didn't always mean as much to the SNCC folk as to some of the local people. Some of the SNCC volunteers who came from the North after the first year struck some local people as truly snobbish. They acted as if Mississippi people were still in slavery, too backwards to do anything for themselves. According to Waite Johnson, his grandmother, Mrs. Holt, had to straighten one or two of them out. As staunch a movement person as Canton's Annie Devine commented on the missionary attitudes. The SNCC workers were seen as having the usual human failings, but the bottom line for many of the local people was that they also had virtues of courage, character, and commitment that more than compensated.

In 1967, Robert Jackall, then a young professor at Georgetown University, spent part of the spring and summer working in Sunflower County. In an essay written years later, he commented on the modern trivialization of the concept of charisma, adding that he had seen real charisma just once, and it was in Mississippi. It was at a mass meeting that was going poorly, speakers droning on in the heat without reaching the audience. Then Mrs. Hamer stood to speak.

> Immediately, an electric atmosphere suffused the entire church. Men and women alike began to stand up, to call out her name, and to urge her on. . . . She went on to speak about the moral evil of racism itself and the grievous harm it was doing to the souls of white people in Mississippi. . . . She did not do so in accusation, but with a kind of redemptive reconciliation, articulating a vision of justice that embraced everyone. She ended by leading the assembly in chorus after chorus of a rousing old Negro spiritual called, appropriately, "This Little Light of Mine." When she finished, the entire assembly was deeply shaken emotionally. People crowded around her to promise they would join the struggle.

Jackall goes on to analyze the specific elements of her charisma:

> her unvarnished, earthy forcefulness, devoid of all pretense; her unshakeable conviction in the justness of her cause, proved by her personal physical sufferings and the risks she continued to take; her ennobling vision of racial harmony and of personal redemption for those who seek it; and her ability to articulate her ideas with a powerful religious rhetoric that had deep resonance for her audience but that had no trace of practiced cant.[10]

In a less concentrated way, similar characteristics among other local people had a similar effect on SNCC workers. The mere fact that joining the movement entailed so many risks meant that early joiners were likely in disproportionate numbers to be men and women with distinctive strengths of character. Moreover, organizers were self-consciously seeking such people. As local people were drawn to much that they saw in the character of SNCC workers, the workers were in turn drawn by, strengthened by, the force of character of some of the local people and by their lavish affection. "If I needed a couple of bucks," one organizer said, "or even a ride for a hundred miles or so, there would be people waiting in line. Their feelings would have been hurt if I didn't let them help me. When there's that kind of push behind you, you can keep going."[11]

The good opinion of others is a form of social control. Having attained it, we tend to conduct ourselves so as to maintain it. Local people set constraints on what organizers could or could not do, in effect operating as a source of moral regulation for the movement. Block, Watkins, Peacock, and the others self-consciously strove to be on their best behavior around local people, best behavior as defined by local people. Organizers tried to present an image of themselves as God-fearing, as respectful to women and the elderly, as men and women of their word, as principled. By demonstrating that they could live up to values that the community respected, organizers legitimated themselves and their program.

BUILDING RELATIONSHIPS

Bob Moses was once asked how you organize a town:

> "By bouncing a ball," he answered quietly.
> "What?"
> "You stand on a street and bounce a ball. Soon all the children come around. You keep on bouncing the ball. Before long, it runs under someone's porch and then you meet the adults."

Charles Sherrod, who directed SNCC's work in southwest Georgia, commented that the whole key to organizing is finding one person other than yourself. One of his coworkers described organizing as slow work, respectful work. Most of us would expect more "political" answers, but SNCC's early organizers often portray much of their work as simply building relationships. Thus, SNCC's MacArthur Cotton thought his morning coffee break was significant enough to deserve mention in a report:

> 8:00 am—I went to get my coffee as every morning. I talk with
> many people as possible in an informal way—trying to get to know
> the people that I work with. . . . After working this area for 6 days
> the same people have [accepted] me as a friend. They have become
> willing to discuss some of their more personal problems.[12]

A staff newsletter from mid-February 1963 suggests something of what the daily work of an organizer was like at that point, less than a year after COFO entered the Delta in force.[13] The newsletter's tone is that of an in-house document. Many people are referred to only by nickname, and there are jokes that only insiders can fully appreciate. ("Dorie 'Elephant' Ladner had 'tea' with Tom Gaither [of CORE]. So now we know why Dorie went to Atlanta.") Overall, the document reflects a sense of people being dug into their communities, experimenting with tactics and strategies.

In Indianola in the Delta, the mayor told workers they could canvass door-to-door, but if they tried to pass out literature on the street or tried to get into churches, they were going to find themselves in jail. In Greenville, Curtis Hayes was trying to arrange a meeting with the mayor to see how far he was going to let them go before arresting them. In Coahoma County, the clerk told one group that they had had the last forty or fifty years to register, so why are they bothering him now? At the very end of January, Hayes tried to get something established in Hollandale. Amzie Moore had advised him that the Black professionals there were pretty backward and he would be better off trying to work with small businessmen like cafe owners. Hayes was staying in a house of prostitution owned by a man who had two such houses. The man—a bisexual, a registered voter, and a bigwig in the Masons—had started carrying people to pay poll taxes as soon as Hayes got there. One never knows where help is to be found. Someone on the Greenville staff noted that Greenville is not the kind of place where canvassing is likely to be productive; more direct action would be needed there.

In Jackson, attorney Bill Higgs filed suit to force the University of Mississippi to admit Dewey Greene, Jr. The next day he was arrested on a morals charge. In Greenville, three COFO staffers were picked up for investigation of a burglary charge. On the social side, Charlie Cobb and Curtis Hayes had just found out they were both being led on romantically by the same girl. (Her version is not reported.) CORE's Dave Dennis had picked up clothing in Jackson, delivered it to Amzie, and gone over to Ruleville, looking for people who needed commodities, then back to Jackson for more clothing. Work in Washington County was being hampered by the lack of a car.

An organizer had just moved into Leland, forewarned by Amzie Moore that the police were especially bad there and that he should expect trouble soon. One of the prominent Black residents had promised to organize a meeting of other leading citizens. The organizer really did not expect his contact to follow through, "but I have to start somewhere. He may surprise me." The organizer was planning a car pool and a citizenship school.

In Holly Springs, in the northern part of the state, Frank Smith had a lot of things going. He had a system with a contact person in every section of the county, and he had organized a speakers' bureau and a welfare relief committee chaired by a professional social worker. The registrar had recently allowed twenty-five people to register, most of them, interestingly enough, schoolteachers. It seemed that someone had let the air out of the tires of a visiting Justice Department official, and Justice had suddenly gotten around to acting on several affidavits that had been filed earlier. Smith was again hearing rumors, from both Black people and white people, that he was to be killed. The county clerk was jerking people around when they tried to pay poll tax— putting dates on the receipts that invalidated them, charging whites less than Blacks. One of Smith's contacts thought he had located at least one white person who might be willing to testify about the latter.

By the end of the month, the weather had turned so cold that it was hard to get anybody to do anything. Smith continued to have problems with people failing to follow through. One night after visiting the home of one of his contacts, a man who lived "seventeen miles from nowhere," Smith stopped by a cafe, met some people, bought them a beer, and got them interested in what he had to say about registration. They promised to meet him at the registrar's at ten the next morning. Next morning, not a soul turned up, so Smith went back to the cafe to wait for them to show up.

The last item in the newsletter reported happily that Mrs. Hamer had finally gotten registered, making a total of six in Ruleville since August. The Ruleville Christian Citizenship Movement had raised $3.85 for transportation. They were expecting some evictions soon on the plantations and planning to set up a tent city if need be. Workshops were well attended, and they were thinking about spreading out into some nearby towns.

Bob Zellner once compared organizing to a juggling act—how many plates can you keep spinning at once? Organizers had to be morale boosters, teachers, welfare agents, transportation coordinators, canvassers, public speakers, negotiators, lawyers, all while communicating with people ranging from illiterate sharecroppers to well-off professionals and while enduring harassment from the agents of the law and listening with one ear for the threats of violence. Exciting days and major victories are rare. Progress is a few dollars raised, a few more people coming to pay poll tax.

The newsletter reflects the specificity of the organizing experience. Local situations could vary greatly from one another. There were general patterns, but organizers worked with individuals, not generalities. Maybe this was a police chief with whom you could reason, maybe here you could get help from schoolteachers. In general, you knew ministers were unreliable, but not all of them and not everywhere. In Hattiesburg, ministers responded to the movement very early on, which Hollis Watkins attributes to spadework done by Vernon Dahmer and others. People will sometimes surprise you, as the one organizer said, but mostly only if you are open to it. A 1964 handbook for volunteers tells them "No one can give you specific instructions on what to do in your area this summer. . . . There is no set one way. Fake it." At this stage in its history, SNCC, in the tradition of Septima Clark and Ella Baker, was still taking a let's-try-it-and-see stance. That stance was institutionalized. According to Willie Peacock, over the winter of 1962–1963, "different projects were taking different approaches to organizing, sort of an experiment and we'd have workshops on a regular basis on the weekends," allowing experiences to be sifted and analyzed.[14] Their openness to learning from experience meant they could more fully exploit whatever sources of strength a particular locality offered, whether found in a pulpit or a whorehouse. It was a climate that militated against writing off this or that group in advance on the basis of what "people like that" were *likely* to do.

Their ability to exploit the human resources they found in these various towns was contingent on how well organizers came to know the individuals in them. If you knew your town well enough, even Uncle Toms had their uses. When Frank Smith was called from Holly Springs to Greenwood in response to the Jimmy Travis shooting, he first carefully explained why he was leaving to local movement supporters. Then: "You have got to let the white folks know why you are leaving, so you find a local 'Tom' and explain the plan in detail." As soon as your back was turned, Tom could be counted on to run and tell the white folks everything he knew.[15]

By this time, some organizers had been dug into their towns for six months or more, and they had an enormous store of information about who was likely to do what, but their knowledge could hardly compare with that of local people like Amzie Moore or Cleve Jordan. Across the South, VEP's experience time and again was that registration drives were more successful to the degree they could be locally organized and staffed, which they attributed in part to the importance of "intimate knowledge of [the] conditions, psychology and people" involved.[16]

Organizers were particularly exposed when trying to open up some of the smaller Delta towns, especially if they were without local contacts. COFO's manpower was always stretched thin, so going into a new town often fell on just one or two persons. In the fall of 1963, for example, Ivanhoe Donaldson (he who had organized food caravans into Leflore) and Charlie Cobb (he who had found himself in the midst of a shooting a few days after coming into the state) paid their first visit to a town called Rolling Fork, intending to start by going door to door. A police car watched them for a while and then disappeared. Donaldson was standing on the steps of some man's house, trying to get him to talk about registering. A pickup with two white men inside pulled up and began taking down the tag number of the rented car Donaldson and Cobb were driving. The driver, a man who had been sitting in the police car a few minutes earlier, then drove the pickup right over the man's lawn, nearly running Donaldson down. He threw a shotgun into Donaldson's face. "Nigger, we aren't going to have any more of this agitation 'round here. Niggers 'round here don't need to vote, so you and your damned buddy get out of here. Goddamn it, Nigger! I'll give you one minute to get out of town or I'll kill you!!" Then he drove off. The old man they had been talking to disappeared into his home as soon as he saw the shotgun, and no one else would so much as speak to them after the incident with the pickup. They left town and returned that evening after dark.[17]

In small towns it was frequently impossible even to place a phone call for help. Local operators might refuse to take the calls, or they might tell the local police where the organizers were calling from. Operators across the state recognized "movement" phone numbers—the COFO or NAACP offices, Amzie Moore's home or Aaron Henry's—and anyone placing a call to one of those numbers from a small town endangered the people whose phone had been used.

Organizers coming into a new town had to confront immediately the complexities of the local stratification system. One SNCC training document makes it clear that SNCC put a great deal of thought into dealing with the problem. It suggests that prospective organizers engage in a role-playing exercise. Assuming that they have just come into a new town, they are instructed to act out how they would solicit the help of a local businessman. Trainees are first instructed to assume that the businessman is a Tom but is pretending to be friendly, then they are to assume that the businessman is unwilling to share power with young upstarts, and finally they are to assume that the businessman is sincerely committed to the movement but thinks SNCC people are working for personal glory.[18] Trainees are encouraged to think about not only overcoming fear but also neutralizing deception, distrust, and arrogance while avoiding pigeonholing people stereotypically.

Identifying informal leaders was often the most efficient way to open up a town. Registration workers

> frequently found that the real leaders were not the people in places of position. An elderly woman of no title and with no organiza-

tional support might be highly influential simply because she was noted as a kind of personal problem-solver. Sometimes, such a person, because of her effectiveness in small matters and the trust consequently built, could be a key figure in efforts to persuade people to register to vote in a difficult area.[19]

When such people were identified they were often sent to Septima Clark's citizenship training center in Dorchester, Georgia. The trip helped people develop a sense of the larger movement and of themselves as movement people.

It was seldom advisable, though, just to ignore the traditional leadership class. Organizers were encouraged to respect traditional leadership without depending on it. One VEP field worker, described as very experienced, describes how he would go about organizing a new town:

> He would go first to the "independents," the undertaker, the grocers, the preachers. Then he would go to the school principal. ("In some cases you can go to the principal, ask who his enemies are, and you have the leaders.") Having made contact with these, he would assume that he had discovered the principal community leaders. He would assume, too, that the Negro church was at the center of the community because "the church belongs to the folks." He would regard the deacons of the churches ("because they're the preachers' men") as very important to anything he undertook. Finally, he would assume that for action, a strong outside stimulus probably would be necessary to break what frequently was a local paralysis.

Another worker, probably also thinking about the problem of paralysis, puts the issue of contacting middle-class traditional leaders in a different light.

> I would do this to neutralize them. They do not usually oppose having the job done—they want it done, but they don't want to be embarrassed if someone else does it and they are left out. After seeing

them, I would find people prepared to work hard for recognition. Then I'd try to wed the two together and monitor the group.[20]

No matter what the response from the established leadership, mobilizing a town ordinarily involved a great deal of canvassing, going door-to-door, trying to draw people in. "There is nothing dramatic about the work. There are no emotional releases. The tension is constant. Every passing car is a threat, every white face a mask for violence, every back road a potential trap."[21] Many Blacks were less than welcoming. Will Henry Rogers recalls that he and the other canvassers "got thrown out of people's homes, got knocked in the head with skillets, got knives and guns throwed in our faces."[22]

In Greenwood as in most places, the volunteer canvassers initially tended to be young people like Rogers. Bob Moses wrote:

> We can't count on adults. Very few who "have the time" and are economically independent of the white man are willing to join the struggle, and are not afraid of the tremendous pressure they will face. This leaves the young people to be the organizers, the agents of social and political change. . . . They operate at extreme disadvantage; they suffer from the most backward educational system in the United States; they very seldom are free to work in their own home towns because of the pressures brought to bear on their parents and their relatives. . . . They have little knowledge of procedures and skills involved in writing newsletters, press releases, reports, etc., so their ability to analyze and report on their activities is limited; they do not have a functioning adult structure to provide a framework for their operations. Such structures as exist are usually paper organizations with no active program. . . . It is a sign of hope that we have been able to find young people to shoulder the responsibility for carrying out the voting drive. They are the seeds of change.[23]

Among the initial group of youthful canvassers in Greenwood were some, like George, Dewey, and Freddie Greene, who came from families with a history of political activism, and others, like Al Garner, who had been involved in founding the NAACP Youth Council. Others were drawn in gradually by the SNCC workers. SNCC workers simply hung out wherever young people did. In the fall of 1962 Waite Johnson, Lula Belle's son, was a high school sophomore. His first contact with the movement was in the person of Sam Block, who made it a practice in the afternoons to hang out in the poolroom frequented by Waite and some of his friends. Waite found Sam interesting, captivating; he talked about things that Waite had not heard of before, and he told Sam and the other boys that they were going to be a part of the movement whether they wanted to be or not. The boys laughed at that, but they kept listening, and a number of them did eventually begin canvassing, which did not mean that they had bought the whole message that Block, Peacock, and the others were preaching. When Waite first started canvassing, he still believed that even if blacks were allowed to vote, their votes wouldn't be counted. Again, SNCC workers knew that participation could precede ideological commitment as well as follow it.

When Waite Johnson describes his initial reaction to Block and Peacock, he uses the word "skeptical" a lot, but the word he uses most is "curious." They were just interesting to listen to. They were equally interesting to some young women. The SNCC workers, in their late teens or early twenties, were marketable items romantically. They were from out of town, they were courageous, they were intelligent, everybody in town was talking about them, and some of them were "soft talkers."

At least some young women, then, began hanging out at the SNCC office for reasons that were not entirely political, and young men followed them. Indeed, there were at least a few arguments among SNCC staff over whether some of them were keeping the right balance between the social and the political. In any case, some young people initially drawn to the movement partly for social reasons became a part of the initial cadre of canvassers. The movement also offered opportunities for travel that were unusual for Black youth growing up in small Delta towns. Alberta Barnet, who was in her early twenties when SNCC came to Greenwood, remembers traveling to other parts of Mississippi, to Georgia, Ohio, Indiana, New York, and to the 1964 National Democratic Convention in Atlantic City.

Field reports are filled with stories of spending day after day dragging from house to house without a single positive response to show for it. Most people were simply afraid and confused but reluctant to admit it. Some of the excuses people gave were repeated so often that some workers simply developed a checklist:

Feel votes of Negroes not counted.
Thinks politics are un-Christian.
Just not interested.
Don't have the time to discuss voting.
Feel the politicians are going to do whatever they want, regardless of votes cast.
Too busy, engaged in personal affairs.
Feels Negroes should not become involved.
Must consult with someone else.
Fear of being embarrassed at the registrar's office.
Wants time to think it over.
Feel poll tax should be abolished.
Don't like the way things are carried out.
Been advised not to register.
Satisfied with things as they are.[24]

One young worker commented on the same problem with inventive syntax and unintentional irony:

I canvassed, while I was canvassing we discussed that the problems of some of the Negro race are afraid and do not understand their rights as citizens simply because all their lives they have been taught that the Negro race isn't as good as any other race in the South which in most cases that's true.[25]

Producing one warm body at the courthouse took a great deal of knocking on doors. Luvaughn Brown reported that on one day in August of 1962, a hundred people were contacted, ten agreed to go register, three actually showed up, and those three were frightened away from the courthouse by the sheriff.[26] The yield probably varied a great deal from community to community. At about the same time

Block went to Greenwood, Frank Smith went to Holly Springs in the northern part of the state, an area where economic reprisals were quite severe but reputedly somewhat less violent than Leflore and other counties near the heart of the Delta. After his first meeting, he was able to get adult volunteer workers, unlike the experience in Green-wood. After contacting over one thousand people, they got about one hundred fifty actually to take the test.[27]

Some COFO workers in Greenwood developed reputations as being especially successful canvassers, and no one style of work characterizes them. When I interviewed George Greene, he impressed me as a man who genuinely enjoyed talking with people and particularly enjoyed a friendly argument. According to Waite Johnson, Greene was a re-markably patient and persistent organizer, with a response for every excuse:

> I have seen people slam doors in his face, but he said I'm going to be back. . . . he'd go every day, every hour, every week. Like he would knock on that person's door, they would see him at least 3 or 4 times a week. He'd say, "This is something you should do. It's free and won't cost you nothing. I got the gas, I got a ride—you ain't got to walk. I've got the paper here. . . . I'll hold your hand." He took time with them.

Canvassers had to be patient. Silas McGhee remarked that people, especially on the plantations, had only known one way of life, and you couldn't expect them to change overnight. Guyot, talking about how one might approach a potential local leader, said, "Don't speed him up too much, dialogue with him, find out what his tempo is, what his objectives are. Then you might alter them a little bit, but . . . be careful."[28] Willie Peacock recalled that canvassers were instructed not to worry about numbers; the idea was to reach individuals, and you did that by returning over and over to the same people. Eventu-ally, he said, people would start telling you some of the negative things they heard about you. As that suggests, returning repeatedly to people who had rejected you was partly a matter of developing trust. Re-peated visits also meant that canvassers could gradually get a feel for what line of argument might best move a particular individual. Alberta Barnet recalled that among older residents who had little or no conception of electoral politics, you could sometimes get their attention by talking about Franklin Roosevelt and explaining that if they wanted to see programs like those Roosevelt started, they would have to vote. Older canvassers who were residents of Greenwood had the advantage, of course, of frequently talking to people they had known all their lives. In such cases, Alberta Barnet said, you would pretty much know in advance what kind of argument the person might listen to and you had the important advantage that "he already has a little trust and confidence in you—just from the way that you live." Guyot noted that when you got a door slammed in your face, "It just takes a day or two of talking to people to find out whose face the door won't be slammed in."[29] Thus, getting even a few reliable adult volunteers was a significant turning point in the development of each local movement.

Sam Block's effectiveness as a canvasser seemed to be related to his "preacher's air," according to Waite Johnson. He was especially good with older people. "He was always saying my grandfather told me this, my grandmother told me this and the Bible says so and so. . . . Once people got to know him naturally they thought he was Jesus. They would sit down and I heard them say 'I'll go down with you, Block. Go ahead, my boy!'"

The handbook that COFO prepared for the volunteers for the 1964 summer program summarizes what the organization had learned about canvassing from nearly three years in the field. It starts by warning volunteers to be careful how they present themselves; you have to make people want to talk to you. Everybody can be approached, but some people will require a lot of time. If a person seems reluctant, come back later, try to soften them up through repeated exposure. Try to build a relationship. If a person asks you in but doesn't really seem to be listening, try asking questions to focus their attention. If a person shows any interest, try to give them something to do right away, perhaps helping you contact others. If a person already knows what you are telling them, try to find out how they learned. Do not overwhelm people. Give them a single idea—attending a mass meeting or helping with a workshop.[30]

In the city of Greenwood itself, canvassing might only be a matter of taking a group to a section of town and assigning a different street to each person, or it might be a matter of going to the basketball court to see who was willing to canvass that day. "Out in the rural" was a different matter. The plantations were white-owned, and civil rights workers were trespassing. They had to either sneak past the landlord or lie their way past ("I'm just going to visit my cousin.") There was always the possibility that someone would tell the owner what was really going on, and if plantation workers were even suspected of talking to civil rights workers, they would be fired and evicted. When people did decide to register, civil rights workers might slip onto the plantations at night and help them move before the landlords got wind of what was happening. Sometimes it was better to wait until people came to town on the weekend. Even then, there remained the problem of what civil rights workers called the "plantation mentality," an ingrained sense of helplessness and dependence on whites.

George Greene, who for all of his long career in the movement seemed to wind up in the hardest and most dangerous places to work, was among those who spent the most time canvassing on the plantations. So did Silas McGhee. Silas, who lived on a farm himself, knew a great many of the people on the plantations and was able to build on that, translating their personal regard for him and his family into political capital.

Some people left no doubt that they didn't want to be bothered. Arance Morgan and Dot Johnson were canvassing together once, when a lady pulled a gun on them. The girls got out of there quick. The first time Jake and Silas McGhee visited the Willard home, Mr. Willard pulled a gun on them. They went back anyway, though, eventually convincing him to register. It was a pyrrhic victory. Mr. Willard was thrown off the plantation he lived on and eventually left the area.

Maybe canvassing is the prototypical organizing act. It is the initial reaching out to the community, the first step toward building relationships outside the circle of those favorably predisposed to the movement. Mass meetings were another step in that process. If canvassers could awaken an initial curiosity in people, mass meetings could weld curiosity into commitment.

MASS MEETINGS: LEANING ON THE EVERLASTING ARMS

"It is said that these people accumulate into crowds and then by their speeches are exhorted into frenzy and then seek to march in a body to register."

GREENWOOD COMMONWEALTH
April 1, 1963

I once heard a journalist who had covered the movement remark that two decades after its height the civil rights movement had inspired no great works of art—no great novels or films, no great plays. He rather missed the point. The movement was its own work of art, and mass meetings were among the places where that might most easily be seen. Mass meetings, which had the overall tone and structure of a church service, were grounded in the religious traditions and the esthetic sensibilities of the Black South. If the drudgery of canvassing accounted for much of an organizer's time on a day-to-day basis, mass meetings, when they were good, were a part of the pay-off, emotionally and politically.

The Montgomery, Alabama, bus boycott of 1955 is one of the turning points of the modern movement. According to Ralph Abernathy, the first song at the first mass meeting there was "Leaning on the Everlasting Arms": What a fellowship, what a joy divine, leaning, leaning on the everlasting arms. What have I to fear, what have I to dread, leaning on the everlasting arms? It was an appropriate choice. Emile Durkheim wrote:

> The believer who has communicated with his god is not merely a man who sees new truths of which the unbeliever is ignorant; he is a man who is stronger. He feels within him more force, either to endure the trials of existence or to conquer them.[31]

The religious traditions of the Black South were an important part of what empowered members of the movement, especially the older members, allowing them to endure and conquer. In bending Afro-American Christianity toward emancipatory ends the movement took it back to its origins. For much of the twentieth century, the Black church, especially in rural areas, turned people away from this-worldly concerns.[32] The preacherocracy, as one critic termed it, urged patience in the face of suffering. "They saw the church as a way to escape the pains of the world, not as a moral force that could help heal them."[33] This view was a far cry from the Christianity of the slaves. As described by Lawrence Levine among others, slave Christianity was a liberation theology. It is true that those slavemasters who pushed Christianity generally hoped it would make slaves more manageable, but as Herbert Gutman points out, the important question is not just what masters did to slaves but what slaves did with what was done to them. In this case, they were to take what was intended to be a theology of accommodation and fashion from it a theology of liberation.

If masters were fond of the Bible verse that urges, "Servants, obey thy masters," slaves tended to be fonder of the verse that held the laborer is worthy of his hire. Levine notes that slaves identified more strongly with the Old Testament than the New, and within the Old Testament they identified themselves with the Hebrew children held in bondage by Egypt. Their sacred music referred more frequently to Moses than to Christ, and their Moses was the Deliverer, more than the Lawgiver. They seem to have preferred slave preachers to white ones, in part because white ones were too likely to present an order-serving interpretation of the Bible. Similarly, Du Bois argues that in the world view of the slaves, emancipation, when it finally came, was seen as fulfillment of prophecy. "My Lord delivered Daniel, Daniel, Daniel. My Lord delivered Daniel, then why not every man?"[34]

sncc had deliberately made a policy of recruiting Mississippi field secretaries from within the state, so many of them were steeped in the religious traditions of the South. Sam Block could slip into his "preacher's air" at will. Many people in Greenwood thought Hollis Watkins was the Reverend Hollis Watkins, and he did not try to discourage them from thinking so. Willie Peacock grew up in a family that was very involved in the AME church and was able to use his knowledge of its politics to prod reluctant ministers. All of them took pride in their knowledge of the Bible and their ability to find the verses and the parables that made the points they needed to make.

Meetings in Greenwood were frequently opened with a prayer by Cleve Jordan, who had an enviable reputation as a prayer leader. His prayers were part-chant, part-song, with the audience murmuring assent and agreement at the end of every line.

> Oh Father, Oh Lord,
> Now, now, now, Lordie, Oh Lord
> When we get through drinking tears for water
> When we get through eatin' at the unwelcome table
> When we get through shakin' unwelcome hands
> We've got to meet Death somewhere
> Don't let us be afraid to die. . . .
> Father, I stretch my hand to thee
> No other help I know.[35]

Fannie Lou Hamer was such a powerful public speaker that Lyndon Johnson once called a news conference solely to stop television coverage of her. One of the most popular speakers at mass meetings in Greenwood, she stressed that God walks with the courageous. A meeting taped at Tougaloo is a good example of her style.[36] The meeting began with Hollis Watkins leading a vigorous rendition of "Before I'll be a slave, I'll be buried in my grave and go home to my Lord and be free." Mrs. Hamer follows the singing, giving a history of her involvement in the movement, including the kinds of harassment she was subjected to. Lately, the cops in her hometown have taken to coming by late at night with their dogs, letting the dogs bark so she will know she's being watched. They have done it so much she has gotten used to it. "Look like now the dogs help me get to sleep." She then pointed out the need for people to be serious about their religion. There are plenty of people, she says, always talking about "Sure, I'm a Christian," but if you're not doing anything about being a

Christian, if you can't stand some kind of test, you need to stop shouting because the 17th chapter of Acts, 26th verse, says that the Lord made of one blood all nations. After giving some examples of how some people in the movement were making their faith concrete, she ends by leading the meeting in a freedom song: "I'm on my way to the freedom land / If you don't go, don't hinder me / I'm on my way, praise God, I'm on my way / If you don't go, let the children go."

The mixture of spirituality and music had a special impact on some of those raised outside the traditions of Afro-Christianity. Jean Wheeler Smith had never so much as heard gospel music before she went to Howard. When she got to Mississippi,

> the religious, the spiritual was like an explosion to me, an emotional explosion. I didn't have that available to me [before]. It just lit up my mind. . . . The music and the religion provided a contact between our logic and our feelings . . . and gave the logic of what we were doing emotional and human power to make us go forward.

Mass meetings partook of the mundane as well as of the sacred. New workers in town might be introduced, internal problems ironed out, tactics debated and explained.[37] They were also educational. At one meeting in February 1963, James Bevel gave what amounted to a lecture on political economy, talking about the separation of Negroes from the land, outmigration to the North, the implications of automation, Negro self-hatred, and the broader purposes of education. Speakers brought news of what was going on in other places. Medgar Evers, for example, a frequent and popular speaker in Greenwood, might bring word of what was happening in Jackson or at the NAACP national office. Meetings broke down the debilitating sense of isolation by bringing local people out so they could see that growing numbers of their neighbors were with them. At the same time, the news from other places reinforced their sense of being part of something larger and more potent than just what was going on in Greenwood.

In some respects, mass meetings resembled meetings of Alcoholics Anonymous or Weight Watchers. Groups like these try to change the behavior of their members by offering a supportive social environment, public recognition for living up to group norms, and public pressure to continue doing so. They create an environment in which you feel that if you stumble, you are letting down not only yourself but all of your friends. One might be afraid to go to a particular demonstration or be tired of demonstrations, period, but not going would mean disappointing those people who were counting on you.

From its inception, SNCC was sensitive to the need to motivate people by giving them public recognition. Ella Baker often stressed the point. At mass meetings in Greenwood, local activists might find themselves sharing a platform with heroes like Medgar Evers or Dick Gregory, or later with Harry Belafonte or Sidney Poitier, or perhaps even with Martin Luther King himself. On one of his trips to Greenwood, King asked to meet Dewey Greene, about whom he had heard so much.[38] Within the movement, the traditional status system was relatively inoperative. Belle Johnson belonged to Strangers Home Baptist Church, which thought itself a high-class church. Not everyone thought she was the kind of person who belonged there. The "dicty" attitude of the church toward her angered her daughter June.[39] In the movement, Belle Johnson was respected for her dedication; her income and education did not matter.

Pressure at mass meetings could be overt or friendly. At one, Hollis Watkins asked for a show of hands from people who had tried to register. Then he asked how they felt about what they had done. People shouted back that they felt good about it. He asked to see the hands of those who had not yet been down ("Don't fool us now") and, after a short pep talk on the importance of what they were trying to do, urged them all to meet him at 8:30 in the morning so they could all go to the courthouse together.

A part of the meeting might be devoted to having people simply recite their life histories, histories inevitably full of deprivation and injustice. At one Greenwood meeting, Cleve Jordan, who had been born near the turn of the century, spoke of how he had spent forty years sawing and hauling logs for a dollar and a quarter a day, working such long days that he only saw his children on Sundays, making forty bales of cotton in a year and having nothing to show for it except the dubious satisfaction of having made some more white people rich.

Other speakers continued in the same vein.[40] In his analysis of the Chinese revolution, William Hinton argues that an important element in reconstructing the consciousness of peasants was simply having them publicly recite their biographies. Doing so helped turn private and individual grievances into a collective consciousness of systematic oppression. Mass meetings seem to have served a similar function. They also created a context in which individuals created a public face for themselves, which they then had to try to live up to. In his heart, Reverend Such-and-Such may not feel nearly as militant as the speech he gives at the mass meeting, but once he gives it, he has created an image of himself that he will not want contradicted. After playing the role he has defined for himself for a while—and getting patted on the back for it—he may find that the role becomes natural. Before you know it, he may be shaking his head at how rabbit-hearted these other ministers are. What God can cowards know?

Depending on the situation at a given moment, it might be very easy or very difficult to get people to come to mass meetings. When necessary, canvassers went door to door, passing out handbills. Most people seem to have come initially out of sheer curiosity. The meetings were something new, the regular speakers, including Mrs. Hamer, Medgar Evers, Dick Gregory, and Aaron Henry, could hold an audience, and sometimes the speakers were nationally known celebrities.

Then, too, there was the music. It would be hard to overestimate the significance of the music of the movement. The changing fortunes of the movement and the morale of its participants could have been gauged by the intensity of the singing at the meetings. Music has always been a central part of the Black religious experience. Ministers knew that a good choir was a good recruiting device. In the same fashion, many who came to meetings came just to hear the singing. Bernice Reagon calls the freedom songs "the language that focused the energy of the people who filled the streets." She tells of an incident in Georgia in which a sheriff and his deputies tried to intimidate a mass meeting by their presence. "A song began. And the song made sure that the sheriff and his deputies knew we were there. We became visible, our image was enlarged, when the sounds of the freedom songs filled all the space in that church."[41] When things were hopping in Greenwood, SNCC's Worth Long sometimes brought people over from Little Rock or Pine Bluff to help on the weekends. The mass meetings he saw in Greenwood were different from the ones in Arkansas. Greenwood had more of a singing movement, and the meetings had more of an emotional tone; it was like comparing a Holiness church to a Methodist church. He tried to take some of that feeling back to Arkansas with him.[42]

People in Greenwood were similarly enlarged by the singing and the emotional intensity of the meetings. Among their other talents, Hollis Watkins, Willie Peacock, and Sam Block were all songleaders. Arance Brooks, recalling the period when meetings were always packed, says, "I loved it. I just felt so much better when everybody would go. Looked like I slept better. The singing and everything. I just loved it." In spite of threats to his life, the Reverend Aaron Johnson, during a particularly tense period, opened his church for a meeting after the church that was supposed to have it backed down. People were afraid to come in at first, but when they did "We rocked the church. We rocked that church that night. Ha, Ha, Ha. I said, 'Well, if I die, I had a good time tonight. I had a *good* time tonight.'"

The music operated as a kind of litany against fear. Mass meeting offered a context in which the mystique of fear could be chipped away. At one Greenwood meeting, a speaker noted with satisfaction that at a recent demonstration where it looked as though things might get out of hand, Police Chief Lary was visibly scared; Lary's voice had trembled as he asked demonstrators to break it up. Even the police chief is human. At another meeting a boy who had spent thirty-nine days in jail with Hollis Watkins and Curtis Hayes talked about how jail was not as terrible as most people thought. He had kind of enjoyed it, actually. The community sent them baked chickens and pies and cakes and things, so they just sent the jail food on back.[43]

Much of the humor at mass meetings was an attack on fear. A song could bring the Citizens' Council down to size. To the tune of "Jesus Loves Me, This I Know," they might sing:

Jesus loves me cause I'm white.
Lynch me a nigger every night. Hate the Jews and I hate the Pope,
Jes' me and my rope.
Jesus loves me, The Citizens' Council told me so.

"We Shall Overcome" could become:

Deep in my heart, I do believe
We shall keep the niggers down
They will never be free—eee—eee
They will never be registered,
We shall keep the niggers down.[44]

Mixtures of the sacred and the profane, the mass meetings could be a very powerful social ritual. They attracted people to the movement and then helped them develop a sense of involvement and solidarity. By ritually acting out new definitions of their individual and collective selves, people helped make those selves become real. Informed and challenged by the speakers, pumped up by the singing and the laughing and the sense of community, many of those who only meant to go once out of curiosity left that first meeting thinking they might come once more, just to see.

By late 1963, women like Lula Belle Johnson and Susie Morgan and Lou Emma Allen often stopped by the SNCC office just to sit around and visit with one another and the staff and maybe do a little sewing. Old men stopped by to listen to the ballgames or just to argue with one another. For a segment of Greenwood's Black population, the movement had become as integrated into their lives as the barbershop or beauty parlor. It was not the least significant of the movement's achievements. Most of the people we are talking about we would have called apolitical twelve months earlier. Within a year, a radical political movement had become woven into their personal and communal patterns.

Of Nate Shaw, a Black Alabama sharecropper who joined a

communist-led attempt to create a sharecroppers' union in the 1930s, Theodore Rosengarten says "Shaw admits he learned little about the origins of the union. He was less concerned with where it came from than with its spirit, which he recognized as his own."[45] Similarly, local people in Greenwood recognized something of their own best spirit reflected in the early COFO cadre.

Courage was only the most visible part of what accounts for the dynamism of this period. We also have to consider the depth and richness of the personal relationships between organizers and local people, the flexibility of the organizers, their willingness to experiment, their ability to project themselves as men and women of character and the well-honed ability of the local people to read character, to recognize "fullness" when it was there. We also have to consider simple persistence. Our collective imagery of the movement does not include George Greene returning to talk to some frightened farmer for the tenth time or a Mary Lane, taking the registration test eleven times before she is allowed to pass, or Donaldson and Cobb returning at night to a town they were run out of that day. Overemphasizing the movement's more dramatic features, we undervalue the patient and sustained effort, the slow, respectful work, that made the dramatic moments possible.

"Spadework" was a pet phrase of Ella Baker's, popping up with regularity in the reports she filed while traveling the South in the 1940s:

> I must leave now for one of those small church night meetings which are usually more exhausting than the immediate returns seem to warrant but it's a part of the spade work, so let it be.

> Yes, Madison seems to have done a good job in N.C. He is to be congratulated because it was mostly spade work.[46]

Ironically, later in the decade, as the struggle became, in some ways, more sophisticated, activists seemed less and less willing to engage in the kind of spadework that had made Greenwood possible.

Nine

A WOMAN'S WAR

Ah wanted to preach a great sermon about colored women sittin'
on high, but they wasn't no pulpit for me.

ZORA NEALE HURSTON
Their Eyes Were Watching God

Women all over the world are less active in politics than men.

MATTHEWS AND PROTHRO
Negroes and the New Southern Politics, 1966

It was women going door to door, speaking with their neighbors,
meeting in voter-registration classes together, organizing through their
churches that gave the vital momentum and energy to the movement,
that made it a mass movement.

ANDY YOUNG
SCLC[1]

Those who trust in the Lord are like Mount Zion, which can
never be shaken, never be moved.

PSALM 125

ASKED TO NAME ALL THE women they can think of who were associated with the civil rights movement of the 1960s, most audiences are hard-pressed after Rosa Parks and Coretta King. In the South, a few may remember Mrs. Hamer. That so few women are remembered is ironic, to understate it. In the Delta, in the rural South generally, women were in fact much more politically active than men, at least in the early sixties. According to COFO organizers, women took civil rights workers into their homes, of course, giving them a place to eat and sleep, but women also canvassed more than men, showed up more frequently at mass meetings and demonstrations and more frequently attempted to register to vote. There appears to be no disagreement with Lawrence Guyot's comment that "It's no secret that young people and women led organizationally."[2] Another organizer called the war in the Delta a woman's war.

The greater responsiveness of women represents a departure from the 1950s. Traditional wisdom among political scientists holds that across the Western world men are more politically involved than women.[3] The pattern in Mississippi during the 1950s appears consistent with that. In that especially dangerous period, Black political activism in rural Mississippi seems to have been dominated by men. There were women at all levels of the state NAACP hierarchy, but when they had official positions they tended to have those traditionally assigned to women—hospitality committee, secretary, membership committee—and they did not dominate the membership rolls in the way they would come to dominate many COFO-initiated movements.

The gender-related pattern of participation in the 1960s seems to have been age-specific. That is, among older folks, there is no clear imbalance. We saw earlier that in the earliest days of the movement in Greenwood, a number of older men, men in their fifties and sixties, played important roles in getting the movement off the ground. Similarly, there does not seem to be any clear difference between teenage boys and teenage girls. The gender difference appears to be strongest in the years in between, the "settle-aged" years from, roughly, thirty to fifty. In that age range, some of my respondents estimated that women were three or four times more likely to participate than men.

The first citizenship classes in Greenwood averaged about fifteen students, typically five men and ten women.[4]

While there was virtually no disagreement among the people I spoke with about the nature of the pattern, there was no consensus at all about what explains it. I heard a variety of conflicting, sometimes contradictory, explanations, and many said simply they had no idea what accounted for the differences. Even those who did offer explanations were not very confident about them or anxious to defend them. These gender differences were not something to which people had given a lot of thought, even though they were aware of them. This is not surprising, given that in 1962 or 1963 gender was not as politicized a social category as it became a few years later.

Joyce Ladner offered an explanation that made sense to several people:

> The same types of women were the backbone of the Black churches. Women in the rural South have a long history of being doers. This is what set them apart from a lot of white women who came into the movement. . . . If they were employed it was as a maid and not necessarily as major breadwinners in their families. They weren't as beholden to a paycheck. White people considered them less threatening. . . . Because Southern white men discounted women, period. Because of their strong sexism, they didn't see Black women as much more threatening than they did white women.

Hollis Watkins also thought it had to do with the fact that historically Black women have had to adapt to so many different expectations and pressures they became relatively open to new situations:

> I really believe it's the fact that women are more flexible than men. Because of that, they are more susceptible to change. . . . Especially Black women, many of them started out supporting the family and abruptly they are the full supporters of the family. So they have to accept and be flexible and adjust to that change.

Although not mentioned by anyone I interviewed, one factor that probably played some role was SNCC's operating style. Founded by a woman, in its early years, women were always involved in the development of policy and the execution of the group's program. Its distaste for bureaucracy and hierarchy meant a willingness to work with anyone who was willing to work with them, traditional considerations of status and propriety notwithstanding. SNCC organizers were concerned with finding and helping to develop nontraditional sources of leadership. Women obviously represented an enormous pool of untapped leadership potential. Much of SNCC's organizing activity in the Delta involved door-to-door canvassing, which meant that women were as likely as men to encounter organizers. SNCC, despite the traditional expectations of sex roles held by many of its members,[5] was structurally and philosophically open to female participation in a way that many older organizations would not have been. Had SNCC employed a more traditional style of organizing—e.g., working primarily through previously established leadership—it might not have achieved the degree of female participation it did. Still, SNCC's openness to the participation of women does not explain why women were so responsive.

One explanation that might initially seem plausible can be rejected. This is the argument that there were just more women than men in the Delta. The argument here goes that the massive migrations out of the South in the 1940s and 1950s drew away more men than women in the twenty-to-forty age range. Thus, there were simply more Black women around in the Deep South when the movement of the sixties began. It is true that the migrations, especially in the early stages, took a large number of men out of the Delta, but in Greenwood at least, even when one looks at families where both husband and wife are present in the early sixties, wives were more likely to participate.

As Joyce Ladner noted, historically, Black women, especially poor Black women in rural areas, have had to fulfill social roles not commonly played by more privileged women. Zora Neale Hurston called southern Black women the mules of the world; they did whatever needed doing. Still, that has not always led to the kind of dominance of political activity that we seem to have in the rural South in the sixties. As recently as the 1950s, we had a different pattern. We might best think of the expanded social roles played by Black women as a predisposing factor rather than a complete explanation.

The notion that women were less exposed to reprisals than men has a certain plausibility. Southern whites, the argument goes, were less afraid of Black women and thus less likely to initiate either physical violence or economic reprisals against women. Even when economic reprisals were used, the wife's salary was likely to be less important to the family than the husband's. If anyone was going to be fired, better it be the wife. In short, it was simply safer, more cost-effective, for women to participate. Writing in the 1940s, E. Franklin Frazier had said that "in the South, the middle-class Negro male is not only prevented from playing a masculine role, but generally he must let the Negro woman assume the lead in any show of militancy."[6] It is true that many parents thought they had to whip the fear of white folks into their children at an early age, especially into their sons. "Oh, how many times," one woman told an interviewer, "have I heard my grandmother say, I've heard old colored women say, when they were whipping kids with a stick: 'Now I'm gonna beat the hell out of you to keep that white man from killing you! I'm gonna bend you now!'"[7] We know that in general, quite apart from considerations of gender, how free people were from economic reprisal had a great deal to do with who joined the movement in its early days. Nonetheless, it does not follow that differences between men and women can be explained in the same way. If, under normal circumstances, whites were more indulgent of transgressions of the racial norms when they came from Black women, it does not follow that the same indulgence would extend to the quite abnormal situation of 1962 and 1963. By that time, whites in the Delta clearly felt threatened, and it seems likely that they would have struck back at whomever they associated with the threat, old indulgences notwithstanding.

Moreover, the differential-exposure thesis minimizes the very substantial risks that women who joined the movement were running. Reprisals against women in the rural South were constant and were highly visible. SNCC's newsletters in 1962 and 1963 suggest that some of the most violent incidents of reprisals took place against women.

Women who were even rumored to be a part of the movement lost their jobs. Every adult woman I interviewed got fired, except for those who quit because they expected to get fired. Any woman in Greenwood who contemplated joining the early movement had to be aware of all this. She would have also been aware of the absolutely brutal beating that Annell Ponder, Mrs. Hamer, June Johnson, and Euvester Simpson had received in jail. In Greenwood, women were regularly clubbed at demonstrations, beaten in jail, and subjected to electric cattle prods. In at least one case, a cattle prod was used on a pregnant woman.[8] Everyone knew that Mrs. Laura McGhee's home, a home with no adult man, was being fired on by nightriders almost every other week, and the same thing was happening to other women. The women who had to make the decision to join or not join had to do so knowing full well that there was a virtual guarantee of economic reprisal and a high probability of worse.

Moreover, it is misleading to think of reprisals as being directed against merely the individual who was involved. Anyone who joined the movement placed his or her whole family at risk. When someone got evicted, the whole family was evicted. True, the man pressured by his boss to get his wife out of the movement could say "Gee, boss, I can't do anything with that woman. You know how women are," and hope for a sympathetic response. It was likely to be only a hope, though. The Citizens' Council in particular made it a point to put pressure on the entire family. If anyone in a family was known to be a part of the movement, any adult in that family might have trouble finding work or getting credit. Similarly, the most popular forms of violence in that period—arson, drive-by shootings into homes, and bombings—were reprisals against family units, not just individuals. One of the earliest shootings connected to COFO's work in the Delta involved nightriders in Ruleville, who shot up the homes of people who had supported the local voter-registration drive; the only people they hit were two teenage girls.[9]

As the severity of reprisals eventually lessened, there was not necessarily a corresponding increase in male participation. "As the violence petered down," noted SNCC's Lawrence Guyot, drawing on his experience organizing the Mississippi Freedom Democratic Party, "I did not see a correlative surging forward by Black males into leadership positions." He recalls telling a group of women that included Fannie Lou Hamer, Victoria Gray, and Unita Blackwell, "'Y'all step back a little bit and let the men move in now.' Fortunately, they didn't kill me." He made a similar comment at a meeting, probably around 1965, at which Ella Baker was present.

> Ella Baker told me, "You have proven that there are *some* men who can do a very good job but you have to learn never, never make the mistake of substituting men in quantity for women of quality." I haven't done that shit anymore. In fact, I've gone the other way around.

Finally, the differential-reprisal interpretation strikes me as suspicious because no woman to whom I spoke ever suggested, even indirectly, that *her own* involvement could be explained in such terms. Nor did anyone to whom I spoke ever identify any specific woman whose participation was affected by the reprisal issue. In fact, I find in my interviews with women very little thinking that I would consider calculation, whether calculation of probable harm to oneself or of the movement's chances of success.

When explaining their own decision to join the movement, my respondents constructed answers primarily in terms of either religious belief or pre-existing social networks of kinship and friendship.[10] For many women, both factors seem operative. Thus, Lou Emma Allen was drawn into the movement by her son, a junior-college student. Though she was often afraid, she was sure the Lord would see her through. Lula Belle Johnson got involved after June, her fourteen-year-old daughter, was arrested along with Fannie Lou Hamer and beaten. Mrs. Laura McGhee explained that she was initially interested in the movement because of her brother, Gus Courts, who had been shot for his organizing activity. Susie Morgan was drawn in partly by the activity of her daughters. She prayed and prayed over the decision to join, and finally she could see that it was what the Lord wanted her to do. Ethel Gray was drawn into the movement by an old friend. After she had joined, people would drive by and shoot into her home and on at least one occasion threw rattlesnakes on her porch, but "we stood up. Me and God stood up." The pattern in their histories is one of being drawn in initially by relatives or friends and feeling that the movement was God's work.

The religious issue raises a series of important questions. One line of explanation for the overparticipation of women might go as follows: the movement grew out of the church. Women participate in the church more than men do. (One contemporary estimate is that across all varieties of Black religious activities, women represent seventy-five to ninety percent of the participants.[11]) Therefore, women were naturally more drawn to the movement.

This argument is probably more applicable to the urban South. In urban areas, the churches certainly were an early focal point of organizing activity.[12] It is not surprising that there would be a high level of participation by women in the activities of the Southern Christian Leadership Conference, because many of that organization's affiliates were large, urban churches populated largely by women. Their rural counterparts, however, were far less supportive of the movement. In Greenwood, as we have seen, the early movement grew despite the opposition of the church. Those who joined the movement in the early days ordinarily did so in defiance of their church leadership. Nonetheless, if the church as an organization did not lead people into the movement, the religiosity of the population may have been much more important. Here it may be especially important to make a distinction between the pre- and post-1964 periods. The victories that affected the daily life of the average person began in the summer of 1964, with the public-accommodations bill. After that came the Voting Rights Act of 1965, bringing federal registrars to the South. The same period saw a decline in the frequency of both economic and physical reprisals and increasingly vigorous federal prosecution of those who persisted in violence.

Those who joined the movement in its early days could not have known that things would work out as they did. What they knew for certain was that those who joined were going to suffer for it. From the viewpoint of most rural Black southerners in 1962 or 1963, the overwhelming preponderance of evidence must have suggested that the movement was going to fail. Joining a movement under such circumstances may literally require an act of faith. Faith in the Lord made it easier to have faith in the possibility of social change. As the slaves of a century ago, according to Du Bois, saw the fulfillment of Biblical prophecy in the coming of the Civil War,[13] residents of the Delta may have seen the civil rights movement as a sign that God was stirring. Civil rights workers had long made a practice of using religion to challenge people. Ruby Hurley, who started working for the NAACP in the South in the early 1950s, noted:

> I found [using the Bible] to be effective in saying to our people, "You go to church on Sunday or you go every time the church doors are open. You say 'amen' before the minister even has the word out of his mouth. . . . Yet you tell me you're afraid. Now how can you be afraid and be honest when you say 'My faith looks up to Thee' or when you sing that God's going to take care of you? If you don't believe it, then you not really the Christian you say you are."[14]

Most of the organizers in the Delta in the early sixties were native Mississippians, fully aware of the motivating power of religion. Such appeals would have the most impact on the most religious—women rather than men, older men rather than younger ones.

It might be helpful to know more about why women, regardless of race, age, or education, are more religious than men in the first place. Despite considerable research, there is no clear answer. The pattern seems to hold, by any measure of religiosity, for all major Western religions other than Judaism.[15] On the other hand, previous research has ordinarily been interpreted to suggest that strong religious feelings ought to militate against participation in a change-oriented movement. One review of the literature concludes that the values reinforced by traditional churches

> include a world view focused on the private sector of life and with such immediate social orientations as the family, ethnic group or local community. They are associated with conformity and conserva-

tism in all attitude realms and with personal and privatistic commitments not oriented to social change. They value conformity and tradition more than individual freedom and tolerance of diversity, social conservatism more than social change, and definite moral codes more than individualized moral orientations.[16]

This interpretation, consistent with the idea of religion as opiate, obviously does not cover the situation of southern Blacks in the 1960s. If the pre-1950 history of the rural Black church conforms to this model,[17] its history since then suggests that there is nothing inherently conservative about the church, that its message can as easily be packaged in order-threatening as in order-serving ways. Similarly, it is ironic that investment in "personal and privatistic commitments" should be thought to be conservatizing. Among the women in Greenwood, it is just such commitments that seem to have played a large role in drawing them into the movement.

A more flexible model might hold that involvement in such commitments ordinarily militates against involvement in social movements, but once any one person in the network becomes politically involved, the strength of the social ties within the network is likely to draw other members in. In the Delta, there were sub-populations predisposed from the beginning to the message that SNCC conveyed. One such subgroup consisted of those, mostly older men associated with the NAACP, who had been community activists before SNCC came—Cleve Jordan, Dewey Greene, Reverend Johnson, Ed Cochrane. People like Robert Burns, Laurie McGhee, and Hattie Miller might be taken to represent a different subgroup of people who, while not active organizationally, were, for individual reasons, favorably predisposed to the new movement. The other group that responded quickly were young people. Thus, the situation that SNCC usually encountered in the Delta was that while most people were initially afraid, there were some who were interested right away, and it seems that given the tightly knit social bonds of rural communities, they were able to pull others in. If we assume that women tend to be more deeply invested than men in networks of kin and community, it is not surprising that more women tended to be drawn in during the early stages. When teenage children were drawn in, for example, that seems to have had a greater effect on their mothers and aunts than on their male relatives.

It seems likely that the greater investment of women in kin and communal networks would also affect the nature of their work inside the movement, an idea elaborated in Karen Sacks's analysis of a 1980s union-organizing drive among Black women in a southern hospital. Sacks was particularly concerned with the differing styles of leadership exhibited by men and women. In the traditional sense of leadership, men did the leading despite the fact that women were responsible for the actual building of the organization, for making people feel a part of it, as well as doing the everyday work. Men, on the other hand, were the public spokespersons, and they confronted and negotiated with management, which is what traditionally gets defined as leadership. In fact, women were offering leadership in very important ways. Certain women operated as network centers, to use Sacks's term, mobilizing already existing social networks around the organizing goals, mediating conflicts, conveying information, coordinating activity, creating and sustaining good relations within the group. Many of these skills seemed to be rooted in the way these women operated in their families.[18] Sacks's description of the leadership style of the women she studied would fit very well the role played by rural women in the civil rights movement, which raises another question.

How do such high levels of female participation change the tone of the movement? Drake and Cayton claimed in their study of Chicago's Black community in the thirties and forties that Black women community leaders—Race Women—were more trusted than Race Men, at least in part because of the perception that women could not as easily capitalize off of their activism.[19] Similarly, the preponderance of female participation in the movement may have had the effect of helping to create an atmosphere in which it was relatively easy to establish and maintain trust. At a guess, one would think that the participation of so many women meant that relationships inside the movement would have been less competitive, more nurturing than might have been the case otherwise. These women very clearly came to see SNCC organizers and some of the other out-of-town volunteers as their children. A movement with these familistic overtones, overtones reinforced in early SNCC by its ideal of the Beloved Community, must have been a relatively supportive and empowering political environment. At a point in the movement's history when the prospects for success seemed poor, when the stresses and tensions involved in organizing were great, such a climate may have done much to sustain the activists.

In the spring of 1940, E. Frederick Morrow of the NAACP's national office wrote Horatio Thompson, president of Baton Rouge's very active branch, offering advice on how to organize a membership drive:

> Select a campaign committee and select for chairman (if possible) a prominent person, who has a following and who will take the responsibility seriously. Preferably a woman—for they have a deeper sense of something-or-other than men.[20]

We still don't know very clearly what that something-or-other is. We know beyond dispute that women were frequently the dominant force in the movement. Their historical invisibility is perhaps the most compelling example of the way our shared images of the movement distort and confuse the historical reality.[21] There is a parallel with the way in which we typically fail to see women's work in other spheres. Arlene Daniels, among others, has noted that what we socially define as "work" are those activities that are public rather than private and those activities for which we get paid. Under this taken-for-granted understanding, much of the activity in which women are expected to specialize—caring for children and home, seeing to the fabric of day-to-day relationships—does not qualify as "work" and is thus effectively devalued.[22] In the same way, the tendency in the popular imagination and in much scholarship has been to reduce the movement to stirring speeches—given by men—and dramatic demonstrations—led by men. The everyday maintenance of the movement, women's work, overwhelmingly, is effectively devalued, sinking beneath the level of our sight.

As important as religious belief is for these women, it may be an error to take it too literally. Alberta Barnet, who started working in the Greenwood movement while still a teenager, suggested that the pattern of disproportionate female participation was not restricted to movement activities:

> Round here women just go out for meetings and things more than men. Men just don't do it. They don't participate in a lot of things. The most they participate in is a trade. So I guess that's one reason. It's like the church. You find more women there than you find men. . . . I guess women are probably easier to get to. . . . Men just don't fall for stuff that quick.

Arance Williamson, speaking to me in 1981, noted that even then women took more of a role in community politics than men. She suggested that much of the organizational life of Black Greenwood, not just the church and the movement, was dependent upon women. Ella Baker, with her decades of experience as an organizer in the South, felt much the same way. Cheryl Gilkes has found that in the contemporary urban North, Black women community workers are more common than men, which is consistent with my own experience with community organizations and with what Lawrence Guyot says about his experience as an organizer in contemporary Washington, D.C.[23]

The pattern of relatively high levels of female participation among either Black or working-class women seems to exist in several types of non-traditional political activities in widely differing circumstances. Even without a more precise description than that, it seems unlikely that religion would have the centrality in all of these circumstances that it had in the Delta. The important element, then, may not be so much religion itself as the sense of efficacy it engenders under certain circumstances. One way to get at this would be to look at situations in which men did participate in large numbers. In the Delta, one such place was Holmes County. While women were involved there—including Bernice Montgomery, one of the few schoolteachers in the Delta to join the early movement—Holmes County was one place where the movement was dominated by men from the very beginning. Indeed, the men of Holmes County did not wait for organizers to get around to them. They went to Greenwood and invited organizers to Holmes. According to Lawrence Guyot, in the mid-60s, when many FDP chapters were dominated by women, the Holmes County chapter continued to be dominated by men.

Holmes County is directly south of Leflore. In 1960, Blacks constituted seventy-two percent of the county population and owned fifty percent of the land in the county. A particularly important concentration of landowners was the community around Mileston. Blacks there had numerous advantages. When the school calendar for Black children in the rest of the Delta was still constructed around the cotton season, Black children in most of Holmes County attended school on a normal calendar. Howard Taft Bailey, one of the farmers who became involved with the movement, recalls that his father, a landowner, never allowed the children to work for whites and never allowed white peddlers on his land, common practices in Holmes County.

During the spring of 1963, when the situation in Greenwood was so intense, some Holmes County farmers, including some from Mileston, started attending mass meetings in Greenwood. According to Hollis Watkins, Amzie Moore had encouraged some of them to come. Eventually, Ozelle Mitchell, a long-time NAACP member, requested that someone be sent from Greenwood to help Holmes County get organized, concentrating especially on the Mileston area. COFO sent John Ball, a young man from nearby Itta Bena who had become a SNCC field secretary. A committee was formed that included Ozelle Mitchell, the Reverend J. J. Russell, Ralthus Hayes, Shadrach Davis, and Hartman Turnbow. Thus, in contrast to Greenwood, the movement in Holmes was in the hands of adult men from its inception, not teenage volunteers. In April, John Ball, sometimes with the assistance of Sam Block and Hollis Watkins, began teaching citizenship classes. They were immediately able to use the Reverend Russell's church.

Hartman Turnbow was in the first group of fourteen that went to register. They were careful not to give offense, parking their trucks on the outskirts of Lexington, the county seat, and walking to the courthouse in groups of two or three, instead of in a "big drove." Sheriff Andrew P. Smith tried to intimidate them. "He slapped one hand on his pistol and the other one on his blackjack and then raised his voice. . . . 'Now, who will be first?'" At that, Turnbow volunteered to be first, and the registration proceeded from there. The next day, Turnbow was surprised to find that "it was a write-up that Hartman Turnbow was an integration leader." A week later, at three in the morning, his home was attacked. Shots were fired from the front and the back of the house, and the living room and bedroom were firebombed. His wife and daughter ran outside. So did he, carrying a .22-caliber Remington automatic rifle with him. There were two white men outside, and after an exchange of fire, they fled. (Turnbow: "I don't know where all that there braveness come from. . . . I just found myself with it. . . . I had a wife and I had a daughter and I loved my wife just like a white man loves his'n and I loved my daughter just like a white man loves his'n and a white man will die for his'n and I say I'll die for mine.")[24] The next day, Turnbow was arrested and charged with firebombing and shooting up his own home. Turnbow told the sheriff and everybody else that anybody he caught on his land after dark was going to get lit up like a Christmas tree. Hazel Brannon Smith, owner of the Lexington *Advertiser* and a well-known and courageous moderate, published a notice that people would be well-advised to stay away from the Turnbow farm. His arrest, the firebombing of the home of Mr. Howard, another movement supporter, and the arrests of John Ball and Hollis Watkins, failed to make a significant dent in the level of local activism. Local people increasingly took on the functions of the organizers. By July, regular mass meetings in Mileston were attracting seventy-five to two hundred people, and with no COFO organizer working with them—many of the organizers were in jail again—the local leaders were spreading the movement through the rest of the county.[25]

Hollis Watkins thinks it was difficult to intimidate these people once they had been activated because they were used to cooperating with one another. They habitually shared tools and exchanged labor. They had made a success of a cooperatively owned cotton gin. White gin-owners had been unable to put them out of business even by undercutting their prices. Most of those active in the movement were also members of the cooperative gin. Watkins feels it was the fact that these country people had such a sense of solidarity among themselves that made Holmes County special.

The following year, during the summer of 1964, the people of Mileston established an armed community patrol that made sure no one got into the community without being known. SNCC's policy of nonviolence notwithstanding, Watkins and some of the other organizers were willing to take their turn on guard. Their successful patrol contrasts with the experience of Robert Burns, who had tried to do something similar with his neighbors in Greenwood but found them unreliable.

John Ball also found a different sense of solidarity in Holmes. People in the country may be slower to come around, but once they do, the sense of community among them makes them easier to organize. In that respect, Ball says, the difference between Greenwood and Mileston was the difference between daylight and dark. Once the country people did make a commitment, it was solid. Ball recalls marches in Greenwood where a lot of those who promised to show up didn't. In Holmes County, it was just the opposite. Once they had given their word, they tended not to back down, and would go out and recruit their neighbors. *More* people would show up for a march than had promised to. One could make distinctions even within the county. As small as they were, little towns like Durant didn't have the solidarity that organizers found out on the farms.

Later in the decade, other organizers would take note of the solidarity of people "out in the rural." In 1968, Blacks were boycotting businesses in downtown Greenwood. The Reverend William Wallace, a boycott leader, noted at the time that the people violating the boycott were from the city; from the rural areas they were getting almost one hundred percent cooperation. Both groups were poor, he added, "but usually there is a kind of loyalty that exists in a rural section that doesn't exist in some cities."[26]

The Mileston community has a special history. During the Depression, the Farm Security Administration had purchased 1.8 million acres of land and established a series of experimental farming and industrial communities. Some of these projects were intended to elevate sharecroppers and tenants to landowner status by allowing them to purchase government-owned land. Thirteen of these projects were reserved for Blacks, one of them being Mileston, where in 1936, 110 families were settled on their own land. Program policy was to give preference to those tenants who were already on the land when the government acquired it. After a five-year trial period, tenants were given low-interest mortgages. Federal officials provided technical assistance, helped construct community buildings, schools, and cooperative enterprises like cotton gins, and developed activities specifically designed to foster a sense of community. "The aim throughout was to transform a depressed class of agricultural tenants and laborers into viable communities of small farmers and entrepreneurs in possession of the resources they needed to avoid falling back into sharecropper status."[27]

In an evaluation of the experiment conducted thirty years later, Lester Salamon examined eight of the thirteen all-Black projects, Mileston among them. His conclusions support the possibility that owning land tended to shape a distinctive world view. As compared to a group of sharecroppers Salamon interviewed, the landowners—sometimes the descendants of the original participants—were more optimistic about the future, had a higher sense of personal efficacy, and were more likely to feel that they had been of help to others. The landowners themselves said that owning land made them feel like somebody, made them more independent and self-reliant. Significantly, they also reported higher rates of civic participation in ways ranging from holding offices in churches and fraternal groups to taking part in some kind of economic cooperative.

The landowners were distinctly more likely than the sharecroppers to have been active in the civil rights movement, no matter how activity was measured—attending meetings, joining a civil rights organization, working in a voter-registration drive, letting workers stay with them, or running for office. As the degree of danger in an activity increased, the disparity between landowners and croppers grew. Thus, landowners were roughly twice as likely as tenants to attend a civil rights meeting, but were four times as likely to work on a voter-registration campaign. Landowners were more likely to become involved early on. Three-fifths of the landowners, against one-fifth of the croppers, were involved prior to 1965.

Salamon's data suggest that the experience of those Mississippi SNCC workers who found independent landowners easier to organize may have been true across much of the South. Any difference between landowners and others might be attributed solely to their greater freedom from economic reprisals, but it seems very likely that Salamon is correct in thinking that there is more to it than that, that the experience of owning land within relatively cooperative communities contributed to a greater sense of efficacy, independent of the issue of reprisals. This would have been true for individual landowners, no doubt, but the effect must have especially pronounced when there were whole communities of Black landowners. Salamon refers to T. J. Woofter's study of the South Carolina Sea Islands, which concluded that in such communities Blacks exhibited a more independent and confident spirit.[28] Even in the late 1980s, people who knew both Holmes and Leflore counties found substantial differences between the populations. In Leflore schools, for example, Black parents tended to accept what the teacher did. When parents in Holmes had doubts about what their children were getting, they weren't shy about saying so.

Landownership—or more broadly, a tradition of economic independence—may do for men what religion seems to do for women—provide them with a sense of personal efficacy that in turn leads to a greater willingness to be socially involved.[29]

Holmes County is an extreme example, but the hill and piney-woods counties of Mississippi are similar in some pertinent ways. Southwest Mississippi, where SNCC's work in the state began, generally considered the most dangerous part of the state, was also a place that had relatively high rates of participation by men. Similarly, according to SNCC's MacArthur Cotton, in Attala County, the hill county where he grew up, civic leadership including movement leadership, has always been much more in male than in female hands. (Joking: "Oh, we might let the women have a Women's Day at the church or something like that.") Men in those counties didn't have the kind of independence and range of control in their work life that characterized Holmes County, but neither did they suffer from the near-total dependency of many Black men in the Delta. The typical jobs available to Black men in the Delta were sharecropping and field labor. If you were a plantation Negro, it would not be at all unusual for one man to control virtually your whole life outside your family. One man controlled your work, told you what to plant and where, where to shop for groceries and what you could spend on them, where to take your children if they were ill, where you lived, and, of course, what if anything your labor had been worth during the year. A word from your landlord to the sheriff could buy you more trouble than you needed in a lifetime. As oppressed as Blacks were in the hill counties, some of the jobs available to Black men there—woodcutting, lumber hauling, running small farms—offered a degree of independence, allowed for some personal initiative, and offered a better chance of bringing in some reward for one's labor. The mechanisms of social control could be brutal, but they were also fragmented. It was potentially a significantly less alienated existence, under conditions that were more likely than those in the plantation counties to allow men to develop a sense of personal efficacy.[30]

Perhaps the important thing to understand is not why men were less likely to participate in the civil rights movement of the sixties but why in the 1950s Richard West and Louie Redd had so much trouble getting men to help with their Black Boy Scout troop. Fear was so obviously a hurdle to participating in the movement that it can easily become an all-purpose explanation. It may be another case of the most dramatic features in a situation distracting us from other features that were perhaps equally important but more mundane. There is nothing particularly dramatic about thinking that one's own efforts can make a difference, but the presence or absence of that feeling—whether it comes from religion or a strong sense of community or traditions of economic independence—probably has a great deal to do with who participated and how.

Ten

TRANSITIONS

*Before the summer project last year
we watched five Negroes murdered in two counties
in Mississippi with no reaction from the country. We couldn't get
the news out. Then we saw that when three civil rights workers were
killed, and two of them were white, the whole country reacted, went
into motion. There's a deep problem behind that, and I think if you
can begin to understand what that problem is—why you don't move
when a Negro is killed the same way you move when a white
person is killed—then maybe you can begin to understand
this country in relation to Vietnam and the third world,
the Congo and Santo Domingo.*

BOB MOSES
1965

*And those two murders, Herbert Lee and Louis Allen, really punctuate
this little piece of the movement in Mississippi.*

BOB MOSES
1991[1]

Happy is she who fights without hating.

THE LAY OF SUNDIATA

THE PERIOD FROM THE SUMMER of 1963 through the summer of 1964 appears, at first glance, to have been a time of stalemate. White power could no longer completely suppress Black activism, but Black activism could make no major dents in the structure of oppression. It was a stalemate punctuated by dramatic moments: the assassinations of Medgar Evers and Louis Allen, Freedom Summer, with its own assassinations, and the disillusionment of the 1964 Democratic National Convention. Ironically, as the fear that had initially made organizing so difficult began to wither, growing disillusionment made activists increasingly impatient with some of the tenets of the community organizing tradition.

It was June 1963 when June Johnson, Mrs. Hamer, Annell Ponder, Euvester Simpson, and the others were arrested in Winona and brutally beaten (see Chapter 7). As soon as he found out where they were, SNCC's Lawrence Guyot called the Winona jail and was told that if he wanted to know their bail, he'd have to come over to find that out. He walked into one of the worst beatings of his life. He was forced to strip, and several policemen using gun butts and the like gave him a going-over for hours until a doctor told them he didn't want to be responsible if they kept it up. When Guyot didn't return to Greenwood, SNCC had friends from around the country flood the Winona jail with calls: "Where's Lawrence Guyot? I want to speak with Guyot?" The doctor and the phone calls may have made his captors nervous. Charged with attempted murder, he was taken to a cell where, oddly, the radio had been cut off. He found out why the next day, when they were all released. While they had been undergoing their own ordeal, Medgar Evers had been shot and killed down in Jackson.[2]

For a twenty-month period in 1961 and 1962, Evers had worked on the Meredith admission to Ole Miss. Meredith said later that he didn't think the whole thing would have come off at all without Evers. As his responsibilities in that case were winding down, direct action was slowly getting off the ground in Jackson. Just before Christmas, 1962, after months of discussions and a false start the previous year, a vigorous boycott had finally been launched against downtown merchants in Jackson. Initially, young people carried the spirit of the movement.

Dorie and Joyce Ladner (Chapters 2 and 5) were heavily involved. At a time when bail money was unpredictable and most Mississippi-born students were afraid of reprisals against their parents, Dorie was among the first to go to jail for picketing. Joyce's work building support for the campaign on Tougaloo's campus won her an award as Student Citizen of the Year.

The boycott held firm into the spring. By that time, a movement was in full bloom in Jackson. There were mass meetings, marches, and picket lines, and over six hundred arrests, much of the action initiated by NAACP youth members. A school-desegregation suit, with the Evers children among the plaintiffs, was pending. On May 28, Tougaloo students held a sit-in at the downtown Woolworth's; it became a mob scene. John Salter, a Tougaloo professor, part white and part Native American, who acted as adviser to the student activists there, joined his students at the lunch counter:

> Someone struck me several hard blows on the side of my face. I almost passed out and had to grip the counter for support. My face was bleeding. Then I was struck on the back of the head and almost passed out again. I was dizzy and could hardly hear myself talking, but I asked [Tougaloo student] Annie Moody what she thought of the final examination questions that I had asked in Introduction to Social Studies. She smiled and said that she felt they were much too tough. Joan [Trumpauer, another Tougaloo student] began to talk about her final exams. More ketchup and mustard were poured over us. Then sugar was dumped in our hair. We talked on.[3]

After it was over, Evers found out that several FBI officers had been in the crowd, observing. The violence generated national publicity and shook the local power structure. In its immediate aftermath, Mayor Allen Thompson, an unreconstructed segregationist, showed some signs of being willing to make concessions to the movement—opening parks and libraries to Blacks, taking down segregation signs, hiring more Black policemen and crossing guards. Before the movement could celebrate, Thompson, who was probably being pushed from different sides, recanted. The boycott had generated a momentum within the Black community that continued, however. Roy Wilkins came to town and got himself arrested in a demonstration, bringing more national attention. That did not mean that the NAACP national office was fully comfortable with direct action. They still worried about the financial burden of finding bail money and about the possibility that demonstrations would get out of hand. The national officers were able to pack the local strategy committee with people, largely ministers, who shared their more conservative viewpoint.

The success of the boycott and the media attention made Medgar Evers more vulnerable than ever; telephone threats were coming on an hourly basis. Evers often seemed drawn and worried that spring. Several of his friends have said that he was unusually brooding and spoke frequently of his own death and what it would do to his family. When Myrlie suggested that he needed a new suit, he snapped at her, saying he wouldn't get to use it if he bought it. A workaholic in any case, the increased pace of movement activity meant he was stringing together many workdays of eighteen hours or more. There was a great deal of in-fighting within the movement about pace and tactics, and he had to referee it. Several regional or national NAACP officers came to town late in the spring, so he didn't have as much decision-making authority as he normally did, and he was caught again in the middle of the ill feeling between the people from the national office and local youth leaders and CORE and SNCC members. According to John Salter, Evers had half-a-dozen firearms in his home, he sometimes carried a .45 or a rifle in the car, and he had gotten a German shepherd to patrol the yard. Myrlie slept with a small revolver on the nightstand. The house had bullet-proof blinds. The children—ages three, eight, and nine—had all been taught to stay away from windows at night and to hit the floor or jump in the bathtub as soon as they heard anything that might be a gunshot. There was talk within the NAACP of getting him a bodyguard, but nothing ever came of it, even after someone threw a firebomb against the carport one evening when Evers was at a mass meeting. Myrlie put the fire out with the garden hose. Characteristically, once he knew the family was safe, Evers contacted the media before he went home.

The movement ebbed and flowed in early June. The city obtained an injunction against further demonstrations, and movement leadership was divided about whether to defy it. The movement's sagging spirit received a boost when Lena Horne and Dick Gregory appeared at a mass meeting, but that was hardly enough to make people forget the constant threats of reprisal. One of the activist ministers had shotgun blasts fired into his grocery store. Cars were driving by the Tougaloo campus firing randomly. Salter decided to send his wife and child out of state. The national NAACP office had recently taken steps to end mass demonstration in Jackson, working through the conservative local ministers. Mayor Thompson was also taking steps to divide Black leadership, with some success.

On Sunday, June 9, Evers spent the entire day with his family, something he seldom took time to do. On Tuesday, the 11th, John Kennedy gave the strongest civil rights speech of his administration and asked the nation's support for the civil rights legislation that he would be sending to Congress. Medgar was very pleased with the speech. There was a mass meeting that night, but it was not a good one. Attendance was poor, and the spirit was weak. Evers got home after midnight. Police officers frequently followed him home, but apparently they did not do so that night. Myrlie had let the children stay up to wait for him. They heard the car pull up and the door slam, and immediately after, they heard the gunshot. As he stepped out of his car, carrying a stack of "Jim Crow Must Go" t-shirts, he was hit by a shot from a high-powered rifle fired from a nearby vacant lot. Houston Wells, his next-door neighbor, heard the shot and Myrlie's scream. Looking out of his bedroom window, he saw the body lying there. He got his pistol, ran outside and fired a shot in the air to frighten the gunman away. Evers died shortly after he reached the hospital. He had his new poll-tax receipt in his pocket.[4]

Many white officials condemned the killing, after a fashion. Governor Ross Barnett said, "Apparently, it was a dastardly act."[5] Apparently. The fingerprint on the rifle found in the vacant lot belonged to Byron de la Beckwith, a Greenwood fertilizer salesman, son of an old Delta family, self-anointed defender of segregation and member of the Greenwood Citizens' Council. It was proven that he had owned a rifle and a scope that matched the murder weapon. Two cab drivers testified that he had asked for Evers's address a few days before the shooting. Beckwith's attorney, Hardy Lott, past president of Greenwood's Citizens' Council, produced testimony from two Greenwood policemen who swore they saw Beckwith in Greenwood—ninety miles from Jackson—the evening of the slaying. Beckwith contended that his rifle had been stolen a few days before the killing. The trial reflected both the old Mississippi and the emerging one. On the one hand, the prosecutor, to Myrlie Evers's surprise, really tried for a conviction. On the other, Beckwith treated the trial as a royal joke.

> The accused killer appeared to enjoy himself immensely. He rested his legs on another chair while he drank soda pop, scowled at Negro newsmen, and waved gaily to white friends. At one point, a bailiff had to escort him back to his place when he strode over to chat with members of the jury. With a courtly flourish he offered cigars to Prosecutor William L. Waller.[6]

The trial ended in a hung jury. When he got home to Greenwood, the town gave him a rousing parade. Subsequently, a second trial also ended in a hung jury and Beckwith was freed.

The reaction of Jackson's Black community also reflected both the accommodationist past and the defiant future. The morning after the murder, Anne Moody—from the Woolworth sit-in—and Dorie Ladner decided to go to Jackson State to recruit students for a protest march. "We begged students to participate. They didn't respond in any way," a reaction that enraged Moody: "How could Negroes be so pitiful? . . . I just didn't understand." President Jacob Reddix found them and ordered them off campus immediately. Dorie asked him if he didn't have some feelings about what had happened. He responded, "I am doing a job. I can't do this job and have feelings about everything happening in Jackson. . . . Now you two get off this campus before I have you arrested."[7]

On the other hand, thirteen Negro ministers and businessmen, people who had been reluctant to march before, held a protest march of their own, getting arrested before they had gone very far. On the day of the funeral, perhaps three thousand people followed the casket to the funeral home, many of them not the usual movement types, young men more comfortable in a pool hall than in a demonstration. Things were supposed to end at the funeral home, but some of the crowd decided to march on the business district. They were met with police dogs and arrests, but the crowd wouldn't be intimidated. Several observers felt that only the intervention of several civil rights workers and the Justice Department's John Doar prevented the anger from boiling over into a full anti-police riot.

In Greenwood, there was a special edge to the sense of loss. If white people had spies in the Black community, the movement probably had a much larger number of eyes and ears in the white community. "Certain people," according to Willie Peacock, were afraid to do one thing but they weren't afraid to do another. Like these people working in these big white folks' homes. . . . We had allies in their homes"— and, he might have added, in their places of business, including one janitor at the bus station, a man who had lost an earlier job for movement activity. Beckwith was regarded as a dangerous character, someone to keep an eye on. In the weeks preceding the killing of Evers, the janitor warned them "that Beckwith and some woman and a white kid of about 17 from Sidon were meeting at the bus station regularly . . . talking about how they were going to do this job in Jackson." The custodian was never able to catch any names, so there was no way to act on the information.

For years after Evers's death, there were stories in the Delta about con men who raised money by claiming the funds were going to be used to bring Medgar Evers's killer back to trial. It is a testament to the stature Evers held among ordinary folk; if there was one cause to which you could get people to contribute money they couldn't afford, it was the cause of bringing his murderer to justice. Many of Greenwood's younger activists were in jail at the time of the killing. After the influx of out-of-town organizers had left in April, young people in Greenwood were, if anything, more aggressive than they had been earlier, leading to two mass arrests in June. By July, thirteen hundred county residents had attempted to register, unsuccessfully, of course, in all but a few cases. COFO found an alternative way of encouraging political participation. Some volunteer law students found a Reconstruction era law that allowed unregistered citizens to vote provided they submitted an affidavit asserting they were qualified to vote. On that basis, COFO decided to participate in the gubernatorial primary scheduled for August 6.

The idea was to encourage as many people as possible to vote by affidavit. COFO people would serve as poll watchers. People reluctant to go to the polls could cast a freedom ballot that would be collected and disposed of by COFO. For six weeks, they explained the idea through canvassing and mass meetings, teaching people to prepare sample affidavits, how to find polling places, and the like. Response was good. During the week before the primary mass meetings were held nightly with an average attendance of two hundred.

A few days before the election, the whole plan was threatened by state Attorney General Joe Patterson, who announced that those trying to vote under section 3114 would be "summarily" arrested. He had waited so long to make the announcement that there was no chance to inform everyone of the possibility of arrest until the day of the election itself.

Mass meetings had been set for 7 A.M. on election day so that people could receive final instructions. In Itta Bena, just outside Greenwood, eighty-five people were gathered by that hour at Hopewell Baptist. After COFO workers explained the new threat, some people began to leave. Mr. Bevel—father of SCLC's James Bevel—said he would go. When he came back and reported, "They scared. . . . They were so polite, I didn't know how to act," a lot more people were willing to go. COFO workers ferried one hundred fifty of them to the polls. As more and more of them went down, the clerks became more hostile and the crowd of whites that had gathered became more threatening, eventually placing themselves so as to block the entrance, which wasn't going to stop Stokely Carmichael, who said he "merely directed the group courteously through the middle of them," despite the cursing and swearing. "Two years ago," Carmichael noted in his report, "we would have been shot for a stunt like this."[8]

Things were tougher in neighboring Ruleville, where police quickly arrested three SNCC workers and turned Blacks away at the polls, which may have been less troubling than the groups of hostile white men aiming shotguns at them. Only a couple of dozen people got to vote. One of them was Joe McDonald, who had been among the first to welcome COFO workers and whose house had been shot into the previous fall: "I voted all I could," he said.[9]

No one could know how the Greenwood police were going to act. The 7 A.M. meetings in Greenwood were at Jennings Temple, Union Grove, and Turners Chapel, and between one hundred and two hundred people showed up at each. Some early arrivals left when they heard about the possibility of arrest, and even many of those who stayed were clearly afraid but determined to go through with it. At Union Grove, Martha Prescod Norman and one of the SCLC citizenship teachers, spent an hour going over the affidavit procedure with people:

> I was surprised to see so many people ready to go to jail. I imagine that there were more than seventy people in the church who had come expecting to be arrested. They were mostly old people, people with arthritis and things, that came to the church. Before we left the church we sang "Is That Freedom Train A-coming." One old man behind me on a cane said, "Here's what hurts a man, if he's scared; but the trouble of it is, I ain't scared."

They weren't all older people. The night before, after Bob Moses had asked for volunteers to go to jail, Billie Johnson, one of Lula Belle's daughters, went home, took off her good clothes, and put out something suitable for jail, fearing the worst.

> I had fear in my heart because as soon as morning came, I had to face a big problem. That was going downtown and getting a beating. I know when the police see me they will hit me. I had it all in my mind how it was going to be: one [policeman] would hit me on the head with a night stick, and the other would hit me in the mouth. Another was going to sic five or six dogs on me. I knew they were going to knock me down and kick me in the face. The moment came for me to go downtown. My mind was made up; I looked at the clock—quarter to nine. I was going at nine. If they whipped me for my freedom, I would not mind. And all at once

Sam Block came in and said the police said they would not arrest anyone. . . . I said "Thank God" three times.[10]

Earlier that morning, the police commissioner had found Block and promised him no arrests in Greenwood. The Reverend Aaron Johnson led the first group down and the police kept their word. The reception was actually polite at first, but a hostile white crowd gathered as Negroes continued to show up. Crowd or no crowd, once it was clear there were going to be no arrests, people poured in. Freddie Greene in the office answered a flood of phone calls for information about what was going on. By 11 A.M., people were coming through so rapidly the staff couldn't keep an adequate count. People were no longer waiting on a ride; they were walking. Between five hundred and seven hundred ballots were cast in Greenwood, and the polls closed before everyone got there. Those turned away "were extremely disappointed at being unable to cast their votes."[11]

The decision not to arrest seems consistent with a strategy of holding on to power through moderation. The Leflore Democratic party maintained that it had examined each ballot and found each invalid, preserving the semblance of legality without running any of the risks entailed in open police harassment.[12]

The night of the election, SCLC's Andy Young and SNCC chairman John Lewis spoke at mass meeting that reflected the celebratory air of the day. "Difficult to capture," SNCC's Mike Miller wrote, "is the mood of the day—the air of jubilation at going to vote, and the infusion of this spirit in the Greenwood staff." Willie Peacock's brother, James, got so wrapped up in the people's excitement that he forgot what he was supposed to be doing. He was especially struck by the fact that some of the same people who had been negative before had changed, including one man who had cursed him out just a day ago—"He even sounds different now, not much, but you can tell it's a change in his voice, he is interested in what's going on."[13] Registration attempts picked up after the election, with more people going down without COFO escorts.

To judge from the reports Sam Block submitted, Greenwood by

early fall of 1963 was a stabilizing situation. By October they had opened a library, a better library than anything available to Negroes in that part of the Delta, and it was bringing new people into contact with the movement. Billie, Lula Belle Johnson's daughter, was in charge of it. More older people were canvassing regularly. The staff was also experimenting with what amounted to passive canvassing, sending postcards to people who had gotten food the previous spring announcing that the office was signing up people who wanted food in 1964 and was also asking them to try to register again. Block was pleased with the response. On the other hand, he was getting complaints about having too many mass meetings. He admitted that he was so happy about having five churches regularly open to the movement that "I guess I went Mass Meeting crazy." They were broke again; there wasn't even money for food. In that respect and others, Greenwood staff felt they weren't getting enough support from the Atlanta office, a long-running complaint. One staff member had been transferred to Jackson. His heavy drinking was getting the best of him, and he was embarrassing them with the local people. Another had written $147 in NAACP memberships and failed to turn in the money, so SNCC had to cover for him. The Citizenship Schools had more people applying for teacher-training than they could handle. SCLC's Dorothy Cotton urged Annell Ponder to take advantage of that and be a little more selective in the people she sent for training at Dorchester. "There were some in the last group who couldn't hear, and one who couldn't see so well or write." The reports suggest a genuinely dug-in movement. There were problems, large and small, but with the high drama of the spring behind them, there was a still-growing core of people who were making some kind of long-term commitment to being a part of the process of change.[14]

Against the backdrop of steady growth, there was one exciting initiative, the continuation of that summer's Freedom Vote. Encouraged by the participation in the primary, COFO decided to take part in the election that fall by holding its own registration and running its own candidates. The Freedom Vote was intended, first, to show that the masses of Negroes did in fact want to vote. (Polls at the time showed that forty percent of white southerners did not think Negroes really wanted to vote.) Second, it was intended to mock the legitimacy of the regular election by making the point that the candidates elected did not represent hundreds of thousands of Negroes. Aaron Henry ran for governor, with Ed King, a white native Mississippian and chaplain at Tougaloo, as his running mate. If Henry had suffered less than other leaders from repression in the 1950s, he made up for it in the sixties. He was arrested for leading a boycott of Clarksdale stores, his wife lost her job, he was arrested on allegations of child molestation, his home had been either firebombed or hit by lightning, and in July 1963 he spent a week on the chain gang for parading without a permit.

Those who were registered—fewer than twenty-five thousand Negroes statewide—were encouraged to vote in the regular election and write in the names of the Freedom candidates. Everyone else was encouraged to vote in COFO's mock election, allowing them to register their opinions without exposing themselves to much danger.

There was nothing mock about the way COFO approached the election. They set up an elaborate statewide campaign organization, took out newspaper and television ads, and held rallies across the state. By October, Aaron Henry was making a speech a night. In mid-month, the campaign received some extra manpower. Eighty to ninety college students recruited by Allard Lowenstein from Stanford and Yale took two weeks off to help with the campaign. Previously, it was thought that having whites work openly in the Delta was likely to be too dangerous for all (though exceptions had been made), and not everyone thought it was a good idea now. Sam Block and Willie Peacock were opposed to the idea from the very beginning. When the students assigned to Leflore County showed up, they promptly took them over to Indianola in neighboring Sunflower County and got them arrested.

Registration workers were harassed across the state. Greenwood's police department engaged in its share of harassment, but beyond that, it is difficult to gauge the state of mind of local law enforcement officials during the fall of 1963. While the movement was constantly evolving new tactics, the powers-that-be frequently seem to have continued almost ritualistically with the same old responses.

On November 2, for example, Dick Frey and Jane Stembridge set up a ballot box on Johnson Street in downtown Greenwood, hoping to catch people coming downtown to shop, being careful not to block the sidewalk. While they manned the polling place, local high school students, including June Johnson, Dorothy Higgins, and Willie James Earl, did most of the "floating"—

> moving about and talking with the people. . . . For the better part of an hour we had people voting constantly. Then the police showed up . . . and finally parked just across Johnson Street and watched us. The crowd thinned. We started singing freedom songs to keep the spirit up. A few people kept coming up to vote. Chief Curtis Lary appeared in his car and parked in front of the first police car. . . . We sang "Ain't Gonna Let Chief Lary Turn Me 'Round" and Chief Lary walked up to Dorothy Higgins and said something like "You're asking for it."

Most of them were arrested, although someone got away with the ballots so the police couldn't get the names of those who voted. At the station, they were cursed, threatened, and shoved around. No one told them what the charges were. They spent the weekend in jail, and Monday morning Sam Block, Chico Neblett, James Forman, and Willie McGee came to bail them out. As Sam was paying the bail, Captain Ussery, who had a reputation for being especially aggressive about harassing movement workers, started cursing them and told the others to leave.

> They started out the door. . . . Forman was in the rear. Just as he got to the door, this Captain Ussery reached for his pistol and cursed the goddamn niggers . . . [and] then all of a sudden he kicked Jim—kicked him just as hard as you can kick a man and said, I said get out. . . . niggers. Forman stopped . . . and looked at the man . . . for a split second, looked like he was deciding whether to kill him or what . . . [and] then Forman just walked out and got in the car. No gesture from Forman—just his eyes. . . . After [the] Captain had kicked Forman, Dick walked up to him and looked at the nameplate. . . . The Captain said, "That's right . . . get my name. I don't give a goddamn . . ." then something about not giv-

ing a goddamn about any of us and niggers and cursing some
more. . . . It was unintelligible.

Police response seems almost petty in its meanness. No doubt they
had originally expected to be able to stamp out the local movement
pretty quickly. Almost a year and a half had passed and the movement
showed no signs of going anywhere anytime soon. It would not be
surprising if they were frustrated and confused. They were certainly
not all of one mind. After the incident cited above, the police did not
follow the workers back home, a switch from the usual pattern. Jane
Stembridge thought it might have been because Chief Lary ("He is at
least sane most of the time") drove up as they were leaving. Lary seems
on several occasions to have restrained some of his more aggressive
officers.[15]

The vote was a great success across the state. Perhaps eighty thousand Freedom ballots were cast in COFO's first statewide organizing
campaign, less than half of what COFO had hoped for but enough to
make the point. National media coverage was considerable, due in no
small part to the media's considerable interest in the white students
from Yale and Stanford. Given that, why not bring an even larger
number of students into the state for the following summer? The idea
was first fully broached at a meeting in Greenville in November 1963.
More media attention could lead to a greater degree of protection for
civil rights workers. Most COFO staff, including MacArthur Cotton,
Charlie Cobb, Ivanhoe Donaldson, Hollis Watkins, Willie Peacock,
and Sam Block, opposed the idea. Even before the idea was raised,
there had been some discomfort among veteran staff about the slowly
growing role of whites in the movement. It contradicted the principle
of developing organizers where they found them. Given their education, whites coming into the movement were going to gravitate to
leadership positions, supplanting local people, who were beginning to
take on more leadership responsibility. If lives were at risk, it was
largely the lives of COFO organizers, and most COFO staff preferred
continuing running that risk to risking the long-term viability of their
community-building efforts. Tactical issues aside, there were some

who just plain didn't want to be bothered with a bunch of white folks on a daily basis. For that matter, the idea of bringing in outsiders, had that been Black staff from the Atlanta office, didn't sit well with some veteran staff members, mostly southern Blacks, who had done the most and risked the most to build a viable movement.

Bob Moses, Lawrence Guyot, Mrs. Hamer, and CORE's Dave Dennis were among the proponents. Mrs. Hamer told opponents, "If we're trying to break down segregation, we can't segregate ourselves."[16] Other proponents saw real risks in the idea but thought that the potential benefits outweighed them and that some way had to be found to offer some protection to the local people with whom they were working. Older local leaders were generally very much in favor of bringing the students in. The debate, in SNCC style, went on over the course of that winter.[17]

SNCC's initial community-organizing venture in the state had been brought to a halt by the murder of Herbert Lee. Another series of killings in the same part of the state, the Southwest, ultimately ended the arguments over Freedom Summer. Anne Moody, who had grown up in that part of the state, was touched by some of the murders. When the Jackson movement began, college students there were afraid that their participation would bring reprisals against their families at home. These were realistic fears. Anne Moody was from Centreville in the Southwest. After she started doing movement work in Jackson, the sheriff visited her mother back home in Centreville and told her it would be a good idea for Anne not to come home any more unless she changed her ways; they didn't intend to have any of that NAACP stuff in Centreville. After Moody took part in the Woolworth sit-in, the sheriff paid her mother another harassing visit. A group of white boys cornered her younger brother, and he was saved from a beating or worse only because a friend came by in a car and got him away from the scene. Her uncle was not so lucky; a group of white men caught him alone and gave him a good beating. Moody spent that spring of 1963 waiting to hear that a member of her family had been killed.[18]

Three Negroes in the area were killed in December 1963, found dead in their car. The local paper at first stated that Eli Jackson, Dennis Jones, and Lula Mae Anderson had all fallen asleep with the motor running and been poisoned by fumes. In fact, two of them had been shot and one had had his neck broken. In late February, one of Anne Moody's relatives was killed. As he was coming home from work one night, someone ambushed him; buckshot took off most of his face. Bob Moses believed the killings were simply terror killings intended to keep the Negroes in their place.[19]

Against the backdrop of the other killings, the murder of Louis Allen from Amite County had the greatest impact on the ongoing discussion about white volunteers. Allen was a logger with a seventh-grade education who had served in the South Pacific in World War II. A witness to Herbert Lee's murder in Liberty in the early fall of 1961 (Chapter 4), he initially told the coroner's jury—which was held in a room full of armed white men—what he had been told to say—that Lee had a tire tool in his hand and had threatened E. H. Hurst with it. That had not been true, and Allen was willing to change his testimony—"to let the hide go with the hair," he said—in exchange for a promise of federal protection. The Justice Department told him in no uncertain terms that no such promise could be given. Word about Allen's willingness to recant apparently reached some local whites, including the sheriff. Allen knew he was a marked man and thought about leaving. Unfortunately, he had elderly parents who were very ill, and he had debts to pay off. The next couple of years alternated between periods when whites harassed him and periods when they left him alone. He had trouble selling his logs, was arrested twice on dubious charges, and frequently received direct or indirect death threats. The second arrest was in November 1963. While he was in jail, a Negro trustee heard that a lynch mob was forming. Allen managed to get word to his sons, Henry and Tommy, who came to the jail and stood guard outside all night. When he got out of jail, Allen decided it was time to get out of the state as soon as he could. His mother died in January, releasing him from one responsibility. He determined that he would leave February 1 for Milwaukee, where his brother lived. He spent the last day of January trying to get his business straight and get some letters of reference to take with him. The latter proved difficult. By evening, he had not found anyone willing to write a letter for him, and he decided to go ask one more of his former employers. His son Henry suggested he take a pistol with him and volunteered to go with him, but Allen turned down both suggestions. He got back home around 8:30 that evening and got out of his truck to open the gate to his property. He must have suddenly realized he was in danger and tried to dive under his truck. When Henry returned home that evening, he found his father under the truck, hit by two loads of buckshot.[20]

Talking to Mrs. Allen made up Bob Moses's mind about the Summer Project. They had watched Herbert Lee get gunned down and couldn't do anything about it. Now at least they were in a position to force some national attention onto Mississippi, thereby putting pressure on the federal government to protect Black life in the state. It was self-consciously an attempt to use the nation's racism, its tendency to react only when white life was endangered, as a point of leverage. Moses and Dave Dennis put all of their authority behind the Summer Project.[21]

As the plans for the summer evolved, Mississippi officialdom geared up for war. In early June, Sam Block, Willie Peacock, James Black, Charles McLaurin, and James Jones set off for a SNCC meeting in Atlanta, with Black driving. Heading West from Greenwood, they realized that they were being followed. Several efforts to shake their company failed, and the car, a white and black Mercury, was still behind them when they approached Columbus, playing cat-and-mouse games, roaring right up to their rear bumper and cutting its headlights, falling back, catching up, passing and pulling over to the side of the road until the SNCC workers caught up. Finally, the car turned off onto a side road. In Columbus, they were stopped by a police car and asked why they had been trying to run that Mercury off the road. It was clear that one of the officers, Roy Elders, knew them as "the niggers who are going to change our way of life." On the way to the jail, James Black was separated from the others. When he showed up twenty minutes later, "one side of his face was swollen out of shape; one of his eyes was blackened and bloodshot, and blood was running from his swollen mouth. His clothes were also torn and disarranged."

Black, Elders explained, had fallen getting out of the car. Sam Block was taken out for an "interview." As he remembered it, "Elders hit me on the cheek with his fist. I staggered and fell back to the window and he grabbed me and hit me in the groin with his fist very hard. I fell down and he kicked me hard in the shin." Block passed out when he got back to his cell. Peacock, McLaurin, and James Jones were beaten in turn. The next day Black was charged with reckless driving and running a stop sign, fined $28, and they were all released.[22]

The Greenwood staff had the feeling that national SNCC didn't particularly care about the fact that they had been beaten, which is a measure of what staff morale was like in Greenwood that spring. They were frustrated by a lack of money, saw themselves as being taken for granted by the central office, and not exactly anticipating the summer project with joy.[23]

The beating was reflection of the hair-trigger temper of the state's official and unofficial forces of repression as they contemplated the summer "invasion"—Mississippi newspapers hardly used any other word in referring to the Summer Project. In just the first two weeks of the summer project, in addition to the murder of Mickey Schwerner, James Chaney, and Andrew Goodman in Philadelphia, Mississippi, there were at least seven bombings or fire-bombings of movement-related businesses and four shootings and a larger number of serious beatings.[24] The state was clearly primed for violence, and the final tally might have been far worse had it not been for the hundreds of federal officers who swarmed over the state after the Philadelphia murders. (Once, that is, the FBI took the murders seriously, which took a while.)

Since the summer involved large numbers of white people, we have a great deal of literature on it, far more than on the three years of organizing that preceded it.[25] Two aspects of that period are especially interesting here: Freedom Schools, and the reception given volunteers by local Blacks. The schools offer another example of the developmental aspect of the community-organizing tradition; the response of local people to the volunteers suggests another way of thinking about the influence of southern Black culture on the movement.

When Ella Baker first went to New York in 1927 she organized a Negro history club for youngsters at the Harlem Y. This may have been her first "political" act in the city. No doubt, she saw it as a way to raise consciousness, to help people develop themselves. The Freedom Schools in Mississippi were an experiment in the same tradition. By late 1963, strategic thinking in SNCC was increasingly concerned with "parallel institutions."

If existing institutions did not meet the needs of Black Mississippians, what kinds of institutions would? Freedom Schools were one reflection of that thinking, but they also exemplified a much older tendency within the community-organizing tradition. During one of the early planning sessions for the summer, Charlie Cobb, the Howard University student who had first come to the Delta in the fall of 1962, proposed a summer Freedom School program "to fill an intellectual and creative vacuum in the lives of young Negro Mississippians, and to get them to articulate their own desires, demands and questions . . . to stand up in classrooms around the state and ask their teachers a real question." The schools were expected to be "an educational experience for students which will make it possible for them to challenge the myths of our society, to perceive more clearly its realities and to find alternatives and ultimately, new directions for action."[26] Cobb envisioned the schools handling perhaps a thousand students of high school age. In fact, somewhere between twenty-five hundred and three thousand students actually showed up, and their ages ranged from seven to seventy. Cobb's original idea of having one teacher for every four or five kids had to be dropped, and the number of schools was increased from twenty-five to forty-one.

Part of the classwork consisted of traditional academic subjects. In Mississippi, though, traditional subjects were often not available in Black schools. Publicly supported Black schools tended not to offer typing, foreign languages, art, drama, or college-preparatory mathematics. Apart from whatever intrinsic interest they held, these subjects were popular with students partly because they symbolized equality.

It was the Citizenship Curriculum that made the schools distinctive. It was built around a set of core questions, including:

1. What does the majority culture have that we want?

2. What does the majority culture have that we don't want?

3. What do we have that we want to keep?

One unit of the curriculum asked students to compare their social reality with that of others in terms of education, housing, and employment; one section called for them to compare the adjustment of Negroes to Mississippi with the adjustment of Jews to Nazi Germany. Another unit was intended to convince students that "running away" to the North wasn't going to solve anything. The "Introducing the Power Structure" unit tried "to create an awareness that some people profit by the pain of others or by misleading them." The unit on poor whites tried to help students understand how the power structure manipulated the fears of poor whites. "Material Things and Soul Things" was a critique of materialism. The last area of the curriculum was a study of the movement itself. The section on nonviolence made sure to present it as something beyond a mere refraining from doing anyone physical harm; students were admonished to practice nonviolence of speech and thought as well. The curriculum reflects how far discussion within SNCC had progressed beyond a narrow concern with civil rights. A full analysis of society was embedded in the thinking behind the schools, an analysis that went beyond racial problems and public policy about them. What was actually taught and how it got taught varied from situation to situation. Teachers were encouraged to use a Socratic style of teaching, asking questions that drew on the experiences of students and trying to help them develop a larger perspective. Volunteers who were professional teachers often had more trouble adjusting to the teaching style than did the inexperienced.

At their best the schools were an electric experience for teachers and students alike.

The atmosphere in class is unbelievable. It is what every teacher dreams about—real, honest enthusiasm and desire to learn anything and everything. The girls come to class of their own free will. They respond to everything that is said. They are excited about learning. They drain me of everything that I have to offer. . . .

If reading levels are not always the highest, the "philosophical" understanding is almost alarming: some of the things that our 11 and 12 year olds will come out with would never be expected from someone of that age in the North. . . .

Classes in voter registration work and political play-acting were a success everywhere. With innate sophistication about their own plight, the kids pretended to be a Congressional Committee discussing the pro's and con's of a bill to raise Negro wages and "the con's" would discover neat parliamentary tricks for tabling it. Or they'd act out Senator Stennis and his wife having cocktails with Senator and Mrs. Eastland, all talking about their "uppity niggers." Sometimes they played white cops at the courthouse, clobbering applicants with rolled-up newspapers.[27]

The schools were more successful in rural areas and in those urban areas where the movement had been strong. With so little for youngsters to do in rural areas, the schools became the focal point of teenage social life and an activity in which whole communities felt invested. ("When the Freedom School staff arrived in Carthage, the entire Negro community was assembled at the church to greet them; when, two days later the staff was evicted from its school, the community again appeared with pick up trucks to help move the library to a new school site.") In urban areas with little movement history and alternative ways for young people to spend their time, places like Greenville or Gulfport, it was much more difficult for the schools to have an impact.[28]

There is some suggestive anecdotal evidence about the political effectiveness of the schools. In August, students from around the state held a conference at which they worked on the platform for the youth program of the Mississippi Freedom Democratic Party, and according to one observer "the kids did a fantastic job of it." They developed guidelines for housing and health programs, suggested that repressive school districts be boycotted, and after a particularly bitter debate decided not to endorse a boycott of Cuba. There were other expressions of political consciousness in the fall. In Philadelphia, where Schwerner, Chaney, and Goodman had been killed, students returned to school wearing "ONE MAN, ONE VOTE" buttons. In Issaquena and Sharkey counties, after the principal told them they could not wear their SNCC buttons, students launched a boycott that lasted eight months.

Within the movement, Freedom School work always had relatively low status value, at least for some. In part this was because women did much of the Freedom School work and because it wasn't as dangerous as other work. Voter registration was the prestige assignment. Looking back at the Freedom Schools with the hindsight of the last three decades is disturbing. Of all the models generated by the movement, it seems tragic that this one, an institution specifically attentive to the developmental needs of Black youngsters as a movement issue, was accorded relatively little respect. At the time, though, for young people with a sense of urgency, Freedom Schools seemed a long, slow road. The school in the small Delta town of Shaw, for example, got off to a horrendous start. Discouraged, one volunteer wrote:

> Furthermore [the kids] don't see how we can help them to be free. At this point, neither do we. Slow change is unthinkable when so much change is needed, when there is so much hurt. . . . Things are so terrible here that I want to change it all NOW. I mean this as sincerely as I can. Running a freedom school is an absurd waste of time. I don't want to sit around in a classroom; I want to go out and throw a few office buildings, not to injure people but to shake them up, destroy their stolen property, convince them we mean business. . . . I really can't stand it here.[29]

In part the Freedom School model got lost in the desire to do something bigger, something that would have more impact sooner. This was emblematic of a larger impatience. Just as Negro communities were shedding their fear, some in SNCC-COFO were losing their patience with the pace of change. At least implicit in the thinking behind the community-organizing tradition has been a warning that big, dramatic actions may not produce the most substantial change over the long term. Miss Baker, for example, was not a big fan of demonstrations because she thought the gains they produced often proved short-term. In the politically tumultuous years after 1964, that kind of skepticism seemed to hold less sway in the movement, and that may have something to do with the inattention to the slow processes of helping people develop their powers.[30]

AND PRAY FOR THOSE WHO SPITEFULLY USE YOU

The first essay in James Baldwin's *Fire Next Time* takes the form of a letter of advice to his young nephew. There is, he tells the boy, no reason for you to become like white people

> and there is no basis for their impertinent assumption that *they* must accept *you*. The really terrible thing, old buddy, is that *you* must accept *them*. And I mean that very seriously. You must accept them and accept them with love. For these innocent people have no other hope. They are, in effect, still trapped in a history which they do not understand; and until they understand it, they cannot be released from it.[31]

Much of the literature on Freedom Summer gets part of the story backwards. Every work of any length comments on the racial friction within the movement, and particularly on the hostility volunteers encountered from some of the SNCC-COFO workers. It is frequently discussed and explained at some length; that is, it is treated as an intellectual problematic. The fact that some young Blacks were distrustful of whites is not one of life's great puzzles. Intramovement racial friction is less surprising than the fact that the volunteers were so warmly received by so many of the local residents across the state, especially the older ones and children. The volunteers were generally accepted, and accepted with affection.

Batesville welcomed us triumphantly—at least Black Batesville did. Children and adults waved from the porches and shouted hello as we walked. . . . In a few days, scores of children knew us and called to us by name. . . . I found it difficult to be cynical. Sometimes when we pass by the children cheer. . . .

[From Gulfport:] Fifty times a day people come up to us and thank us and tell us what we're doing is so fine, so good.

[From Greenville:] The Negro community has been so receptive and welcoming. The other night, a woman who has 17 children invited 20 of us over for dinner. It was a good dinner, too.

[From Canton:] When we go walking with [the two] widows [we're staying with] one of them invariably greets each passerby with "Have you seen my girls yet?"

[From Meridian:] There are the old men and women in old clothing whom you know have little money and none to spare, who stop you as you are leaving the church . . . and press a dollar into your hand and say, "I've waited 80 years for you to come and I just have to give you this little bit to let you know how much we appreciate your coming. I prays for your safety every night, son. God bless you all." And then they move down the stone steps and disappear along the red clay road lined with tall green trees and houses tumbling down.

[From Gulfport:] Time and time again we go into a restaurant or bar, we start to pay, only to be told that the bill has been taken care of. People bring over a dozen eggs or cake or invite us to dinner.

[From Hattiesburg:] Sometimes I think that all the decency the Mississippi human contains is encased in black walls. They're slow and talkative, but they'd shake hands with a mule if it came up to speak to them; if they had one cigarette left, they'd offer to halve it with you before they'd smoke it in front of your face. All this from people to whom $20 is a fortune.[32]

In southern tradition, many of the volunteers were "adopted" by the families to whom they were closest, and some of these relationships lasted years after the volunteers had left the South. Why were so many local residents willing to accept the volunteers at face value, substantially more willing to do so than young adults in the Black community? After all, the older people had suffered a good deal more at white hands than had their children. In other historical circumstances, even leaving aside the particular nature of racial oppression, we would expect an older, rural population with minimal education to be a group prone to prejudicial feelings. It certainly wasn't the case that the volunteers were entirely free of ugly racial feelings themselves; some of them could be patronizing, some thought themselves the great white saviors and communicated that, some were indifferent to local mores concerning sexual and religious behavior, some were by local standards not particularly mannerly.

Perhaps the older people were just more practical than the younger ones. They had seen more of Mississippi racism at its worst, and they were grateful for help wherever it came from. Given the history they had lived through, they had pretty low expectations of white people, and by those standards the volunteers looked pretty good. There is probably some truth to this, but pragmatism doesn't necessarily explain the affection and love so often extended to the volunteers. Being grateful to people is one thing; accepting them with affection is another. Their acceptance was in the spirit of nonviolence, but that is not a plausible explanation. Nonviolence as an ideology never penetrated that deeply into the older Deep South rural population. The one thing that is certain is that some of the willingness to accept white volunteers at face value can be attributed to a kind of worshipful servility that still existed among some of the older people. White would always be right for them. They thought so much of the white volunteers because they thought so little of themselves. It was for this reason that some COFO workers found the ready acceptance of whites offensive.

None of this, though, offers a very complete explanation. The volunteers were interacting largely with the strongest, most self-regarding individuals in the community. Susie Morgan and Lula Belle Johnson and Dewey Greene were proud people, capable of being quite critical of whites as a whole and critical of some of the behavior of the volunteers as well. Whatever they thought of whites as a category, whatever flaws they saw in the volunteers, they were still willing to accept them into their hearts and families. Their ability to do so is certainly in part a reflection of how Black southerners saw God. In a conversation with me, Lou Emma Allen, after recounting some of what she had suffered from whites while growing up, ended the discussion by saying she still couldn't hate whites: "Of course, there is no way I can hate anybody and hope to see God's face."

Mrs. Hamer used to say that as well. During the beating at Winona, before Mrs. Hamer was taken out of her cell for her beating, she could hear the beating being administered to Annell Ponder—the blows falling, Miss Ponder screaming, the demands from the officers that Miss Ponder call them "sir" and her refusal to do so. Then she could hear Miss Ponder start to pray. "But anyway, she kept screamin', and they kept beating on her, and finally she started prayin' for 'em, and she asked God to have mercy on 'em, because they didn't know what they was doin'."[33] Shortly after, Mrs. Hamer was beaten herself and then returned to her cell. She could tell when the jailer and the other men went out for something; the jailer's wife and the jailer's daughter would bring them cold water and ice.

> And I told them, "Y'all is nice. You must be Christian people." The jailer's wife told me she tried to live a Christian life. And I told her I would like for her to read two scriptures in the Bible, and I tol' her to read the 26th Chapter of Proverbs and the 26th Verse ["Whose hatred is covered by deceit, his wickedness shall be showed before the whole congregation"]. She taken it down on a paper. And then I told her to read the [17th] Chapter of Acts and the 26th Verse ["Hath made of one blood all nations of men for to dwell on all the face of the earth"]. And she taken that down. And she never did come back after then.[34]

Annell Ponder always understood evils like those she had endured as "examples of man's separation from God and from his own truest self." It followed that people like the ones who beat her weren't hopeless, but they did, in her words, "need training and rehabilitation."[35]

If there was a specifically Christian tradition of southern Black humanism, there were secular forces reinforcing it. The structure of racial interaction in the old South taught some Blacks how superficial racial differences were. On the one hand, the traditional system was designed to convince them of their inferiority, and the sheer weight of it necessarily defeated a great many people psychologically. When a man with Amzie Moore's strength of character says that he was once convinced that the inferiority of Blacks was ordained by God, that is testimony to the power of the system. Still, no system crushes everyone. For many older Blacks, the system also meant living much of their lives in constant and complex daily contact with whites. They saw white people under every conceivable circumstance, and they were able to see them change over time, to see weaknesses as well as strengths. That density of contact would have allowed, in Baldwin's terms, some of them to understand whites as trapped in their own history.

Consider the complexity of Aaron Henry's relations with white people. Henry once ordered by mail a copy of *Black Monday,* the famous racist tract of the Citizens' Council. Late one evening, the book was hand-delivered to him by Robert Patterson, founder of the council. Patterson was afraid that a mailed copy might fall into the wrong hands, and some of Henry's people might misunderstand why Henry would be reading Council literature. It was the same "Tut" Patterson who as a youngster had been Henry's best friend growing up in Clarksdale. Apparently, enough of the memory of that friendship survived that the head of the Council cared a little about the reputation of the head of the NAACP. Myrlie Evers, who tells that story, says there is nothing unusual about it; one could find similar stories in small towns across the south.[36]

If, as was suggested earlier, Henry seemed to have an especially acute sense of white folks, perhaps it was because his early life could provide the material for a textbook on the complexities of interracial relations in the Delta. Part of his education came when he worked as night clerk at a Clarksdale motor inn. "I saw white people do things that I had been told were done only by Negroes, I heard prominent white men who stood staunchly with the system tell me to stand up and be a man, although I'm sure their advice did not mean for me to consider myself their equal."[37] The owner of the motel encouraged him to go to college and helped him learn to do simultaneous equa-

Mileston Plantation School in Holmes County, November 1939. In the 1960s, Mileston, with an unusually large number of landowning Blacks, became an important center of movement activity. (Marion Post, Farm Security Administration, Library of Congress)

Above: Sharecropper who had been evicted for trying to organize other tenants into a union in Hillhouse, Miss., June 1936. (Dorothea Lange, Farm Security Administration, Library of Congress)

Opposite, top: Dice game on the Marcella Plantation, October 1939. (Marion Post, Farm Security Administration, Library of Congress)

Opposite, bottom: Juke joint in Clarksdale, November 1939. Aaron Henry grew up in the Clarksdale area. (Marion Post, Farm Security Administration, Library of Congress)

Two generations of activists: Bob Moses, Julian Bond, Curtis Hayes, unidentified man, Hollis Watkins, Amzie Moore, and E. W. Steptoe. (Courtesy of Mary Lee Moore-Chatman)

Ella Baker in workshop at the Highlander Center. (Courtesy of
Highlander Research and Education Center)

Esau Jenkins and Myles Horton in front room of Citizenship
School, 1959. The front room had been set up as a grocery to hide
the voter-registration activities going on in the back. (Courtesy of
Ida Berman)

Citizenship School on Johns Island, with Alice Wine (*second from left*), Septima Clark (*center*), and Bernice Robinson (*standing*), 1959. Robinson had to be convinced that she could teach. (Courtesy of Ida Berman)

June Johnson at mass meeting, probably 1963 or 1964. (Danny
Lyon/Magnum)

Above: Lou Emma Allen.
(Courtesy of Lou Emma
Allen)

Left: Mary Boothe. (Courtesy
of Mary Boothe)

Right: James Moore.
(Courtesy of James Moore)

Below: Susie Morgan, with her daughter Arance Williamson, who started working in the movement in 1962 and was elected to the Greenwood City Council in 1993. (Courtesy of Arance Williamson)

Greenwood police trying to turn demonstration. (Charles Moore,
Blackstar)

Mass meeting in Greenwood, March or April 1963.
(*New York Times*)

Herbert Lee. SNCC's initial organizing
campaign in Mississippi led to Lee's
murder in September 1961. (Courtesy of
Herbert Lee, Jr.)

Fannie Lou Hamer. (Library of Congress)

Aaron Henry, chair of the Mississippi Freedom Democratic Party delegation, speaking at the 1964 Democratic National Convention, August 1964. (Library of Congress)

Bob Moses talking to Mr. Cleve Jordan. (*New York Times*)

Annell Ponder came to Greenwood to work with Citizenship Schools. (*New York Times*)

Hollis Watkins working with Freedom Summer
volunteers, Oxford, Ohio, June 1964. (Steve Schapiro,
Blackstar)

Bob Moses, Sam Block, and (*far right*) Willie Peacock at Amzie
Moore's house. (Lyon/Magnum)

Jimmy Travis, who was ambushed and shot just outside
of Greenwood. (Danny Lyon/Magnum)

Stokely Carmichael, Charlie Cobb, and George Greene at Atlanta demonstration, December 1963. (Danny Lyon/Magnum)

Medgar Evers. (Library of Congress)

Funeral procession for Medgar Evers. Dick Gregory: "It looked like we had enough folks to march on God that day." (Charles Moore, Blackstar)

Youths challenging police after Medgar Evers's funeral.
(UPI/Bettmann)

tions, in itself an enormous breech of the racial norms, yet the owner himself was a firm believer in the existing racial system. On the other hand, some white men thought it so insulting to have to hand their money to a nigger clerk that they refused to do it; others took personal pleasure in publicly degrading Henry in front of their friends. He found that the very poorest whites, contrary to their redneck image, were often willing to get along with Blacks. When he returned home from the service, the registrar refused three times to let him register. He was able to get a white veteran to help him register. His first business partner was white, and the two of them always maintained a generally egalitarian relationship, with his partner willing to stick out his neck a little in Henry's defense when Henry was accused of being a communist. Henry knew white people who pretended to be friendly to Blacks because it was good business and others who acted more racist than they felt because they were in situations where that was expedient. Aaron Henry had seen white people from a variety of angles; he had seem them change for the better and for the worse. It is not a background that easily lends itself to thinking that race, in and of itself, is determinative. The rich, complex experience with whites that Henry had is very much a generational experience. With each succeeding cohort, urbanization, the changes in the structure of work, the increasing tendency of younger Blacks to keep white contacts to a minimum, meant that fewer Blacks had the complexity of interracial experience Henry had been exposed to.

In the evolution of African American culture, the most influential form of sustained and complex interaction with whites may have involved black women domestic workers. Few jobs offer such potential for personal humiliation and sexual abuse, few are so obviously exploitative. On the other hand, the sheer frequency of contact meant that domestics acquired enormous amounts of information about their families. They knew far more about their white folks than the white folks could ever know about themselves. It is also true that reciprocal affective ties sometimes developed between domestics and their families (if hardly with the frequency and depth southern whites liked to assume). Domestics were in the position that Patricia Hill Collins calls "outsider-within," forced to see the world from two very different social perspectives.[38] As with any form of social marginality, we may be sure that some of the women thrust into such a position found it disorienting and confusing, but it is equally sure that many others were able to use their position to develop a profound understanding of race and social behavior.

One of the people sociologist Robert Blauner interviewed for his study of American racial attitudes was Florence Grier, a Black woman who began doing domestic work at the age of eleven during the Depression. Even at that age the experience quickly demystified white people for her:

> It didn't take me very long to learn that there was *nobody* . . . better than Negroes. As a girl, I'd walk into [white people's] homes, and they didn't know how to cook, they didn't know how to talk, they were more stupid than I. And it just didn't take me very long to find out that the only difference in this particular woman and myself was that she was white—and that she had the opportunity to live on the other side of town—and she could have access to better jobs.

The work gave her a perspective on class nuances among whites. Once upper-class women knew you were qualified, they would give you your instructions and leave you alone. Women who had just clawed their way into the middle class were all wrapped up in their possessions, so they watched everything the maid did with them. Poor whites were the worst, keeping their foot on your neck all the time, always reminding you that they were your betters.

Florence Grier helped to raise many a white child, which gave her a perspective on how racial contempt was systematically nurtured:

> I've seen youngsters that I've taken care of until they got three or four years old, I've seen the youngster gradually withdraw. . . . He would be just as sweet as he wanted to be when I came in the back door, but then when I went to town that would be a different little boy! Now this little boy had been sitting in my lap, this little boy had been sleeping in my bed . . . but when we would get to town

he would have to change his whole attitude. And this is the way that they teach these youngsters prejudice and selfishness. He learns by the time he is five years old that "Florence is a nigger."[39]

Florence Grier was not altogether powerless. If white people were using her, she took "a kind of pleasure" in manipulating them. With the men, this was sometimes a matter of playing off their sexual desires. "[A] man is a man. And I [*wry laugh*] really haven't found any difference in 'em. Only that the white man will want an undercover situation. It's not to be talked about or anything." White men had a complete repertoire of tactics for trying to maneuver Black maids into a sexual situation—"Wouldn't you like to make your check a little bigger?" "What do you think about white men?" Race made only a superficial difference: "A colored man would do the same things. I honestly don't see any difference other than the color of the man's skin." In her experience, men either had moral principles or they didn't.

As with Aaron Henry, Florence Grier's intense and varied experiences with whites helped her to develop early in life a sophisticated understanding of how her world worked and how race fit in. She understood so much that it almost hurt.

> When I was a girl I would always say to God, "I don't want to know this much." Because if you know so much and you can't do anything about it, it's very, very hard for you. It's better to not understand.

She finished high school, and in the 1940s moved to California. In the late 1960s, she became increasingly involved in community activities, especially in monitoring police behavior and protesting police brutality, work she found so frustrating that she came to appreciate

> the Black Panther route. And that's killing, isn't it? . . . I'm going to be frank with you, because I'm frustrated now! But if we can't get this white man to think no other way—and I'm a mother—if we

can't get him to see any other way—kill some policemen, the way they're killing us.

Thinking that some whites need killing does not mean that one hates them:

> I don't hate . . . the white man. Something inside of me under-stands that he was taught that. And I have a real deep smirk of, some sense of satisfaction—it might be self-righteousness—but I have a real good feeling that I love him—and I feel bigger than he is. You can't make me hate *every* white man! Even though I'd kill a policeman! . . . And I feel that by them beating us and doing all the ugly things that they did to us, we've had an experience of learning what it really feels to have empathy with people.[40]

At one level, there is something inconsistent about Medgar Evers contemplating guerrilla warfare against whites in the Delta and simul-taneously believing that if he can talk to hate callers long enough, he might be able to change them. The inconsistency is only apparent, a function of the breadth of social vision some southern Blacks devel-oped. They could, like Malcolm X, contemplate the broadest range of oppositional tactics, but like Martin Luther King, they never lost a larger sense of a common humanity. It is a dialectical world view, sen-sitive to how contradictions in social structure shape contradictions in people, and also sensitive to people as at least potentially changing and evolving.

If humanism is belief in the essential oneness of humankind, then one traditional strand of southern Black culture was a visceral human-ism, a dearly bought, broad perspective on human behavior that mili-tated against thinking about people in one-dimensional terms. CORE's Matt Suarez stressed that one of the contributions southern Blacks made to the movement had to do with their diplomatic skills, skills that allowed them to get along with people from a wide range of social backgrounds and helped those people get along with one another. They served as buffer and link between, say, youngsters who were beginning to question every social form they could think of and preachers who thought dancing was a dark sin. If part of the movement's dynamism was its ability to accept the contributions of people from diverse backgrounds, part of the reason it was able to do so had to do with the fact that at the movement's core were many people who saw people pretty much as people, despite whatever baggage and blind spots they brought with them.

If praying for those who spitefully use you is one tradition of the Black South, damning their nasty souls to hell is another, with roots that are easy to understand. Some of the older adults who were at the movement's core, however, had woven from their faith and their collective experiences with whites a broader vision, one that helped the movement maintain its humane spirit so long as they were a part of it.

The period from the summer of 1963 to the fall of 1964 was a time of transitions on many levels. Nationally, the movement had won the Civil Rights Act of 1964, a major legislative and psychological victory. The federal government was moving in the direction of more visible and aggressive protection of civil rights workers. The summer of 1964 had exposed the worst state in the South to the scrutiny of the entire nation. Still, the victories, in some senses, may have come too late and at too great a price. The end of the period was characterized by disillusionment and confusion. In that mood, it may have been difficult for some of the actors to see what the community-organizing tradition had accomplished.

SNCC-COFO members were seriously questioning the extent to which liberal America in general and the federal government in particular could be thought of as allies. Having achieved a degree of local organization that seemed improbable a few months earlier, SNCC, after 1964, began to put more of its energies into other issues and priorities. They did not immediately abandon the philosophy and practice of the community-organizing approach—witness the work spearheaded by Stokely Carmichael in Lowndes County, Alabama, in 1965 and the election of several grassroots Mississippians to the SNCC executive committee the same year. Nonetheless, after 1964, in Mississippi, SNCC-COFO workers, including some of those born in the state, began leaving the rural communities, drifting back to the cities. At just the historical moment when all the pieces seemed to be in place, other issues pushed community organizing to the side.

White Mississippi in the fall of 1964 looked unchanged, but only at first glance. The monolithic structure of white supremacy was in fact cracking. White Citizens' Councils were beginning to lose influence. The state was purging klan members from the highway patrol (or, in other cases, retaining them provided they brought in a note from their local klavern releasing them from klan vows). The state seemed to be making some good-faith efforts to investigate bombings and arsons. In November, the *New York Times* noted that in McComb, tough McComb, more than six hundred fifty white citizens signed a petition calling for an end to racial violence and to harassment of civil rights workers by law enforcement officials. If that could happen in bloody McComb, the state really was changing.[41]

The transformation that mattered most was the transformation in the local people themselves. At the beginning of the summer of 1963, open defiance by significant numbers of rural Blacks was a new phenomenon. White terrorism was still a potent weapon, its existence conditioning every step the movement took. By the end of the summer of 1964, defiance of white supremacy had been institutionalized. It was going to continue, reprisals notwithstanding. Wedded to the weapons they knew best, white supremacists continued to employ terrorism as a weapon for several more years (see Chapter 14), but it was no longer a determinative factor. Largely unembittered, with the confidence of people who have faced and passed a great test, local people in Greenwood and elsewhere increasingly took on the work of leading the movement.

Eleven

CARRYING ON

The Politics of Empowerment

I want to tell you about Mrs. Hazel Palmer, who is a lady who works with the Freedom Democratic Party in Mississippi. She was working for ten, fifteen dollars a week as a maid most of her life. She stopped and changed last summer. And if you want to write her, and I suggest you do—a lot of you—drop her a line. . . . Ask her, "What did you use to do? What do you do now? How come you changed? What gave you the courage to do that? What makes you think that instead of being a cook in somebody's kitchen you could help run a political party? Where did you go to learn how to do that? Did you go to school?"

BOB MOSES
1965

SNCC demonstrated the possibility of taking uninitiated people and working with them to the point that they began to understand where their interest really was and the relationship to their own capacity to do something about it.

ELLA BAKER[1]

SNCC is the best school there ever was.

JUNE JOHNSON

IT IS POPULAR NOWADAYS to count the number of Black elected officials in Mississippi—690 in 1991, second only to Alabama—and use that as a yardstick of progress, as a measure of what the movement of the sixties ultimately wrought.[2] Who in 1962 thought that Jesse Jackson would carry the state in the 1988 presidential primaries? (Hollis Watkins and Willie Peacock both worked for Jackson in that campaign, by the way.)

Counting politicians is not the best way to assess the work of SNCC-COFO. For many early SNCC members the proper measure of their labor would not be the number of Black officeholders, nor the influence they had on national policy, nor the number of local institutions they desegregated, nor the number of people they registered. At a conference in 1979, Bob Moses noted with pride that there were still counties in Mississippi where the Freedom Democratic Party was meeting. Hollis Watkins recalls hurrying up to a church where he was supposed to be leading a mass meeting and hearing the freedom songs come out of the building. The people hadn't felt they had to wait for him to start the meeting. That for him was a moment of accomplishment. Charles Sherrod of SNCC's Southwest Georgia Project said, "Our criterion for success is not how many people we register but how many we can get to begin initiating decisions solely on the basis of their personal opinion."[3]

For many in SNCC the proper measure of their work is the extent to which the people they helped bring into political activity became leaders themselves. In Greenwood, more than in some other SNCC projects, that happened to a considerable degree. Through the NAACP, the Freedom Democratic Party, the Child Development Group of Mississippi, the Greenwood Voters League, and the Greenwood Movement, local people carried on the struggle even as the direct influence of SNCC was waning.

One of those who continued the struggle was James Moore, a relative of the McGhee clan. In 1962, Moore, a native of Greenwood, was living in Chicago. He moved back to Greenwood that year, partly because he was intrigued by the movement. Once there he put off talking to Sam Block and the others, always planning to get around to it. His involvement was triggered in the spring of 1963 when Block and Peacock and two local residents were fired on from a passing station wagon. Moore was a witness to the shooting. "The FBI was running around trying to find people that they thought might have seen something. I went down and volunteered to give the little information that I had." From that point on, Moore would be fully involved with the movement. His father, who worked for the city, was told to get his son out of "that mess" or else. Instead, Moore's father just retired. The city refused to give him his retirement pay until he sued them.

In April 1963, Moore was part of the group that reactivated the NAACP. Some of the adults felt that SNCC was so much oriented to young people that the adults needed an organization that was more oriented to them, an organization that could provide legal help when needed. They got fifty members, the minimum needed for a branch, very quickly, perhaps in a month. Dewey Greene was involved, and so were Reverend Aaron Johnson, Reverend Redd, W. J. Bishop and Ed Cochrane. The one schoolteacher who was involved, Andrew Jordan, Cleve Jordan's son, was soon fired.

Medgar Evers helped the group get a new charter from the national office. Moore thought very highly of Medgar: "He was always here. If we called in the middle of the night he was here. Whatever the situation, he was always here." After Medgar's death, the branch worked with his brother Charles, which Moore found to be a very different experience. According to Moore, Charles Evers was always trying to interfere in the operations of the local branch and always uncomfortable with its militance. Unlike Medgar, Charles seemed to think like the people in the national office.

Some of the local chapter's militance was displayed in connection with the 1964 Civil Rights Act. The McGhees were not the only people in Greenwood who realized that just the passage of the law wouldn't mean much unless people were willing to force the issue at the local level. Near the end of the summer, the NAACP formed a testing committee, with Silas McGhee as the chair and Jake McGhee as assistant chair. The committee, six or seven strong, would go up one side of Howard Street, the main business street, and down the other, testing each business in turn. In the beginning, they were consistently refused service, they were ignored, had hot coffee thrown on them, and were attacked by mobs. One of the wealthiest white businessmen in town was supposed to have told other businessmen that the fine for refusing to serve Blacks was only five hundred dollars, and he would pay it for any business that needed it. When they heard that, the testing team doubled its activity, trying to make sure there were a lot of five-hundred-dollar fines to pay. In some cases, they made it virtually impossible for merchants to conduct their normal business. They would go to the Holiday Inn, for example, just before noon and take up all the seats. They didn't get served, but no whites could be served either. The Inn came around after a month or so of that. While all of this was going on, the national office of the NAACP repeatedly expressed its displeasure with the testing activity, and the Greenwood chapter just ignored it.

By the end of a year, most businesses were at least trying to look like they were complying with the law, though there were still holdouts. Some converted into private clubs, including the Krystal Klub, the restaurant Silas had intended to integrate on his first foray into town. Traveler's Inn announced that its accommodations were henceforth available only to those holding memberships. Lusco's, an exclusive restaurant, would serve Blacks but at prices that started at five dollars for a cup of coffee. As the testing teams were able to bring more and more legal and financial pressure to bear, the holdouts either went out of business or decided to conform, more or less, to the law. Businesspeople were between the hard place and the rock. If they did desegregate, they might face retribution from other whites. One movie theater that desegregated was hit with a boycott, led by the son of Byron de la Beckwith, and had to go out of business.

White Greenwood's reaction to the 1964 Public Accommodations Act was repeated across the Deep South. The mere passage of a law in far-away Washington did not immediately lead to any dramatic changes in local mores. It did, though, give local activists a new weapon, and they used it to wage a restaurant-by-restaurant, bowling-alley-by-bowling-alley campaign against segregation. They did this without any significant direction from local SNCC-COFO people. Although SNCC was supportive, testing public accommodations was not high on its agenda. Local people, many of whom had become active because of COFO, put it on the agenda.

During the spring of 1964, after futile attempts to get local branches of the state Democratic party to accept Black participation, SNCC organized the Mississippi Freedom Democratic Party as a vehicle for the political expression of Mississippi Blacks. Lawrence Guyot was state chairman, and Ella Baker gave the keynote address at the founding conference. Miss Baker talked about the way the rest of the country had tacitly supported white supremacy in Mississippi: "At no point were the southern states denied their representation on the basis of the fact that they had denied other people the right to participate in the election of those who govern them." She warned the delegates that when they were able to elect their own representatives, that wouldn't be the end of their troubles; elected representatives had to be watched: "Now this is not the kind of keynote speech, perhaps, you like. But I'm not trying to make you feel good." She urged them to spend less time watching television and more time reading about political and social issues; uninformed people cannot participate in a democracy. She reminded them that young people want some meaning in their lives, and they weren't going to get it from owning big cars and having a place in the power structure. Echoing the theme of the summer project, she said, "Until the killing of Black mothers' sons is as important as the killing of white mothers' sons, we must keep on." The delegates, one journalist observed, gave "Miss Baker, the party, themselves a traditional placard-waving march, the first in American political history that stepped off to the tune 'Go Tell It On the Mountain' and 'This Little Light of Mine, Boys, I'm Gonna Let It Shine.'"[4]

In November 1964, MFDP organized another statewide mock election, at which Victoria Gray and Mrs. Hamer were elected congresspersons. For much of the next year, most of the organization's effort went into challenging the seating of the five persons elected from Mississippi to the U.S. House of Representatives, again on the grounds that nearly half of the state's electorate had been prevented from participating in their election. At one point, FDP had a respectable 149 votes for its position, but both the House leadership, much of it southern, and the White House were appalled at the idea. The issue was repeatedly stalled in committee. At the same time, both the Congress and the national Democratic party indicated that in the future they would not tolerate discrimination in the selection either of members of Congress or of delegates to the national convention. Mississippi politicians were alarmed enough to send letters to the state's local enforcement agents and registrars, asking for a halt in violence related to registration efforts (sentiments echoed by Governor Paul Johnson "at least for the next six months.") For the first time in seventy-five years, Mississippi Negroes began receiving routine communications from their putative congressional representatives.[5] All of a sudden, they were constituents. The challenge failed, but it gave Mississippi's political establishment further evidence that it would have to restructure itself and gave the leadership of FDP and others close to the movement further evidence that Mississippi's racism was predicated on the tolerance of forces outside the state, including forces once thought of as movement allies.

The formation of the Leflore County FDP reflected a good deal of continuity with earlier cohorts of activists. The first county convention was held July 27, 1964 at a Baptist church, interestingly enough. SNCC workers, including Bob Zellner, Stokely Carmichael, and Eli Zaretsky, opened the meeting, but after explaining the FDP idea they pretty much turned the meetings over to the delegates, most of whom had already gone through smaller workshops about FDP. There were forty-seven delegates at the meeting, representing the five precincts of the county, and one hundred fifty observers. Rural areas were underrepresented because of the dangers of working there, but fifteen of the delegates came from rural communities or plantations. The Reverend Aaron Johnson was the unanimous selection for chair, and Mary Lane was elected secretary. Of the sixteen people selected as delegates or alternates to the district convention, at least five had been Citizenship School teachers, including Mary Diggs, Alice Blackwell, Laura McGhee, Ethel Brady, and Pinkie Pilcher, who had been a supervisor of teachers for the schools. Most of the others came from among those who had supported SNCC in 1962 and 1963, including Alma Henderson, Dewey Greene's daughter; Lula Belle Johnson; Eddye Lane; the Reverend Johnson; Will McGee; and Cleveland Jordan, who garnered more votes than anybody. The resolutions they passed reflected movement concerns as well as more traditional bread-and-butter political issues. They asked for more federal protection, for the removal of Byron de la Beckwith from his position as auxiliary policeman, for better housing, for school crossing guards, better street lighting, and garbage disposal.[6] Later, Jake McGhee became the county chairman, James Moore the secretary, and Susie Morgan, Lou Emma Allen, and Dewey Greene all became very active members.

Both at the state level and locally, friction frequently developed between SNCC and the organization it had created. Moore thought it was partly a matter of jealousy, of who should get credit for what: "Some workers in Snick didn't particularly like FDP and they'd try to show FDP up. . . . Snick wanted to get all the credit." Moore may be right, but some of the friction was also due to squabbling over which organization was going to get what part of the scarce available resources, and some to ideological disagreements. In the fall of 1964, FDP members generally supported Lyndon Johnson; by that time, many SNCC members felt he had betrayed the movement. What is important here about the disagreements is that they show that FDP was in fact a substantially independent entity, just what SNCC said it was going to create, even though some SNCC workers, faced with the reality, weren't always satisfied with the result.

The local FDP engaged in some tactics that SNCC was not particularly known for, including boycotts, which became the focal point of movement activity in Greenwood in the middle and late sixties. White merchants were still hiring Blacks only as porters, laborers, window washers, and the like. Significantly, by the middle sixties, merchants were less likely, in their discussions with movement representatives, to take a blunt racist stand. Rather, some of them argued that if they hired Blacks for non-laboring jobs, they would lose all of their white customers or, in the tradition of doublethink, they argued that they would hire Blacks if they could find any with experience. Many merchants still refused to use courtesy titles—Mr., Miss, or Mrs.—when addressing Blacks; most still served white customers first. FDP initiated a series of boycotts around these issues.

One of the first targets was a large food store called Liberty Cash. James Moore went around to the social clubs, the churches, the Elks, the veterans' organization, asking each to designate a member to serve as liaison to the boycott. Methodist ministers openly supported the boycott; Baptists generally did not. At first, white businessmen openly scoffed at the idea of a boycott. When Moore first told the owner of Liberty Cash that there would be a boycott if the store did not begin offering better jobs to Blacks, the owner replied "You can't run these niggers away from me; they love me." That was not altogether false. When the boycott did start, Moore had plenty of Black people tell him things like "I wish that white man would come out here and break your damn neck. What business you got trying to ruin his business? You can't tell me where to spend my money." On one occasion Moore had to punch one of the store's black employees, who, trying to stand up for his boss, threatened Moore. Many poor Blacks had credit accounts at the store and were reluctant to let them go. Others, especially some of the older people, really did believe that the white store owner had always treated them right. Others just didn't believe it was possible to put a white man out of business. As things turned out, the boycott did put the store out of business. The next owner was more willing to cooperate with FDP's demands.

A second boycott against a larger number of downtown businesses was not very effective, for reasons that are not clear. By November 1965, FDP agitation had led to the hiring of three Negro crossing guards at the elementary school and the installation of sidewalks at the high school. In December, FDP launched a Black Easter boycott against downtown merchants. A few weeks into the boycott, James Moore bragged, "Last Saturday, you could see from one end of the downtown area to the other, the street was so empty." By the beginning of 1966, the first two Black students had integrated Greenwood Junior High, and there were five in the senior high. By that fall, though, the movement seemed in something of a lull. There were only two full-time workers in town, and one of them thought the glamor was gone and "the shadow of fear" was returning, but there were still some mass meetings and the boycott was holding well.[7]

In the fall of 1967, Moore and other boycott leaders found an important new ally in Father Nathaniel Machesky. Father Machesky, a white priest, was in charge of Saint Francis, the local Black Catholic church. Just before he and Moore talked, Father Machesky had tried unsuccessfully to talk the mayor into meeting some of the demands of the Black community. Moore and Machesky decided to launch another boycott. Since some people had problems with the fact that the earlier boycott was sponsored by FDP, the name was eventually changed to the Greenwood Movement.[8] Merchants were the direct target of the boycott, but city hall was an indirect target. The leaders of the Greenwood Movement believed that if they put enough pressure on the local merchants, the merchants in turn would pressure the local government.

The movement lasted with varying degrees of effectiveness for a year and a half. During most of that time, it was chaired by a triumvirate of Father Machesky, the Reverend William Wallace, a Colored Methodist Episcopal minister who had moved to town in late 1964, and M. J. Black, an AME minister. They went back to the old practice of holding regular mass meetings, sometimes as often as three times a week. They made use of the highly efficient block-captain system that the NAACP and FDP had set up earlier and a system of telephone trees. In a pinch, they could organize a mass meeting in a couple of hours. One of the block captains was Susie Morgan, who with her two daughters and a niece could cover just about her whole side of town. Another was Lula Belle Johnson. So many of the other captains were drawn from among Citizenship School teachers that there weren't enough people left to teach classes.[9] Previously, the Catholics had had an on-again, off-again relationship with the movement, but they became deeply involved in the boycott. The movement was administered from the offices of the Saint Francis Center, the church's community-outreach arm. Nuns from the Center were very active on the picket line. Mary Boothe, a parishioner at Saint Francis and the young woman who in 1963 had been stationed by SNCC every day at the registrar's office, eventually became the director of the Greenwood Movement.

There was not a great deal of violence or harassment from the police. Occasionally, a store owner might sit in his window with a shotgun, or leaders might receive threatening phone calls, and the McGhee home was firebombed at least once during the period, but it was nothing like the situation of 1962 or 1963, a change the Reverend Wallace attributed to SNCC's earlier work "because through the troubles that Snick had, the brutality that they faced, we didn't have to face."[10] Instead of violence, whites tried to out-maneuver the movement legally. They were successful in obtaining a court order against picketing within three hundred feet of any store. Jake McGhee violated the order repeatedly and got arrested repeatedly.

The assassination of Martin Luther King in April 1968 gave the Greenwood Movement a boost. The day after the assassination, six or seven hundred students poured out of the high school, determined to have a protest march downtown. They passed by the Reverend Aaron Johnson's barbershop. As soon as he saw them, he locked up the shop and managed to get the crowd to stop. He made an impromptu speech, saying that he was not against demonstrating—no one could challenge him on that—but the downtown area was crawling with local police and highway patrolmen, and they were liable to hurt someone. It made more sense to take some time to think about what their demands were going to be, how they were going to organize themselves, and then have an orderly march.

Some of the kids didn't want to listen, but the Reverend Johnson managed to get most of them to crowd into the Reverend Wallace's church. Johnson and Father Machesky went downtown and got an instant march permit. Mayor Sampson appeared frightened by the thought of what an unorganized march could lead to. They held the march that same afternoon, with no one on the street except National Guard units. Subsequently, the leaders of the Greenwood Movement were able to turn some of the anger and energy generated by King's death into a higher level of support for the boycott. The Greenwood Movement eventually became an SCLC affiliate.

At its strongest, the boycott may have been close to ninety percent effective. Some rural people who hadn't gotten the word might come into town, but once they knew about the boycott, they were even more supportive than people in Greenwood, according to the Reverend Wallace. Some of the city folk would get store owners to let them in during hours when the stores were normally closed. Others called their orders in and had them delivered.

The most recalcitrant might be visited by Spirit. Spirit was organized by a young man who had moved to Greenwood from Hattiesburg, where he had worked in boycotts. People who repeatedly violated the boycott might find that when they hung laundry out to dry, somehow it got thrown onto the ground when they weren't looking. When they walked down the street with bags of groceries, someone might bump into them, spilling the groceries. People might have a brick thrown through their windshields. Spirit, a small secret group, was never approved by the official boycott leaders, but at least one member of the board of directors knew about it and did not strongly disapprove. So far as I know, Spirit represented the first time local activists took any form of reprisals against non-activist neighbors.

Supporting the movement put Father Machesky in an awkward position with local whites. In 1966, for example, he bailed Stokely Carmichael out of jail—ironically, Carmichael gave his first "Black Power" speech as soon as he got out—and was particularly vilified for that. The effectiveness of the boycott further aggravated the problem, the more so since many of the whites being boycotted were Catholic. At one point, one hundred thirty white Catholics signed a petition asking that Machesky never again be allowed to set foot in Greenwood's white Catholic church. There were whites who privately expressed their sympathy for the boycotts to Father Machesky, but that was as far as they were willing to go. The Saint Francis Center, from which the movement was being run, was shot up by nightriders several times and firebombed once.

The poorer white store owners were the first to begin negotiating with the Greenwood Movement. By early 1969, others were beginning to come around. Finally, the head of the Chamber of Commerce hired a Black sales clerk in the drug store he managed, just to see if it could be done, as he explained it. According to James Moore, when a woman known to be active in the Ku Klux Klan came in and didn't bat an eye at the presence of a Black clerk, the store manager knew that Greenwood was ready. Other store owners followed suit. The city, pressured by the boycott as well as by lawsuits filed by the various civil rights groups, began hiring Blacks, paving streets in Black neighborhoods, putting up street lights, and so forth. It was hardly the millennium; whites continued to employ a variety of strategies to hold on to power, but by the end of the decade raw white supremacy was going out of style. It would have been difficult—but not impossible—to find a local politician still willing to say publicly that he couldn't think of anything to meet with niggers about. Charles Sampson, the mayor who had made that remark, was voted out of office in 1969.

Most Greenwood activists feel strongly that the immediate cause of real change, change that they could feel in their daily lives, came in response to economic pressure. It is a point worth noting, because most histories of the movement, with the exception of Aldon Morris's, pay little attention to economic pressure, stressing a more normative interpretation—change coming as the result of new laws and a changing national social climate. It did not always appear that way to those most immediately involved in the Deep South.

We should note, too, that the fruits of the struggle were not necessarily distributed evenly. When new jobs did begin to open up, some employers made a conscious effort not to hire people who had been actively a part of the movement. If they had to hire Blacks, at least they could hire "safe" ones.

A rejuvenated NAACP, MFDP, and the Greenwood Movement were not the only organizational offspring of SNCC-COFO. Before he left town in 1965, Sam Block helped organize the Greenwood Voters League, seeing it as a forum in which poor Blacks could discuss candidates and issues. He recruited David Jordan, another son of Cleve Jordan to help him organize it. Block, according to James Moore, specifically wanted a schoolteacher like David Jordan to be involved with the organization. It could not have hurt that while David had not himself been previously involved with the movement, he came from one of the town's most visible and vocal activist families. The Voters League outlived many of the other organizations and by the 1990s had grown into one of the most visible and influential Black organizations in the Delta.

The Child Development Group of Mississippi (CDGM), another organization that grew indirectly out of the early organizing efforts, was short-lived compared to the Voters League, but while it lasted it, perhaps more than the other groups mentioned, seemed to generate a level of emotional involvement comparable to the pre-1964 years.

Among the most popular of the projects developed during the summer of 1964 were the Freedom Schools, and there was some sentiment, both among the volunteers and within COFO, for finding some way to continue them. The most active person pushing the idea was probably Tom Levin, a forty-one-year-old psychoanalyst who had taken part in Freedom Summer and who envisioned setting up a group of preschools in the spirit of the Freedom Schools. The schools would stress innovative teaching methods, and parents would be trained to run them. While Levin was discussing these ideas with civil rights workers over the winter of 1964–65, officials of the recently-formed Office of Economic Opportunity (OEO), which was just beginning the Head Start project, heard about the discussions and tried to convince the Levin group to become a part of Head Start. The CDGM planners were skeptical, partly because of the fear of being co-opted by federal money and ruined by federal control, but they finally decided to go along with OEO.

At a SNCC conference in the spring of 1965, Levin failed to get the organization's endorsement but was successful in getting a number of SNCC workers to start canvassing local communities for support. The local people they were able to interest in the project turned out, to no one's surprise, to be movement people, frequently FDP members, although FDP's statewide leadership was not initially enthusiastic about the project. CDGM's central staff of forty people were largely young and inexperienced, and the program was always somewhat chaotic administratively. Nonetheless, by July 12, opening day of the eight-week session, eighty-four centers opened across the state, serving fifty-six hundred children.[11]

Although the intensity of repression seems to have declined by 1965, it had hardly disappeared. Sharecroppers were threatened with eviction for enrolling their children, buildings used as centers were burned, and there were sporadic shooting incidents. Local centers found they could get no credit from local businesses and no peace from local cops. In its first week of operation, CDGM staffers were hit with over a thousand dollars in traffic fines. Partly to deflect local hostility, OEO agreed to fund a second series of Head Starts to be operated by local school boards.

CDGM is another case where an idea was more enthusiastically received by local people than by some SNCC members or by the FDP leadership. In Greenwood, the people most involved were largely the core FDP members—Lou Emma Allen, Lula Belle Johnson, Susie Morgan, Mary Boothe, Mary Lane, and James Moore among them. In addition to providing a vital service for children, they saw the program as something that could provide work for people who had rendered themselves unemployable by their activism. They, like Tom Levin, also saw it as an organizing tool, a way to draw more people into some of the other movement activities, which proved to be the case. Some people who weren't very interested in the more explicitly political parts of FDP programs or who weren't altogether comfortable with FDP's militant image were interested in a program that would give their children a better start in life.

They had no trouble getting the initial group of children, but they didn't get funding right away. For a year, the Greenwood program was run entirely on a volunteer basis, after which they did get funding through Head Start. The funding itself, though, created other problems, as we shall see later, leading eventually to the demise of the group statewide and locally. But while it lasted, local people in Greenwood thought they had a tool that was going to help them create long-term change in the Delta.

In the NAACP, CDGM, MFDP, and the Greenwood Movement, people, most of whom had initially been activated by COFO-SNCC prior to 1964, not only carried the movement forward despite declining levels of direct support from SNCC staff but were able to expand the base of the movement, gradually drawing in individuals, including ministers, who had not been a part of the early days, the marching days. They were able to employ successfully tactics that had not been a part of SNCC's repertoire and to address issues like public accommodations that were not high on the agenda of Mississippi SNCC. By 1966, local women, say, who a few years before had not organized much more than church socials were arguing with Washington bureaucrats about how programs should be shaped. No matter what came out of the process, the activation of the local people was itself an important achievement. To some degree, SNCC members had been

program and ask him or her to tell others about it. You may need to do all of the arranging and contacting for setting up the opportunity in some cases (often spelling out or rehearsing with the local person what he should get over, or going along with him) but if people see one of their neighbors either alone or with one of the volunteers making a bold step forward, they are more likely to see such action as possible for themselves. . . . *Talk to them* with confidence, with [a] sense of "expectation." . . . Remember that they are adult, though many of them will be overly dependent because of this repressive culture. . . . As you work you must somehow resist the temptation to do things for the people, but share the work, the planning and the decision-making with them, so they realize that if the center is to continue after the summer, they will have to do it.[14]

The memo walks a line between romanticizing local people by assuming that they could do everything and infantilizing them by doing everything for them. Volunteers have a clear role, but it is more a coaching role than a doing role.

Bob Moses feels that part of what the movement did was credentialize people. Organizers gave people a kind of support that makes them feel entitled to do things and able to do them, much in the same way that educational credentials work for those who have them. The process that made that most likely to happen, he thinks, is one that gives people broad social exposure:

It can't happen if the framework is narrow. You've got to be exposed to a lot. Part of what the Movement did is just expose people to a lot. Exposing people to all different kinds of people who were coming in and out of Mississippi . . . all people who are somehow part of this movement culture, sharing certain values, talking about certain things. . . . If all those activities are really trying to get across the same message which is that people have to take ownership over what they are doing, they have to commit themselves and there has to be this element of persistence and also an element of trying to figure out how to work with other people. If all of that is happening everywhere then it gets to be more than just the sum of the parts. Something begins to take hold which becomes sort of a culture which becomes a place where people can grow and emerge.

If that kind of culture especially characterized the Mississippi movement, a large part of the explanation for that has to go to Moses, who tried to turn everything into a lesson, according to Willie Peacock. Peacock said that instead of writing reports himself, Moses would teach others, often just kids, to do them. A capable speaker himself, he preferred finding local people to do whatever public speaking was necessary. Worth Long, who directed SNCC's work in Arkansas, speculates that Moses deliberately rejected the role of orator because it was the traditional role of Black leadership. Long also recalls that:

> A kid would come in off the street and say "I want to help out," and [Bob would] say "What can you do?" Kid would say, "I can sing Freedom songs" and such and such, and Bob would say, "Well, I need to have this letter typed. Why don't you go and type it?" Kid had never typed, and he [Bob] would say, "Well, you know, you just type the letters. [Laughing] It's very simple. You just type the letters." And he would have someone answer his mail like that. Someone who had never typed before.

Long adds that Moses won a tremendous respect

> for his ability to listen and to think and more than anything else to consolidate. . . . Bob is the kind of dude who would lay back and let you talk about what you wanted to talk about. He would facilitate that process. . . . You would always seek to ask him a question but he would take it back to the group or back to you. He would facilitate a process where you would solve your own problems, but he would summarize. I tried to copy some elements of his style. Everybody did. It wound up getting a whole lot of people involved for a long period of time. Everybody that I know that came in touch with Bob ended up feeling that they could change the world or they could at least change the part that they were in. He took the attitude that anybody, regardless of their education or whatever, could do whatever anybody else could do.[15]

Amzie Moore and Bob Moses had a kind of father-son relationship, but Moore once commented to an interviewer that he had a hard time explaining Bob. He struck Moore as unassuming, quiet, but a deep thinker on the one hand and as ordinary as a common shoe on the other.

> He didn't project leadership. He didn't say, "I'm the man and you do this, that and the other." He didn't even argue with you on a point except where people were involved . . . [and] he also wanted people to be recognized as individuals who possess the capabilities and the intellect to actually do things for themselves once they are shown.[16]

Maintaining a focus on developing leadership was, of course, more difficult in practice than in theory. Mary Lane remembers SNCC staff meetings in Greenwood at which no local people were present. Some SNCC staff had such forceful personalities—Stokely Carmichael and Lawrence Guyot are sometimes described this way—that people working with them sometimes felt they didn't get enough time to make up their own minds. On the other hand, Mary Boothe recalls that if she didn't know something, Carmichael would take her aside, explain it to her, and then let her go on back in front of the people as if she'd always known it. Organizers have to see that there are some short-term victories if they are not to lose all but the most committed of their constituency, and this may mean that some decisions will have to be made by those with most experience. On the other hand, "Let the people decide," as Clayborne Carson has noted, could easily be taken to such extremes that nothing got done—a form of poor-people-itis, as some called it. There seems to be fairly strong agreement among both SNCC staff and local residents that Greenwood was one of the more successful cases of developing local leadership. There is no agreement on the reasons for that. Some argue that it was because there were relatively large numbers of SNCC staff in Greenwood and they stayed for a relatively long period of time, but others take the opposite stance, arguing that the strong SNCC presence militated against developing local leadership. There seems to be more agreement, at least among younger local residents, that while the 1964 summer project was tactically justified and produced a number of positive outcomes, it also worked against the development of local leadership. Mary Lane, for example, acknowledged the value of the summer project but also noted that:

> There were local people that were holding positions in SNCC before the summer of '64. And you know, after these [summer volunteers] came in, you could see it every day, the man moving up a little more, you know. And he knew more. And he had it, where maybe you didn't. But you [had been] learning. . . . You sit down and work with them everyday and you find out that they can do a much better job of it than you could.[17]

Thus some local people began pulling away from the movement that summer, and a good deal of effort that fall had to be devoted to drawing them back.

By the end of the decade, the idea of developing leadership in others was no longer a prominent element in local Black politics. In a 1968 interview, Mary Boothe noted that people in Greenwood were no longer talking about developing leadership. Local people themselves were not necessarily as concerned with leadership development as some SNCC staff had been. No one ever questioned the courage of Silas McGhee, for example, but some of those who worked with him felt that as a leader he could be just as hard-headed dealing with his own people as he was dealing with white racists. He was still in his early twenties, after all, and not always patient about listening to the viewpoints of other people.

More recently, at political meetings I attended in Greenwood in the late 1980s and early 1990s, the style of contemporary Black leadership struck me as rigorously top-down. Political candidates were presented rather than discussed. The leaders told the people who the "right" candidates were, talked about how wonderful they were, and disparaged the candidates of the other side. There was no sense of trying to get people to think through issues on their own, no sense of making a genuine attempt to present more than one side of a question, no attempt to involve less experienced people in the running of the meeting. This, of course, could describe a political meeting almost anywhere in the country, but in the Delta, against the history of Black struggle and growth in the Delta, it seemed to have a special poignancy.

Still, SNCC's style of thinking and organizing had an impact that far outlasted its active presence in the Delta. That they could not plant the seeds of that style of thinking even more deeply was, in no small part, a function of how successful both the organization and the broader movement had been.

Twelve

FROM SNCC TO SLICK

The Demoralization of the Movement

*And another thing is that when the lunch counters finally integrated
. . . these guys and women [who had not supported the sit-in movement]
fought to be the first to eat at Woolworth's or Rich's and came to the
church in furs . . . sad, sad, sad. Elbowing the students aside.*

JULIAN BOND

CDGM *[Child Development Group of Mississippi] was one
of the best . . . community action programs that the Office of Economic
Opportunity funded. . . . It really exceeded the wildest expectations
of the community action programs. Therein lies its difficulties
and the source of its downfall.*

ELMER J. MOORE
OEO economist

*And so help me God nothing in the world is so unjust as this poverty
program in Mississippi. It's a disgrace and it's a shame before God for
people to operate this kind of thing and call it a poverty program.*

FANNIE LOU HAMER

*I want you all to think about the fact that there's a direct relationship
between the fact that we [SNCC] don't have money and the fact that
we're doing something real.*

PRATHIA HALL
1964[1]

When Silas McGhee returned home in 1968 after his hitch in the service, he found that his brother Jake had lost faith in the movement. "He didn't have any confidence in himself or anybody. If anybody was going to do anything, it was going to be without Jake. Jake was totally devastated."

For five or six years after her first talk with Bob Moses, Mary Lane was completely immersed in movement activity—as SNCC's local project director, a candidate for office on the FDP ticket, one of the people most instrumental in bringing CDGM to Greenwood, one of the first organizers for the Voters League, local director of Friends of Children, an outgrowth of CDGM. At one point she couldn't picture herself doing any work but movement work, getting involved, working with people. By 1969, though, she didn't find the movement as satisfying as it had been. "You become disgusted," she said, "with the people and yourself."[2]

After about four years as a full-time activist, George Greene was working in Alabama when he decided he'd had enough. The final straw was an incident in which another SNCC worker stole a rifle and let George take the blame for it, at a time when George already had several other charges hanging over his head.

Individuals like these and organizations like the Freedom Democratic Party, the Greenwood Movement, and the Child Development Group of Mississippi ran into the contradictions created by their own success and that of the broader movement. The energies they unleashed made participation in movement-generated activities attractive to groups and individuals that had previously stood on the sidelines. When it became clear that the movement was going to bear some fruit, those who had worked hardest to make it happen were systematically pushed aside.

The newcomers came in part because of changes in the rewards available for movement participants. Those same changes altered the internal moral climate of the movement, undercutting the sense of community and identity among activists. The movement had become alien to the people who had built it, and many of them didn't wait to be pushed out by the new leaders; they simply withdrew.

In Greenwood during 1962 and 1963, there was always movement participation, both open and sub rosa, from individuals who were middle class. As a group, though, the middle classes, teachers and preachers in particular, either sat out the early years or spoke against the movement. Nonetheless, statewide, according to John Dittmer, class tensions were kept reasonably well in check until the 1964 convention challenge in Atlantic City. Dittmer finds that traditional Black leaders initially scoffed at the idea of the challenge, but when it became clear that FDP was winning support from important national leaders, "established ministers and well-to-do businessmen attempted to jump on the bandwagon."[3] In the delegate-selection process, steps were taken to ensure that most delegates would come from the rural poor, keeping the more urban and middle-class component to a fifth of the delegation. The vote on the compromise split along these lines, with the rural people voting against it and the more conservative urban element tending to favor it. The latter group included many NAACP people, including Aaron Henry.

Tensions deepened after the convention. "Atlantic City had given legitimacy to people like Mrs. Hamer, Hartman Turnbow and E. W. Steptoe, and the black middle class resented it" and began taking steps to do something about it.[4] In this process they would repeatedly have the support of the Johnson administration, of white liberals from outside the state and of a social category that barely existed prior to 1964—Mississippi white moderates. ("A white moderate in Mississippi," Dick Gregory used to quip, "is a cat who wants to lynch you from a *low* tree.")

After the convention, FDP worked to support the Johnson ticket in the fall election, much to the disappointment of many SNCC workers, who could not so quickly overlook the betrayal of Atlantic City. Mary Lane remembered the confusion of being in meetings where people railed against the perfidy of the administration and then having to go out and drum up votes for Johnson-Humphrey. Doing the politic thing did not come easily to people whose initial orientation to the movement had not been political. The Johnson administration successfully beat back FDP's 1964 Atlantic City challenge to the seating of Mississippi's delegation, but the compromise worked out was that the 1968 convention would not seat a segregationist delegation.[5]

The expected exclusion of the regular Democratic party of the state hardly meant that FDP would be seated. A new group had formed, an integrated group called the Young Democrats of Mississippi, under the leadership of Charles Evers, one of the state's most visible Blacks, Aaron Henry, and Hodding Carter III, arguably the most visible white moderate in the state. According to FDP's Ed King, this group was repeatedly successful at presenting itself to opinion-makers and policy-makers outside the state as the new face of the freedom movement in Mississippi. Both Charles Evers and Aaron Henry had substantial legitimacy with several of the relevant constituencies, and many within those constituencies were not sophisticated enough to realize that they represented a wing of the movement, not the whole of it.

By 1968, the Young Democrats had generated an organizational clone called the Loyal Democrats, pledged to support the national ticket and poised to replace the old segregationist Democratic party. This left FDP in a bind. Many of its members were reluctant to work with Evers and Carter, but they were even more reluctant to have Evers and Carter representing Mississippi at the convention. An FDP-sponsored delegation would have been totally unacceptable to the national party. The result was a coalition delegation, half white and half Black, with the NAACP appointing half the Black delegates and FDP the other half. After the convention, FDP was purged from the leadership of the coalition, leaving the party's machinery in the hands of people who, with exceptions like Aaron Henry, had little or no connection with the early movement in the state, although they never ceased to wrap themselves in the mantle of the movement.[6] Dittmer notes:

> When the Loyalists were in fact seated at the stormy Chicago convention the national media trumpeted the victory as a triumph for the civil rights forces in Mississippi, and in a sense it was. But a different breed had captured the movement banner: urban, edu-

cated, and affluent, these new leaders had their own agenda. Few of them were organizers, and they had little contact with the black masses, for whom they professed to speak.[7]

In Greenwood, the Loyalists' supporters included the Reverend Wallace, who became county chair for the party, and Father Machesky, who served on the state credentials committee in 1968. Machesky had some misgivings about clergy being so directly involved in politics but agreed to serve because it was a tense moment and both Aaron Henry and Charles Evers felt that some white representation would help the larger cause. Both Machesky and Wallace were cool to the idea of an independent, Black-led political party. Both were leaders of the Greenwood Movement, but neither could claim any connection to the early movement.

After 1965, the Leflore FDP chapter seems not to have been an effective organization. There were acrimonious fights over whether they should continue to support the national Democratic party, over whether they should merge with the state party or try to create a separate structure representing poor whites and poor Blacks; there were fights over leadership positions and fights that seemed to reduce to nothing more than unresolvable personality disputes. As we shall see, these fights took place in an atmosphere in which people were increasingly questioning one another's motives, and not without reason. For members like James Moore and Mary Lane, there was little that looked like program direction and, in the development of the Loyalist Party, a lot that looked like outright betrayal of all that they had fought for.

The history of the Child Development Group of Mississippi is similar to that of MFDP. CDGM operated for a year without any outside funding at all. Those who brought the program to Greenwood were very happy with how it performed there that first year. After they did receive Head Start funding from OEO, problems developed. Some people who had been defiant on the picket lines and in demonstrations continued to be defiant as employees hired by CDGM, refusing to come to work on time, refusing to acknowledge the authority of their supervisors.[8] Still, people continued to feel very good about the program.

The larger problems came from outside Greenwood. OEO signaled its stance while CDGM was still under consideration for funding. CDGM plans called for local governance councils—i.e., elected poor people—to run each center. OEO decided that there would have to be some "respectable, responsible" people—i.e., not poor—in the governing structure. CDGM did what it could to create the appearance of complying.[9] Meanwhile, OEO itself showed more and more willingness to comply with the demands of Mississippi's political establishment. Although the political establishment had at first wanted nothing to do with poverty-program money, the possibility that millions of dollars might go to what was thought of as a SNCC-COFO project frightened them into action. Senators Stennis and Eastland, among others, led a witch hunt against CDGM, accusing them of being communist, of funneling funds to the revolution, and, in a new twist, of being racist by excluding whites. In fact, most CDGM projects had made strenuous efforts to recruit white students and hire local white teachers, with predictably minimal results. In many cases, those whites who showed any interest at all in the program found themselves the objects of threats from their neighbors. Most CDGM centers did have white staff members, but these were people from the North. Still, to those unfamiliar with the social realities of Mississippi, the charge of racism carried some weight, particularly in the context of the then-developing furor over Black Power. Since Stennis was chairing the Senate Appropriations Committee, OEO was under considerable pressure to placate him. Thus, OEO sent white southerners to conduct investigations of local CDGM projects and invested the authority to run local poverty projects in such well-known friends of the poor as Delta planters.[10]

By September 1966, when CDGM was operating in about thirty counties, a new organizational entity was formed to compete with it. Formed without the knowledge or input of CDGM or of any other group that could be called close to poor Mississippians, it was called MAP, Mississippi Action for Progress. MAP was a recycling of the Loyal Democrats, not only in the social constituency it represented but even down to the individuals involved. Its leading actors included Owen Cooper, a businessman from Yazoo City, and Leroy Percy, a plantation owner from the Delta, in addition to Hodding Carter III, Aaron Henry, and Charles Evers. Its board was appointed rather than elected, and its membership was approved by Stennis and by Mississippi's bluntly segregationist Governor Paul Johnson, as well as by the White House. (Governor Johnson on poverty: "Nobody is starving in Mississippi. The nigra women I see are so fat they shine.") In Greenwood, MAP supporters included Father Machesky, who got involved because of his friendship with Aaron Henry.[11] MAP was able to establish a beachhead in Greenwood by opening a program in Wesley Methodist church. Apparently, they were in town for several weeks before anyone associated with CDGM knew anything about it, and according to James Moore, they took in mostly children from financially ineligible families.

Aaron Henry's "defection" was a particularly bitter pill for CDGM people. Henry was still state NAACP president, a man who had been struggling against white supremacy in Mississippi when the SNCC kids had still been in grammar school; he had been a vital part of the early COFO coalition, and dozens of SNCC-COFO activists could have told stories about being bailed out of jail or otherwise personally helped by Doc Henry. His relationships with some COFO activists, though, had been somewhat strained since the Atlantic City convention, where he had been among those leaning toward accepting the compromise offered by the administration.[12] Many in CDGM could accept the idea that from his perspective a chance to participate with whites in state and national politics represented genuine progress. Others were just angry with him, all the more so after he issued a statement accepting the accuracy of the various charges against CDGM without giving them a chance to respond.[13]

At the state level, MAP had some relatively credible figures like Henry and Hodding Carter III, but some of its local units tended to be composed of traditional members of the power structure, people defined as safe by both the White House and Mississippi politicians, often people deeply distrusted by local Blacks, especially by movement people.[14] Where CDGM boards always had a majority of members locally elected, MAP boards usually allowed only one-third of their members to be elected locally.[15] In the miraculously short time of three weeks, MAP was able to get OEO funding.

Meantime, Sargent Shriver of OEO let it be known that when CDGM funding expired in October 1966, it would not be renewed, partly because of alleged financial irregularities, a charge that had dogged the program from the beginning, often coming from Senator Stennis. In fact, in the opinion of Elmer Moore, an OEO economist, such problems as existed were trivial and well within the bounds of what would be expected from any new program. When a New York accounting firm agreed with that opinion, OEO separated the firm from the project. Shriver released the various allegations against CDGM to the press without ever having afforded CDGM a chance to respond to them, a move that backfired when some members of the press questioned its propriety.[16]

There had never been much question about the quality of the program CDGM was running. In earlier days, Shriver himself had praised their work; many people on his staff thought it the best Head Start program in the country. OEO had approved funding for a film on the teacher-training methods used by CDGM as a model for other programs. Troops of well-known educators had visited centers and come away praising how much was being done with so little. All of this was being done while spending only eighty percent of what OEO itself recommended per child. The preferences of local people were clear. During the fall of 1966, MAP, with three million dollars, was only able to establish five centers in two counties, serving one hundred children. CDGM, meanwhile, operating without any funds at all, was running sixty centers serving four thousand children.[17]

Certainly there were some quite bad centers. During the first year, one of the weakest programs was in Cleveland, a disorganized center where "they taught nothing, the children just ran to hell and back." Some program evaluators were convinced that Amzie Moore, who had helped organize the program, was a large part of what was wrong with it. He struck some of them as being interested primarily in maintaining control of the program and its resources. The Leflore County programs ran the gamut. One evaluator found some of them to be near-perfect and thought they were getting "smart, reasonable" leadership from Mary Lane. On the other hand, Polly Greenberg, in charge of the program's teacher development, found the program at the American Legion Hut barely above the level of a bad baby-sitting service, with several hostile and inept staff members who did little teaching, and that badly, a place where children were always being "scolded at for not understanding that which is never explained." Some of the worst staff had impeccable movement credentials, and one suspects they were hired as thanks for services already rendered rather than for any predisposition toward working with children.[18]

Greenberg was not reluctant to point out shabby work where she saw it, but at the end of the first summer she found the overall program to be in good health. She thought there were fifteen very poor centers, sullen, joyless places; fifty were good, by which she meant good enough for children and parents anywhere, not just in the Delta; twenty-one were outstanding, places where: "warmth, human contact and person-child endorsement abounded." Another evaluator noted how rewarding it was "to hear the parents talk about how much the centers had meant to their children; [to] hear them ask very relevant questions about what and how their children best learn." It seems to have been a remarkable beginning for any social program.[19]

That fall saw a massive lobbying campaign on behalf of CDGM. Busloads of poor Mississippi Negroes arrived in Washington to demonstrate and lobby. FDP, which at the state level had always had ambivalent feelings about CDGM, became an aggressive defender of the program. Shriver, who had been a member in good standing of the liberal community, found both himself and OEO under sharp attack from that community, including attacks from church and labor groups. OEO employees circulated petitions for CDGM. It was one of the last stands of the liberal coalition of the sixties, and it was ultimately successful. By the end of 1966, OEO reversed itself and refunded CDGM, although five counties, Leflore included, were dropped from the program.

The excluded counties reorganized themselves under the name Friends of Children (FCM) and continued to operate highly popular volunteer programs. In Greenwood, FCM was directed by Mary Lane and was able to keep its center in operation for two years after OEO funding was cut off. During part of that time, FCM was able to get a small grant from the Field Foundation, but it remained essentially a volunteer program.

At the state level, it became increasingly difficult for CDGM and FCM to compete with MAP after 1967. OEO continued to take counties away from CDGM and harass it in other ways, some CDGM employees went over to MAP, and MAP became more skillful at using its political muscle. With its greater funding, MAP was able to influence the churches that provided space for many of the centers. They could provide new plumbing, new wiring, new bathroom facilities, and so on. In some parts of the state, churches that wanted Head Starts were not allowed to have them if the building was also being used for voter-registration work or any other kind of movement work, unless sponsored by the NAACP, which because of its newly acceptable political status, was increasingly becoming a patronage operation using poverty-program jobs. At one point, poverty-program job applicants were told to apply directly to the NAACP office. In most communities, as Head Start became less controversial, schoolteachers and others were able to argue successfully that jobs should go only to people with qualifications, and for that matter, only educated people should be involved in the governing of local programs.[20] The original intention under CDGM was that centers would be connected with movement activity and imbued with movement values—a spirit of volunteerism, recognition of the need of the poor to represent themselves, minimal hierarchy, respect for the ability of the untrained to be trained, concern with teaching people how the issues that touch them are impinged upon by wider social issues. What they got under MAP was an educational program dominated at best by a traditional social-welfare mentality. Let's-have-some-experts-do-something-for-poor-people. Stripped of the movement spirit, a program that was clearly politicizing people at the beginning wound up doing just the opposite. CDGM supporters across the state were deeply embittered. One man from Forrest County said of the people who had worked so hard to kill the program: "You can't blame 'em for being dumb; they're just a bunch of federal jerks, but you cin blame 'em for bein' a bunch of dirty, dishonest politicians playin' with us little people."[21]

The Greenwood Movement similarly came to its end amid charges and counter-charges of dishonesty, hypocrisy, and betrayal. During the earliest boycotts, one of the SNCC workers who had been coming in and out of town left town under a cloud of suspicion. Although he was not in charge of the boycotts, some people believed that he had represented himself to one of the Chinese merchants as being the person who determined who got boycotted and had accepted payoffs from that merchant supposedly in exchange for not boycotting him. One of the members of the board of directors of the Greenwood Movement, again a minister who had not been involved in the early movement, was found to have quietly purchased a new station wagon from a merchant who was being boycotted. He claimed that he had ordered it before the boycott, but many people didn't believe that. Jake McGhee, rummaging around in the office one day, stumbled upon a letter that suggested that one of the movement leaders was being paid off by one of the merchants. The accused minister argued that the funds were either a donation or legitimate payment for advertising in the movement's newsletter, but that hardly satisfied members of the movement, who felt that, were that the case, everyone should have been told about it up front. In a move that suggested how much the leadership had come to be distrusted, the Reverend Louis Redd got people to agree that there would be no more of this business of individual leaders negotiating with individual businessmen. Instead, a group was delegated to negotiate.

For idealistic young people like Mary Lane, the movement was no longer the kind of sustaining experience it had once been. Working with people who appear to be dramatically self-sacrificing is one thing; working with the self-serving is another, and working in situations where the lines between the two are blurred and shifting may be worst of all. From the viewpoint of the early participants, all of the particular allegations of misdeeds took place in the context of all these new people joining the movement. On the one hand, early participants wanted to expand the base of the movement. On the other, doing so created a situation where it was more difficult to judge the motives of the newcomers, especially of those who did not become involved until after the problem of reprisals had abated, after it was clear that a certain kind of prestige could be had from being a movement leader, after it became possible for movement leaders to profit financially and politically from their participation.

Even after Mary Boothe became director of the Greenwood Movement, she couldn't forget that many of the people in the Movement had sat out the early sixties. "There are a lot of people working now [1968] that just weren't interested in the old days." Mary Boothe had spent much of the decade of the sixties working to secure the right to vote. In her interview with me, she said that after all that, she actually stopped voting for several years. Too many of the people running were the same middle-class people who hadn't wanted anything to do with the movement in 1962. They had all gotten real Black after the late sixties, they were all talking bad about the white folks, but in the days when the white folks really were dangerous, they didn't have anything to say. Mary Lane was not very active in the boycott movement, at least partly because she couldn't forget that some of the leaders of the boycotts, including the Catholic leaders, hadn't wanted anything to do with COFO when it first came to Greenwood. In 1969 she said:

> I remember when SNCC first came into Greenwood, the [current] leaders of the [Greenwood] Movement wouldn't have anything to do with SNCC, you know. And this sort of thing hurts. . . . They [the Catholics] still have a paper, the *Centerlight*. You know, we went to them and we pleaded with them to print something about SNCC in the paper. And they refused to do it. And the poverty money started coming in and the Catholics were the first ones in the state to get the poverty money, you know. . . . And then, all at once they are saying like, we are brothers and we love you.[22]

Teachers and preachers were the objects of most of the ambivalence about newcomers. Some of the movement veterans think that David Jordan, the schoolteacher who became head of the Voters League, has done a good job with the organization, but some of them still see him as exploiting the reputation of his very active and very visible father and brother. Several local teachers became involved with MAP (which by Mississippi standards, was paying very good wages), which not only meant that they were seen by local activists as being among the first to profit tangibly from the development of movement-stimulated programs but that they did so by cooperating with a group perceived as a tool of the power structure. A number of ministers who had not participated in the early movement also cooperated with MAP and with the Greenwood Movement and its boycott programs, and some of them rose to leadership positions. The ministers were there in part because FDP activists made explicit attempts to recruit them in order to have the broadest possible base of support. Professional participation was desired, but it was still a source of smoldering resentment.

Sue Lorenzi, an organizer who worked with FDP in neighboring Holmes County, captures much of this ambivalence in her description of that county during this period. There, as in most places, teachers, with the exception of a woman named Bernice Montgomery, preachers, and most of the successful businessmen generally stayed away from the movement until preparations began for the 1967 elections, in which it appeared that Blacks might win some significant local posts. As in Greenwood, organizers made deliberate efforts to get professionals involved. When a few of them did begin attending meetings, "they were treated with a mixture of . . . ridicule overlaid with a great deal of respect." FDP leaders, few of whom had much education to speak of, talked among themselves about whether it was appropriate for an uneducated person to run for office. They continued to try to build a coalition that would include all organizations and social classes. When more middle-class people did come to meetings, "deference was paid to the preachers and professionals attending and an attempt was made to allow them into leadership positions. They were sought out to speak up."[23] As in Greenwood, their presence was both desired and resented.

The problem wasn't necessarily that the people who came into the movement in its latter days were of an inferior caliber morally to those who joined earlier. Among the early-movement joiners one can find all the character flaws that flesh is heir to. One of the stalwarts of the

NAACP chapter in the early sixties, a man who had sacrificed much, is believed to have left town taking with him all the NAACP membership dues. One of the courageous older men who was among the first to support SNCC workers was also widely believed to regularly skim money out of the collection plate at mass meetings. Another is supposed to have gone into the rural areas after Byron de la Beckwith was acquitted, telling people that if enough money could be raised, they would be able to bring Beckwith to trial again. No one ever heard anything about what happened to the money raised. Mrs. McGhee was convinced that when she was having her troubles, SCLC raised money in her name which she never saw. Even when food and clothing were being distributed in Greenwood in the winter of 1962–63, rumors went around suggesting that SNCC staff and the local people working with them took their pick from what came in before they started distributing it. One of the SNCC people who was in and out of town acquired a reputation for being a kleptomaniac.

Outright dishonesty may have been less a problem than egotism. One of the women most beloved by SNCC workers was thought by other local residents to be hell to work with, just impossibly hardheaded. She would go to meetings, present her position, shout down the opposition, and generally disrupt things. When the block-captain system was very strong, she wanted to be in charge of it. The block captains tried having meetings without notifying her, but she would find out and show up to disrupt them, weakening the system as more and more people decided they didn't want to come to meetings just to see her perform. People who were upstanding and courageous in their public demeanor might be small and vindictive in their private lives. Early members of the movement were likely to have some measure of courage, but they could be courageous egotists or courageous knaves or worse.

Dishonesty and egotism—in this case, probably two ways of saying one thing—were always present but seem clearly not to have been as demoralizing in the early years. For one thing, judging from my interviews, allegations of self-serving behavior were not as common in the early years and were more likely to be directed against people who were peripheral to the movement. I would suspect, too, that when the movement was young, with only a couple of hundred people at its core, people could be generally more trusting of one another because they knew so much about what was going on. Someone may have been skimming something from the collection plate, but the fact that everyone in Greenwood seems to have known it was going on and who was doing it suggests that it was unlikely to get out of hand. People can be relatively tolerant of one another's shortcomings in that situation. In addition whatever shortcomings were exhibited were balanced by the fact that the same people were exhibiting inspiring levels of self-sacrifice and heroism in other contexts. If it was true that some SNCC workers took items for themselves from the clothing distribution, most of the local people in the movement's core would have said they were more than entitled to whatever it was. If the man stealing from the collection plate is also a leader in defying the police, is taking in families that have been evicted, people can balance his faults against his contributions.

Had the movement of the early sixties been composed of nothing but saints, there would have still been accusations against the activists, if only because those who were not part of the movement had a vested interest in believing that activists had nefarious motives. Much in the same way that white Greenwood had a vested interest in believing that COFO was communist, the non-active part of Black Greenwood, especially those who had traditionally been thought of as community leaders, had an interest in believing that COFO workers were irresponsible, sexually immoral, and out for their own ends. If the people leading the movement are devoid of character, one cannot be blamed for not participating. Thus, as with white Greenwood, whatever evidence supported that image of SNCC was focused on or, if necessary, imagined into existence.

Accusations of self-serving behavior were inevitable, but their credibility was probably much greater in the late 1960s, irrespective of any real differences in behavior patterns. The first SNCC workers were accused of being interested only in publicity for themselves, but that was difficult to believe because they weren't getting any publicity in 1962. Even in the 1950s, there were people in Amzie Moore's hometown who said he was in it primarily for personal glory or personal gain, but under the conditions of that time, it would have been hard to convince most people of that. Any sane person could have found safer paths to personal gain. By the late 1960s, though, he was connected with several poverty programs in ways that gave him potential influence over money and jobs. During his tenure as chair of Bolivar County's Head Start, the program was renting property that Moore owned, a goodly sum of federal money went into fixing up some of those properties, and friends of his were on the payroll. Allegations that he was just lining his own pockets became more frequent, and now they sounded a good deal more plausible.

Mary Lane commented that when she first started working all anyone got out of it was satisfaction, and that was enough. Bob Moses thought that for the first few years in Mississippi, the local young people who had been recruited across the state—Guyot, Curtis Hayes, Hollis Watkins, the Peacock brothers, Sam Block, and the others—were kept going primarily by their own sense of self-growth and by the sense that the people they were working with were growing as well. They were not getting the ordinary forms of tangible rewards, and that itself helped to make them trusted. If they were willing to be jailed, beaten, and shot at, willing to leave school, willing to live on virtually no money, then it was likely that they were serious about the beliefs they espoused. The reward structure—that is, the lack of tangible rewards and the certainty of harsh reprisals—constituted a kind of screening device. By the middle of the decade, the reward structure was such as to make it very plausible that some people were out primarily for themselves.

Ruby Hurley had a unique perspective from which to observe these changes. She was probably the first professional civil rights organizer to be stationed in the South, having gone to Birmingham in 1951 to open the NAACP's regional office. Except for a few years when the NAACP had been declared illegal in Alabama, she continued to be the regional director well into the 1970s. Although her political perspective was very different from that of many people in groups like CDGM or MFDP, she too saw real differences in the movement's constituency over time. Referring to the people across the South she had begun working with in the fifties, she said that with few exceptions, "the

Negroes in those days were working for their people without any feelings of self-aggrandizement or anything selfish." On the other hand, in 1968 she said:

> In recent years, with the new laws, the money that can be made in the business of fighting for civil rights. . . . You have different kinds of motivations, I think a variety of motivations on the part of persons who are working in the field—a little different from the old days.[24]

Veterans of the early days have a vested interest in believing themselves better men and women than the johnny-come-latelys, but it is clear that later entrants to the movement were exposed to temptations that earlier members did not have to worry about, and it certainly seems likely that taken collectively they had different patterns of motivation from the early participants. Taken together, those two factors—a different structure of opportunity and different patterns of motivation for participating—probably did mean real differences in the level of demoralizing behavior. At the same time, some of the early participants changed their own patterns of behavior as the opportunity structure changed. It is difficult to believe that those who were active in 1962 or 1963 were motivated by self-aggrandizement in any useful sense of that term, but once some people, even people who had not been involved in the early days, began to reap rewards from the movement, once some people became national celebrities, flying all over the country to give speeches and be lauded, once some people began to get decent jobs, once some people began to acquire a degree of political influence, it is easy to imagine some of the early participants saying, "Well, why not me?" Who had a better claim? The very fact that they had sacrificed as much as or more than others who were profiting from the movement might have created some sense of personal entitlement. Even selflessness can become its own contradiction.

Worth Long, a veteran of SNCC's work in Alabama and Arkansas, describes one of the local Mississippi SNCC leaders as going through just this kind of corrupting process. A successful local leader, he let the success go to his head. SNCC started sending him on speaking tours to California and other places, and he started getting hung up on the attention and the publicity, which was diametrically opposed to what SNCC was about. Being a leader simply went to his head. Owen Brooks of the Delta Ministry saw the same process many times, often among the veterans, the old leaders who had been sticking their necks out when everybody else was afraid. That very fact became a problem: "That becomes a self-serving kind of attitude. The next thing that flows from that is, I paid my dues and it's time for me now to collect some premium on the dues."[25]

Subtler corruptions of the spirit were more troubling to some SNCC workers, who had found themselves on the cutting edge of history—making decisions to which United States presidents had to respond—while they were still in their early twenties. It was hard for some of them not to develop a sense of themselves as special people, as celebrities. SNCC's MacArthur Cotton, who never left the state, spoke of the need to struggle against the temptation to see yourself as a person apart:

> I had to learn my way back, so to speak, to the community, to the community from which I had come. I had to work my way back to being accepted as a peer. . . . You had a peculiar status in the minds of a lot of people. [*Laughter*] You had to kind of work all that out so you could become an ordinary citizen working with the people.

Even if one did not try to trade on celebrity status for tangible rewards, just allowing others to see you in that light interfered with their process of development.

Ruby Hurley is probably right when she says the fifties were different, but the differences are relative, of course. One can certainly find examples of fifties activists developing a potentially problematic sense of personal entitlement. When activists fell out among themselves, for example, one of the weapons they used on one another was the stick of Selfless Dedication. C. R. Darden, president of the Meridian NAACP branch, was involved in a number of scrapes with other NAACP leaders, dating back at least to the middle 1950s. At one point, Aaron Henry wrote him to clear up charges that Darden was being insufficiently cooperative with the state conference. Bristling, Darden wrote back, pointing out that no one needed to remind him of his responsibilities.

> Nor would anyone need to remind me of the years of stern agony, intimidation, economic reprisals, threats of violence, personal sacrifice and anxiety that I endured during those rugged years when [almost] everyone . . . refused to accept the challenge. I need no reminder that today my wife could not get employment in the school system if she desired work, my two sons are still denied employment because of my activities with the NAACP. . . . Yes, you have seen me when I was more than four thousand dollars ($4,000.00) in the red with my company, plus I was on the verge of losing my home. I still laid down everything and responded to every call by the NAACP anywhere in the nation. Do I need a reminder?[26]

Darden did not exaggerate his sacrifices at all, but his admirable record was not particularly pertinent to the issue at hand. It would have been possible for him to respond to any criticism by reciting his activist contribution, and there were activists who did exactly that.

In the 1950s some observers would have said that staff members of the NAACP's national office didn't seem to appreciate the sacrifices made by a few heroic souls in the South. The NAACP had enough experience in the management of near-martyrs or the survivors of people who had been martyred to know how difficult it could be to work with them. Some people got invested in the role of being professional heroes.

Gus Courts—Laura McGhee's brother and the man who survived a shooting in Belzoni in 1955—believed that God had saved him to tell "the Naked Truth to the World." Before he was fully healed, he was speaking to Black churches and NAACP branches, exposing the horrors of Mississippi and extolling the virtues of the NAACP. Somehow, the national office lost track of him for a while until he showed up in Chicago in the fall of 1956, destitute, in ill health, as was his wife, living in a hovel and blaming the Association for not doing more to help him. Gloster Current in the New York office worried about how that kind of criticism would sound coming from a near-martyr:

> Once again we are faced with a problem situation and in Mr. Courts' case we may have to handle him very carefully. He has made a marvelous contribution to our cause and [our] utilization of his services has given him a great sense of importance.

The Association was able to give him some short-term aid. The following spring he requested a five-thousand-dollar loan from the Association to enable him to purchase a grocery store in Chicago. When more than a month passed without his receiving a clear reply, Courts wrote an angry, threatening letter to Roy Wilkins:

> It is against my grain to beg and continue to do so and accept small collections from churches which are growing much less interested in me . . . I MUST do something. Must I go back to Mississippi, denounce the NAACP and accept the offers of the South? No, I must not do that. . . . Am I to understand that after I have done my best and given my all—nobody cares? I worked hard for the NAACP and it profited by my work. Has it now deserted me?

The NAACP found it difficult to draw the line between reasonable requests for help and activism-as-larceny. Being reconstructed as a hero did seem to change Courts. While in Chicago, he had business cards printed up that read:

> Gus Courts
> —Formerly of—
> Belzoni, Mississippi
> Who was shot because he refused to remove his
> name from the Voting List[27]

The accusations and counter-accusations of self-seeking behavior in Greenwood in the sixties constitute what Black southerners call a Who-Struck-John?—a discussion so tangled that there is little hope of ever straightening it out. While I do not doubt that there was a rise in the level of unprincipled behavior, I would also suspect that the accusations of cutting deals and selling out were overused. In an emotionally charged situation, it too easily becomes the all-purpose explanation for whatever one does not understand or like; it is too easily used to discredit any opponent with whom one disagrees. Leaders have to negotiate with the other side, but once the bonds of trust begin unraveling, any negotiation can look like deal-cutting to people who have been dealt on all their lives.

Poverty-program jobs did pull some activists out of their old orbits, but that did not necessarily mean they had been coopted. Militant local activists don't immediately become tame and conservative because they are getting a paycheck. Indeed, ex-COFO people were often the worst employees imaginable, precisely because they went on agitating inside their new organizations, often against their own bosses. What was destructive was not necessarily the fact that they were hired but that it happened at a time in the movement's history when many people were almost predisposed to distrust the motives of others.

Some of the charges of selling out also overlook the fact that it had become more difficult to say what the movement was trying to do. Skipping the cases of outright dishonesty, some of what was called selling out in 1968 would have been called progress had it happened in 1963. In 1963, working with something like the Loyalist party, had that been possible, would not necessarily have been seen as wrong. Indeed, most people at that time would have agreed that the whole point was to open up the system to those who had been excluded from it. Some of the people who took jobs with MAP—which eventually came to include Hollis Watkins, MacArthur Cotton, Al Garner, and Silas McGhee—clearly felt that in doing so they were only taking advantage of the kinds of opportunities for a better life that the movement had been trying to create. Aaron Henry and Charles Evers, increasingly vilified as Uncle Toms, seem to have felt this way, as did people like Father Machesky in Greenwood. What was selling-out from one perspective was just moving on from another, becoming a part of the structure so that one could change it even more.

Lawrence Guyot, FDP's first chair, was among those who argued most forcefully for moving on. He never accepted the idea that cooperation with the regular Democratic party was evil. He understood what the establishment was trying to do, he understood that he was getting into partnerships with people who were going to be tough to deal with, people he would have to fight tooth and nail on a thousand issues, but he also believed that the movement had reached a point where it had to institutionalize some of what it had done. The fight wasn't about being politically pure; it was a fight to get in and take over. What would have happened had SNCC decided in 1962 to remain outside the Black church because the church was so backwards? They had decided to go into the churches and change them, and that's just what they did. In 1966, there was every reason to believe that an influx of movement energies could begin to change national political structures. Guyot's personal history inclined him to this view. For fifty years, his great-uncle was the chairman of the Republican party in Hancock County. Guyot thus had a personal feel for the possibilities of Black participation in national parties that few other Black Mississippians could have had.

A part of what divides the two perspectives is the bitterness created by the fact that the new opportunities were least available to movement veterans. Another part of it, though, is that many of the veterans had changed so much because of their activism. Marx noted that those who try to change the world are certain to at least transform themselves.[28] Many of those who in the early years would have thought integrating the Democratic party a worthwhile goal had, by the middle sixties, become much more skeptical about both the state and the national parties, much more cautious about trusting white moderates or traditional Negro leaders. These were the sources of betrayal, and one tainted oneself merely by being close to them. Younger activists were more likely to undergo this kind of radicalization than older ones like Charles Evers and Aaron Henry.

Commenting on this contentious period, one CDGM supporter noted that most people tended to see the groups they liked as entirely virtuous and the groups they disliked as completely evil. Translating the dialectics into the idiom of Mississippi, she added "Life ain't like that, chile—there's Jesus and the Devil all mixed together in each thing you look at." In these arguments about who sold out whom, there was sincere belief and good intent on both sides, and some self-serving motives on both. Nonetheless, it is also true that when veteran activists legitimated vehicles like the MAP and the Loyalist Democrats, they departed from the SNCC-COFO-FDP tradition that the poor have to define their own self-interest, marking an important change in the political philosophy that underlay much of the activist upsurge in the state since 1961, a change would not have been possible without the help of political elites within the state and outside of it. In 1961, the Kennedy administration had erred seriously in thinking that it could control the movement by channeling it into voter registration. The Johnson administration was much more successful in its policy of splitting off the movement's right wing and using it to build company unions.

The transition from Medgar to Charles Evers illustrates the state-wide change to a more morally ambiguous climate. By the middle sixties, Charles Evers had a sizeable and devoted following among poor Blacks, particularly in Fayette and Jefferson counties. Statewide, feelings about him were always more divided than they had been about his brother. No one doubted his nerve. Returning to the state to take his dead brother's job as NAACP field secretary was courageous in 1963. Even some of those who admired him for that, though, found him abrasive and egotistical. Personality conflicts aside, many people in COFO or FDP also found him opportunistic—exploiting the popularity of a martyred brother, opening a grocery store of his own when white stores were being boycotted, using poverty funds as a form of patronage to build his own political machine, making alliances with powerful politicians with segregationist records. He has also been accused of causing people unwilling to go along with his program to lose their jobs. Ed King, the Tougaloo chaplain who had been a good friend of Medgar's, attended a mass meeting at which it became clear that people who were not supporting the boycott Charles Evers was then leading were pressured with tactics that might have been borrowed from the klan. Evers has called charges of this sort distortions. He has responded to charges of opportunism by claiming that his critics don't understand pragmatic political and economic development.[29] There were certainly people who disliked Medgar Evers, and plenty who thought his politics ill-considered, but he was almost universally seen as a symbol of personal integrity. However one judges the charges and counter-charges surrounding his brother, Charles is a more ambiguous figure, and in that sense the transition from Medgar to Charles is a metaphor for a change, a loss of moral clarity, that affected the entire movement.

Considering what happened to initiatives like the Freedom Democratic Party and the Child Development Group, it is easy to see why some observers see the process as fundamentally a history of cooptation. That is true as far as it goes, but it is also a history of demoralization. It simply became harder to know what to believe in or whom to trust. Had it not been for the demoralization, it might have been more difficult for outside elites to coopt so much of the movement's energy.

It is said frequently that the movement's loss of energy and direction in the post-1965 period came because the movement had achieved its goals. Civil rights had been achieved, more or less. From the viewpoint of local people in Greenwood, that makes little sense. It puts too much emphasis on legal changes, which, while welcomed, were only part of what local people wanted. For local people, the movement was about freedom, not just civil rights. At the very least, their conception of freedom would have included decent jobs, housing, and education. In 1966, local activists in Greenwood still had a clear agenda of things they wanted changed, and they had organizational vehicles they thought might do the job.

No one would suggest that the reciprocal processes of demoralization and cooptation were the sole factors explaining the decline of activist politics in Greenwood. From the viewpoint of the people I interviewed, however, these are the ones that emerge with the greatest clarity, the ones that are remembered when they look back after a quarter-century. Nothing they said to me could be construed as meaning they were largely content with what the movement had achieved by 1965 or that they didn't know what they wanted to do next. In fact, the opposite seems more likely; the visible legislative victories, in which they felt they had played a role, whetted their appetite for further change.

Ironically, the demoralization was itself a by-product of the movement's success. Bringing new people into the movement was only possible because the movement had been more successful than seemed possible in 1962. Participation had been made relatively safe, for one thing, and potentially worthwhile in terms of economic rewards, prestige, or political influence. The newcomers often differed from the older activists in their sense of how leaders should act and how they should be rewarded. Even though the old-timers wanted to draw new people into the movement, the presence of the newcomers created distrust and resentment, all the more so because the newcomers were often more acceptable than movement veterans to those who were in a position to affect the distribution of benefits. Local politicians in Greenwood much preferred having previously apolitical teachers running Head Starts to having CDGM people run them. As the Loyalist Democrats ascended to power, they were more comfortable sharing political influence with the more conservative and traditional types of Black leaders than with the unpredictable FDP types. All the doors newly opened by the movement created new temptations for self-seeking behavior, and it seems that both movement veterans and newcomers succumbed at times.

The essence of the demoralization in Greenwood probably had more to do with uncertainty than with dishonesty or truly self-seeking behavior. What to believe? Whom to trust? Courage was essential to the early movement, but so was the ability of movement people to trust one another. In the changed conditions of the middle sixties, trust was more important than physical courage, and it could not be sustained. What had been a politics of community became increasingly just a politics.

Thirteen

MRS. HAMER IS NO LONGER RELEVANT

The Loss of the Organizing Tradition

Even the hatred of squalor
Makes the brow grow stern.
Even anger against injustice
Makes the voice grow harsh. Alas, we
Who wished to lay the foundations of kindness
Could not ourselves be kind.

BERTOLT BRECHT

So my rationalization for it is that the kids tried the established
methods and they tried at the expense of their lives, which is much
different from the accommodating role of trying that had previously
been used. . . . So they began to look for other answers.

ELLA BAKER[1]

ON MANY COLLEGE CAMPUSES today, Black student organizations do not use traditional titles for their officers. Instead of presidents and treasurers they have "facilitators" or "coordinators." On some campuses, there is not a single member of the organization with any idea why Black students forming organizations in the late 1960s didn't use the more common terms. The language chosen by the students of the sixties reflects the fact that they were still in touch, in greatly varying degrees, with an entire philosophy about social change that cautioned against hierarchy and centralized leadership. Contemporary students are almost entirely unaware of that heritage.

To take another example, columnist Clarence Page opens a recent Public Broadcasting documentary on Black conservatives by claiming that for most of this century civil rights leaders have focused on outside help rather than the Black community's own resources; now, he says, in the 1990s some conservative Black leaders are focusing on Black self-help. I suspect few viewers, including few Black viewers, will question his premise: that the civil rights movement was something that had little to do with the Black community's own sacrifices and resources. The ideological right has successfully appropriated the movement's history and reinscribed it to support the conservative line, and even contemporary Black activists are often sufficiently alienated from their own history as to not recognize its theft.[2]

In the late sixties and early seventies, the themes of the community-organizing tradition—the developmental perspective, an emphasis on building relationships, respect for collective leadership, for bottom-up change, the expansive sense of how democracy ought to operate in everyday life, the emphasis on building for the long haul, the anti-bureaucratic ethos, the preference for addressing local issues—were reflected, in varying combinations, in some anti-poverty campaigns, in various forms of nationalist organizing, in struggles on college campuses. In some cases, Deep South organizers carried the organizing philosophy with them as they moved on to other struggles. One can certainly find contemporary examples of activists self-consciously working within the organizing tradition (and far more of activists using that tradition's rhetoric). It is still fair to say that the organizing tradition as a political and intellectual legacy of Black activists has been effectively lost, pushed away from the table by more top-down models.

In the sixties, organizing represented just one culture of activism among the several that made up the movement. It never had much visibility to those outside the movement. Outsiders saw the sit-ins, the Freedom Rides, Freedom Summer, Atlantic City, but not deeper traditions that lay underneath them. Nonetheless, at a critical juncture in our history, some of the country's most innovative and influential activists were working within and redefining an organizing tradition, and through them, the concerns of that tradition were part of the larger dialogue in the Black community about direction and means. That is seldom the case now.

In part certainly, organizing lost ground because to people hungry for change it often looked like such a tortuously slow road that people began experimenting with other activist styles. The radical-nationalist thrusts that came to dominate much Black activism after the mid-sixties represent not one but several distinguishable activist cultures, some of them diametrically opposed to the assumptions of the organizing tradition. Some—I stress the *some* here—of those operating under the new political banners had no problem with hierarchy so long as they could be at the top of it, no problem with cults of personality so long as they got to pick the personalities, little conception of individual growth as a political issue, more interest in the dramatic gesture than in building at the base, and little concern with building interpersonal relationships that reflected their larger values. The basic metaphor of solidarity became "nation," not "family." The last may be especially important. The larger movement—not just SNCC and not just the civil rights movement—underwent a loss of community similar to what happened at the local level in Greenwood. While their analysis was in fact growing sharper in many ways, movement activists increasingly lost the ability to relate to one another in human terms. Even had there been no other changes, that alone would probably have been enough to prevent much organizing. In the movement's sense of "organize," in the transformative sense, it is probably safe to say that you cannot organize people you do not respect. You can lead them, you can inspire them, you can make speeches at them, but you cannot organize them. Some of the more self-consciously radical thrusts, notwithstanding rhetoric to the contrary, were simply contemptuous of the individual.[3]

Near the end of 1964, Bob Moses wrote that SNCC was like a boat in the water that had to be repaired to stay afloat but had to stay afloat in order to be repaired. Too many issues needed to be addressed simultaneously. Between the fall of 1964 and the spring of 1966, SNCC was trying to resolve a staggering number of questions, many of them products of the organization's disillusionment with American society. What did "integration" mean, and was the country worth integrating into? How would it be possible to accommodate both the need of individual members for freedom of conscience and action and the need of the organization for discipline? What was the proper role of whites in the context of increasing race consciousness among Blacks? How is it possible to provide leadership without being manipulative? Is it possible to be both moral and politically effective? How could the organization speak to economic inequalities, rural and urban? If neither the federal government nor liberals could be trusted, where were the movement's allies? Could allies or models be found in the Third World? How should the organization respond to the anger in the urban ghettoes and the periodic violent uprisings it generated? What are the limits on what local leadership can accomplish? Should existing social structures be reformed or new ones created? What was to be the role of women in the movement? What should be the movement's position on Vietnam?

Even had there been fewer questions, discussion about them was increasingly taking place in an atmosphere of mutual distrust and recriminations, a deteriorating social climate that would ultimately lead to SNCC members threatening one another with weapons, to members calling the police to settle disputes among themselves, to the members of one faction "firing" all the members of another faction and being "fired" by them in turn. We are still far from fully understanding the causes of these changes, but an important part of the explanation may be that the transition from the Beloved Community to Black Power was accompanied by a jettisoning of some of the moral and social anchors that had helped regulate relationships among activists when SNCC was in its community-organizing phase.

Even allowing for some nostalgic exaggeration on the part of early SNCC members, there is not much doubt that most members at that time really did find the movement an oasis of personal trust, an extended family more sustaining than some real families. Joyce Ladner remembers Medgar Evers introducing her to a CORE worker who had come into the state to lay groundwork for the Freedom Rides. "We didn't ask questions. You didn't ask questions back then. We just accepted him as he was." Bob Moses compared SNCC's ability to release from its members levels of personal energy that they themselves never knew they had to nuclear fusion. The sense of trust and community was an important part of that, and its erosion was an important part of the organization's growing ineffectiveness. Instead of making individuals feel larger and stronger, it made them weaker. "They began to sort of eat on each other," Ella Baker put it.[4]

Jim Forman and Bob Moses always represented somewhat opposite tendencies in SNCC. Forman, while aware of the need for field workers to have considerable autonomy, thought the organization needed to be run like a real organization if it was going to be effective. Moses, while aware of the need for some minimal level of organizational discipline, was much more afraid of the possibility of too much organization suffocating the spirit. These differences did not prevent them from working together. In the wake of the 1964 Summer Project, they jointly developed a plan to expand SNCC's range of operation and to take advantage of the momentum created by the Summer Project. Called the Black Belt Project, the intention was to establish new projects in counties with large Black populations, from Virginia to Texas, this time using Black volunteers to minimize racial conflict as well as the chances of undermining the confidence of local participants. Preliminary inquiries suggested that both Black college students and local Black communities were going to be receptive to the idea. The plan was introduced for approval at a staff meeting that fall but never fully discussed. As soon as it was introduced, some members began questioning the motives of its authors and arguing that there should have been more staff input in its development, reacting as if it were a final decision rather than a proposal. Discussion got side-tracked into a consideration of the basic issue of decision-making. Some members objected to the plan, apparently without revealing their real motives for doing so. Some took the plan to be a power-play on the part of those who had done the preliminary planning. Apparently, in that climate, neither Forman nor Moses felt comfortable pushing the plan. The plan was tabled. Forman later wrote that the kind of confusion that characterized discussion of the Black Belt plan would have been "unimaginable" one or two years earlier. SNCC had then been a smaller, more tightly knit group, "moving on the assumption of great unity of purpose and good intentions as well as a willingness to compromise."[5]

The inability to implement the Black Belt Project was a sign of things to come. Time and again, the substance of ideas could not be discussed because of a climate of suspicion and emotional strain, so that the organization was unable to implement any new projects or even effectively maintain old ones. The climate would become progressively more debilitating. Mary King noted:

> Until late 1965 it was possible to disagree in SNCC and yet not feel reviled, because the underlying bonds were strong. Personal hostility was now [in 1965] being expressed. This did not feel like SNCC to me. It was foreign—dissonant.

Mrs. Hamer commented on the changes at least once. In late 1966 at a dinner at which SNCC workers were honoring her, Mrs. Hamer "turned upon her old friends, as much in sadness as in anger, for growing 'cold' and unloving."[6]

One of the factors contributing to the new and unhealthy climate was the expansion of the staff. At the end of the Summer Project, about eighty volunteers elected to stay on, a decision approved with some misgiving by the staff. The Mississippi staff almost doubled in size. At the same time, the increased national visibility of SNCC following the Summer Project attracted new members to SNCC projects across the South and outside of it. In late 1963, the organization only had about one hundred fifty full-time staff. By the summer of 1965, it had swollen to more than two hundred staff and two hundred fifty full-time volunteers. According to SNCC's Cleveland Sellers:

> This growth, coupled with the changing nature of struggle, was responsible for the emergence of several opposing factions. Although SNCC had always contained individuals who strongly disagreed with each other on various minor issues, it had never really had to contend with large factions divided by basic political differences. I spent much of the spring and summer of 1965 attending long, in-

volved staff meetings where the various factions haggled and argued over everything from the "true nature of freedom" to the cost of insurance.[7]

It is misleading to suggest that early SNCC members disagreed only over "minor" matters, but disagreements in the early years seldom led to the rigid, politicized factions, each quick to suspect the worst of the other factions, that developed after 1964. If the expansion had not occurred so rapidly, or if it had come when the organization had a stable direction programmatically, or if SNCC had been a more hierarchical organization, or if the people coming in had come from social backgrounds more like those of the veterans, the effects might not have been so damaging. At the same time it was trying to reassess its entire program, respond to the morale problems caused by disillusionment with liberal America and by the lingering resentments from the debate over whether there should have even been a Summer Project, SNCC was adding a group of largely upper-middle-class white northerners to what had been predominantly a southern Black movement.

SNCC's membership had always come from diverse backgrounds. Mary King notes that the early members included rural Blacks, northern middle-class blacks, upper-class southern Blacks, New England Quakers, Jews, white ethnics, members of the Left, and southern whites. "Our heterogeneity—a strength while we were small . . . — was strained to the breaking point when we expanded quickly. It resulted in irreconcilable schisms."[8]

Organizational size was always an important consideration to Ella Baker. She generally preferred smaller organizations. She was much impressed by cell structures like that of the Communist party: "I don't think we had any more effective demonstration of organizing people for whatever purpose."[9] She envisioned small groups of people working together but also retaining contact in some form with other such groups, so that coordinated action would be possible whenever large numbers really were necessary. I know of no place where she fully explains her thinking, but, given her values, it is almost certain that she would have been put off by the undemocratic tendencies of larger organizations as well as by their usual failure to provide the kind of environment that encouraged individual growth. I suspect that she also favored smaller organizations precisely because they were less likely to factionalize or develop climates of distrust.

The changing social base of its membership, as well as the rapid expansion in the number of members, contributed to the increasingly negative social climate. That climate, then, contributed to its inability to execute its program, which in turn aggravated internal relations even further. After 1964 there are more reports of staff members acting irresponsibly or just not working at all. In Greenwood, Mary Boothe remembers the post-1964 period as a time when there were staff meetings all the time but very little follow-up. There were similar problems across the state. Referring to the fall of 1964, Clayborne Carson writes:

> Some of those involved in the Summer Project abandoned their responsibilities, citing fatigue and a desire to allow local black residents to assume greater control over civil rights activities in their communities. Freedom schools and community centers in Mississippi were closed, owing to the absence of dependable personnel. "People were wandering in and out of the organization," Marion Barry recalled. "Some worked, some didn't work." There was a noticeable increase in marijuana usage, which contributed to the discipline problems.

In the years between 1964 and 1966, Jack Newfield notes, "drinking, auto accidents, petty thievery, pot smoking, personality clashes, inefficiency and anti-white outbursts all increased." According to Forman, even some of those "who had come to SNCC as disciplined, dedicated workers became dysfunctional and disgusted within a year or two." After the winter of 1965, Cleveland Sellers remembers, "Although most of us were under twenty-five, we seemed to have aged. Our faces were haggard, our nerves overwrought. Arguments over trifles dominated all our meetings." He recalls relationships deteriorating to a point where two factions had a stand-off involving "pool cues, baseball bats, knives and a couple of pistols." The issue at stake was whether people at a conference could be admitted to breakfast without a meal ticket.

When Cleveland Sellers was elected program secretary in 1965 he was determined to set the house back in order, and he quickly sent letters to all staffers asking them to explain what they were doing. The move generated substantial resentment among some old members, who thought SNCC should still operate like an extended family, and some newer members, who thought it smacked of authoritarianism. The various initiatives by Sellers and others were insufficient to halt the decline. By 1966, SNCC projects in Mississippi had weakened to the point where both the NAACP and SCLC were considering expanding their activities to take advantage of the vacuum.[10]

Factions contributed to programmatic ineffectiveness. Sellers describes two of the important factions as the Floaters and the Hardliners, putting himself in the latter group. His admittedly biased description portrays Floaters as equally divided between Blacks and whites, generally well-educated and committed to integrationist ideals. They were resistant to organizational discipline, upholding the right of the individual to follow the dictates of individual conscience, an important principle in early SNCC. "Go where the spirit say go," they used to say, "Do what the spirit say do." In the early years, the small size of the organization and the fact that the membership was so highly self-selected probably ensured that personal freedom wouldn't too often become personal license. In later years, according to Miss Baker, "the right of people to participate in the decisions that affect their lives . . . began to be translated into the idea that each person working had a right to decide what ought to be done. So you began to do your own thing."[11]

Hardliners tended to be Blacks, with less formal education than Floaters, were more likely to be field organizers, and were less concerned with personal freedom than with organizational effectiveness, which they saw as requiring a greater degree of centralization and accountability. In retrospect, Mary King thought that while the problems were difficult ones, they could have been resolved had the discussion not taken place in an atmosphere of suspicion and paranoia.[12]

Program ineffectiveness was probably also a function of the reluctance of some new members to work with local leaders in the old way. On the one hand, Ivanhoe Donaldson, who had driven truckloads of food to Leflore during the winter of 1962–63, had moved to Columbus and, cooperating with local leaders, had set up what appeared to be a very promising community development corporation. On the other hand, Carson attributes the modest success of the attempt to organize in Vine City ghetto in Atlanta to the failure of the leadership "to acquire the support of strong, indigenous adult leaders who had traditionally provided entree for SNCC field secretaries." Many of those in the leadership of the project were relatively recent members of SNCC. Where the veterans were almost always respectful of local leadership, sometimes to the point of romanticizing it, some of the new members had no respect for local leaders at all, seeing them as clear examples of political backwardness. At a 1966 meeting where the expulsion of whites had been proposed, Mrs. Hamer fought the idea. A few separatists discounted her position since she was "no longer relevant" and not at their level of development.[13]

Attitudes like that may have been part of the reason organizers began leaving rural areas. At the same time, ghetto uprisings and the passage of the civil rights bill caused more concern with taking the movement to the cities. Traditionally, the great majority of staff members had been stationed in the rural South. By October of 1966, only a third of the staff remained in such areas, the rest being placed in urban centers in the South or outside of it. According to Carson, most of those who joined in 1966 were urban Blacks drawn to the militant image of SNCC rather than to the kind of organizing it had done in rural areas, and "few wanted to engage in the difficult work of gaining the trust and support of southern black people who were older than themselves and less aware of the new currents of black nationalist thought." More harshly, Forman claims that too many of the newcomers were simply middle-class Black elitists, unwilling to work with poor people.[14]

Drifting away from the close ties they had once shared with local people meant that the movement was drifting away from one of its moral anchors. In earlier years, Bob Moses had noted that being rooted in the lives of local people kept the movement from going off on tangents. Similarly, Martha Prescod Norman pointed out that the decision to work with people like Mrs. Hamer and Amzie Moore implied a decision to conduct oneself in a manner acceptable within their moral code. Some of the contentious and dogmatic behavior that came to characterize the movement in the middle sixties would never have been tolerated by local people. For many of the local people with whom SNCC had worked, nothing excused a lack of personal courtesy, and abstract ideas about political direction were less important than relationships with concrete individuals.

The loss of faith in nonviolence meant the loss of another moral anchor. Nonviolence is frequently talked about in tactical terms, in terms of its impact on the outside world, but the internal effects of the nonviolent, Christian tradition may have been equally important. Although not a proponent of nonviolence herself, Ella Baker noted with approval that in SNCC's early days the kids "were so keen about the concept of nonviolence that they were trying to exercise a degree of consciousness and care about not being violent in their judgment of others."[15] So long as significant numbers of members were making an effort to live their daily lives according to the dictates of stringent moral codes, there was something to balance whatever forces might have generated interpersonal bitterness. As organizers generally lost faith in American values, rejected the nonviolent, Christian tradition, and drifted away from their close contacts with the rural poor, they failed to create or find any functionally equivalent system for regulating their day-to-day behavior with one another. Without some such system, activists could become as much a danger to one another as to the social order.

The increasingly dogmatic style represents an especially important break with SNCC's heritage. It is quite different from the attitude with which the first organizers entered Mississippi. SNCC members had often prided themselves on their non-ideological character, on the way in which they developed ideas out of action. By the mid-sixties, ideas were taking on a primacy of their own, which meant a tendency to be unable to learn further from experience.

As a counter-example, consider Charlie Cobb's experience with the

Julian Bond campaign. During the spring of 1965 Bond, at the urging of Ivanhoe Donaldson, ran for a seat in the Georgia House. By this time, probably a majority of SNCC members had deep doubts about participating in the political system. Some of those who did not participate in Bond's campaign called those who did sell-outs, symbolized by the exchange of overalls for coats and ties among campaign workers. Charles Cobb decided to participate despite his own misgivings: "I will confess that I was also worried about the corrupting influence of politics in general. I felt, and I still feel, the threat . . . American 'politics' has on people who 'play the game'—you know, like touch . . . and be tainted." At the time, according to Cobb, most of the staff thought that city people were hardest to organize; they were "too apathetic." "We don't know yet what can tap and sustain the energies of the people locked up in the city ghettoes." Bond ran a campaign very much in the SNCC tradition. His workers went door to door, asking people what their problems were and what they wanted from a state representative (which often required explaining what a state representative was, since these people had never really had one before). On the basis of their responses, Bond fashioned a platform that stressed economic issues. He won the primary and the election by comfortable margins. Cobb learned a good deal from the effort. In the final analysis, he wrote, urban organizing is the same as rural: "What people need—all over!—is something they can grab hold of, or build, that is their own." He found that his own fears "about controlling people or manipulating them blurred in the give and take dialogue (which implies give and take of decision-making and ideas) with the community." After the campaign he was fascinated by the idea of communities "moving in and out of traditional American political forms. It implies a creation of instability of these political forms, created by people whose needs are not being and probably will not be met by the forms anyway. I think it is to our advantage to have oppressive government unstable."

Cobb's stance was open-ended. He took part in the campaign despite misgivings; he was willing to experiment with a tactic he thought dubious. The experiment then changed his thinking to something more complex than an either-or choice about whether to participate in the system. Much of what was dynamic in SNCC is reflected in Cobb's attitude, and that dynamism would be lost in a more dogmatic climate.[16]

The more doctrinaire climate also meant a tendency to see one another in increasingly stereotypical, one-dimensional terms. Ella Baker and Septima Clark understood clearly that the matron in the fur coat or the self-important preacher were hardly models of progressive thought, but they still assumed that such people could be worked with and could make a contribution. This ability to see people in their full complexity was increasingly lost in the more dogmatic phase of the movement, and as had been the case with southern racists, labels came increasingly to substitute for an awareness of the contradictions and complexities of individuals. Once, in the context of an argument within SNCC over who had the right to participate in the movement, Miss Baker, with uncharacteristic rhetorical flourish, said, "We need to penetrate the mystery of life and perfect the mastery of life and the latter requires understanding that human beings are human beings."[17] Making allowances for the ordinary human imperfections and contradictions of one's comrade became increasingly unlikely as the movement became increasingly dogmatic.

SNCC's increasing radicalism meant increasingly problematic relations with former allies. In the wake of the Atlantic City convention, they found relations with northern liberals and funding sources strained. In November 1964, the NAACP, still very angry over Atlantic City, left the COFO coalition, citing SNCC dominance. COFO disbanded altogether a year later. After Atlantic City, SNCC also found itself redbaited more frequently, a problem exacerbated even more in early 1966, when SNCC spoke out officially against the Vietnam War, the first major civil rights group to do so (although King as an individual had earlier made known his opposition). Most SNCC members seem to have opposed the war from the very beginning but the organization refrained from taking a stand until Sammy Younge, an Alabama SNCC worker and a navy veteran, was killed for trying to use a white restroom. Their statement on Vietnam argued that "the murder of Samuel Younge in Tuskegee, Alabama, is no different from the murder of people in Vietnam." In 1966, the liberal establishment was still largely behind the war. Even a year later, when Martin Luther King, against the advice of his staff, spoke out very aggressively against the war, he was sharply criticized by much of the liberal community. For SNCC, liberal reaction to its position on the war was more evidence of liberal hypocrisy. All apart from the war issue, SNCC's increasing emphasis on economic issues meant that it was going to have more trouble with liberals. "We are raising fundamental questions," Bob Moses said, "about how the poor sharecropper can achieve the Good Life, questions liberalism is incapable of answering." By 1967, most members thought of themselves as anti-capitalist, anti-imperialist members of the Third World.[18]

Reconciling the more global concerns with the daily problems of the sharecropper and the ghetto dweller did not prove easy. The deepening radicalism led to Stokely Carmichael's election as chairman. In 1965, when few SNCC projects were going well, he had led an effort in Lowndes County, Alabama, that resulted in the creation of what was becoming a very powerful Black political party. His work there was very much in the community-organizing tradition, basic door-to-door organizing to create vehicles to empower the powerless. His success increased his prestige within the organization. His election in May 1966 reflected that, and it was also a repudiation of the tradition of Christian nonviolence symbolized by John Lewis, who had been chair since 1963. The shift from the religious Alabaman to the brasher, more eloquent New Yorker also symbolized a shift in the organization's self-presentation. Carmichael was seen as more militant on racial issues than Lewis, although his nationalism never precluded effective working relations with whites, a distinction largely lost on the press.

Traditionally, SNCC chairmen had not become media figures, but that changed under Carmichael, primarily because of the Black Power controversy. In early June, less than a month after the election, James Meredith began his March Against Fear, intending to walk from Memphis to Jackson to prove that it could be done. He was shot from ambush on the second day. A coalition of civil rights groups quickly formed to continue the march. Almost as quickly, the NAACP and Urban League, deliberately baited by Carmichael, pulled out. He refused

stop using white SNCC members as punching bags against whom they could release pent-up racial frustrations.

There was broad agreement within the organization, including among many white members, that some of these were valid problems, but different people took different lessons from that. Many, probably a majority, thought that it was time that white organizers started working in white communities. Others thought that whites had to go altogether. Among those taking the hardest line were the members of the Atlanta Project, an attempt to demonstrate that urban areas could be successfully organized. Half of the members were from the North, many were veterans, but only a few had been with SNCC in its earliest years. Most had not been as exposed to the nonviolent, Christian period of the movement and were not as likely to have long-standing personal relations with individual whites. Black members who had gone through that earlier period even as they adopted nationalist ideology were more likely to envision a continuing role for at least those individual whites with whom they had shared jail cells, cigarette butts, and beatings.[28]

Members of the Atlanta Project were among those within the organization engaging in a new form of race-baiting. While members of the press kept the organization on the defensive by constantly raising the specter of Black racism, members of the Atlanta Project kept other Black SNCC members on the defensive by constantly questioning their loyalty to the race. The Atlanta separatists also acquired a general reputation for being difficult to work with. "They ignored memos, refused to return phone calls and rarely attended general staff meetings," according to Cleveland Sellers. Some of the lack of cooperation may be attributable to the fact that some members were jealous of Carmichael or to the fact that from their perspective, the persons running the organization, even though largely nationalist, had not achieved the level of consciousness they had reached.[29]

Members of the Atlanta Project forced a "final" resolution of the racial question at a staff meeting in upstate New York in December 1966. To the chagrin of many present, they refused to allow any other business to be discussed until that issue was disposed of. Debate went on for several frustrating and emotional days. Carmichael argued for the whites-organizing-whites idea rather than exclusion. In the end, the vote was for exclusion of whites, with nineteen voting for the motion, eighteen against, and twenty-four official abstentions. (Perhaps another twenty-odd members were not present for the vote, held at two in the morning.)[30]

The December vote did not lay the race question to rest. In May of 1967, Bob and Dottie Zellner presented the central committee with a proposal under which they would organize a poor white community in New Orleans. They had already acquired their own funding, but they wanted to operate the project as SNCC members without any special restrictions because of their race. Zellner had been in SNCC almost since its inception and held a special status. Sellers, one of the leaders of the nationalist thrust, said Zellner "commanded the unqualified respect of everyone in the organization. He was a damned good man. No one questioned his courage or his commitment." During the uneasy debate over the proposal, Forman, also an architect of SNCC's nationalist position, called Zellner his best friend. The decision not to accept the Zellners' proposal was painfully made by the committee, most of whose members, with the exception of Forman, had not been in the organization as long as Zellner. Someone wanted to deliver the decision by mail rather than look the Zellners in the face. Forman condemned that proposal for cowardice. What comes through from all accounts of the meeting is the ambivalence of SNCC's officers, committed though they were to the nationalist path. In the name of ideological principle, they were doing something that just did not sit right in the gut. Like nearly all of the whites expelled from the organization, the Zellners refused to talk with an eager national press.[31]

The Zellners stayed in the organization longer than did many members of the Atlanta Project. A few months after the December meeting at which they had pushed the expulsion of whites, Atlanta Project staff were themselves fired from SNCC after they had responded to a disagreement over use of a staff car by sending Jim Forman a threatening letter. There was talk among the Project members of settling their expulsion with force, but that was averted. They had, though, made a contribution to the growing pattern of dogmatism within SNCC that would outlast their actual presence. "In their uncompromising effort to impose their ideas on other SNCC workers, they further undermined the trust, mutual respect, and interdependence without which SNCC could not survive," according to Carson.[32] Still, it is not clear that they were any more dogmatic than any of the other factions.

The expulsion of whites from SNCC and from some other movement organizations is taken to be a watershed in our social history, but emphasizing racial antagonisms in this way can be misleading. American intellectuals have often stressed the interracial to the exclusion of the intraracial.[33] For the same reason that the deaths of Black activists never had the public impact of the deaths of white activists, social commentary on the movement in the middle of the decade sometimes focused on how Blacks and whites were interacting almost to the exclusion of looking at how Blacks were interacting with one another. Thus, we don't fully appreciate one of the central ironies of the period, that while elaborating an ideology that gave a new primacy to racial unity, Black activists increasingly lost the capacity to work effectively with one another. Once that happened, the status of whites in the movement was more or less beside the point. The expulsion of whites has to be understood as one expression of a more pervasive deterioration in social relationships. Charlie Cobb refers to it as a period of tribalism, a time when activists began making invidious distinctions among themselves based on educational background, region of origin, philosophy of organization, placement on the field or office staff, length of movement service.[34]

One important dividing line was that between northern and southern Blacks. Tensions had been present from the beginning. At SNCC's founding conference in 1960, Miss Baker had been at some pains to keep southern students and northern ones apart, precisely because the northern students were better schooled and exposed to a broader range of social philosophies. Miss Baker thought it important that the basically southern character of the early struggle not be suddenly overwhelmed by all these ideas the southern students weren't yet prepared to discuss.

Even among Black students, each group came to Raleigh conference with its own reputation. The North Carolina kids had been the most activist and had the prestige that went with that. The Atlanta kids were seen as swell-heads, and they did have a pretty high opinion of themselves. They quickly learned that in this context, they lost points because they hadn't engaged in much direct action, and no one at the conference was especially impressed with the ringing proclamations they had issued. The Nashville group was the most steeped in the study of nonviolence and civil disobedience, probably the only group to have a regular pattern of workshops, and like the North Carolina kids, they already had a great deal of practical experience. The Howard group was thought to be more articulate than any of the others in a formal sense and better prepared to argue their positions. Miss Baker noted that kids from the southern tradition were strong on the flowery oratory but less good at reasoned dialogue. The Howard group was also seen as more aggressive than the other students, often inappropriately aggressive, a reputation that would follow them and other northern students so long as the movement in the South lasted.[35]

Joyce Ladner, who appreciated the students, white and Black, who came from the North and once thought they might be the South's salvation, still felt a deeper sense of communion with students who shared her southern background.

> I strongly agreed with the southerners, Black southerners in the movement much more than I did with northerners because they understood more. I used to feel that there were occasions when northerners didn't fully understand and they could go back to their own homes. So I had a special affinity with people like MacArthur Cotton, Sam Block, Willie Peacock, James Peacock, Hollis and Curtis. They were people like me. I always felt we had much more of a stake in what happened in the South, in Mississippi.

Hollis Watkins expressed the differences more sharply. He referred to northern students as "the children of those who ran" from the South. He found northern Black students less dependable, more given to rash behavior. They were great philosophers, he said; they could rap for days, but they might or might not be around when something serious had to be done. Those who had not been politically active in the North were actually less trouble than those who came down with some prior experience. If they already had any kind of civil rights experience, you couldn't tell them anything. They already had all the answers. Willie Peacock noted that "we [Southerners] had spiritual values; most of them did not. . . . They tried to rationalize everything. Because of our different realities, we clashed on many issues." Other southern-born organizers expressed similar feelings. Northerners had too little respect for the local people and their customs. Above all, perhaps, they were simply seen as arrogant and pushy, too prone to seeing themselves as saviors.[36]

Similarly, James Forman has been sharply critical of certain attitudes that he attributed to middle-class northerners, whatever their color. He attributes much of the disorder of the post-1964 period to their increasing influence within the organization, and the egotism and elitism they brought with them. He also sees them as the source of a kind of bourgeois liberalism that made them so concerned with retaining a kind of moral purity they were unwilling to exercise the power they might have exercised.

As with race, these antagonisms were at least partly a struggle over ownership of the movement. According to Mary King, the involvement of the white and powerful tended to make local field staff, those who had risked the most to build the movement, feel excluded. That is no doubt true, but it does not apply only to the involvement of whites. When the Summer Project was still under debate, local staff objected to the idea of large numbers of white students coming down, but many were also uncomfortable with the idea of large numbers of Black students coming down, and the Greenwood staff objected to SNCC's national office coming to Greenwood. Although they differed in intensity, there were objections to outsiders, period, and the objections were almost certainly related to the fact that the outsiders, white or Black, were perceived as taking the movement away from the people who had built it at the local level. As had been expected, national attention focused on the outsiders. There are any number of stories from the Summer Project in which a reporter is in a room with several veterans of the Mississippi movement and Susie Sophomore from Swarthmore, who has been in Mississippi all week. The reporter, of course, wants to talk with Susie. Similarly, as some SNCC members became nationally known spokespersons, they tended not to be the southern-born members of the field staff, but northern Blacks. The southern-born staff was pushed aside inside their own movement, and their resentment showed at times in quite visible disdain for johnny-come-latelys, some of whom had never organized anything and never put their bodies on the line. Fighting back, newcomers sometimes treated whatever SNCC had done prior to their coming as irrelevant and old-fashioned anyway. It was the kind of escalating spiral that could go on endlessly with the real issues never being discussed.

At their most destructive, the various manifestations of tribalism encouraged subgroups of activists to try to establish some higher legitimacy by playing games of moral superiority—Blacker Than Thou, More Dedicated Than Thou, More Revolutionary Than Anybody. In the absence of successful program, it allowed one to maintain a self-identity as being on the side of the angels. Of course, it also helped make organizational life, or even rational discussion, virtually impossible.

The social and political atmosphere of the late sixties was inimical in so many ways to the organizing tradition that it is impossible to be precise about just which of many factors were most important. The social climate that developed in much of the movement community after 1965 was certainly a very important problem. The social climate of the Mississippi movement in the early sixties was developmental in several different respects. In the latter period, it was much more judgmental, more divisive, more negative, sometimes characterized by a dogmatism that militated against thinking freely and experimenting widely. In the name of radicalism, people started destroying their friends. Political work became increasingly media-mediated, increasingly focused on charismatic personalities. The patient path of actual organizing seemed much less attractive. At their worst, the new militant spokespersons were just the modern version of the old southern preacher, Reverend Chickenwing transformed into Brother Abdullah. Rushing off into brave new forms of struggle, activists frequently left behind some of the forms of thinking and doing, some of the relationships that had sustained and anchored activists in Mississippi and elsewhere.

Black Power was and is an unsettling idea. While there is much truth in characterizing it a radical slogan that, at least within SNCC, seldom developed a comparably radical program, the idea of Black Power was a central element in a national debate that changed, probably permanently, the way Americans think about race. For substantial numbers of Black activists and intellectuals, it legitimated their right to think without constant reference to what pleased whites. It added legitimacy to the idea that Blacks have as much right to defend themselves as anyone else, that the legal rights of Blacks cannot be dependent on how loving and nonviolent they are, that Blacks need not beg and plead for what white Americans take for granted. It helped make it possible for an important minority of Black Americans to identify with non-white people the world over and with their own African backgrounds and to begin looking for reasons to take pride in a history that had too often been treated as stigma and degradation. It was a part of several social currents that encouraged Black and white intellectuals to think about social problems in terms that were more institutional and less personal. If it developed in ways that represented a turning away from the styles of many older, rural Blacks, it also captured and gave expression to a growing mood of frustration and urgency among younger Blacks.

The benefits were not without costs. Although few in number, SNCC and CORE organizers had great impact on the shape of political discourse among Blacks nationally. In the best of worlds, as those who had been a part of the organizing tradition began moving to other political styles, some thought would have been given to preserving and passing on whatever had been learned from years of struggle in Deep South communities. In fact, real-world urgencies and the emotional climate of the time left little time for calm reflection. The idealism and high hopes of the early years had been thrown back in their faces. Joyce Ladner said:

> I think a lot of the acting out that people have gone through, the turning on each other, came about in part because of the big, idealistic bubble having been burst in so many places. . . . If this that I

believed and in which I've invested so much psychic energy all these years doesn't work, then what am I to believe?

In turning on one another, they were turning away from the local people of the South and the sense of community that local people had done so much to create within the movement. If the movement's formally radical phase achieved less than it might have, the erosion of community is at least partly responsible for that.

However unwittingly, however compelling the reasons, the activist tradition in the Black community lost touch with the kinds of questions raised by the organizing experience in Mississippi, a loss that has certainly contributed to the impoverishment of political discussion in that community for the last two decades.

Fourteen

Just as people as workers *have no voice in what they make . . .*
so do people as producers of meaning *have no voice in what the*
media make of what they say or do, or in the context in which the media
frame their activity. . . . The processed image then tends to become
"the movement" for wider publics and institutions who have few
alternative sources of information.

TODD GITLIN
The Whole World is Watching[1]

THE FIRST PARAGRAPH OF Richard Kluger's remarkable history of the
1954 Supreme Court decision outlawing school segregation reads:

> Before it was over, they fired him from the little schoolhouse at
> which he had taught devotedly for ten years. And they fired his wife
> and two of his sisters and a niece. And they threatened him with
> bodily harm. And they sued him on trumped up charges and con-
> victed him in a kangaroo court and left with a judgment that de-
> nied him credit from any bank. And they burned his house to the
> ground while the fire department stood around watching the flames
> consume the night. And they stoned the church at which he pas-
> tored. And fired shotguns at him out of the dark. But he was not
> Job, and so he fired back and called the police, who did not come
> and kept not coming. Then he fled, driving north at eighty-five
> miles an hour over country roads, until he was across the state line.
> Soon after, they burned his church to the ground and charged him,

for having shot back that night, with felonious assault with a deadly weapon, and so he became an official fugitive from justice.[2]

The passage refers to the Reverend Joseph Albert Delaine, who in the late 1940s led the Blacks of Clarendon County, South Carolina, in their fight for the equalization of school facilities, a fight that became one of the cases addressed by *Brown v. Board of Education.*

Brown is the kind of Big Event upon which journalists and historians have generally concentrated. By beginning his discussion not with the Event itself but with the people at the bottom of the process—not with lawyers or presidents or judges or civil rights organizations—Kluger makes it clear that the Big Event grew out of a tradition of struggle, that much of the historical initiative was in the hands of the socially obscure, that they were willing to face enormous repressive powers in order to change their world, that the leadership that led to *Brown* was very much a collective leadership, some of whom lived only because they took for granted the right to armed self-defense. He conveys a sense of what may be the central theme of the community-organizing tradition—that people who think they matter, might. Media coverage of the movement—overwhelmingly sympathetic and a crucial part of the movement's success—was seldom able to capture those themes. The Reverend Delaines were invisible to the media. Journalists refer to themselves as doing the rough draft of history. In this case, rushing to tell the story, they missed much of its substance.

In his analysis of media coverage of the New Left, Todd Gitlin explains media "framing" as the principles of "selection, emphasis and presentation" that determine what gets defined as news.[3] The frames used to cover the civil rights movement were multiple and shifting, but they were always such as to obscure the organizing process. One of the persistent movement criticisms of the national press corps—the very idea of a "national press corps" grew partly out of the movement—is that the press focused on big, dramatic events while neglecting the processes that led to them. Paul Good, an ABC reporter in the early 1960s, thought that the focus on events was largely due to competition among understaffed networks, which led to a policy of crisis reporting, moving on a story as it boiled up, quickly dropping it the moment its supposed public interest had died and racing off to a newer crisis. . . . Our procedure crimped perspective and often substituted the superficial glance for the needed long look.[4]

Thus Good spent much time interviewing a Black Alabama family about their motives for sending their son to an integrated school over the protests of a howling mob, but that was the kind of background story there was seldom interest in running. A rock-throwing mob would be more likely to attract attention than the motivations of the people being thrown at or those of the mob itself. Similarly, Mary King, who worked in SNCC's communications office, recalls that in the fall of 1963 organizer Frank Smith was very excited because in his area of Mississippi local adults, as opposed to youth, were beginning to play a larger role. From an organizer's viewpoint, this is a pivotal moment in the process, but it was hardly the kind of thing the press deemed important. "Part of the difference," King wrote, "about what was important and what was not lay in the difficulty the news media always face when confronted with a process rather than an incident."[5]

The inability to convey a sense of process meant that much of what the movement was could not be presented. The media generally seem to have been surprised by Black Power, suggesting they did not have a very clear sense of how the thinking of people in the movement was changing. The emphasis on what Joyce Ladner calls the "Big Events" instead of process is particularly distorting from SNCC's viewpoint.[6] The questions SNCC was raising about the nature of leadership and how leadership potential might be developed, the sheer persistence of organizers, the continuity of 1960s organizing with that done in earlier years, the questioning of the basic premises of American society— none of these were likely to become a key part of the story as framed by the press, and partly for that reason they never became a part of collective consciousness about the movement in the way that the "Big Events" did.

Editors and reporters could be quite rigid in their conceptions of what constituted the story. By 1964, when Paul Good was trying to interest his editors and producers in background pieces on the Atlanta sit-ins, he found them uninterested:

> I received the impression that they were weary of civil rights stories, they were in basic sympathy with the [progressive] image Atlanta presented, and they did not want or need any analyses of current black-white attitudes or projections of how these attitudes could affect the course of the civil rights story in the days ahead. Their attitude was that clear when you cleared away the evasions.[7]

Any incident involving violence, according to Good, was more likely to be considered a story. In 1962, Sheriff Laurie Pritchett of Albany, Georgia, earned a southwide reputation as the man who had whipped Martin Luther King by meeting nonviolence with nonviolence, at least in public. As expected, the press did lose interest in the Albany Movement. Later, Hattiesburg, Mississippi, adopted the same tactics, with the same reaction from the press. Nick Von Hoffman, of the *Chicago Daily News,* quotes one magazine cameraman who had been given marching orders by his editor:

> Know what my picture editor told me? He said the Klan didn't scare him and that I should get a shot of them burning a cross in front of a Negro's house. Says he'd like the Negro on his knees begging and the Klan should have their pillow cases . . . and in color yet.[8]

Similarly, historians Pat Watters and Reese Cleghorn claim that the wire services, with their dependence on formula writing, "contributed to the fixation on violence, and the amoral tendency to view a profound moral crisis in the South in cliche perspective, so that it came to seem like a baseball game, complete with box scores of broken heads."[9]

In order to play, the story had to be packaged with violence or with white involvement or with the involvement of nationally known celebrities. Where violence was present, the press could be counted on to be more attentive, but that didn't mean that they would convey the messages the movement wanted conveyed. Despite enormous coverage of the Schwerner-Chaney-Goodman killings, Rita Schwerner, Mickey's widow, felt that "the news media had, in general, not used her numerous statements and the tapes she had made because she refused to be maudlin, sentimental, or tearful and had instead tried to discuss the [political] issues involved." Watters and Cleghorn, referring to Greenwood during the turmoil of the spring of 1963, wrote: "In Greenwood, there was the whole basic constitutional issue and one police dog. The nation noticed the latter."[10]

No one should doubt that the nation did notice the violence and was repulsed by it. David Garrow's careful analysis of reactions to the Selma and Birmingham campaigns leaves little doubt that violence, especially if photographed, moved both average citizens and congressional decision-makers.[11] However salutary it may have been for the passage of civil rights legislation, however, the focus on violence bore its own costs by discouraging the development of a more complex understanding of the movement and its evolution.

Paul Good thought that all but a few of the journalists coming into Mississippi for the 1964 Summer Project came in wanting to collect stories of "violence, police brutality, volunteer heroism, Negro suffering." Good felt that such stories were necessary but did not convey all that needed to be conveyed. A couple of years later, on the Meredith March, Good found that the sought-after theme was dissension among civil rights groups. "I once saw them [a group of newsmen] shoot from the truck like flushed quail when two marchers almost came to blows." There was no interest in the fieldhands they were passing who were making three dollars a day.

There was a natural tension between editors back in New York and reporters in the field. Even at the liberal *Reporter,* Good found "editors who never left Madison Avenue but thought they had the southern (and northern) racial situations down cold." One of the stories he submitted on Selma was altered by the editors to make it appear that "militant" blacks had forced "moderates" to knuckle under, which had not been the case at all "but *Reporter* editors—and they were not alone—loved to highlight supposed black militant-moderate controversy."[12] It would appear that the *only* time intraracial relationships became a part of the story, as far as most editors were concerned, was when they involved squabbling among the perceived leadership.

An argument over what constituted news led to Paul Good's leaving ABC. Immediately after the Schwerner-Chaney-Goodman disappearance, Good wanted to stay at the scene while one of his out-of-state editors wanted him to go back to Jackson in order to get a statement from the governor, in the time-honored tradition of defining anything a public official says as news. In the course of the argument, Good, who had had several similar run-ins with his supervisors, both resigned and got fired.

The 1961 killing of Herbert Lee in McComb was pivotal in shaping the world view of Mississippi-SNCC. The boldness of the assassin, the timidity of the federal government, its failure to protect witnesses, its possible involvement even in exposing those witnesses to danger, the weak reaction from the media—taught organizers just what Black life—especially life that was poor and Black and southern—was really worth. Much of SNCC's organizing was a response to their assumption that national institutions, including the press, were more interested in what happened to whites than to Blacks. The press had shown little interest in the mock elections that SNCC was running in Mississippi in the fall of 1963, but when white volunteers—the students from Yale and Stanford—came, the elections became a "story." Freedom Summer, of course, was predicated on the idea that privileged white volunteers would bring the concern of the nation with them. The unprecedented media coverage of the summer concentrated not on local Blacks or experienced organizers but on the volunteers. That surprised no one in SNCC, but it was nonetheless embittering because it reflected the same underlying disregard for Black people that had made it possible for the nation to ignore the murders of Herbert Lee and Louis Allen.

The last movement assassinations to embed themselves fully in popular memory were the Schwerner-Chaney-Goodman killings in the summer of 1964 and the killings around Selma in 1965—Mrs. Liuzzo, the Reverend Daniels, Jimmie Lee Jackson, the Reverend Reeb. There were in fact later killings, but they received little attention. In Mississippi there were at least four movement-related killings in 1966 and 1967. In June 1966, during the Meredith march, a group of Natchez klansmen calling themselves the Cottonmouth Moccasin Gang decided that by killing a local Black person they might lure Martin Luther King to the area where they intended to assassinate him. The victim they chose was sixty-seven-year-old Ben Chester White, an inoffensive plantation caretaker with no activist history at all. Three men picked White up at his home, drove him to a secluded area, and shot him, dumping the body in a creek.

In contrast to White, Wharlest Jackson, also of Natchez, was an activist, treasurer for the local NAACP, and he was an employee of Armstrong Rubber. In 1967, responding to pressure from civil rights groups, Armstrong began opening jobs that had been reserved for whites. It was rumored that any Blacks accepting such positions would be killed. Jackson nevertheless accepted a job as a chemical mixer which got him a raise of 17 cents per hour. George Metcalf, the local NAACP president, who had barely survived a bombing of his car, impressed on Jackson the importance of regularly checking his truck for explosives. One evening in February, three weeks after he had started the new position, Jackson clocked out of work at 8 P.M. There was a pouring rainstorm. Given the weather, he may have failed to check the truck. In any case, a time-delay bomb went off as he was driving home, killing him.

Ben Brown of Jackson also had an activist history. A teenager at the time of the 1961 Freedom Riders, he took part in protests against the treatment of the Freedom Riders and subsequently organized boycotts against discriminating businesses and worked on voter-registration campaigns before becoming a full-time worker for the Delta Ministry, a spiritual successor to SNCC. By the spring of 1967, he was settling out of activism, newly married, expecting his first child, and working as a truck driver. On May 10 and 11, Jackson State students were demonstrating against police activity on their campus. Brown, for once, was not part of the demonstration. On the 11th, he went out to get a sandwich for his wife, and he had to walk by the demonstration. Some of the demonstrators threw rocks and bottles at the police, who responded by firing on the crowd. Brown was hit by a shotgun blast. Police refused to let anyone help him as he lay bleeding on the sidewalk. He died the following day, his twenty-second birthday.

Vernon Dahmer's death may have carried the heaviest weight of symbolism. President of the Hattiesburg NAACP since the early 1950s, mentor to the Ladner sisters, supporter of Hollis Watkins and Curtis Hayes when they first came to Hattiesburg, Dahmer was a prosperous farmer and businessman and the father of eight children (see Chapter 2). In 1966, in the wake of the Voting Rights Act of 1965, he continued to push Blacks to vote. Over the radio, he offered to collect poll taxes for anyone uncomfortable about going to the courthouse, and to pay poll taxes for anyone who couldn't afford to do so. The night of the broadcast, his home was shotgunned and firebombed. Dahmer returned the gunfire while his family escaped. His home and nearby store were destroyed, his ten-year-old daughter was badly burned, and his own lungs were scorched. From his hospital bed, he continued to urge people to register: "People who don't vote are deadbeats on the state." He died in the hospital. Three members of the White Knights of Mississippi were eventually convicted.[13]

These stories are not lacking in drama or human appeal. The people involved were just not socially significant. It is also true that the frame for race-relations stories by 1966 was shifting elsewhere—to the North, to the new militants, to the riots. The irony is that part of what underlay the new anger was cumulative frustration with the societal undervaluing of Black life. There was never a time when the simple deprivation of constitutional guarantees or the murders of Black activists were enough to seize and hold national attention.

There is no reason to believe that personal prejudice within the press corps played a major role in shaping patterns of coverage. Southern dailies naturally gave the movement either slanted coverage or none. When something happened outside one of the larger metropolitan areas, the national wire services were ordinarily dependent on local reporters, who tended to share local sentiments and edited their material accordingly, which often meant that allegations of anti-movement violence never got to the wire services. (SNCC learned to have their Friends of SNCC chapters around the country call their local

AP or UPI office and ask "What about that violence in So-and-So, Alabama?" which often led to a more accurate version from the people on the scene.)

Still, so far as the national press corps is concerned, there is little reason to believe that personal prejudice in any simple sense determined how the story was presented, this despite the fact that a number of the most visible reporters covering the South were native southerners—Turner Catledge, Claude Sitton, and John Popham of the *New York Times,* Roy Reed of the *Arkansas Gazette* and later the *New York Times,* Karl Fleming of *Newsweek,* Jack Nelson of the *Los Angeles Times,* Reese Cleghorn of the *Detroit Free Press* and the *Atlanta Journal.*[14] In 1987 the University of Mississippi, of all places, held a symposium called "Covering the South," bringing together many of the journalists who had covered the movement. In the course of the symposium many stories were told about individual struggles to overcome inbred prejudices. The fact that the southern-born reporters had to fight through some of these issues in their personal lives may even have had a positive impact on their work (though one could see how it could also lead to the self-congratulatory condescension of the newly reformed). In any case, the collective image of the movement created by these journalists was overwhelmingly sympathetic, particularly prior to 1964.

Racial prejudice is only one form of condescension. Journalists, clearly very proud of their own racial liberality, might reflect elitist views in other ways. Paul Good found coverage of SNCC's 1964 Challenge at the Democratic National Convention patronizing and ill-informed, which he attributed partly to arrogance and partly to a subjective identification with the establishment. NBC's Chet Huntley, according to Good, delivered himself of the opinion that the Mississippi Democratic Party was "entirely open to Negroes." Journalists seemed to favor acceptance of the compromise offered by the White House and seemed to find SNCC's demonstrations out of place. John Scali of ABC asked one FDP woman:

> "Ma'am, now that you've made your point, don't you think it would be best to leave? We don't mean to advise you. . . ."

"I intend to stay here as long as I can," replied the woman, who did not mean to be advised. "Till someone comes in to carry me out."

Scali later asked another demonstrator, "Do you think by sitting here in this manner you will be dramatizing your case?" ABC's Bill Downs also trivialized the protest, remarking "The educational factors of sitdowns, are, I suppose, questionable. But they get a lot of attention." In the print media, FDP's refusal to accept the compromise was widely seen as a clear sign of political immaturity, which of course journalists were quite competent to judge in the Mississippi context. Overall, with the exception of CBS, Good thought the convention coverage had a tendency to

> patronize the Mississippi Negro insurgents, to assume that commentators' judgments carried a certain sophisticated superiority over the judgments of these well-meaning, morally motivated, but rather childishly stubborn Negroes. These people had something vital to say about the American democracy, its philosophy and practice; but power and hoopla carried the day.[15]

However much they struggled against racial prejudice within themselves, I would think that most of these men still found it hard to take seriously the idea that uneducated southern Blacks could be important political thinkers and actors. They could more easily be sympathetic than respectful.

The undervaluation of the leadership role played by ordinary people corresponded to an overconcentration on the role of national leaders, Dr. King in particular. In 1963, when SCLC was about to announce the accords that had been reached with the power structure in Birmingham, it was decided that Fred Shuttlesworth, by far the most important local leader, should speak first at the press conference. The national press corps had hardly assembled to hear Fred Shuttlesworth. "Although Shuttlesworth announced the terms of the settlement, the reporters would not be satisfied until they heard it from

King himself, as most of their readers knew nothing of Shuttlesworth."[16] Anyone who wanted to understand Birmingham should have known Shuttlesworth. A Baptist minister, he had been the center of the struggle against white supremacy in Birmingham during the 1950s. In 1956, he was an officer in the local NAACP when the State of Alabama declared it illegal. Shuttlesworth's response was to organize the Alabama Christian Movement for Human Rights which used both mass direct-action protests and lawsuits to attack discriminatory hiring practices, segregated public facilities, segregated transportation, and segregated schools. His personal courage was legendary. He survived the bombing of his home Christmas night, 1956, announcing "I wasn't saved to run." He was given a thorough beating with chains and brass knuckles, and his wife was stabbed when they tried to wade through a mob to enroll their children in a white high school. His church was bombed again.[17] He had his enemies among Black leaders in Birmingham, but his dramatic courage had won him a loyal following among ordinary people, a factor that played a role in SCLC's decision to come into Birmingham. In deciding that Shuttlesworth was not a part of the story, the press missed an opportunity to learn something about the historical depth of the struggle and the variety of leadership styles that sustained it.

At the 1987 symposium on civil rights journalism, Jack Nelson opened the proceedings by referring to Dr. King as having "launched the civil rights movement." As an explanation for how the movement began, that borders on the useless, and it suggests again how unsophisticated journalists were about the political dynamics of the 1950s South. Most reporters were hampered by their own backgrounds. With few exceptions, white journalists, southerners included, did not come from backgrounds that would have allowed them to know much about political activity in Black communities since World War II. They would have known little about the activist generation symbolized by Amzie Moore and Steptoe and Gus Courts and Shuttlesworth. Unfamiliar with that history, the 1960s movement itself and King in particular seemed more a qualitative break with the past than was in fact the case. At the same time, it is likely that many journalists felt more comfortable dealing with the well-educated

King, a man so much like themselves, than with many local leaders. Additionally, King and SCLC fulfilled an important function for the press, providing one place they could go to and get *the* movement perspective. King's leadership was certainly not a media creation, but the media certainly enhanced his role.[18]

King played another kind of symbolic role as well. In *Symbols, The Newsmagazines, and Martin Luther King* Richard Lentz analyzes the use of King as normative icon, tracing the coverage given his career by three major newsmagazines.[19] While he restricted himself to the South and refrained from sticking his nose into American foreign policy (White Folks' Business), *Time* and *Newsweek* were generally laudatory and used King as a symbol to counter more militant spokespersons. *U.S. News and World Report,* on the other hand, treated him as a dangerous demagogue until the day he died, after which it too started holding him up as the standard more militant Blacks should emulate.

Comments made by journalists at the "Covering the South" meeting suggest that some of them are aware, at least in retrospect, that Dr. King's role was expanded. Callie Crossley, who searched media film archives in connection with the "Eyes on the Prize" documentary on the movement found that the archives of national broadcasters had little footage on anything but King, not even John Lewis's speech at the March on Washington. There was almost nothing on SNCC prior to the mid-sixties and the advent of Black Power. Before that, stories tended to be told as if SCLC were the movement standard.

John Herbers (UPI, *New York Times*) allowed that perhaps the media had covered national leaders too much, but it was hard not to in the case of a figure like King, a figure who simply drew attention to himself like a magnet. He acknowledged that a more diffuse coverage might have been better but was not sure it was possible under the circumstances. Similarly, Marianne Means (White House correspondent for the Hearst newspapers) noted that we have to communicate with symbols, and King became the symbol of the movement. In general, I left the symposium with the feeling that the reporters there had some sense of the discrepancy between what they were reporting and what was going on but could not easily conceive of having done it differently. One might point out that other social movements—modern feminism and the labor movement included—have in fact been covered by the press in ways that did not imply they had a single central leader.

Reporters varied among themselves, of course. According to Mary King of SNCC's communications office, Claude Sitton was among the reporters most respected within the movement, not least because of his willingness to take seriously stories most reporters ignored, including the discovery of five Black bodies in the river near Natchez in late 1963. SNCC believed them to be terror killings, but only Sitton and a few others showed any interest at all. It may be too pat an explanation, but King believes that after Sitton's car was vandalized while he was attending a 1963 mass meeting in Georgia his "coverage lost the distant, flat quality of most news reportage of the time and leaped to life."[20] Sitton was also among the few who consistently filed stories about local people like E. W. Steptoe, and one of the few, along with Roy Reed of the *New York Times,* who did not join in the general practice of treating segregationists as the objects of friendly derision.

In the fall of 1961 in McComb a group of determined high-school students decided to have a protest march despite the fact that it looked like the march would be met with violence. Bob Zellner, relatively new in town, decided reluctantly and at the last minute that if the kids were going to put their lives on the line, he had to go too. Twenty-five years later, looking back at old newspaper clippings, Zellner found that the *New York Times* had described him as the leader of the march. What that reflects, he says, is the assumption that if a white man is around, he must be in charge. That kind of assumption is an example of what Gitlin calls the "tacit little theories" that are embedded in media frames. Despite their sympathy for the movement and their frequent displays of courage in getting the story out, those most involved in interpreting the movement to the world were often unable to see beyond their own background assumptions. Their collective tendency to frame the story in terms of Big Events, in terms of what white people did, in terms of traditional leaders and organizations, in terms of what happened after 1955, in terms of southern backwardness, in terms of violence-nonviolence, replicated biases of race, gender and class, and relegated to secondary importance the themes that would have been important from a community-organizing perspective.[21]

The roots of that perspective are deep and complex, and it would be unfair to expect reporters suddenly caught up in the movement to fully understand them. One strand of those roots was the generation of leadership that came out of World War II hungering for freedom and willing to take enormous risks to see it come about. It was they who groomed the youngsters of the Emmett Till generation to think of themselves as the vehicles of change, who created the social and political networks that later activists could exploit, who set the standards by which later activists would judge themselves, and who offered those later activists family and a tempering humanism.

Those younger organizers themselves became important models of courage, but that represents only the most visible part of their work. We have to remember that they immersed themselves in their communities—Bob Moses liked to call them deep-sea divers—learning those communities from the inside and developing relationships in which people learned to care about one another as individuals in ways that cut through issues of ideology and social status, militating against the tribalism that worked so much evil in the later movement. We have to remember how much of themselves they invested in learning, slowly and painstakingly, how to help other people recognize and develop their own potentials. We have to remember their persistence and their willingness to do the spadework, the undramatic, actual work of organizing.

The philosophic roots of the movement reach farther back than World War II, farther back even than the thinking of Ella Baker or Septima Clark. Much in SNCC's early style—its celebration of the potential of ordinary men and women, its desire to valorize as many voices as possible, its rejection of individual celebrity, its striving for consensus, its disdain of credentials and hierarchy—reflected, in the words of SNCC's Casey Hayden, the "old SNCC axiom that everyone is as valuable as everyone else."[22] The Black South had its own expressions of that axiom. If contemporary Black youth think at all about the elaborate rituals of courtesy that meant so much to their grandparents, they are likely, I am afraid, to find in them a symbol of servility. That is, they reduce courtesy to what they think it meant for relations *between* the races, ignoring the equally important question of what it meant inside the race. They are not likely to understand it as one part of a code of conduct which helped an oppressed people give back to one another some of the self-respect the racial system was trying to squeeze out of them, a profoundly democratic tradition holding that every man and woman, merely by virtue of being that, is entitled to some regard. Similarly, the expansive sense of family, the predisposition to see whatever is positive in people, the emphasis on character rather than wealth, are all egalitarian traditions, as empowering as anything SNCC ever devised. The ability to affirm the moral worth of even the most hateful, to look at the oppressor and think without irony "There but for the grace of God go I" affirms our ultimately equivalent moral status, even in the face of evidence that seems to contradict it.

The correspondence between the ethos of SNCC and deeply rooted egalitarian themes from the folk culture of the Black South is hardly accidental. Ella Baker and Septima Clark were born into turn-of-the-century southern Black communities, scarcely a generation removed from slavery, and they knew all the faces those communities could present. They were intimately acquainted with their destructive elements—the petty status-striving, the internalized self-hatred of which it was an expression, the parochialism. In their different ways, they tried to shape a style of social action, as Miss Baker might call it, that took those weaknesses into account but built on the communal strengths with which they were also intimately acquainted. The young activists of the 1960s trying to work within the organizing tradition were bringing back to the rural Black South a refined, codified version of something that had begun there, an expression of the historical vision of ex-slaves, men and women who understood that, for them, maintaining a deep sense of community was itself an act of resistance.

EPILOGUE

ELLA BAKER AND SEPTIMA CLARK died within a year of one another, Miss Baker on her eighty-third birthday in December 1986, Mrs. Clark in December of 1987. Before she died Mrs. Clark was twice elected to the Charleston School Board, and the South Carolina legislature voted to compensate her for being fired in 1956 when she refused to deny that she was an NAACP member. Miss Baker's funeral brought together SNCC members who had long been out of touch with one another or had been at odds with one another since the turmoil of the late sixties. Appropriately enough, coming together for her funeral started a process of rebuilding some of those relationships. Myles Horton died in 1990; Highlander continues to represent the same progressive ideals upon which it was founded in 1932.

Amzie Moore died in 1982. Aaron Henry, the true long-distance runner, is still the state NAACP president, still a member of the SCLC board, and is now a member of the Mississippi state legislature. In 1994, Byron de la Beckwith was again tried, and finally convicted, for the murder of Medgar Evers. Darrell Kenyatta Evers is a grown man now. His mother says that at one point she had an argument with Darrell, when he claimed that he didn't see the point of voting. She ended the argument by showing him the bloodied poll-tax receipt his father had been carrying the night of his murder.

Mrs. Hamer died of heart failure in March 1977. For some in SNCC-COFO her funeral ceremony was an embarrassment, a media event with dignitaries from around the country competing with one another to be seen on camera, pushing her neighbors into the background. It seemed the perfect contradiction of the values she tried to live by.

The Reverend Aaron Johnson still pastors his church in Greenwood, still cuts hair, and is still active in the community. When Richard West was run out of Greenwood in the mid-fifties, he went to California. In 1975, he returned to a Mississippi different from the one he left and became the mayor of the small, racially integrated town of West, Mississippi. At the age of seventy-nine, Lou Emma Allen is still doing domestic work, still very active in her church and community, living in the pleasant subdivision of Rising Sun. In a sign of the times, she has seen street-gang symbols painted near her home, which saddened her more than it frightened her. She is absolutely disgusted with the way some of the people currently associated with Head Start in Greenwood pretend that they brought it there. She is still in close contact with Miss Susie Morgan, whose daughter Arance Williamson sits on Greenwood's city council. James Moore, who used to picket by himself, also served several terms on the council, but in general, in Greenwood as elsewhere, ex-activists trying to enter politics have not been well received. Both Silas McGhee and June Johnson failed in attempts at office. Silas is running a gas station in Greenwood; June has moved to Washington. The Greenwood Voters League that Sam Block rejuvenated is still headed by Cleveland Jordan's son, David, who was recently elected to the state senate of Mississippi.

Some of those who were young adults in the early sixties seem to have had real difficulty finding something to replace the movement in their lives, leading in some cases to bouts with drugs or alcohol. Some have recovered in recent years. Some members of old movement families are now believed by others to be involved in selling drugs in Greenwood. Some of the younger people went through periods of withdrawal from activism. Al Garner, who helped start Greenwood's NAACP youth group, found that organizing in urban areas where Black people had little sense of community was harder than working in supposedly backwards Greenwood. In Chicago, he organized tenants in the Henry Horner projects and helped set up the Miles Square Health Federation in the West Side ghetto before a period of disillusionment set in. For ten years, he refused to work with civil rights organizations, thinking they had let themselves become irrelevant. Now in Gary, Indiana, he has recently become re-involved in community activities. Mary Boothe, who went to the registrar's office every day for much of the spring of 1963, went through a long period when she just stopped voting because she didn't see anybody worth voting for.

The older activists also frequently voice their displeasure with contemporary leadership. Herman Perry, still living on the land his father bought in 1937 in Bolivar County, doesn't see any leadership now that compares to Medgar Evers or Amzie Moore. He sees a lot of small people aspiring to big jobs, but "there's a difference between filling a space and fitting a place. Anybody can fill a space but don't everybody fit the place."

In the early 1950s the Reverend George Lee of Belzoni had a stock speech he used to give about how the day was going to come when the Negroes of the Delta were going to rise up and elect someone to the United States Congress. In 1986, thirty-one years after George Lee's devotion to that dream got him killed, Mike Espy became the first African American to represent Mississippi in Congress since Reconstruction. In 1992, Bill Clinton appointed Espy Secretary of Agriculture, making him the first African American to hold that post as well. In 1994, Espy resigned amid allegations of corruption. His career illustrates yet again why Miss Baker was reluctant to see people entrust too many of their dreams to individual leaders.

SNCC's decision to grow organizers where they found them bore fruit. Willie Peacock, MacArthur Cotton, and Hollis Watkins, among others, continued to be politically active in Mississippi through the 1980s. Watkins played a significant role in a successful fight to redistrict state legislative districts in Mississippi. Peacock, now Wazir Peacock, stayed in Mississippi until 1991, when he moved to California, suspecting that his reputation as movement troublemaker would always follow him in Mississippi. Sam Block is also in California.

Bob Moses feels that the problems plaguing inner-city youth are central organizing issues for these times, in the same way that the right to vote was in 1960. He had been teaching math when the movement caught him up. In 1982, he was living in Cambridge, Massachusetts, the father of four children. Not satisfied with the mathematics they were getting in school, he required that they do additional math with him. As his daughter Maisha was entering eighth grade, she rebelled at having to do both. The compromise was that he started coming to her school to teach math to her and a few other students, initially students hand-picked as being ready for more difficult mathematics. Uncomfortable with the elitism implied in that, he began trying to find ways to teach children who were not defined as "ready." Over a period of years, that led to the development of the Algebra Project, a program for introducing algebra to inner-city children by changing the way mathematics is taught. The program is built on the egalitarian, non-hierarchical values that informed the organizing tradition, and it was developed in that tradition's step-by-step, bottom-up fashion. Like any good organizer, the program starts where children are, taking things students understand intuitively—a trip on the subway, trading possessions, playing musical chairs—and helping them see the mathematics inherent in those activities. Teachers are more facilitators than teachers in the traditional sense. They are expected to not give direct answers to students' questions but to help students find questions that will lead them to discover their own answers. Teachers are also expected to present themselves as learners, as people who don't always know the answers. The program encourages parents to think about the politics of mathematics, the way in which too many Black, Hispanic, or poor children are shunted into dummy math before the middle-school years, putting them on a track that goes nowhere. As we end the twentieth century, Moses argues, mathematical literacy has to be regarded as a right. Those who do not develop it are excluded from full participation in society.

Algebra may seem far removed from the civil rights movement but the error there may be in our tendency to reduce the movement to a "civil rights" movement, taking that narrow label more seriously than did the people who participated in the movement. To many of them, the overriding question is still, How do you open up the society? As of 1993, the Algebra Project was serving children in such cities as Chicago, San Francisco, Milwaukee, Los Angeles, Boston, and Oakland. One of the places where the project is growing fastest is the Mississippi Delta, where it has revived some of the old COFO network. The Mississippi project is directed by Dave Dennis, CORE's Mississippi director in the sixties; MacArthur Cotton and Hollis Watkins have worked on its development. Nationally, a number of major foundations are now supporting the Algebra Project, it has been recognized as a model by the National Science Foundation, and it shows every promise of developing into something that can have a significant impact on the lives of a great many children. Bob Moses emphasizes that it all began with one parent worrying about one child:

> The main thing is not to set out with grand projects. Everything starts at your doorstep. Just get deeply involved in something. . . . You throw a stone in one place and the ripples spread.[1]

BIBLIOGRAPHIC ESSAY

The Social Construction of History

*These federal, state, and municipal civil rights acts were mainly
due to the efforts of the black professional groups (ministers, lawyers,
teachers), students, and, particularly in the 1960s sympathetic
white liberals. Lower-income blacks had little involvement in
civil rights politics up to the mid-1960s.*

WILLIAM JULIUS WILSON[1]

SCHOLARLY AND POPULAR histories of the movement have traditionally reflected the same underlying analytical frames as did contempo-
raneous media. That has begun to change within the last decade, encouraged by a chorus of complaints from movement participants that
they could not recognize their own movement in most histories. Even
taking recent improvements into account, we are far short of what we
might hope for. The issues that are invisible to the media and to the
current generation of Black activists are still almost as invisible to
scholars.

In a 1991 review article on civil rights historiography, Steven Lawson
sees three generations of scholarship.[2] The early work was top-down,
focused on the movement as a national phenomenon that secured legislative and judicial victories. That was followed in the late 1970s and
the 1980s by a second generation of studies taking local communities
and grassroots work as their focal point. More recently still, we have

seen the emergence of a third generation of work that is interactive, trying "to connect the local with the national, the social with the political."

Lawson doesn't name the community studies he thinks of as representative of the second wave of scholarship, but the obvious choices would include Robert Norrell's *Reaping the Whirlwind* (Knopf, 1985) on Tuskegee, William Chafe's *Civilities and Civil Liberties* (Oxford, 1980) on Greensboro, and David Colburn's *Racial Change and Community Crisis* (Columbia, 1985) on St. Augustine. In an article calling for still more concentrated attention to local struggles, Clayborne Carson notes that studies like Chafe's and Norrell's have shown that local movements often developed independently of national civil rights organizations and pursued goals and strategies bearing little relation to national campaigns. One might add that Norrell offers an especially useful portrait of more aggressive middle-class leadership in a case where the Black middle-class was larger and better-insulated than was typically the case in rural counties, while Chafe's work, looking at race relations in Greensboro over thirty years, contains an important and still very relevant analysis of the ways in which a culture of civility operated to support the racial status quo. Colburn's work on St. Augustine is interesting partly because both Black leadership and white segregationist leadership there were distinctly militant. More to Carson's point, St. Augustine was a case where the priorities of local and national leaders were emphatically different. All of these are respected studies for good reason. Nonetheless, if we are considering civil rights scholarship as a whole, the works on communities, individually or collectively, seem to have had relatively limited visibility outside the circle of civil rights specialists. Indeed, it is not even clear how much real impact they are having inside that circle. The same anthology that contains the Carson article features a David Levering Lewis discussion of "The Origins and Causes of the Civil Rights Movement," which reflects virtually no awareness of the community studies, consistently taking a top-down stance except for a two-sentence reference to a new African American leadership emerging in the South.

Carson may actually overstate his case for the importance of community studies when he maintains that national organizations and leaders "played only minor roles" in bringing about local insurgencies. If we place the strictest interpretation on "bringing about," what he says is often true, but that does not do justice to the complex ways in which local and national movements fed off one another. Carson, for example, rightly calls Montgomery an "unplanned act of defiance," meaning, I take it, unplanned at the national level. On the other hand, many of the people who made Montgomery work had honed their activist skills as members of national groups like the NAACP or the Brotherhood of Sleeping Car Porters.[3]

In several respects, Aldon Morris's *Origins of the Civil Rights Movement* (1984) represents one relatively early work that falls into Lawson's interactive category. While concerned with the national movement, its focus is on Southern Black communities. Concentrating on the decade from 1953 to 1963, a period he sees as distinguished from earlier protest activity by the development of sustained mass confrontation and the use of nonviolent tactics, Morris's analysis stresses the ability of southern Black communities, essentially urban communities, to mobilize indigenous resources, institutions, and leadership. Much of the book is on the Black church and SCLC, which he sees as "the force that developed the infrastructure of the civil rights movement" (p. 77). His analysis of the church stresses its progressive side, which perhaps is a consequence of his concentration on urban areas. Similarly, the degree of centrality he attributes to SCLC is dubious. Between 1957 and 1962, SCLC was hardly a dynamic organization. Adam Fairclough calls the 1957–1959 period, the "fallow years" for SCLC, adding that "although it had been founded to promote direct action in the South, SCLC was itself caught unawares by the mushrooming of nonviolent protests in 1960–61. It found itself a marginal participant in events initiated by other people and other organizations."[4] What seems safe to say is that SCLC developed a special role in communicating a vision of the southern movement to outside audiences, even when it was only marginally involved in what was happening at the ground level.

Morris's perspective is a clear break with the traditional top-down focus. His analysis of Montgomery, for example, is among those that point out its connectedness to earlier struggles, making it clear that the people who initially shaped the boycott had long activist careers. E. D. Nixon, a Pullman porter with a sixth-grade education, in his mid-fifties at the time of the boycott, was probably the most influential Black man in town, at least in the eyes of the Black masses. He had given Montgomery almost three decades of outspoken activist leadership, dating back to his organizing the state branch of the Brotherhood of Sleeping Car Porters in 1928. He started working with the NAACP at the same time, but his hero continued to be A. Philip Randolph, founder of the Brotherhood and the man who successfully used the threat of mass action against both FDR and Truman. He attributed much of what he had learned about organizing to Randolph. In the thirties Nixon, along with Myles Horton at Highlander, tried to organize Alabama cucumber pickers, and he organized a committee to make sure that Alabama Blacks got their fair share of benefits from federal programs; in 1940, he helped organize the Montgomery Voters League; in 1944 he led a march of seven hundred fifty people on the registrar's office; from 1939 to 1951, he headed the Montgomery NAACP, and from 1951 to 1953, the state conference.

Morris is also among those pointing out that Mrs. Parks also had deep roots in the protest tradition; she was not some simple woman who happened to be tired. In 1943, she joined the NAACP under Nixon, became its secretary and worked in voter-registration campaigns; she first registered herself in 1945, she ran the local NAACP youth council and served as secretary to the state NAACP conference of branches. She had attended one of Ella Baker's leadership training conferences in the 1940s and had spent a week at the Highlander Folk School in 1955. Since the 1940s, she had refused on several occasions to comply with bus-segregation laws, frequently enough that some bus drivers recognized her on sight and simply refused to stop for her. King's comment about her—"She was tracked down by the Zeitgeist—the spirit of the times"—is precisely wrong. She, like Nixon, had spent much of her adult life actively seeking levers of change, not waiting until the times were right.

Another initiator of the boycott was Jo Ann Robinson, an English professor at nearby Alabama State College and president of the Women's Political Caucus, a group of three hundred educated Black women who had been concerned with voter registration and segregated public facilities since 1946. They had been agitating the city commission about segregated buses since the early 1950s and in May of 1954 had sent a letter to the mayor threatening a boycott if improvements weren't made. Between the spring of 1955 and the time of the Parks arrest in December, Nixon and the Caucus had considered three bus incidents as potential test cases but decided against them on various tactical grounds. The Parks incident gave them the case they wanted. Nixon and Robinson's group were largely responsible for the initial mobilization of Black Montgomery. Robinson's group, with members in virtually every significant Black institution, was especially well suited for accomplishing a rapid mobilization. Mrs. Parks was arrested on Thursday; Nixon started organizing the first meeting of Negro leadership on Friday; by Monday they had organized a boycott that was nearly completely effective. That they could mobilize the Black community so rapidly is also in part a testimony to how thoroughly people like Nixon and Robinson knew their community, knowledge acquired through long years of working it.[5]

Maintaining, as Morris does, a sense of the continuity between the two generations of activism is crucial for several reasons. It broadens our conception of leadership, ranging in this case from a woman with a college education to a man educated by working the railroads to a woman who worked as a seamstress. Top-down analyses and those that look at the movement as having been spontaneously generated are more likely to give us the usual view of leadership—white, male, and elite. The continuity of this history is also important because it restores a sense of human agency, the idea, as Frances Fox Piven puts it "that reflective and purposeful people matter in the patterning of social life." Montgomery was largely a willed phenomenon, a history made by everyday people who were willing to do their spadework, not one shaped entirely by impersonal social forces or great individual leadership. Finding Dr. King to take the leadership of the movement was fortuitous, but the local activists had put themselves in a position to be lucky through lifetimes of purposeful planning and striving. Lastly, whether in Mississippi or Montgomery, taking the high drama of the mid-fifties and early sixties out of the longer historical context implicitly overvalues those dramatic moments and undervalues the more mundane activities that helped make them possible—the network-building, the grooming of another generation of leadership, the sheer persistence. The result is a history more theatrical than instructive. The popular conception of Montgomery—a tired woman refused to give up her seat and a prophet rose up to lead the grateful masses—is a good story but useless history.[6]

Among less formal histories, the books that are compilations either of documents or of interviews with movement participants give a clear view of the collective, multi-faceted nature of leadership. These include Howell Raines's recently reissued *My Soul Is Rested,* the several volumes based on the "Eyes on the Prize Series" film series, and Fred Powledge's *Free At Last?* (HarperCollins, 1991), which alternates between a journalistic narrative history and interviews with a wide range of participants. He notes at the outset that

> In the minds of untold numbers of Americans, for example, the Reverend Dr. Martin Luther King Jr., *was* the civil rights movement. Thought it up, led it, produced its victories, became its sole martyr. Schoolchildren—including Black schoolchildren—are taught this. (p. xiv)

Powledge thus wants his narrative to demonstrate that the "people who made up the Movement were almost as diverse as America itself" (p. xi). I am particularly thankful he doesn't hold southern racists up to ridicule; he gives them credit for being complex and makes some attempt at understanding the cross-pressures under which they were operating. The opposite tradition, in which racists are pictured as stupid, vulgar, and one-dimensional, is one of the hoariest conventions of writing about civil rights and one of the more destructive. I take it to be a device by which authors certify their own enlightened status by distancing themselves from the grosser expressions of racism, thus giving racism the face of the ignorant, the pot-bellied, and the tobacco-chewing, an image with which almost no one can identify and which easily supplants more complex and realistic images of racism.[7] On the other hand, Powledge is especially well suited to do a retrospective critique of media coverage of the movement, and I, at least, was disappointed that, brief introductory comments aside, he did not attempt it.

Among both scholarly and popular works, those with the greatest visibility still continue to be King-centric, notably Pulitzer Prize–winning efforts by David Garrow and Taylor Branch.[8] Garrow's *Bearing the Cross* is almost overwhelming in its command of detail and documentation. Garrow is at some pains in the text to point out that the movement cannot be reduced to King. Interestingly, the last two people quoted in the epilogue are Ella Baker and Diane Nash, with Miss Baker saying that King didn't make the movement; the movement made him, and Nash saying that if people understood the movement they wouldn't ask "When will we get another leader like that?"; they would ask "What can I do?" Elsewhere, Garrow has written very forcefully about the need to study the level of leadership represented by Bob Moses and Diane Nash, arguing that sustained movement in the South was contingent on the development of an organizing cadre and that "the somewhat precipitous decline of the southern freedom struggle between 1966 and 1968 can also largely be traced to the burnout and eventual departure from full-time organizing of most of that crucial cadre."[9]

Like Garrow, Taylor Branch's *Parting the Waters* invokes the familiar messianic imagery, but the book goes into significant detail about people other than King. "The text moves from King to people far removed, at the highest and lowest stations . . . seeking at least a degree of intimacy with all of them" (p. xii). The effect is that of reading a well-crafted novel; few writers have done a better job of conveying a sense of the movement as human drama. Garrow and Branch have complementary flaws. Like the cop in *Dragnet*, Garrow sticks to "the facts, ma'am, just the facts." One yearns for a little more guidance as to the larger meaning of it all. Branch, on the other hand, wrings deep meanings from raised eyebrows. The work is aggressively, sometimes gratuitously, interpretive. I'm not sure what it means to say that Jim Forman was both more subtle and less subtle than other SNCC workers (p. 723). I do know that to say that the Delta movement evolved "almost unconsciously" (p. 711) strains more than credibility. It is hard for me to imagine how movement organizers could be more conscious of what they were doing than were the Mississippi organizers. In the winter of 1962–63, remember, they were having workshops to sift through their experiences, according to Willie Peacock, which amounts to institutionalized self-consciousness. Similarly, saying that SNCC in 1963 had no realistic goals beyond surviving the year (p. 712) seems completely out of touch, and his attitude toward Black activism in Mississippi before the 1960s strikes me as dismissive. The loose interpretations are the more worrisome because Branch can be less than careful with his facts. He errs by several years about the date of the raid on the Amite County NAACP; he is confused about which member of the Greene family was shot at in Greenwood; he gets the founding of COFO wrong by several months. Some of the factual errors are slight, but some do matter. He tells a great story, but not always the one that happened.

Normative history is history premised on the assumption that national institutions work more or less as advertised, that shared values are the key to understanding change. In most popular discourse about the movement, King serves a normative role—the apostle of nonviolence, advocate of interracial brotherhood and Christian patience. One of the virtues of Garrow is that he traces the evolution of King's thinking, generating a picture not so easily turned to normative uses. In the last years of his life, King consistently spoke out against militarism and, against the advice of most of his staff, condemned our adventure in Vietnam. He came to doubt the viability of a purely capitalist economy and frequently expressed the belief that we would have to move toward some form of democratic socialism. In the last months of his life he was planning a campaign of Poor People in Washington intended to be "dislocative and disruptive."[10] The radicalization of the young may look more reasonable if one knows that even the centrist King had begun to ask far more searching questions about what it would take to bring about meaningful social change.

Top-down interpretations are strongly predisposed toward the normative, and in movement studies that tendency can show up in several ways beyond simply artificially expanding the roles of national leaders and institutions—downplaying the role of pressure, economic or otherwise,[11] reducing the movement to a "protest" movement, treating nonviolence as if it were somehow natural while treating militance as inevitably doomed to failure, overestimating the degree of national consensus about the movement's goals, framing any radicalism as irrational, stressing the interracial aspects of the movement to the exclusion of the intraracial.

A normative interpretation of the movement's origins is likely to stress the general liberalization of postwar America. *New Directions in Civil Rights Studies* (1991) is a collection of essays growing out of a conference of scholars and activists at the University of Virginia. Several of the conferees call for more community studies, for more emphasis on the study of activist networks, and there are numerous warnings against starting the analysis with Montgomery or *Brown;* there are calls to heed studies of voter-registration efforts during the New Deal, of the North Carolina NAACP during the same period, and of political fissures among white leadership in southern cities before they were hit with mass mobilizations. Robert Norrell's essay, "One Thing We Did Right: Reflections on the Movement," raises a fundamental question: Why were direct-action protests so successful for a brief period of our history? Norrell's answer, in the tradition of Myrdal, stresses changes in basic American values growing partly out of the war. The confrontation with Hitler forced many Americans to reconsider the question of racism and its place in American life. By itself, that was not enough to create sustained activism but after the decline of McCarthyism, "the year 1960 initiated a brief but shining era when American ideals moved political structures into alignment in order that the nation's race relations might undergo a fundamental transformation"(p. 71).

Without more context than Norrell provides, this kind of interpretation is potentially hegemonic. Attributing large social changes to the American ability to respond to moral challenge reaffirms what most Americans would like to think of their country. One wonders what Amzie Moore or Medgar Evers would have said in 1957 or 1958 had someone told him that the country was getting more liberal. I think the issue would have looked different from their perspective, not necessarily wrong, but different. This is why it is crucial to have a clear sense of the great price paid by people at the bottom to make change possible, the price they paid in lives lost or disrupted. If we undervalue their contributions, we are likely to overvalue the impact of changes in the moral climate, again removing human agency from the analysis. Granted that changes in values probably had significant effect, their relative importance still has to be treated as an open question. With the federal government certainly, it may be that a rather minimal federal response was enough to have a real impact because of the maximum possible response from so many "ordinary" people. Because they were willing to give everything they had, it wasn't necessary for the federal government to do more than act half-right once in a while. That is a plausible line of argument, one that ought at least to be considered before quick judgments are made about the importance of normative change. Uncritically granting primacy to changes in social norms enshrines the viewpoint of the privileged as self-evident.[12]

From inside the movement, Freedom Summer represented a tactical response to the erosion of normative thinking within the movement, premised as it was on the disheartening realization that the government was in the business of protecting white life only. Ironically, in retrospect, the summer serves as a normative token, a time when integration worked, or seemed to, a time when privileged people were involved. It continues, of course, to attract attention. Sally Belfrage's beautifully written *Freedom Summer* has been reissued by the University Press of Virginia, and we have had at least three new books in the last five years to add to at least seven that had been published earlier. Among the most important is Doug McAdams's very carefully done *Freedom Summer* (1988), which concentrates on the impact the summer had on the volunteers and the subsequent important impact those volunteers had on the other social movements of the sixties. SNCC's Bernice Reagon calls the civil rights movement the "borning struggle" because of its generative and shaping influence on the other social upheavals of the time.[13] McAdams brings that idea to life, detailing the crucial roles Freedom Summer volunteers subsequently played in other social movements. Moreover, he documents the longevity of their activist careers. As a group, they led activist lives throughout the seventies.[14] The question McAdams is pursuing is important in its own right, but it also plays a particular and peculiar role in popular discourse about the movements of the sixties. Popular media periodically run smug stories about former activists who are now selling insurance and voting Republican and otherwise betraying the principles they once espoused. (Hoary Convention of Civil Rights Writing No. 2.) Such stories are probably best understood as a device by which people discomfited by the penetrating questions posed by social activism protect themselves from having to think about them. If even former activists have rejected them, the questions can't have much legitimacy. It is not enough for people to sacrifice a few or many years of their lives trying to live up to their best ideals—more than most of us will ever do—we insist that they do it forever or be denounced as counterfeit.

Another book on Freedom Summer, Seth Cagin and Philip Dray's *We Are Not Afraid* (1988), focuses on the Schwerner, Chaney, Goodman murders, making a clear attempt to place those murders in the context of the larger movement. Despite that, Cagin and Dray sometimes show little understanding of the indigenous movement, referring (p. 89) to Black Mississippians in 1961 as "waiting for deliverance in the isolated hamlets of the Black Belt." Nicolaus Mills's *Like a Holy Crusade: Mississippi, 1964—The Turning of the Civil Rights Movement in America* (1992) has that flavor even more strongly. His summary of the status of the Mississippi movement in late 1963 makes it sound like a pretty complete disaster:

> As 1963 drew to a close, the question for SNCC was where to turn. . . . The one bright spot in the picture was the willingness of young college-educated whites to come to Mississippi for civil rights work. In the fall of 1963 COFO held a "Freedom Vote" . . . and as a result of help provided by one hundred students recruited from Stanford and Yale, scored an important political victory (p. 20).

I'm not sure which is more absurd, the suggestion that white students were the only bright spot in late 1963 or the idea that the success of the Freedom Vote was a result of their help. Recall that in Greenwood, after the demonstrations in the spring of 1963, substantial numbers of local people were willing to go to jail, that during that fall more older people started canvassing, that there were more applicants for citizenship teacher-training than could be accommodated. Statewide, Bob Moses estimated that in the wake of the November Freedom Vote they had ten times the voter-registration workers they had had previously.[15] Growing numbers of people were committing themselves to the struggle. It is certainly true that the movement had found no answer to racist violence or to the willingness of the federal government to tolerate it, but the Mississippi movement in late 1963 was hardly in a state of disaster. The role played by the white students was a heroic one that contributed measurably to the success of the project, especially in attracting funds and publicity, but that success was above all a result of how well SNCC had penetrated the state's Black communities. Ironically, Mills's book, which contains a clarion call for a return to the days of interracial cooperation, has embedded within it the same sort of colonial attitudes that made Black organizers unwilling to work with even whites of good intent.

Similarly, Taylor Branch (p. 725) refers to the "collapse" of the Greenwood movement after April 1963. The mass meetings shriveled, he says, workers continued to take large numbers of people to try to register, but with little success, Claude Sitton of the *New York Times* left town because the news evaporated. "On election day [Blacks] were still invisible." The latter remark is particularly ironic. The next election was the August primary in which five to seven hundred Greenwood Negroes voted in protest, and did so in a spirit of jubilation. It was the most visible Greenwood Negroes had been in an election since Reconstruction. As news is defined, it may not have been news, but if we wish to understand the process of community empowerment, it was a very important step. Both Branch and Mills are giving us Columbus Discovered America all over again; history is something that happens when the White Folks show up and stops when they leave. Were these conclusions that flowed from some careful sifting of the evidence, there could be no objection, but that is hardly the case.

The role of women in the movement, especially that of Black women, is still an area where little progress has been made, although every conference on the movement calls attention to the need. A useful beginning is the 1990 collection of essays edited by Vicki Crawford, Jacqueline Rouse, and Barbara Woods, *Black Women in the Civil Rights Movement: Trailblazers and Torchbearers.* Two biographies of Ella Baker are in progress, one by Barbara Ransby, the other by Joanne Grant.

We now have the first full-length biography of Mrs. Hamer, Kay Mills's *This Little Light of Mine* (1993).[16] In addition to pulling together information from the standard sources on Mrs. Hamer, the book draws on a great deal of material that is either new or not easily accessible, including several dozen interviews, not all of them with fans of Mrs. Hamer. The treatment of Mrs. Hamer's pre-movement life is less extensive than one might hope, but that is compensated for by the careful discussion of Mrs. Hamer's activism after the mid-sixties, when national attention had turned elsewhere. That discussion underscores some of the problematic sides of bottom-up organizing. Much of her energy in the last years of her life was poured into the attempt to make a reality of Freedom Farm, a cooperative venture to provide jobs for the poor, Black and white. The farm failed, in part because of a lack of management skills, in part because of Mrs. Hamer's tendency to trust people who did not necessarily deserve it. Mills notes that "there was no remaining central civil rights movement organization, no group like the Student Non-Violent Coordinating Committee, that was both attuned to her gifts and able to support her in areas in which she was weak" (p. 272), an apt characterization of how the relationship between organizers and local people had worked at its best.

CORE's Matt Suarez has made a comment that would be a useful guide to students of the impact of gender on leadership style. He suggested that statewide, there were five people who were key to the grassroots effort in Mississippi—Aaron Henry, Amzie Moore, Annie Devine of Canton, Victoria Gray of Hattiesburg, and Mrs. Hamer. A comparative study of the five of them might shed a great deal of light on the variety of forms that effective grassroots leadership can play while militating against the tendency to merely lionize. Comparing one to the other will highlight relative weaknesses as well as strengths. At the same time, the comparison should suggest something about how gender affects leadership styles. The latter is a critical issue. Many of the developments that came to bedevil some movement organizations after the mid-sixties—the loss of emphasis on developing others, the inability to maintain effective human relationships, the romanticizing of violence and confrontation, the shift from movement-as-community to movement-as-political-party, the development of more self-aggrandizing, self-publicizing leadership styles—could all be thought of as shifts away from behavior patterns that in this society are socially coded as feminine and toward patterns socially coded as masculine, expressed most vividly by those nationalist organizations that as a matter of policy expected women to take a step back. That is, we might think of the decline in effective activism as representing an imbalance between "feminine" and "masculine" patterns. Whether that is anything more than an interesting metaphor depends on what we can learn about how gender actually influenced styles of leadership and participation.

The most recent overall scholarly examination of the movement from a major publisher is Robert Weisbrot's *Freedom Bound: A History of the Civil Rights Movement in America* (Norton, 1990), and it is a good benchmark for movement scholarship. My comments here focus on how he frames the movement's origins, the Mississippi movement, and Black radicalism.

His chapter on movement origins begins with an overview of the 1960 Greensboro sit-ins, a beginning that does create a sense of the potency of individuals; four college freshmen did something that mattered. The first subsection is appropriately headed, *The American Dilemma,* after Gunnar Myrdal's work. Myrdal's analysis, giving primacy to the role of moral values in shaping the American racial situation, is a model of normative thinking, and Weisbrot's is certainly slanted in that direction. As we moved toward the 1960s, the southern caste system "still flourished on the margins of conscience," but it was not so impregnable as it once was, partly because white people, responding to demographic changes, were beginning to feel differently about it. As the South began to urbanize,

> the logic of business growth favored a more widely educated labor force, employed by merit rather than color, and a domestic market unhampered by racial division of consumers or disruptive social tensions. To a rising if reticent minority of merchants, manufacturers, and professionals, Jim Crow was becoming an embarrassing, and costly, anachronism. (p. 6)

These were real changes, but they are presented out of their context. Exactly, how did these changes work themselves out on the ground? If we examine that, we are frequently going to see southern Black activists pushing the system and northern activists creating the conditions for embarrassment. Without that context, it sounds too much as if no one had to do anything. Weisbrot goes on to mention other relevant changes—the migrations, the changing political status of Blacks, unionization, and particularly, "the ascendancy of liberal politics." Scholars like Otto Klineberg and Franz Boaz and artists like Richard Wright began stripping racism of some of its intellectual legitimacy. "Negroes assisted these developments with escalating protests against discrimination" (p. 8), including the NAACP's campaign against school segregation. Unlike Kluger in *Simple Justice,* Weisbrot gives no sense of the campaign from the bottom-up; it is all a matter of smart lawyers and liberal justices.

As he moves into the war years, he pays some attention to mass activism, but in a way I found almost denigrating:

> That summer [1941] the Negro union leader, A. Philip Randolph, founder of the Brotherhood of Sleeping Car Porters, warned President Roosevelt that over fifty thousand black men would rally at the capital against Jim Crow in the armed forces and war-production industries. Randolph's prediction was more a desperate gambit than an informed estimate, given the paucity of Negro activism outside the Northern ghettoes. But in a time of approaching

war, Roosevelt chose not to test this rippling of black political muscle. (p. 9)

Actually, Randolph initially planned a march of ten thousand and then raised it to one hundred thousand because there was so much enthusiasm on the streets, which hardly sounds like the act of a desperate man. This is one of the few references to mass action in the chapter and it comprises less than a paragraph. Given that, it is curious that Weisbrot chooses to frame it as a successful bluff. Whether Randolph in fact could have turned out a hundred thousand is an open question, but we know that Randolph could have led massive numbers to Washington. The following summer, he organized rallies of twenty thousand in New York, twelve thousand in Chicago, and nine thousand in Saint Louis. (In conjunction with the New York and Chicago rallies, Randolph requested that all outside lighting in Black neighborhoods be turned off, symbolizing the way Blacks were blacked out of American democracy. The blackouts were successful, perhaps a greater organizing feat than the rallies themselves.)[17] We have every reason to believe that he could have brought far more Black faces to Washington than FDR wanted to see.

There are questions one might raise about the March on Washington Movement that seem more important than how many people Randolph could have gotten. Suppose he could have gotten "only" 50,000. Who would they have been? Where in the emerging social structure of the ghetto could one find people willing to act? By what networks were they linked? We know that this was another case where there was substantial involvement of women, enough to make one of Randolph's union colleagues grouse, "There are too many women mixed up in this thing, anyhow."[18] Where did they come from? What role did they play? And what was it about Randolph in the first place that made it possible for him to lead a mass movement, anyway?[19] And why did he think it preferable to keep the MOWM all-Black? The role of whites in the movement became one of the central issues of the sixties movement. Knowing how an experienced organizer like Randolph thought about it in the 1940s might give some perspective on the question. What was the class character of the movement? Lewis Killian calls it "a type of black lower-class militance which had not surfaced since Garveryism and would not be seen again until the slogan 'Black Power' echoed throughout the land." Why did this population respond?[20] Someplace in a chapter titled "Origins of the Movement" there should be a discussion that raises some serious analytical questions about mass activism, and there are plenty of questions from which to choose. Instead, Weisbrot frames his discussion in a way that suggests there may have been little to mass activism beyond a clever bluff.

In fact, since Randolph engineered "the first presidential order for civil rights since Reconstruction" (p. 9), led the successful campaign for the desegregation of the armed forces, built the most important Black union, and was, according to one of his biographers, "the most sought-after Black political figure in America" through the 1940s, a reasonable case could be made for presenting a little more background on him. He was a socialist, a man who admired the Bolsheviks, a racial separatist when he thought it tactically useful, a man who eschewed the accommodationist politics that had been common among Black leaders, who believed in the power of putting the people in the street, not placating whites in power. One of the enduring questions in Black struggle has been the fight between proponents of more militant and less militant tactics. If we put the March on Washington Movement in that context, it becomes a case where in retrospect the more radical position was correct. By emphasizing facts that Weisbrot omits or downplays, one can give the story a very different ideological subtext, and a much less normative one.

The desegregation of the armed forces is given the same kind of normative, top-down shadings. After noting that the registration of over two million Blacks by the late 1940s drove one of the deepest wedges into the racial status quo, he notes:

> President Harry Truman, who as a Missouri politician had always welcomed black support as heartily as white, appointed a committee in 1946 to investigate violations of Negro rights. . . . This prestigious task force urged comprehensive federal action to end segrega-

tion. In 1948 Truman acceded to a strong civil rights plank that liberal delegates had inserted in the Democratic national platform. . . . Two years later he began desegregation of the armed forces to heighten military efficiency for the Korean War and to quiet restive black leaders. (p. 11)

"Restive black leaders" are tacked on like an afterthought; it seems that Truman's basic decency is what really drove the process. Truman, compared to most presidents, did have some sense of decency with regard to race, but his actions in 1948 were more politic than Weisbrot implies. Truman did send a strong civil rights message to Congress that year, but in the hope that he would not have to do anything else. According to one historian, "Truman took no further action, hoping that the rhetoric alone would be sufficient to satisfy black demands and that his inaction would appease southern Democrats." Instead, "no sooner had the President delivered his message, however, than Randolph began castigating him for failing to couple his words with action."[21] Randolph promised a campaign of massive civil disobedience modeled after Gandhi, and he pledged to "openly counsel, aid and abet youth, both white and Negro, to quarantine any jimcrow conscription system."[22] During one meeting with Truman, Randolph pushed the president so hard that the president virtually threw him out of his office. Frightened by cries of "Treason!" much established Black leadership, including the NAACP, either attacked Randolph or equivocated, but he had support in the streets. Seventy percent of young Black men polled in Harlem agreed with Randolph; a number did go to jail.[23] As one of Randolph's biographers put it, "Under the combined pressure of the Randolph campaign, the [Hubert] Humphrey civil rights floor fight [at the Democratic convention] and the need to retain the black vote in the November election," Truman issued an executive order calling for an end to discrimination in the military, whereupon Randolph sent him a telegram, praising him for his high order of statesmanship.[24]

Truman, that is, took the action he took within a political context, a context defined partly by the insistent struggle of Black people no longer content with rhetoric and promises. Here and elsewhere, Weisbrot's presentation just does not reflect a sense of struggle. In particular, he has a poor sense of what was happening outside the North. He says that two million Blacks were voting by the late forties but says nothing about what had happened in the South to make that possible. The percentage of Blacks registered in the South went from three percent in 1940 to twenty percent by 1952. How did it happen? Who organized it, and against what resistance? Weisbrot's viewpoint is too top-down for these questions to even enter into discussion.

In the context of the reaction to *Brown,* he does say that "the Ku Klux Klan, the White Citizens' Council, and other fringe vehicles of racial hate experienced overnight revivals after the Court decision" (p. 12). The Councils were not a revival of anything, and calling them fringe is simply ridiculous. The Councils were eminently respectable, and in Mississippi were hard to distinguish from the state government.

In his discussion of Little Rock, Weisbrot points out that the fight there sobered many who thought that a purely legalistic approach might suffice. I don't know if that's true, but at least indirectly the comment points to the need for mass-based activity. Unfortunately, in the next subsection, titled "An Awakening Moment," he continues to demonstrate an uneven appreciation for that activity. Martha Prescod Norman has pointed out that the much-used metaphor of the fifties as some kind of "awakening" implies that everyone was asleep before then. Before *Brown,* Weisbrot maintains, southern Negroes had periodically defied Jim Crow, "though with limited continuity and effect." "Sporadic local protests also sent a message of growing Negro assertiveness, but few, black or white, received it" (p. 13). Here again, this conveys no sense that anything of substance was happening in the South. At the least, he needs some systematic examination of the expanding Black voting population and of the growth in civil rights organizations within the South. Absent that, he is left to try to understand the fifties through those overused historical markers, *Brown* and Montgomery. His discussion of Montgomery makes it very clear that Montgomery was made possible by the collective leadership of experienced activists. The chapter ends by noting that there was a new national mood as the fifties drew to a close, affecting Black youth in the South more keenly than anyone else. "Raised on the promise of *Brown* and the Montgomery campaign, they awaited only a spark to set them against the barricades of segregation, as they heralded their country's reawakening reform spirit" (p. 18). Leaving aside the normative mysticism, this is Big Event history. What were southern Black people doing that contributed to the origins of the movement? Outside of Montgomery, the chapter seems to say, not much worth noticing.

In a chapter on the Great Society, he looks more closely at Mississippi. Revealingly, he titles the section "Freedom Summer," as if the rest of the Mississippi movement were mere prelude. He does start the discussion in the fifties, but some of that discussion is just wrong-headed.

> While Negroes in other Southern states stirred with news of *Brown* and the successful bus boycott in Montgomery, race relations in Mississippi continued much as if the War Between the States had ended at Bull Run rather than Appomattox. There were always isolated Negroes who were prepared to pay the high cost of first-class citizenship in Mississippi.

"Isolated Negroes" does not capture what was happening in Mississippi; in the ten years prior to *Brown,* activists there had made measurable progress against great odds and had created networks that would help make the sixties possible. The isolated Negro Weisbrot chooses to focus half a page on is Medgar Evers, who, we are told, with a handful of other Blacks brought the civil rights movement to insular Mississippi. Even if he conveys little sense of what the movement was about, simply mentioning Evers goes beyond many histories. Weisbrot also discusses the seriousness of white violence, including the Till case and the shootings of the Reverend Lee and Gus Courts in Belzoni, but he ends that paragraph with another example of curious selection of information. Noting that the Reverend Lee's widow refused to take her name off the voting roll even after the two shootings, he then quotes a Black lawyer who said she "wouldn't take that long march through the valley of the shadow of death to the polling place" (p. 94). One wonders why that needed mentioning. A woman engaged in an act of defiance in the wake of the death of her husband and the attempted murder of her husband's friend. In the context of this history, it seems to me that her defiance is the story. For someone to say, "Well, yeah, but she could have been even more defiant," seems misplaced emphasis at best, but it is consistent with the overall message that Weisbrot conveys: southern Black Folk were in pitiful condition; they needed some rescuing. He ends the discussion of the fifties quoting Medgar Evers worrying about "an apparent decline in the activities of many of our branches. Violence and police brutality still have the upper hand in Mississippi" (p. 94). Unless one checks the footnote, one wouldn't know that he's quoting a 1957 report from Evers. Had he quoted any year after that, both NAACP membership and voter-registration numbers would have been rising again, and I doubt that any one individual was any more responsible for that than Medgar Evers. Weisbrot manages to use Evers's own words in ways that negate the force of his life. When he jumps to the sixties, he does mention Herbert Lee and Louis Allen and the 1963 Freedom Vote. The latter, almost necessarily, is presented ahistorically. It is not the result of a process of struggle and growth, it is just "a rare show of political assertiveness by Mississippi's blacks" (p. 96). And not surprisingly, he puts a white man in charge, referring to Allard Lowenstein's "skilled but abrasive direction of the registration effort." He got the "skilled but abrasive" part right, but that's all. Lowenstein helped develop the idea of the Freedom vote, recruited volunteers, and headed the advisory committee, but he did not direct it.[25]

The stage having been so carefully prepared, it is time to bring on the heroes—on to Freedom Summer. Everything from the middle fifties through 1963 is covered in three-and-one-half pages; Freedom Summer gets nine. The White Folks are here, therefore something historically important must be happening, therefore we slow down a little.[26] Weisbrot consistently downplays indigenous Black activism. Thus, it is not surprising that later in the book, discussing the 1980s, he can say: "Southern whites understandably regard black militancy as an urban malady, for only in the cities have blacks developed an independent business and professional class able to lead sustained protests," ignoring the fact that in the most dangerous moments of the rural movement, sustained militant leadership came from the working class and the poor, while the better classes temporized. Weisbrot simply throws away all that we should have learned about the possibilities of developing leadership where it looks unlikely.

Understandably, nationalism is problematic from a top-down, normative perspective. The same faith in the status quo that convinced southern white supremacists in 1961 that outside agitators must be stirring up all the problems, can lead scholars to reduce any radicalism to irrational, inexplicable hatred of white people. Weisbrot tries to take nationalism seriously, but there are indications that he is less than comfortable with it. Weisbrot's discussion of Malcolm X's career struck me as quite balanced, but he mars it with the same kind of contrived ending that mars the section on Medgar Evers, this time suggesting that Malcolm went to his death having lost influence and following. We are told that civil rights leaders shrank from his embrace. "On the left wing of the movement SNCC leaders occasionally spoke with Malcolm . . . but they too pulled back from his overtures, uncomfortable with his harsh treatment of their Gandhian, integrationist ideals" (p. 177). He quotes James Forman saying "Look, man, nobody's worried about Malcolm X."

All this is very misleading. I know of no SNCC rejections of any Malcolm overtures. Indeed, the picture Carson paints in *In Struggle* (pp. 135–36) is one of mutual admiration and growing cooperation in Malcolm's last year—Malcolm speaking at an MFDP rally, SNCC bringing Mississippi teenagers to meet him, Malcolm speaking in Selma at SNCC's invitation. By 1964–65, the period Weisbrot is referring to, many SNCC members could be as harsh on Gandhian idealism as Malcolm ever was, and the value of integration was very much an open question among them. In many places, as in Greenwood, Deep South organizers were either arming themselves or talking about it. Weisbrot's comment suggests again that he is out of touch with the movement's evolution.

Forman's remark notwithstanding, other SNCC members have cited

Malcolm as one of the pivotal influences on their thinking. Carson quotes John Lewis as saying that Malcolm more than any other single person was "able to articulate the aspirations, bitterness, and frustrations of the Negro people." Cleveland Sellers says: "Before his assassination most of us were convinced that his awesome charisma and brilliant insights would have resulted in his becoming one of the first men in history to lead a multi-continental revolutionary movement."[27] In a later chapter, Weisbrot's brief reference to the Black Panther Party—and its brevity seems odd in a chapter on "The Radical Movement"—gives no idea that members of that organization saw themselves as Malcolm's children. According to Huey Newton:

> Our program was structured after the Black Muslim program—minus the religion. I was very impressed with Malcolm X, with the program that Malcolm X followed. I think that I became disillusioned with the Muslims after Malcolm X was assassinated. I think that I was following not Elijah Muhammad or the Muslims, but Malcolm himself.[28]

In his discussion of Eldridge Cleaver (pp. 231–32), Weisbrot does say that Cleaver was greatly influenced by Malcolm but does not identify Cleaver with the Party.

Malcolm, Weisbrot continues, was being criticized in the bars of Harlem for his shifting philosophy, which, given the bars of Harlem, I am willing to believe, but it is hardly substantiation for saying that his "main base of support was slipping away" (p. 178). In one sentence, Weisbrot tells us that six thousand people attended Malcolm's funeral. In the next: "Yet by then Malcolm had few friends and not many more followers." We can only wonder who were the six thousand. For that matter who were the twenty-two thousand the *New York Times* estimated viewed the body in the days before the funeral?[29] The attempt to portray Malcolm as some kind of failure is at best unconvincing. In a later discussion, Weisbrot notes that Malcolm became more influential after his death, but that comment is followed by a discussion that frames a quotation (p. 234) from Malcolm in such a way as to suggest that the post-Mecca Malcolm was less concerned about exploitation than he had been, having grown into a broader vision of humanity.

However silly some of its expressions became, the fundamental question raised by Black Power was, Can American institutions work for Black Americans? Weisbrot frequently treats this as an open question, which I take to be the only intellectually responsible way to treat it. Unfortunately, his discussion of Black radicalism is arguably more top-down than his discussion of the earlier movement, in that it reduces nationalism to its celebrities—Amiri Baraka, Cleaver, Karenga, Harold Cruse, Nikki Giovanni, Albert Cleage, and so on. We learn little about cultural nationalism as a movement. Who came to Spirit House in Newark? Through what networks? What kinds of programs did they construct? What values governed their interactions among themselves? Giving us a string of celebrities doesn't tell us much about the movement as such.[30]

The level of information in the discussion about the radical movement is low. It is simply not true (p. 236) that nationalism for Baraka meant "opposing all ties with whites." When it made political sense to him, Baraka was willing to make significant overtures to whites, including to some of Newark's notoriously racist construction unions.[31] There may be some logic to calling Eldridge Cleaver a cultural nationalist (pp. 231–32), but it is not obvious. While Cleaver certainly wrote things that were in accord with the thinking of cultural nationalists, presumably his main influence on the movement was as minister of information for the Black Panther Party, usually considered the paradigmatic political nationalist group. Under Weisbrot's interpretation, Cleaver and Maulana Karenga come out on the same ideological side, a nice joke on history.[32] On the other hand, saying that Muhammad Ali remained "buoyantly unrepentant" after being stripped of his crown is not funny. It trivializes the injustice done him and is an inaccurate characterization of his reaction.[33]

How has *Freedom Bound* been received by the scholarly community? On the whole, quite favorably, although many of the points I raise have been raised elsewhere.[34] *Antioch Review* found it "sympathetic and balanced," "thorough and illuminating" on many important points. *Choice* called it a "splendid" book, "the finest comprehensive historical synthesis yet written. Evenhanded in ideology and in its portrayal of leading players, sprightly and often witty in style, and probing and balanced in perspective." The review does note a "tendency to weigh more heavily the perspective from the Oval Office than from front lines" in the 1961–64 period, which leaves one wondering how it can be ideologically evenhanded. David Garrow in the *New York Times* judged it a "commendable and often beautifully written effort" to fill the need for a single-volume comprehensive history of the movement, despite a few incidences of insufficient sources, "mangled names and erroneous photo captions." On balance, he finds it a "praiseworthy" job. Ralph E. Luker, writing in *American Quarterly*, predicts that despite several factual errors, *Freedom Bound* should "soon be accepted as the best one-volume history of the civil rights movement."

John Dittmer agrees that Weisbrot omits a number of important sources and identifies several more errors of fact, enough to "leave an impression that the author is not entirely comfortable on southern terrain." Dittmer underscores the difficulty of trying to cover so much history in so few pages—just over three hundred—and the pressure that creates to focus on major civil rights organizations and their relations with the federal government. Still, "what is lost here is the power of the movement at its most basic and dynamic level—the grass roots." The corollary of that is that women are left out. Weisbrot does acknowledge the role of Miss Baker and Mrs. Hamer, "But for the most part, *Freedom Bound* records the exploits of important black and white men," a point not raised in the other reviews. Noting the unfairness of holding Weisbrot responsible for pushing beyond the borders of current historiography, Dittmer concludes that it is still a succinct and convincing overview.[35]

I would agree that the book represents improvement, of sorts.[36] It is not as King-centric nor as Kennedy-centric as it might have been. It does respect the idea of multiple leadership, it endeavors to treat nationalism as a serious political current. It may seem a small point, but I am glad that a book aimed at a general audience avoids Hoary Convention of Writing About Civil Rights No. 3, Celebratory History. This is that style of writing that finds the changes in the South so-ooo amazing, so-ooo astounding, so-ooo beyond belief that we just can't get over it. (See, e.g., the introduction to *My Soul Is Rested*.) The fact that Blacks, after great sacrifice, can now do what other Americans have always taken for granted ought not be the occasion for so much self-congratulation. Malcolm used to say that a man can stick a knife twelve inches deep in your back and then wiggle it out six inches and yell, "Look ! We're making progress!!" (At the other extreme, we want to avoid the tendency among some Black youth to say the movement accomplished nothing after all, or that its only beneficiaries were middle class.)

Whatever its relative virtues, this is still a book with a distinct and uncritical top-down, normative tint, weak in its sense of historical continuity, awkward in its handling of radicalism, less than distinguished in its ability to just get the facts straight, a book that has difficulty just posing a serious question about mass activism and is thus incapable of posing a question about the role women played in that activism. It is not only possible for such a book to be written; it can still be received among scholars as intellectually respectable and perhaps as laudatory. This is emphatically White History, history where the patterns of selection and emphasis are consistent with the underlying vision of history that has always been most comfortable to the socially privileged.[37] It is still possible to write Blacks out of much of the history, to write women out, to write southerners and working-class people out, and be taken seriously, this despite a decade or more of rather pointed criticism of that kind of history.

To say that traditional movement scholarship has been generally elitist and specifically racist and sexist and class-biased is not at all to comment on the political attitudes of scholars. People drawn to writing about the movement probably tend to be people who share some of its values and its hope for a more equitable society. Remember that the northern liberals who went South in the middle sixties believed so strongly in racial justice as to risk their lives for it, but even they would have been naive to think that they were unmarked by having been shaped within a racist society. Race is embedded in our lives in ways more powerful than specific attitudes. Similarly, intellectual elitism has less to do with explicit feelings about race, gender, and class than with the kinds of general models available to scholars, the kinds of questions that will flow from those models, and the background assumptions scholars bring to their work, assumptions about the nature of social structure and political change.[38]

Nonetheless, it is clear that both popular and scholarly movement history are getting better, however slowly, and are opening up questions about the process of change and the role social status plays in that change that have heretofore been closed. One recent work that suggests what we may hope for is *Minds Stayed on Freedom: The Civil Rights Struggle in the Rural South, An Oral History,* authored by the youth of the Rural Organizing and Cultural Center (Westview Press, 1991). Based on interviews with movement participants done by teenagers in Holmes County, Mississippi, it stresses the themes that would be important from an organizing perspective—the legacy of racial terrorism, the centrality of women, the importance of land-ownership, the guidance of outside civil rights workers, the willingness of local people to defend themselves, the distinction between mobilizing and organizing, the bankruptcy of the church and the courage of some of its members—and aside from a very useful introduction by Jay McLeod, it is rendered in the language of the people themselves. Content aside, the way the book was produced—the collective authorship, the attempt (apparently successful) to teach youngsters that people they see every day have unsuspected powers, the attempt to ground youngsters in their own history and culture—is a powerful reminder of what the movement's values were. Judging from the draft chapters I have seen, John Dittmer's *Local People* (Indiana University Press, in press), which looks at Black politics in Mississippi from the mid-fifties through the mid-sixties, promises, as suggested by the title, to have nearly all the virtues of *Minds Stayed on Freedom* as well as the scholar's broader view.

As academic histories come to reflect a greater variety of social perspectives, it is not clear how popular culture will be affected. It may be that the top-down, normative conception of the movement is so deeply ingrained in popular culture, so constantly reinforced and so consistent with our national vanities, that new scholarship will be unable to dent it. We are likely to soon see a wave of scholarship that paints a more careful conception of Martin Luther King's role, but nonetheless, every January, the airwaves will be filled with "I Have a Dream."[39]

Most of us who study the movement want to believe that our work can have some impact. Addressing an audience of scholars and movement activists, CORE's James Farmer said:

> I think that knowledge of the past is vital but historical knowledge is not an end in itself. The more we learn about the past, the more we must recognize that we learn about it in order to bring a more humane society into being in this country. Otherwise, historical knowledge is meaningless.[40]

None of us understands fully how to use what we know of the past to shape a more just present, but we can be sure that social analysis which does not somehow make it clear that ordinary, flawed, everyday sorts of human beings frequently manage to make extraordinary contributions to social change, social analysis which does not make it easier for people to see in themselves and in those around them the potential for controlling their own lives takes us in the wrong direction.[41] Commenting on the general tendency to reduce history to the actions of the elite, Howard Zinn contends:

> All those histories of this country centered on the Founding Fathers and the Presidents weigh oppressively on the capacity of the ordinary citizen to act. They suggest that in times of crisis we must look to someone to save us. . . . The idea of saviors has been built into the entire culture, beyond politics. We have learned to look to stars, leaders, experts in every field, thus surrendering our own strength, demeaning our own ability, obliterating our own selves.[42]

His point applies with special force to the civil rights movement. The traditional view of the movement, popular or scholarly, has failed to help us appreciate the persistence of a George Greene, the sustained courage of the McGhees, the growth of a Lula Belle Johnson or a

Mary Lane, or Mrs. Hamer's sense of community and humanity, or the strengthening faith of an Aaron Johnson. Alice Walker has written that if the movement has done nothing else it has given Blacks a history of men (and women) better than presidents. Perhaps not. Even at this late date, at the level of popular culture the history has been largely homogenized, the men and women better than presidents largely forgotten, which may make it more difficult to produce any more like them.

NOTES

SNCC   Papers of the Student Nonviolent Coordinating Committee, King Center, Atlanta.

SRC   Papers of the Southern Regional Council (microfilm).

VEP   Papers of the Voter Education Project, Woodruff Library, Clark University, Atlanta.

In the case of material taken from microfilmed collections, the initial frame number of each document, if available, is listed in parentheses.

INTRODUCTION

1. Preface to H. Aptheker, *Documentary History of the Negro People in the United States* (New York: Citadel, 1951), p. v.
2. Bayard Rustin, *Down The Line* (Chicago: Quadrangle, 1971), p. 67.
3. In "Commentary," Charles Eagles, ed., *The Civil Rights Movement in America* (Oxford: University Press of Mississippi, 1986), p. 57.
4. R. Moses, M. Kamii, S. Swap, and J. Howard, "The Algebra Project: Organizing in the Spirit of Ella," *Harvard Educational Review* 59 (November 1989): 423–43.
5. L. C. Dorsey, *Freedom Came to Mississippi* (New York: Field Foundation, 1977), p. 24.

CHAPTER I

1. Ruby Hurley, "Economic Pressure in Mississippi," April 1955, NAACP IIA424.
2. On numbers lynched, see Robert Zangrando, *The NAACP Crusade Against Lynching* (Philadelphia: Temple, 1980), p. 5. While Mississippi had the greatest absolute number of lynchings, Georgia had the higher rate, considering population differences. General information on the Mississippi killings can be found in the NAACP's annual supplements to their pamphlet, *Thirty Years of Lynching, 1889–1918;* more detailed information on some lynchings is in NAACP IIA 407, 408, 411; IC359, 360, 361. See also Arthur Raper, *The Tragedy of Lynching* (New York: New American Library, 1969 [1933]) esp. pp. 80–106, and Jessie Daniel Ames, *The Changing Character of Lynching* (New York: Ames Press, 1942). Between 1930 and 1935, Ames (pp. 42–44) lists three Mississippi killings which were not in the NAACP lists, suggesting something of the inconsistencies in lynching records. Her Association of Southern Women for the Prevention of Lynching was particularly concerned with uncovering lynchings that might not otherwise have come to light and had the machinery for doing so. On the his-

tory of racial violence in Mississippi, see Howard Smead, *Blood Justice: The Lynching of Mack Charles Parker* (New York: Oxford, 1986), and Neil McMillen, *Dark Journey* (Urbana: University of Illinois Press, 1989).

3. One apparent 1934 killing may have been left out of the NAACP's final count. In Hernando, a white man came into Henry Wright's house and accused Wright of having stolen some bricks. Wright denied stealing anything and threw the man out. The next day the white man saw Wright in town. A group of ten to fifteen white men chased Wright out of town and shot him to death. NAACP IC360, "Lynching in Hernando, Miss."

4. "Negro Hanged in Mississippi School Yard," *Memphis Press Scimitar,* March 13, 1935.

5. "Lynching By Blow Torch," NAACP IC360; "Lynchings End 15, Mo. Record in Mississippi," *Memphis Press Scimitar,* April 14, 1937. These reports differ in some details, such as the order in which the men died. I have followed the NAACP report—apparently one of Howard Kester's—which seems generally better-informed.

6. NAACP IC361, "Report of Lynching of Wilder McGowan, 24, at Wiggins, Miss., on November 21, 1938"; George Williams to Charles H. Houston, 11/27/39, NAACP IC361.

7. Ames, *Changing Character of Lynching,* p. 8; see also McMillen, *Dark Journey,* pp. 235–36.

8. On the Canton killings, NAACP IIA408, "Lynching Goes Underground." Also Ames, *Changing Character of Lynching,* pp. 5–7.

9. Madison Jones to Walter White, 11/7/42, NAACP IIA408.

10. NAACP IIA408, "Lynching in Liberty, Miss."

11. Daniel Cohn, *Where I Was Born and Raised* (Boston: Houghton-Mifflin, 1948), p. 41.

12. Hortense Powdermaker, *After Freedom* (New York: Atheneum, 1968); McMillen, *Dark Journey,* pp. 123–25. On how closely sharecropping resembled peonage, see pp. 144–50.

13. Powdermaker, *After Freedom,* pp. 28–29, 81.

14. Ibid., p. 80.

15. McMillen, *Dark Journey,* p. 151; Cohn, *Where I Was Born and Raised,* pp. 303–06, 315–24; Arthur Raper, "Machines in the Cotton Field," *New South* 1, no. 9 (September 1946).

16. Doug McAdam, *Political Process and the Development of Black Insurgency, 1930–1970* (Chicago: University of Chicago Press, 1982), p. 80; McMillen, *Dark Journey,* p. 152. In 1930, 78% of all cropland in the Delta was still in cotton; in 1940, 46%. Cohn, *Where I Was Born and Raised,* p. 321.

17. See McAdam, *Black Insurgency,* for elaboration. Also Jack Bloom, *Class,*

Race, and the Civil Rights Movement (Bloomington: Indiana University Press, 1987).

18. Fully 87% of migrants between 1910 and 1960 settled in seven states—New York, New Jersey, Pennsylvania, Ohio, California, Illinois, and Michigan—crucial in presidential elections. See McAdam *Black Insurgency*, p. 79; also Earl Lewis, "The Negro Voter in Mississippi," *Journal of Negro Education* 26 (Summer 1957): 329–50. Of the electoral college votes won by the Democrats in the 1920 and 1924 presidential elections, 90% came from the southern states. By 1936, the figure had declined to 23%. See Bloom, *Class, Race and the Movement*, p. 76. Although they cannot be so directly attributed to electoral forces, changes in the nature of Supreme Court decisions are well documented. Between 1876 and 1930, only 43% of its decisions had been favorable to Blacks (23 of 53); between 1930 and 1955, 91% (68 of 75) were favorable. McAdam, *Black Insurgency*, p. 84.

19. "Statement of Senator Robert F. Wagner of New York regarding recent lynchings," July 12, 1938, NAACP IC361. The year 1922 was also a turning point with respect to lynchings prevented; after that year, the number of lynchings prevented annually began to exceed the number of actual lynchings. Ames, *Changing Character of Lynching*, p. 11.

20. "FBI to Investigate Lynching of Three," *New York Times*, Oct. 12, 1942; Edward R. Dudley to Paul Kattenburg, 11/10/44, NAACP IIA408; "Jury Verdict in Jones Case Doesn't Dissipate This Menace," Jackson *Clarion-Ledger*, April 27, 1943.

21. "The South Lifts Its Head," *New South* 8, no. 1 (January 1953), p. 6.

22. Raper, *Tragedy of Lynching*, pp. 23, 476; Powdermaker, *After Freedom*, p. 55; "Jury Verdict in Jones Case Doesn't Dissipate This Menace," Jackson *Clarion-Ledger*, April 27, 1943.

23. McMillen, *Dark Journey*, p. 395; Raper, *Tragedy of Lynching*, 30–31; Ames, *Changing Character of Lynching*, pp. 61–62.

24. Ames, ibid., p. 62; Ames quoted in Jacquelyn Dowd Hall, *Revolt Against Chivalry: Jessie Daniel Ames and the Women's Campaign Against Lynching* (New York: Columbia University Press, 1979), p. 169.

25. Powdermaker, *After Freedom*, p. 50.

26. Cohn, *Where I Was Born and Raised*, p. 226.

27. Samuel Adams, "The Acculturation of the Delta Negro," *Social Forces* 26 (December 1947), p. 203.

28. Alabama sharecropper Nate Shaw, in Theodore Rosengarten's *All God's Dangers* (New York: Avon, 1974), also comments on the growing tendency to minimize contact with whites in the pre–World War II years.

29. Powdermaker, *After Freedom*, p. 353. See also McMillen, *Dark Journey*, pp. 307–08, for a parallel discussion of generational change.

30. Powdermaker, ibid., p. 321.

31. Steven Lawson, *Black Ballots: Voting Rights in the South, 1944–66* (New York: Columbia, 1985), p. 120.

32. David Garrow, *Protest at Selma* (New Haven: Yale University Press, 1978), pp. 6–7. For background on the decision, see Richard Kluger, *Simple Justice: The History of Brown v. Board of Education and Black America's Struggle for Equality* (New York: Vintage, 1977), pp. 234–37, and Lawson, *Black Ballots,* ch. 2.

33. Lawson, ibid., pp. 102–03; Cohn, *Where I Was Born and Raised,* p. 354–55. There is apparently no substantial study of the growth of voters' leagues across the South during the war years nor of the role that veterans played in that movement.

34. Lawson, *Black Ballots,* pp. 106–07.

35. Earl Lewis, "The Negro Voter in Mississippi," *Journal of Negro Education,* pp. 334–35.

36. Margaret Price, "Negro Registration: Present and Prospective," *New South* 12, no. 9 (September 1957), pp. 1–5.

37. The list is a modified version of one presented by Luther Jackson, "Race and Suffrage in the South Since 1940," *New South* 3, no. 6 (June 1948).

38. Memorandum from Ruby Hurley, "Report From Call Meeting of Mississippi State Conference," May 7, 1951, NAACP Box IIC96.

39. Myrlie Evers, *For Us the Living* (New York: Doubleday, 1967), p. 98. NAACP IIC96, "Mississippi Branches, January 1 to November 25, 1949"; "Membership Status of Mississippi Branches," October 26, 1951; Clarence Mitchell, "Report on Mississippi for Board and Staff Reference." On the early history of the NAACP in the state, see McMillen *Dark Journey,* 314–16.

40. Bethany Swearingen, "Mississippi," *New South* 4, no. 10 (October 1949).

41. "The South Lifts Its Head," *New South* 8, no. 1 (January 1953), p. 6.

42. Jay Milner, "Jackson Negroes Share Desire for Public School Integration," *New South* 9, no. 9 (September 1954); Price, "Negro Registration: Present and Prospective."

43. NAACP IIC96, press release, "NAACP Branches in Mississippi get Threatening Visits, Calls," September 9, 1954; IIA413, Hurley, "Economic Pressure in Mississippi," April 1955; IIC98, E. J. Stringer, "Annual Report by the President of the Mississippi State Conference of NAACP Branches," November 6, 1954; IIA424, "Memorandum To Mr. Wilkins From Mr. Current," December 13, 1954.

CHAPTER 2

1. Michael Garvey, "An Oral History with Amzie Moore," Mississippi Oral History Program, University of Southern Mississippi, 1981. Other sources on Moore include the Amzie Moore Papers, SHSW; Howell Raines, *My Soul Is*

Rested (New York: Putnam, 1977), pp. 233–37: Seth Cagin and Philip Dray, *And We Are Not Afraid* (New York: Macmillan, 1988); James Forman, *The Making of Black Revolutionaries* (Washington: Open Hand, 1985), pp. 277–91; Bayard Rustin, *Down the Line* (Chicago: Quadrangle, 1971); my interviews with Hollis Watkins, Charles Cobb, MacArthur Cotton, Lawrence Guyot, Ruben Smith, Beverly Perkins, Lillie Robinson, Homer Crawford, Ruth Moore.

2. Garvey, "An Oral History"; Malcolm Boyd, "Survival of a Negro Leader," *Ave Maria,* February 27, 1965; Forman, *Black Revolutionaries,* p. 278. Moore told Forman the Delta State meeting was in 1942. Boyd and other sources place it in 1940.

3. Quotations from Forman, ibid., p. 278–79.

4. Ibid., p. 279, and Raines, *My Soul Is Rested,* p. 252.

5. Garvey, "An Oral History," pp. 9–10, 12.

6. Moore's report (Forman, p. 279) is inconsistent with reports from other sources that say racial violence was minimal in the state in the late forties. The discrepancy may be due partly to the isolation of the Delta. Word of much that happened there simply never got out. This silence would have been especially likely with respect to killings by law enforcement officials. One of the killings to which Moore may have been referring could have involved a young man who escaped from jail and was then recaptured and allegedly killed by the sheriff. See Franklin Williams to W. A. Bender, July 11, 1949, NAACP IIA41. Even so, Moore puts the number of Blacks killed at one a week for six to eight months after the war, a figure that seems improbable.

7. Raines, *My Soul Is Rested,* p. 252.

8. Forman, *Black Revolutionaries,* pp. 279–80; Garvey, "An Oral History," p. 20; Aaron Henry, *Inside Agitator,* Aaron Henry Papers, Tougaloo; "The New Fighting South," *Ebony,* August 1955; on Mound Bayou's history, see N. Crockett, *Black Towns* (Lawrence: Regents Press of Kansas, 1979). Moore, perhaps generously, estimated RCNL membership at 100,000 people spread over 40 counties. On the RCNL, see NAACP IIA381, IIA422. Mass meetings in Mississippi date back at least to the early 1940s; Stephen Oates is wrong when he claims that such meetings were a unique contribution of the 1955 Montgomery bus boycott. *Let The Trumpet Sound* (New York: Harper and Row, 1982), p. 74.

9. On the Nixon incident, see Aldon Morris, *Origins of the Civil Rights Movement* (New York: Free Press, 1984), p. 54; see pp. 13–16 and 33–36 for a fuller discussion of the shortcomings of the NAACP as seen by Southern leaders.

10. Raines, *My Soul Is Rested,* p. 256.

11. Stories about people absent from meetings being elected officers of NAACP chapters—some true, some apocryphal—are so common in this period that

they should be regarded as part of the folklore of Black Mississippi. In the Raines interview, Moore puts the date of the election in 1951, which is erroneous. See Moore to Wilkins, 1/17/55, NAACP IIA422.

12. Interviews with Hollis Watkins, Beverly Perkins, and Ruth Moore.

13. Myrlie Evers, *For Us The Living* (New York: Doubleday, 1967), p. 107; Benjamin Muse, *Ten Years of Prelude* (New York: Viking), pp. 16–22; on Mississippi moderates in general, see James Silver, *Mississippi: The Closed Society* (New York: Harcourt, Brace and World), 1963.

14. Rustin, *Down The Line,* p. 64; on the councils in general, see Neil McMillen, *The Citizens' Council* (Urban: University of Illinois Press, 1971), esp. chs. 2, 12, and Hodding Carter III, *The South Strikes Back* (New York: Doubleday, 1959).

15. Carter, ibid., p. 124; NAACP Annual Report, 1995.

16. Rustin, *Down The Line,* pp. 66–69.

17. On the Lee and Courts shootings, see Jack Mendelsohn, *The Martyrs: Sixteen Who Gave Their Lives for Racial Justice* (New York: Harper and Row, 1966), ch. 1; Myrlie Evers, *For Us the Living,* pp. 154–58, 176–80; Simeon Booker, *Black Man's America* (Englewood Cliffs, N.J.: Prentice Hall, 1964), pp. 161–74; interviews with Ruby Hurley and Gus Courts, HU; NAACP IIIA115, Clarence Mitchell, "Report on Mississippi for Board and Staff Reference," n.d.; NAACP IIA422, Hurley Memorandum to Wilkins, April 8, 1955; correspondence in IIIA230, 231; NAACP Annual Report, 1955; "The New Fighting South," *Ebony,* August 1955; *Chicago Defender* (national), May 21, 28, 1955.

18. Some sources refer to Reverend Lee as having served a term as branch president, but I found no references to that in NAACP files.

19. Mendelsohn, *Martyrs,* pp. 9–10.

20. Henry, *Inside Agitator,* p. 169.

21. Mendelsohn, *Martyrs,* p. 14. Black boycotts in retaliation for white violence go back at least as far as the Depression in Mississippi.

22. Courts interview, HU, p. 15. See also NAACP Annual Report, 1955.

23. Mendelsohn, *Martyrs,* p. 18.

24. Myrlie Evers, *For Us the Living,* pp., 169–70; Henry, *Inside Agitator,* p. 175. The arrest of two men in the Smith killing was in itself an act of courage on the part of the local district attorney, as Mrs. Evers noted, but the grand jury refused to indict.

25. In a pattern that was to be repeated with many near-martyrs, Courts always insisted that a great deal of fund-raising was done in his name and that he saw very little of the money. It is also interesting that when he testified before Congress in support of what became the 1957 Civil Rights Act, he left Washington with the feeling that few of the congressmen believed his story. One of the exceptions, he thought, was John Kennedy. HU interview.

26. Hurley, "Economic Pressure in Mississippi," April 1955, NAACP IIA424.

27. Mendelsohn, *Marytrs,* p. 20.

28. "Memorandum to Board of Directors from Mr. Current," December 13, 1954, NAACP IIA424.

29. Quotation from Clarence Mitchell, "Report on Mississippi for Board and Staff Reference," n. d., NAACP IIA424. See also Myrlie Evers, *For Us the Living,* pp. 152–54.

30. Rustin, *Down the Line,* p. 71.

31. Evers, *For Us the Living,* pp. 164–65, 151, and documents in NAACP IIA422. Quotation from David Halberstam, "A County Divided Against Itself," *The Reporter,* December 15, 1955, pp. 30–32. Halberstam finds that the local Citizens' Council leader was somewhat ambivalent about what the Council was doing.

32. *Southern School News,* April 1, 1957.

33. Morris, *Origins of the Civil Rights Movement,* pp. 30–34; Ruby Hurley, "Economic Pressure in Mississippi," April 1955, NAACP IIA424.

34. *Southern School News,* October 1, 1954, p. 9; Tracy Sugarman, *Stranger At the Gates,* (New York: Hill and Wang, 1966), p. 74; interviews with Beverly Perkins and Herman Perry.

35. Interviews with Lillie Robinson, Beverly Perkins, and Herman Perry.

36. Rustin, *Down the Line,* pp. 74–77; Boyd, "Survival of a Negro"; Garvey, "Oral History."

37. Moore's case got enough attention that T. R. M. Howard complained that Moore was starting to make a "racket" out of his persecutions. Howard to Wilkins, 3/15/56, NAACP IIIA232. Gus Courts, on the other hand, thought Howard had made a racket out of Courts's situation. HU interview.

38. Baker to Amzie Moore, 2/5/57, Moore Papers, SHSW.

39. NAACP IIC98, Ruby Hurley to Medgar Evers, November 29, 1954, "Memorandum to Mr. Wilkins from Mr. Current," November 22, 1954; Myrlie Evers, *For Us the Living,* p. 142; Mendelsohn, *Martyrs,* p. 12. Because Tri-State insisted on the usual standards of credit-worthiness, many farmers could not be helped. Small-town farmers were accustomed to getting crop loans on the basis of personal reputation.

40. Baker to Amzie Moore, 2/5/57, Amzie Moore Papers, SHSW.

41. "Note to Jim Dobrowski," n.d, unsigned memorandum in Amzie Moore Papers, SHSW.

42. McMillen, *Dark Journey,* pp. 134–37. Additionally, the most common accusation against Blacks who were lynched prior to 1945 was murder of a white person (p. 236), often in response to racial injustice. There were also particular Black communities that had reputations for resistance. McMillen (p. 226) mentions the Wahalak community in Kemper County, which twice took up arms against invading vigilantes. Mound Bayou was one of the towns in which custom required that whites be out of town by sunset.

43. Some versions of this story put the size of the crowd at a much higher number. The best source of information on Medgar Evers is Myrlie Evers, *For Us The Living*. See also *Remembering Medgar Evers* (Oxford, Miss.: Heritage Publications, 1988); Mendelsohn's *Martyrs;* interview with Myrlie Evers, HU; Medgar Evers, "Why I Live in Mississippi," *Ebony,* November 1958; James Meredith, *Three Years in Mississippi,* (Bloomington: Indiana University Press, 1966); Charles Evers, *Evers,* (New York: World Publishing, 1971); Reed Massengill, *Portrait of a Racist* (New York: St. Martin's, 1994).

44. Myrlie Evers, *For Us The Living*, p. 79.

45. Ibid., p. 78.

46. Hurly interview, HU, pp. 27–8.

47. Henry Hampton and Steve Fayer, *Voices of Freedom: An Oral History of the Civil Rights Movement from the 1950s through the 1980s* (New York: Bantam, 1990), pp. 152–53; Myrlie Evers, *For Us The Living*, p. 248.

48. Myrlie Evers, *For Us The Living*, pp. 127–8.

49. Both quotations from Evers, "Why I Live in Mississippi," p. 70.

50. Myrlie Evers, *For Us The Living*, p. 204; quotation from Myrlie Evers interview, HU, p. 30.

51. Two of the most cold-blooded of the many killings he investigated, one in 1959, the other in 1962, involved Lawrence Rainey, who held a succession of law-enforcement positions in Neshoba County. Myrlie Evers, *For Us The Living*, pp. 210–14. Rainey was later among those convicted for the Schwerner-Chaney-Goodman murders.

52. There has been some confusion about exactly what Till said or did. I am accepting the version given by one of his cousins, an eyewitness, in the "Eyes on the Prize" documentary.

53. Garvey, "An Oral History," p. 21. Three months after the Till murder, the apparent murder of twelve-year-old Tim Holman by a white landowner in north Mississippi attracted no attention. NAACP IIA422, Medgar Evers, "Report on the Death of Tim Holman," 11/3/55.

54. Hurley interview, HU, p. 15.

55. Ladner quoted in Joe Sinsheimer, "Never Turn Back: An Interview with Sam Block," *Southern Exposure,* 25, no. 2 (Summer 1987), p. 42.

56. Myrlie Evers, *For Us The Living*, pp. 214–25; "How Mississippi Southern Stayed White: The Story of Clyde Kennard," SNCC Papers, Box 15.

57. The best source of information on Henry is the draft of his unpublished autobiography *Inside Agitator,* in the Aaron Henry Papers, Box 1, Tougaloo College, Tougaloo, Miss. Also Robert Penn Warren, *Who Speaks for the Negro?* (New York: Random House, 1965), pp. 73–87; Margaret Long, "The Freest Man in Mississippi," *Negro Digest,* February 1964; my interviews with Hollis Watkins and MacArthur Cotton.

58. Henry, *Inside Agitator,* p. 138. The Turner killing would not qualify as a lynching, since it was done under color of law.

59. Patterson was titular head of the Councils, but the real power seems to have been Ellet Lawrence, who owned a printing company in Greenwood. Massengill, *Portrait of a Racist,* pp. 90–91.

60. NAACP Annual Report, 1959. Garrow's *Protest at Selma* shows higher figures—20,000 voters by 1958—p. 11.

61. Myrlie Evers, *For Us the Living,* 251–55; John Dittmer, "The Politics of the Mississippi Movement," in Charles Eagles, ed., *The Civil Rights Movement in America* (Jackson: University Press of Mississippi, 1986), pp. 72–93. On his up-and-down relationship with SCLC, see Garrow, *Bearing the Cross,* pp. 91, 103. As late as 1961, Evers's memoes to New York were hostile in tone toward SNCC and CORE. See "Special Report," 10/12/61, NAACP IIIA231. By 1963, Wilkins was complaining that Evers was not keeping him informed about activities in Mississippi, perhaps a result of the change in Evers. Wilkins to Current, 2/8/63, NAACP IIIA230.

62. Both quotations from Hampton and Fayer, *Voices,* p. 151.

63. Myrlie Evers, *For Us the Living,* pp. 252–4; Hampton and Fayer, *Voices,* pp. 147–8. Evers and Henry had been impressed by the effectiveness of a Jewish united-front organization they had visited in Los Angeles. Moses recently estimated that there were about 25 NAACP branch presidents in the state who showed marked autonomy from the national office. A. Meier, "Epilogue: Toward a Synthesis," in A. Robinson and P. Sullivan, eds., *New Directions in Civil Rights Studies* (Charlottesville: University Press of Virginia, 1991), p. 214.

64. Guyot in Raines, *My Soul Is Rested,* p. 259; Cobb in Raines, ibid., p. 266.

65. Jo Freeman, *The Politics of Women's Liberation: A Case of Study of an Emerging Social Movement and Its Relation to the Policy Process* (New York: David McKay, 1975), pp. 48–49.

66. Freeman suggests that the role of the organizer is most important when the networks are rudimentary. Presumably, it would also be important where the opposition is active and formidable.

67. Quotations from Sinsheimer, "Never Turn Back," p. 43.

68. Hurley interview, HU, p. 10.

69. Dittmer, "Politics of the Mississippi Movement," p. 68.

70. Mendelsohn, *Martyrs,* p. 20.

CHAPTER 3

1. Baker from Lenore Hagan, "Ella Baker Interview, March 4, 1979," p. 77, Highlander. Hart quoted in Frank Adams, "Highlander Folk School: Getting

Information, Going Back and Teaching It," *Harvard Educational Review* 42 (November 1972), p. 502.

2. Bob Moses, for example, describes Amzie Moore as an organizer at the state level but a leader in Cleveland; that is, in his home base, Moore liked to have the last word.

3. Adams, e.g., in "Highlander Folk School," notes the difficulty of talking about Highlander's working style without making it appear more fixed than it was. "Words and sentences, spoken or written, tend to order this synthesis and give it a logic by making it a sequence, when in fact it cannot be and is not sequential or logical," p. 520.

4. The best sources on the life of Mrs. Clark are Cynthia Brown, ed., *Ready From Within: Septima Clark and the Civil Rights Movement* (Navarro, Calif.: Wild Trees Press, 1986); Septima Clark, *Echo in My Soul* (New York: Dutton, 1962); Judy Barton, "Interview with Septima Clark," November 9, 1971, Martin Luther King Oral History Project, King Center; Bill Steverson, "Septima P. Clark, 1898–1987," *Southern Changes* 10, no. 2 (March–April 1988), pp. 12–16.

5. On the Warings, see Richard Kluger, *Simple Justice: The History of Brown v. Board of Education and Black America's Struggle for Equality* (New York: Random House, 1975), pp. 295–305; Brown, *Ready from Within,* pp. 24–29; Carl Rowan, *South of Freedom* (New York: Knopf, 1952), pp. 87–100. If anyone was more elegant than Medgar Evers in handling hate calls, it was Mrs. Waring. See Samuel Grafton, "The Lonesomest Man in Town," *Negro Digest,* March 1951.

6. Aldon Morris, *Origins of the Civil Rights Movement* (New York: Free Press, 1984), pp. 139–40.

7. On Highlander and Horton, see John Glen, *Highlander: No Ordinary School, 1932–1962* (Lexington, University Press of Kentucky, 1988) and Myles Horton, *The Long Haul* (New York: Doubleday, 1990).

8. Myles Horton, quoted by Morris, *Origins,* p. 142. This is almost a perfect restatement of the mass-line theory of the Chinese Communist party, as described by William Hinton in *Fanshen: A Documentary of Revolution in a Chinese Village* (New York: Vintage, 1966), p. 608.

9. Horton quoted in Morris, *Origins,* p. 143.

10. Guy and Candie Carawan, "'We Shall Overcome': An American Freedom Song," *Talkin' Union,* August 1983.

11. Morris, *Origins,* pp. 146–49; Glen, *Highlander,* pp. 149–50.

12. Brown, *Ready,* p. 33. Virginia Durr, who had encouraged Mrs. Parks to go to Highlander, thought that the experience of egalitarian living increased her impatience with segregation.

13. Glen, *Highlander,* pp. 134–35.

14. A remarkable 41 teachers from rural Clarendon County admitted to being NAACP members. Their defiance may have been related to the fact that Clarendon had been one of the counties involved in the *Brown* case.

15. On Esau Jenkins's remarkable life, see Richard Couto, *Ain't Gonna Let Nobody Turn Me Round: The Pursuit of Racial Justice in the Rural South* (Philadelphia: Temple University Press, 1991), pp. 120–22.

16. Brown, *Ready,* p. 49.

17. Ibid., pp. 49–51; Morris, *Origins,* pp. 152–53. Sandra Oldendorf, "South Carolina Sea Island Citizenship Schools, 1957–1961," (Western Carolina University, unpublished).

18. These are Clark's numbers. Different sources cite different numbers for the first class.

19. Oldendorf, "Citizenship Schools," p. 11.

20. Highlander's charter was eventually revoked by the state. It reorganized as the Highlander Research and Education Center and is now located in New Market, Tennessee.

21. Brown, *Ready,* p. 69.

22. Septima Clark, "Literacy and Liberation," in Joanne Grant, ed., *Black Protest* (New York: Fawcett, 1968), p. 297.

23. Brown, *Ready,* p. 63–4.

24. Quotations from Adams, "Highlander Folk School," pp. 518–19, 513. The kinds of tensions that developed between Blacks and whites in the movement of the mid-sixties never seem to have been a problem in terms of Highlander's relations with Blacks. This may be related in part to the fact that some of the relationships had developed over such a long period of time and in part to the fact that Horton and other whites at Highlander were not interested in leading anything.

25. Taylor Branch, *Parting the Waters* (New York: Simon and Schuster, 1988), pp. 576–77, 899; Barton interview, p. 60.

26. Brown, *Ready,* p. 78.

27. Quotations from Barton, pp. 39, 42. See also Adam Fairclough, *To Redeem the Soul of America* (Athens: University of Georgia Press, 1987), pp. 49–50, 169.

28. Cleveland Sellers, *The River of No Return: The Autobiography of a Black Militant and the Life and Death of* SNCC (New York: William Morrow, 1973), p. 57.

29. Howard Zinn, SNCC: *The New Abolitionists* (Boston: Beacon, 1964), pp. 16–17. On sit-ins, see also Miles Wolff, *Lunch at the 5 & 10* (New York: Stein and Day, 1970); William Chafe, *Civilities and Civil Rights* (New York: Oxford University Press, 1980); Harvard Sitkoff, "The Stuggle for Black Equality, 1954–1980" (New York: Hill and Wang, 1981); Lester Sobel, ed., *Civil Rights, 1960–*

66, pp. 5–7 (New York: Facts on File, 1967); Martin Oppenheimer, *The Sit-In Movement of 1960* (Brooklyn, N.Y.: Carlson, 1989).

30. Lester Sobel, *Civil Rights, 1960–66*, p. 45. CORE had used sit-ins in Chicago in the 1940s; there were sit-ins in Oklahoma and Kansas in 1958 and in Nashville and Durham in 1959. Raines, *My Soul is Rested*, pp. 14–15, 86, 101.

31. Quoted in Zinn, SNCC, pp. 27–28.

32. Forman, *Black Revolutionaries*, p. 215.

33. Quotation from "Fundi: The Story of Ella Baker" (New York: First Run Films, 1981), videocassette. There is substantial reason to believe that during the Jim Crow era, towns or settlements that were all-Black and offered some measure of economic or political security produced distinctive levels of racial pride. See discussion of Holmes County in Chapter 7.

34. Quotation from Lenore Hagan interview, p. 15. On her childhood in general, see "Fundi," as well as Ellen Cantarow, *Moving the Mountain: Women Working for Social Change* (Old Westbury: The Feminist Press, 1980). The reference to her grandmother being whipped is from Howard Zinn notes, SHSW.

35. Hagan interview, p. 79.

36. Cantarow, *Moving The Mountain*, p. 60.

37. Ibid., p. 61.

38. In her essay "Notes Toward a Black Balancing of Love and Hatred," June Jordan reminds us how different southern Black communities could be from one another, and she also suggests, comparing Richard Wright to Zora Neale Hurston, that there were gender differences in the ability to appreciate the positive elements of Black folk culture in the South. In Jordan, *Civil Wars* (Boston: Beacon, 1981).

39. Sue Thrasher and Casey Hayden, "Interview with Ella Baker," April 19, 1977, Library, University of North Carolina at Chapel Hill, p. 30.

40. HU interview, p. 1.

41. Cantarow, *Moving The Mountain*, p. 64.

42. "Consumer's Cooperation Among Negroes," NAACP IIA560; "Experience Sheet—Ella J. Baker," NAACP IIA562. As of 1941, Miss Baker thought growing numbers of people of more stable income were becoming involved in the coop movement. It is not clear what actually became of the movement in the more prosperous period of World War II. The lack of research on the movement is interesting, given the great deal of attention given to the philosophical debate between Du Bois and the rest of the NAACP on such parallel-development schemes. On the debate, see Edward Peek, *The Long Struggle for Black Power* (New York: Scribner's, 1971), pp. 221–43, and Du Bois's *Autobiography* (New York: International, 1968), ch. 17.

43. Ella Baker with Marvel Cooke, "The Bronx Slave Market," *Crisis* 42 (November 1935), p. 340.

44. Cantarow, *Moving The Mountain*, pp. 63–64; Baker and Cooke, "Bronx Slave Market."

45. HU interview, p. 69.

46. Paul Good, *The Trouble I've Seen* (Washington: Howard University Press, 1975), p. 173.

47. NAACP IIA572, Ernestine Rose to NAACP, June 11, 1942.

48. EJB to Walter White, September 24, 1938. Paula Giddings, *When and Where I Enter: The Impact of Black Women on Race and Sex in America* (New York: Morrow, 1984), p. 58. Cantarow (p. 54) has Miss Baker starting at the Association in 1938, but the announcement in the NAACP files (IIA572) is dated February 1941.

49. IIA572, EJB to Lucille Black, March 11, 1942; "Campaign Manual for Branches," undated, author's files.

50. NAACP IIA572, EJB to Roy Wilkins, 3/20/41; EJB to Lucille Black, 5/4/42; EJB to Lucille Black, 5/25/42; IIC390, Report of Miss Ella J. Baker, 6/9/41.

51. IIA572, EJB to Roy Wilkins, March 11, 1942.

52. Ibid.

53. Ella Baker, "Conducting Membership Drives" (1942), NAACP Papers (microfilm), reel 11.

54. HU interview, pp. 11–12, pp. 76–82; Hagan interview, p. 21. Others in the Dept. of Branches shared her feelings. One wrote, "The national office pays very little attention to opinions and ideas expressed by branches and Association members." NAACP IIC307, untitled memorandum, E. Fredrick Morrow, July 11, 1941. Also "Report of the the Director of Branches 4/14/41," same box.

55. NAACP IIA572, EJB to Wilkins, March 11, 1942; Baker, "Notes on Houston Conference," June 15, 1941; IIC390, Report of Miss Ella J. Baker, 12/8/41.

56. Cantarow, *Moving The Mountain*, p. 70.

57. Ella Baker to Walter White, April 17, 1943, NAACP IIA575. The high-handed nature of her appointment stuck long in her craw. In her 1946 letter of resignation from the Association, she referred to it as one example of what was wrong with the Association's operating style—disregard for the opinions of people affected by a decision. She also claimed that she accepted the position only because there was no "graceful" way to decline. From such a strong-willed person, that explanation seems disingenuous. Ella Baker to Walter White, May 14, 1946, NAACP IIA573.

58. NAACP IIC394, "Digest of the Regional Leadership Training and In-Service Training Program Conducted by the Branch Department during 1944–1946."

See also boxes IIA573, IIA575, IIC374, IIC375; Hagan, p. 21; Thrasher and Hayden interview, UNC at Chapel Hill, p. 49.

59. NAACP IIC375, "Minutes of the Texas NAACP Board Meeting," n.d. Some of the conferences were arranged on short notice, for which she was sometimes reprimanded by her superiors. Among the other complaints about her work appearing in NAACP files are accusations that she sometimes failed to do enough planning and was too frequently out of the office on personal matters. See IIC374, "Memorandum from Roy Wilkins to Miss Baker," 12/8/44 and IIA573 "Memorandum from Roy Wilkins to Miss Baker," 11/24/45.

60. IIA573, EJB to Walter White, 5/14/46. Her letter did not mention that she had accepted responsibility for raising a niece, making it more difficult to travel; she mentioned this as a factor in interviews done subsequently. Thrasher and Hayden, p. 51; Cantarow, *Moving The Mountain,* pp. 74, 156. She circulated her resignation letter among several members of the Association Board and some branch officers but refused several requests from members of local branches to appear at that year's national conference to explain her departure. Du Bois's characterization of the Association is strikingly similar to hers: "The branches . . . have no . . . program except to raise money and defend cases of injustice. . . . The organization fears the processes of democracy and avoids discussion" (*Autobiography,* p. 339).

61. Ella Baker, "Developing Community Leadership," in Gerda Lerner, *Black Women in White America* (New York: Vintage, 1973).

62. Giddings, *When and Where,* p. 268.

63. Levison and Rustin would remain among King's most important advisers for some years to come. Rustin would have played a more visible role, probably including the role that Miss Baker played, if not for fear that his homosexuality and youthful involvement with "red" organizations would be used to embarrass the embryonic movement.

64. HU interview, pp. 33–34; Hagan, p. 63; David Garrow, *Bearing the Cross: Martin Luther King, Jr., and the Southern Christian Leadership Conference* (New York: William Morrow, 1986), pp. 118–21. Given her focus on mass action, it is not clear that she did all she might have to enhance and exploit King's image.

65. Walker interview, p. 21.

66. HU interview, pp. 34–35.

67. Baker, "Developing Community Leadership," p. 351.

68. Cantarow, *Moving The Mountain,* p. 53.

69. Baker, "Developing Community Leadership," p. 347.

70. Ibid., p. 352.

71. Cantarow, *Moving The Mountain,* p. 82.

72. HU interview, p. 81.

73. "Memorandum from Ella Baker to Committee on Administration," 10/23/59; Ella Baker File, SHSW.

74. Sellers, *The River*, p. 36. On Lawson, see also Zinn, SNCC, pp. 21–22.

75. Sellers, *The River*, p. 45.

76. Cox and Jenkins quotation from "Fundi"; Mary King, *Freedom Song: A Personal Story of the 1960s Civil Rights Movement* (New York: Morrow, 1987), p. 60.

77. Nash, speaking at the Carter Woodson Library, Chicago, April 23, 1991; my interview with Bob Moses.

78. HU interview, p. 45.

79. Re King, see Morris, *Origins,* p. 216–17.

80. Sellers, *The River*, p. 37.

81. Quoted ibid., p. 39.

82. See Sara Evans, *Personal Politics* (New York: Vintage, 1980); Kirkpatrick Sale, *SDS* (New York: Random House, 1978); and esp. Doug McAdam, *Freedom Summer* (New York: Oxford, 1988).

83. On the ways in which the radical organizations strengthened the position of the less radical, see Herbert Haines, *Black Radicals and the Civil Rights Mainstream* (Knoxville: University of Tennessee Press, 1988); also Nancy Weiss, "Creative Tensions in the Civil Rights Movement," in C. Eagles, ed., *The Civil Rights Movement in America* (Jackson: University Press of Mississippi, 1986).

CHAPTER 4

1. Young quoted in Pat Watters, *Down To Now: Reflections on the Southern Civil Rights Movement* (New York: Pantheon, 1971), p. 136. The implication that SNCC was less southern than SCLC at the time it chose to go into Mississippi is dubious. Baker quote from Eugene Walker, Interview with Ella Baker, 9/4/74, Southern Historical Collection, University of North Carolina at Chapel Hill, p. 71. Morgan quoted in A. Meier and E. Rudwick, eds., *Black Protest in the Sixties* (Chicago: Quadrangle, 1970), p. 144. Ladner at "We Shall Not be Moved" Symposium, Trinity College, Hartford, Conn., April 14–15, 1989.

2. Howell Raines, *My Soul Is Rested* (New York: Putnam 1977), p. 253.

3. When he was a child, Moses's family could only afford milk because it was available at a lower price through one of Harlem's co-ops. When he went South, he found out Ella Baker had organized it. Casey Hayden, "Sermonette on the Movement," *Southern Changes* 9, nos. 5, 6 (December 1986), pp. 27–29.

4. Clayborne Carson, *In Struggle: SNCC and the Black Awakening of the 1960s* (Cambridge, Mass.: Harvard University Press, 1981), p. 46.

5. Ibid.

6. Howard Zinn, SNCC: *The New Abolitionists* (Boston: Beacon, 1964), pp. 62–63.

7. The Communist quotation is from Raines, *My Soul is Rested,* p. 109. The longer quotation is from Cleveland Sellers, *River of No Return* (New York: William Morrow, 1973), pp. 41–42.

8. Sellers, *River,* p. 42.

9. Moses and Moore quotations from Henry Hampton and Steve Fayer, eds., *Voices of Freedom: An Oral History of the Civil Rights Movement From the 1950s through the 1980s* (New York: Bantam, 1990), pp. 140–41. See also Anne Romaine, interview with Bob Moses, SHSW. Meier and Rudwick (*Black Protest,* p. 12) are in error when they refer to "the realization, *first grasped by Bob Moses* . . . that without the leverage of the vote*" demonstrations in Mississippi would be useless. (My emphasis.) Meier makes the same error in "Epilogue: Toward a Synthesis of Civil Rights History," in A. Robinson and P. Sullivan, *New Directions in Civil Rights Studies* (Charlottesville: Univ. Press of Virginia, 1991), p. 221. In his stress on the political process, Moore's attitude was common among Mississippi leaders, or perhaps leaders from the hard-core states generally. In 1956 a newspaper article had noted that Mississippi Black leaders thought the vote more important than school integration. Lewis, "The Negro Voter in Mississippi," *Journal of Negro Education* 26 (Summer 1957), pp. 329–50.

10. Moses points out that as exposed as Moore was, Medgar Evers was even more exposed. Moore's deeper contact network afforded him some measure of support that was not available to Evers.

11. Zinn, SNCC, p. 46.

12. Pat Watters and Reese Cleghorn, *Climbing Jacob's Ladder* (New York: Harcourt, Brace and World, 1967), pp. 45–50.

13. James Farmer, *Lay Bare The Heart: An Autobiography of the Civil Rights Movement* (New York: Plume, 1986), p. 220.

14. Mark Stern, *Calculating Vision* (New Brunswick, N.J.: Rutgers University Press, 1992), p. 66.

15. The Jenkins and King quotations are both from Raines, *My Soul is Rested,* p. 228. The Justice Department quotation is from Neil McMillen, "Black Enfranchisement in Mississippi: Federal Enforcement and Black Protest in the 1960s," *Journal of Southern History* 63, no. 3 (August 1977), pp. 351–72.

16. Harris Wofford, identified by Jenkins as one person who made strong promises on behalf of the administration, was probably the upper-level official most personally committed to the movement. He was passed over for the position of head of the Civil Rights Division in the Justice Department because of

Robert Kennedy's fear that he was too committed to be objective. Wofford could easily have put his own spin on the discussion. Administration officials and SNCC activists may also have had different understandings of where the action was going to take place. Chuck McDew quotes Burke Marshall as saying "You go out there [rural Mississippi] and there's nothing we can do." Stern, *Calculating Visions*, pp. 55, 67.

17. HU interview, p. 57.

18. Forman, *The Making of Black Revolutionaries* (Washington: Open Hand, 1985), p. 225. The lack of preparedness in Cleveland may have been related to the fact that Amzie Moore was caught up in personal difficulties during 1959 and had not devoted much time to civil rights work. In addition, a priest who had worked with him and provided a meeting place had been transferred out of the Delta.

19. Jack Newfield, *A Prophetic Minority* (New York: Signet, 1966), pp. 49–50. Newfield's figure of 200 registered in Pike County may be high. Other descriptions of the movement in Southwest Mississippi can be found in Zinn's SNCC, ch. 4; Clayborne Carson's *In Struggle,* ch. 4; Tom Hayden's *Revolution in Mississippi* (New York: Students for a Democratic Society, 1962); Forman's *Making of Black Revolutionaries;* Fred Poweledge's *Free At Last* (New York, HarperCollins, 1991), ch. 19; and Taylor Branch's *Parting the Waters* (New York: Simon and Schuster, 1988), ch. 13.

20. I am ignoring the distinctions between piney-woods counties and other hill counties, as well as some other distinctions of political topography. See Vincent Giroux, "The Rise of Theodore Bilbo," *Journal of Mississippi History* 43 (August 1981), pp. 180–209. Also V. O. Key, *Southern Politics* (New York: Vintage, 1949), ch. 11.

21. Neil McMillen calculates that in the counties with the lowest Black population, Blacks were lynched at a rate of 8 per every 10,000 population, twice the rate of the Delta counties. Still, he notes that the absolute numbers of lynchings were greatest in the Delta, and it would have been the absolute numbers that created fear. *Dark Journey* (Urbana: University of Illinois Press, 1989), pp. 230, 294.

22. NAACP B116, "Police Brutality in Tylertown."

23. Information about Bryant, Steptoe, Webb Owens, and Herbert Lee is taken largely from comments made at a reunion of activists from the area, held in McComb on June 27–29, 1991, and particularly from a meeting held at the Steptoe farm on June 29.

24. Newfield, *Prophetic Minority,* p. 60; Mendelsohn, *The Martyrs* (New York: Harper and Row, 1960), p. 25; *Mississippi Black Paper* (New York: Random

House, 1965), p. 3; NAACP IIA422, A. M. Mackel, "Report," n. d. Branch (*Parting the Waters,* p. 494) dates the confiscation of the membership rolls to 1959, which is wrong, as is his suggestion that the Amite branch ceased to function after the confiscation. See NAACP Annual Report for 1954, p. 12.

25. Steptoe to Wilkins, 11/19/60, author's files.

26. Moses comment at Steptoe farm, June 29, 1961.

27. Bob Moses interview, Carawan Collection, Highlander, tape 32.

28. Newfield, *Prophetic Minority,* p. 54. See also tape 32, Carawan Collection.

29. Dawson's comments at the Steptoe farm, June 29, 1991.

30. Tape 32, Carawan Collection.

31. Newfield, *Prophetic Minority,* p. 56.

32. Moses quotations from *Voices of Freedom;* Mendelsohn, *The Martyrs,* p. 25.

33. Moses, Carawan Collection, tape 32; *Voices of Freedom,* pp, 142–43.

34. Unidentified neighbor speaking at the Steptoe farm, June 29, 1991.

35. On refusal of Justice Department to accept phone calls, see Timothy Jenkins interview in Raines, *My Soul is Rested,* p. 231.

36. Hollis Watkins interview; Tape 32, Carawan Collection; Carson, *In Struggle,* p. 49; *Voices of Freedom,* pp. 145–7.

37. The state later seized Campbell College by right of eminent domain and turned the facilities over to Jackson State College. Hollis Watkins believes this was an act of retribution.

38. Zinn, SNCC, p. 77.

39. Ibid., p. 76.

40. Sally Belfrage, *Freedom Summer* (New York: Viking, 1965), p. 33.

41. Debbie Louis, *And We Are Not Yet Saved: A History of the Movement As People* (Garden City, N.Y.: Doubleday, 1970), p. 57.

42. Forman, *Black Revolutionaries,* p. 238.

43. The first part of quotation is from Moses's comments at the Steptoe farm, June 29, 1991; the second part is from my interview with Moses. I assume not all SNCC workers would have put as much stress on the primacy of relationships as Moses does. The distinction between those who understood the movement as relationships and those who thought more "politically" may be as important, say, as the split between the direct actionists and the voter-registration people.

44. Tom Gaither and Robert Moses, "Report on Voter Registration—Projected Program," January 27, 1962. Zinn Papers, SHSW.

45. In its first incarnation, COFO was an ad hoc committee in support of the Free-dom Riders in 1961 and subsequently evolved an interest in voter registration. By February 1962, they were able to hire their first staff. A meeting at Aaron

Henry's in Clarksdale in August 1962 is sometimes described as the founding meeting; in fact, it was a planning meeting. "What is COFO?," author's files, p. 2.

CHAPTER 5

1. Jean Wheeler Smith, "Mississippi Remembered," *Essence*, October 1977, p. 102.
2. Sally Belfrage, *Freedom Summer* (New York: Viking, 1965), p. 40.
3. "Leflore County, Mississippi—Statistical Profile," Zinn Papers, SHSW; Jane Stembridge, "The Mississippi Delta," SCLC 141:9.
4. Ibid.
5. Randall Luce, "Racial Relations and Political Change: A Social History of a Southern County, 1886–1981" (Ph.D. diss., University of California, Santa Barbara, 1983).
6. James Moore interview. A *Chicago Defender* article suggests the local chapter was fairly active in the Till case: "Till Lynching Displaces Cotton, Jim Crow, As Top Topic in Delta," September 17, 1955, p. 36.
7. West's name was not included on the death list referred to by *Ebony* in August 1955, which would have been about the right time, but it is likely that different lists—and rumors of lists—circulated simultaneously.
8. On the Greenwood NAACP, see NAACP boxes IIC 96, IIIC74, IVC18.
9. Joseph Sinsheimer, "Never Turn Back: An Interview with Sam Block," *Southern Exposure* 25, no. 2 (Summer 1987), p. 42
10. "SNCC Workshop, June, 1962," Highlander Papers.
11. Ibid.
12. Sinsheimer, "Never Turn Back," pp. 41, 43.
13. Bishop interview.
14. Forman, *The Making of Black Revolutionaries* (Washington: Open Hand, 1985), p. 287.
15. Sinsheimer, "Never Turn Back," p. 43.
16. Ibid.
17. Howard Zinn, SNCC: The New Abolitionists (Boston: Beacon, 1964), p. 86. The quotation is from Forman, *Black Revolutionaries,* p. 283.
18. James Moore interview. Cafe owners "Blood" Bullins and Martha Cooley were among the most significant of the businesspeople supporting the movement (along with barbers and beauticians).
19. SNCC news release, n. d., VEP papers.
20. Notes by Jack Minnis, August 15–19, 1962, VEP papers.
21. Forman, *Black Revolutionaries,* p. 284.

22. Zinn, SNCC, pp. 84–85; Forman, *Black Revolutionaries,* pp. 284–86; Peacock interview.

23. Howell Raines, *My Soul Is Rested* (New York: Putnam, 1977), p. 267.

24. Ibid., p. 265.

25. Bob Moses, undated memo, "The Events Surrounding the Voter Registration Drive in Ruleville," Amzie Moore Papers, SHSW.

26. Quotation from Raines, *My Soul Is Rested,* p. 271. The most extensive source on Mrs. Hamer is Kay Mills, *This Little Light of Mine* (New York: Dutton, 1993).

27. Romaine interview, SHSW; Mills, *Light of Mine,* pp. 41–42; Hollis Watkins interview.

28. Raines, *My Soul Is Rested,* p. 268.

29. Pat Watters and Reese Cleghorn, *Climbing Jacob's Ladder* (New York: Harcourt, Brace and World, 1967), pp. 159–60.

30. Peacock quotations from my interviews and Dent's.

31. Willie Peacock interview; Sinsheimer, "Never Turn Back," p. 45.

32. Willie Peacock interview.

33. Raines, *My Soul Is Rested,* pp. 280–84; Dick Gregory, *Nigger* (New York: Dutton, 1964), pp 157–66.

34. Laura McGhee interview; Bob Moses on the "Story of Greenwood," Folkways Records, #fd5593.

35. *Greenwood Commonwealth,* February 4, 1963.

36. Both the Moses quotation and those from Peacock and Block are from Zinn, SNCC, pp. 86–88.

37. Quotation from Essie Lee Marie, field report, n. d., author's files. On the events from February to April, there are numerous reports in SRC VI: 205, 206, and in SCLC 141. See also Taylor Branch, *Parting the Waters* (New York: Simon and Schuster, 1988), ch. 19.

38. Monetta Hancock, field report, n. d., author's files.

39. "Negro Here Hits Food Publicity," *Greenwood Commonwealth,* February 9, 1963.

40. Dent interview.

41. SNCC news release, "Violence Stalks Voter-Registration Workers in Mississippi," March 12, 1963, SHSW, Zinn papers.

42. Zinn, SNCC, p. 89. It was frequently said that the Black Belt South had not seen anything like the crowds in Greenwood since Reconstruction. That ignores the 1940s mobilization, about which sixties activists may not have known. Robert Norrell notes that in Macon County, Alabama, 200 Blacks tried to register on a single day in 1945. *Reaping the Whirlwind* (New York: Knopf, 1985), p. 59.

43. Robert Bird, "How Nonviolent Warrior Feels on Firing Line in Rural Dixie," *Chicago Sun-Times,* May 20, 1963. SNCC news release, "Violence Stalks Voter-Registration Workers in Mississippi," March 12, 1963, SHSW, Zinn papers; Forman, *Black Revolutionaries,* pp. 294–95; Willie Peacock interview. Two white men, one a wholesale gasoline dealer, the other a manager for a heavy-equipment sales company, were charged with "felonious assault" for the shooting but not convicted.

44. Bob Moses, "The Story of Greenwood," Folkways Records.

45. VEP Papers, Minnis notes.

46. *Mississippi Black Papers,* p. 12; Willie Peacock interview; Bob Moses, "The Story of Greenwood."

47. Interviews with Willie Peacock and Aaron Johnson.

48. Jack Minnis, "Miss. Field Trip, 3/20–22/63," SRC, VI: 205. My interview with Mr. and Mrs. Harold Fleming also suggested that many whites knew little of the movement.

49. On Citizenship Schools in the Delta, see various reports in SCLC 141, 155, 161, 162, esp. 155:34, Ponder, "Citizenship Education in the Heart of the Iceberg" 8/2/63; 155:26 Ponder, "Miss. Report to Annual Convention of the SCLC," 1963; SCLC 141:5, Bevel, "Miss. Report SCLC Field Secretary." Estimates of class sizes and student ages calculated from SCLC, box 161. Holland has written a prize-winning play about her movement experience, "From the Mississippi Delta."

50. Frank Smith, "A Second Beginning of the End," SRC VI:204 (0746).

51. Randolph Blackwell, "A Mississippi Field Report," 3/26/63 SRC VI: 205 (1114); Curtis Hayes, "Report on Voter Registration in Greenwood," 3/15/63, SCLC 141:6.

52. Joyce Ladner, "Report on Voter Registration in Greenwood, Mississippi," 3/23–30/63, SRC VI:205.

53. SNCC newsletter, vol. 1, no. 16; interviews with George and Freddie Greene. Branch, *Parting the Waters* (p. 719), errs in saying the shots were fired at Dewey Greene, Sr.

54. In addition to Ladner's report, see Forman, pp. 297–303; Peacock interview in Dent Collection.

55. Ida Holland, report, 3/31/63, SCLC 141:7.

56. *Greenwood Commonwealth,* March 30, 1963; Moses from "The Story of Greenwood."

57. Forman, *Black Revolutionaries,* pp. 299–303.

58. Branton, untitled notes, n. d., SRC VI:115.

59. Gregory, *Nigger,* p. 172.

60. Andrew Jordan to Gloster Current, 4/22/64, NAACP IIIC74.

61. Neil McMillen, "Black Enfranchisement in Mississippi: Federal Enforcement and Black Protest in the 1960's," *Journal of Southern History* 63 no. 3 (August 1977), pp. 351–72.

62. Branch, *Parting the Waters,* pp. 722–25; Carson, *In Struggle,* pp. 86–87; John Dittmer, *Local People: A History of the Mississippi Movement* (University of Illinois, forthcoming) ch. 7.

63. Watters and Cleghorn, *Climbing Jacob's Ladder,* pp. 62–63.

64. Branch, *Parting the Waters,* p. 725; McMillen, "Black Enfranchisement," p. 362.

65. Cobb and Suarez quotations from Dent Collection.

66. Norrell's *Reaping The Whirlwind* reports a different experience with middle-class Blacks in a place where the Black middle class was larger and better insulated. On teachers, see *Hearings Before the U.S. Commission on Civil Rights, Jackson, Miss., Feb. 16–20, 1963* (Washington: GPO, 1963), p. 242. Selma, Alabama, and Holmes County in Mississippi had some involvement of teachers early on.

67. Block from Sinsheimer, "Never Turn Back," p. 43.

68. Eugene Patterson, *Hearings Before the U.S. Commission on Civil Rights, Jackson, Miss., Feb. 16–20, 1963,* p. 169.

CHAPTER 6

1. Clayborne Carson, *In Struggle: SNCC and the Black Awakening of the 1960s* (Cambridge, Mass.: Harvard University Press, 1981), p. 303.

2. Randolph Blackwell, "A Mississippi Field Report," March 26, 1963, SRC VI:205 (1114). See also memos from Garner in SCLC 141:7.

3. Adam Fairclough, *To Redeem the Soul of America* (Athens: University of Georgia Press), p. 119.

4. This section based on interviews with Mrs. Allen and her son, Thomas Benjamin Brown, June Johnson, and Hollis Watkins. Mrs. Allen's singing can be heard on the "Story of Greenwood" phonodisc, Folkways Records #fd5593. For a discussion of a leadership style like Mrs. Allen's, see the discussion on consultative leadership in Eugenia Eng, "A Study of Leadership Among Influentials in Rural Black Neighborhoods and the Church," Ph.D. diss., University of North Carolina at Chapel Hill, 1983. See also the discussion of Annie Devine in Vicky Crawford, "We Shall Not be Moved: Black Female Activism in the Mississippi Civil Rights Movement, 1960–1965," Ph.D. diss., Emory University, 1987.

5. King in Howell Raines, *My Soul Is Rested* (New York: Putnam, 1977), pp. 91–2. See J. L. Chestnut, Jr., and Julia Cass, *Black in Selma* (New York: Farrar, Straus and Giroux, 1990), esp. pp. 198–201.

6. Frank Smith, "A Second Beginning of the End," SRC VI:204 (0746).

7. "Mass Meeting," Caravan tapes, no. 25, Highlander.

8. Bevel, Field Secretary Report, March 31–April 7, SCLC 141:8.

9. "Greenwood, Miss.—1963 or 1964," Caravan tapes, no. 22, Highlander.

10. Untitled petition from ministers, 4/1/63, SNCC Papers, SHSW; various reports filed by Bob Moses in April and May, 1963, VEP Box 37:11.

11. Suarez quoted in Tom Dent, "Annie Devine Remembers," *Freedomways* 22, no. 2 (1982), pp. 87–88; Moses in Robert Penn Warren, *Who Speaks for the Negro* (New York: Random House, 1965), p. 99.

12. Bob Moses interview with Ann Romaine, SHSW, pp. 19–20

13. Youth of the Rural Organizing and Cultural Center, *Minds Stayed on Freedom* (Boulder: Westview Press, 1991), p. 25. There are numerous other examples in this book of the importance of self-defense to Black farmers.

14. King, *Freedom Song* (New York: Morrow, 1987), p. 318.

CHAPTER 7

1. Quoted in J. Anthony Lukacs, *Don't Shoot: We Are Your Children* (New York: Random House, 1968), p. 447.

2. Zellner interview.

3. U.S. Commission on Civil Rights, *Justice in Jackson, Mississippi*, vol. II (Washington: GPO, 1971), pp. 487–88.

4. COFO's running summary of incidents identifies Ed Rudd and George Greene as being the other staff members present and describes them as restraining the policeman. See Doug McAdam, *Freedom Summer* (New York: Oxford, 1988), p. 279.

5. William Wallace interview, HU.

6. On the Ole Miss application, see the *Greenwood Commonwealth* from 1/31/63 and February 2, 4, 5, and 19.

7. No one was ever arrested for the shooting. The description of the car seen leaving the scene matched that of the car used a few months later by the assassin of Medgar Evers, a car presumed to have been driven by Byron de la Beckwith, a Greenwood native.

8. Susie Morgan interview.

9. Various documents in NAACP IIIC74, esp. D. Greene to L. Black, 10/28/64.

10. Nicholas Von Hoffman, *Mississippi Notebook* (New York: D. White, 1964), p. 24.

11. "Statements of Events in Natchez, Miss.—11/1 & 2, 1963,"SCLC 141:12; *Justice in Jackson,* pp. 70–74.

12. Barbara Johnson interview.

13. Howell Raines, *My Soul Is Rested* (New York: Putnam, 1977), p. 253. Like Miss Ponder, Mrs. Hamer expressed no bitterness toward the men who beat her, saying of the Black prisoners, "Nobody know the condition that those prisoners was in, before they were s'posed to beat me." Raines, pp. 253–54.

14. June Johnson interview; Raines, *My Soul Is Rested,* pp. 276–78, 295–98; Watters and Cleghorne, *Climbing Jacob's Ladder* (New York: Harcourt, Brace and World, 1967), pp. 363–75.

15. Jean Wheeler Smith, "Mississippi Remembered," *Essence,* October 1977, p. 82.

16. Ellen Cantarow, *Moving the Mountain,* (Old Westbury: The Feminist Press, 1980), p. 58–60.

17. Mary King, *Freedom Song: A Personal Story of the 1960s Civil Rights Movement* (New York: Simon and Schuster, 1964), p. 351.

18. On Clark, Cynthia Brown, ed., *Ready From Within* (Navarro, Calif.: Wild Trees Press, 1986), pp. 96–98. Clark's father, on the other hand, was less outspoken. When Emancipation came, he wasn't sure it was that good an idea. Jack Newfield, *A Prophetic Minority,* (New York: Signet, 1966), p. 66.

CHAPTER 8

1. Smith and Larry quotations from Jean Wheeler Smith, "Mississippi Remembered," *Essence,* October 1977, p. 7; Ganz from Amite County Newsletter no. 2, April 26, 1965, SNCC Papers A:XIV:81; Moses quoted in Susan Youngblood, "Testing the Current: The Formative Years of Ella J. Baker's Development as an Organizational Leader in the Civil Rights Movement," Master's thesis, University of Virginia (1989), p. 5.

2. David Garrow, "Commentary," in Charles W. Eagles, ed., *The Civil Rights Movement in America* (Oxford: University Press of Mississippi, 1986), pp. 59–60.

3. Howard Zinn, SNCC: *The New Abolitionists* (Boston: Beacon, 1964), pp. 9–10.

4. Ellen Cantarow, *Moving the Mountain,* (Old Westbury: The Feminist Press, 1980), pp. 69–70. The date Miss Baker cites in Cantarow is wrong.

5. Jean Wheeler Smith, "Mississippi Remembered," p. 102.

6. Saurez in Dent Collection.

7. Howell Raines, *My Soul Is Rested* (New York: Putnam, 1977), p. 237.

8. Martha Prescod Norman, comments at the Trinity conference; Lombard in Tom Dent, "Annie Devine Remembers," *Freedomways* 22, no. 2 (1982), p. 88.

9. Lane interview, HU, p. 3. Mary Booth interview, HU, p. 11; Will Henry Rogers interview, HU, p. 14.

10. Robert Jackall, Department of Sociology, Williams College, "Some Reflections on Charisma," unpublished.

11. Quoted in William Beardslee, *The Way Out Must Lead In* (Westport, Conn.: Lawrence Hill, 1977), p. 73. The organizer is not identified.

12. Moses quoted in Mary King, *Freedom Song* (New York: William Morrow, 1987), p. 146; Sherrod and coworker at "We Shall Not Be Moved" Symposium, Trinity College, Hartford, Conn., April 1989. Cotton to Moses, n. d. [June 1963], SRC VI:205.

13. "Mississippi Newsletter," February 12, 1963, SNCC Papers, box 99.

14. "Mississippi Handbook for Political Programs" SNCC, box 98; Peacock in Dent Collection.

15. Frank Smith, "A Second Beginning of the End," SRC VI:204 (0706).

16. Pat Watters and Reese Cleghorn, *Climbing Jacob's Ladder* (New York: Harcourt, Brace and World, 1967), p. 115.

17. Ivanhoe Donaldson, "Field Report covering period 30 October thru 5 November '63," author's files.

18. Untitled document, "Civil Rights in Mississippi" file, Highlander.

19. Watters and Cleghorn, *Climbing Jacob's Ladder,* p. 106.

20. Both quotations ibid., pp. 105–06.

21. Jack Newfield, *A Prophetic Minority,* (New York: Signet, 1966), p. 64.

22. Rogers interview, HU, p. 4.

23. Watters and Cleghorn, *Climbing Jacob's Ladder,* p. 156.

24. Ibid., p. 129. It is not clear from the source where the checklist was developed.

25. Ibid., p. 168.

26. James Forman, *The Making of Black Revolutionaries,* (Washington: Open Hand, 1985), pp. 284–85.

27. Zinn, SNCC, pp. 81–82. The yield from canvassing may have followed a curvilinear pattern. That is, it may have been relatively good when organizers first came to a town, then dropped off sharply after reprisals began, picking up slowly as the movement established itself.

28. Raines, *My Soul Is Rested,* p. 260.

29. Ibid.

30. "Mississippi Handbook for Political Programs," SNCC Papers, Box 98.

31. Emile Durkheim, *Elementary Forms of the Religious Life* (New York: Free Press, 1965), p. 464.

32. McAdam, *Political Process and the Development of Black Insurgency, 1930–1970* (Chicago: University of Chicago Press, 1982), pp. 90–92; Daniel Cohn, *Where I Was Born and Raised* (Houghton-Mifflin: Boston, 1948), pp. 173–84; J. Edward Arbor, "Upon This Rock," *Crisis,* April 1935.

33. Walter Lord, *The Past That Would Not Die* (New York: Harper and Row, 1965), p. 53.

34. W. E. B. Du Bois, *Black Reconstruction* (New York: Atheneum, 1973), ch. 5; Lawrence Levine, *Black Culture and Black Consciousness* (New York: Oxford, 1977, ch. 1; Herbert Gutman, *Black Family in Slavery and Freedom* (New York: Pantheon, 1976).

35. "Story of Greenwood, Mississippi," Folkways Records, no. fd5593.

36. Highlander, Carawan tape 29, "SNCC Conference at Tougaloo."

37. See, for example, Sally Belfrage *Freedom Summer* (New York: Viking, 1965), pp. 58–60.

38. Alma Henderson interview.

39. June Johnson interview.

40. "Story of Greenwood" record.

41. Liner notes, Bernice Johnson Reagon, "Voices of the Civil Rights Movement: Black American Freedom Songs, 1960–1966," Smithsonian, 1980, p. 4.

42. Some in the movement would argue that the singing in the Albany, Georgia campaign of 1962 was at another level of intensity even as compared to Greenwood. See Bernice Reagon's comments in Dick Cluster's, *They Should Have Served That Cup of Coffee* (Boston: South End Press, 1979). These differences in meeting tone and style, if they could be delineated empirically, would provide an interesting point of entry for discussions about variations within southern Black culture.

43. Tapes 25 and 33, Carawan Collection, Highlander.

44. Discussing humor and the oppressed, Lawrence Levine notes that communal laughter helps people place their situation in perspective, thereby giving them a degree of control over it. Thus, the need to laugh often exists most urgently among those who have the least power over their environment. Levine, *Black Culture,* p. 300.

45. Rosengarten, *All God's Dangers* (New York: Avon, 1974), pp. xxi.

46. NAACP IIA572, EB to Walter White, Dec. 3, 1942; EB to Roy Wilkins, April 1, 1942.

CHAPTER 9

1. Hurston, *Their Eyes Were Watching God* (London: Dent) 1938, pp. 31–32; Andy Young quoted in Mary King, *Freedom Song,* (New York: William Morrow,

1987), pp. 469–70; Donald Matthews and James Prothro, *Negroes and the New Southern Politics* (New York: Harcourt, Brace and World), 1966, p 65.

2. Howell Raines, *My Soul Is Rested,* (New York: Putnam 1977), p. 241.

3. In addition to Matthews and Prothro, see Seymour Lipset, *Political Man* (New York: Doubleday, 1960), pp. 189, 193–94. The book, considered a classic, is aptly named; its index contains no entry for "women."

4. Based on calculation of figures from citizenship reports, SCLC box 162.

5. Sara Evans, *Personal Politics* (New York: Vintage, 1980). The degree of sexism among men in SNCC has recently become an ongoing controversy, with Black women who participated saying that some white women participants have blown male chauvinism in the movement out of proportion and that they— Black women—were always able to exercise authority in some rough correspondence to their abilities and desires, and that they ignored or didn't care much about some expressions of chauvinism. See Joyce Ladner, "A Sociology of the Civil Rights Movement: An Insider's Perspective," presented at the annual meeting of the American Sociological Association, August 1988. Ladner points out that while Stokely Carmichael's remark about the position of women in the movement being prone has been much quoted, during his tenure as chair "he encouraged and supported women as project directors and as members of SNCC's Central Committee."

6. E. Franklin Frazier, *Black Bourgeoisie* (New York: Collier, 1962), p. 182.

7. Bob Blauner, *Black Lives, White Lives: Three Decades of Race Relations in America* (Berkeley and Los Angeles: University of California Press, 1989), p. 27.

8. Arance Williamson interview.

9. Pat Watters and Reese Cleghorn, *Climbing Jacob's Ladder* (New York: Harcourt, Brace and World, 1967), p. 159.

10. It is important to note that most of the women I interviewed were in their middle years—generally old enough to have teenage or adult children—at the time of the movement. Thus, I have little sense of how older women would have portrayed themselves.

11. Cheryl Gilkes, "Together and In Harness: Women's Traditions in the Sanctified Church," *Signs* 10 (Summer 1985), p. 679.

12. Aldon Morris, *Origins of the Civil Rights Movement* (New York: Free Press, 1984), esp. chs. 1, 4.

13. W. E. B. Du Bois, *Black Reconstruction* (New York: Atheneum, 1973), ch. 5.

14. Hurley interview, HU, p. 15.

15. The difference does not appear to be related to gender differences in laborforce participation; see H. Ulbrich and M. Wallace, "Women's Work Force Status and Church Attendance," *Journal for the Scientific Study of Religion* 23,

(1984), pp. 341–50, nor to the greater role that women play in the socialization of children, according to Dean Hoge and D. Roozen, *Understanding Church Growth and Decline* (New York: Pilgrim Press, 1979). Another popular notion, in the Marxist tradition, is that the church serves to compensate those most deprived of "real" rewards—women, the poor, the elderly. Attempts to support that interpretation have generally failed to do so, according to Hoge and Roozen. In fact, in many populations, the most economically privileged appear more religious than the least privileged, though among Blacks there seems to be no relationship between religiosity and social status. See Leonard Beeghley, E. Van Velsor, and E. W. Block, "Correlates of Religiosity Among Black and White Americans," *Sociological Quarterly* 22 (Summer 1981), pp. 403–12.

16. Hoge and Roozen, *Understanding Church Growth*, p. 60. The most important recent study finds that for both Blacks and whites religious belief and church participation are positively associated with political participation. Frederick Harris, "Something Within: Religion as a Mobilizer of African-American Political Activism," *Journal of Politics* 56 (February 1994), pp. 42–68. Harris's findings, based on a more adequate sample and focusing on political participation rather than belief, contradict the earlier findings of Gary Marx in *Protest and Prejudice* (New York: Harper and Row, 1969).

17. Harry Richardson, *Dark Glory: A Picture of the Church Among Negroes in the Rural South* (New York: Friendship Press, 1947); Edward Arbor, "Upon This Rock," *Crisis*, April 1935; David Cohn, *Where I Was Born and Raised* (Boston: Houghton-Mifflin, 1948), pp. 173–84.

18. Karen Sacks, "Gender and Grassroots Leadership," in Ann Bookman and Sandra Morgen, eds., *Women and the Politics of Empowerment* (Philadelphia: Temple University Press, 1988).

19. St. Clair Drake and Horace Cayton, *Black Metropolis* (Chicago: University of Chicago Press, 1970), pp. 393–94.

20. E. Frederick Morrow to Horatio Thompson, March 5, 1940, NAACP IIC69.

21. The lack of recognition of women extends even to the local level. In Greenwood, people seemed more likely to remember some of the men who had been involved than the larger number of women.

22. Arlene Daniels, "Invisible Work," *Social Problems* 34 (December 1987), pp. 403–15.

23. Cheryl Gilkes, "Building in Many Places: Multiple Commitments and Ideologies in Black Women's Community Work," in A. Bookman and S. Morgen, eds., *Women and the Politics of Empowerment*. It is not clear how we separate race from class. At least one study of community organizations in a working-class white-ethnic Chicago community found them to be dominated by

women. Kathleen McCourt, *Working Class Women and Grassroots Politics* (Bloomington: Indiana University Press, 1977), pp. 42–43.

24. Raines, *My Soul Is Rested,* p. 294; previous quotations from Leon Friedman, *The Civil Rights Reader* (New York: Walker and Co., 1969), pp. 167–72.

25. Lester Salamon, "The Time Dimension in Policy Evaluation: The Case of the New Deal Land Reform Experiments." *Public Policy* 27 (Spring 1979), pp. 129–83. Mike Miller, "Report on Holmes County," 7/22/63, VEP VI:204 (1237); John Ball interview. Ball, who was supposed to be staying with the Turnbows the night of the firebombing, says that a white informer, a Klansman, had warned him in advance that an attack was likely. The same informant later warned Ball of another planned ambush. The informant claimed that his family had a tradition of working against the Klan from the inside.

26. Wallace interview, HU.

27. Lester Salamon, "The Time Dimension in Policy Evaluation," p. 145.

28. The all-Black community of Harmony, Mississippi, has a reputation similar to Holmes County. See also Elizabeth Bethel's *Promiseland* (Philadelphia: Temple University Press, 1981) about an all-Black, economically independent community in South Carolina. On the other hand, all-Black Mound Bayou, in the Delta, seems never to have had a reputation for aggressive leadership or cooperative behavior.

29. David Schwartz studying political behavior among urban Blacks finds that men are somewhat more likely than women to feel politically alienated—i.e., estranged—but that women are more likely than men to respond to alienation through political activism. *Political Alienation and Political Behavior* (Chicago: Aldine, 1973), p. 73, 172.

30. Within the Delta, those who lived off the plantations were obviously less dependent than those who lived on them. For a discussion of how that changed their behavior, see Randall Luce, "Racial Politics and Political Change: A Social History of a Southern County, 1886–1981," Ph.D. diss., University of California, Santa Barbara, 1983.

CHAPTER 10

1. First quotation from speech by Moses at Berkeley, circa 1965, excerpt in author's file; second from remarks at Steptoe farm, June 29, 1991.

2. Howell Raines, *My Soul Is Rested* (New York: Putnam, 1977), pp. 268–70; Pat Watters and Reese Cleghorn, *Climbing Jacob's Ladder* (New York: Pantheon, 1971), pp. 372–74.

3. John Salter, *Jackson, Mississippi: An American Chronicle of Struggle and Schism* (Hicksville, N.Y.: Exposition, 1979), p. 135.

4. Salter, chs. 6–8; Myrlie Evers, *For Us the Living* (New York: Doubleday, 1967), pp. 16–17; Jack Mendelsohn, *The Martyrs: Sixteen Who Gave Their Lives for Racial Justice* (New York: Harper and Row, 1966), pp. 68–80.

5. Myrlie Evers, *For Us the Living*, p. 308.

6. Mendelsohn, *The Martyrs*, pp. 83–84.

7. Anne Moody, *Coming of Age in Mississippi* (New York: Dell, 1968), p. 277.

8. Stokely Carmichael, "Report on Election Day," SRC VI:205 (1247).

9. Unsigned memo, n.d, SRC VI:205.

10. Norman and Johnson quotations from Mike Miller, "Election Day Report," 8/13/63, SRC VI:205 (1261). Also Watters and Cleghorn, *Climbing Jacob's Ladder*, pp. 66–67; Willie Peacock interview.

11. Miller, "Election Day Report."

12. Similarly, the town voted for Coleman, the more moderate gubernatorial candidate. VEP staff thought that only a fifth of the overall electorate was voting the hard-line racist position; SRC VI:112 (1527).

13. Miller, "Election Day Report."

14. Two different weekly reports from Block, undated, SRC VI: 205 (1297, 1385); Dorothy Cotton to Annell Ponder, 9/11/63, SCLC 155:2.

15. Jane Stembridge, "Harassment and Violence: Greenwood, Mississippi," n. d., SNCC Papers A:XIV:80.

16. Len Holt, *The Summer That Didn't End* (New York: Morrow, 1965), p. 36.

17. My interviews with Watkins, Peacock, Guyot; Dent interviews with Donaldson, Peacock. Zinn, SNCC: *The New Abolitionists* (Boston: Beacon, 1964), pp. 186–89; Henry Hampton and Steve Fayer, *Voices of Freedom: An Oral History of the Civil Rights Movement from the 1950s through the 1980s* (New York: Bantam, 1990), pp. 181–86.

18. Moody, *Coming of Age*, pp. 261–63, 274–75.

19. Ibid., pp. 356–62, 367.

20. Mendelsohn, *The Martyrs*, pp. 30–39.

21. The way in which Moses and Dennis forced the issue was a long-term source of anger within COFO precisely because it was the opposite of SNCC's usual consensual style.

22. Holt, *Summer That Didn't End*, pp. 258–260; Affidavit from Sam Block, FDP, 10:1.

23. Danny Lyon, *Memories of the Southern Civil Rights Movement* (Chapel Hill: University of North Carolina Press, 1992), pp. 142–46

24. Holt, *Summer That Didn't End*, pp. 206–10, 266.

25. Doug McAdam, *Freedom Summer* (New York: Oxford, 1988); William McCord, *Mississippi: The Long, Hot Summer* (New York: Norton, 1965); Holt, *Summer That Didn't End;* Sally Belfrage, *Freedom Summer* (New York: Viking, 1965); Elizabeth Sutherland, *Letters From Mississippi* (New York: McGraw-Hill, 1965); Seth Cagin and Philip Dray, *We Are Not Afraid* (New York: Macmillan, 1988); Mary Aickin Rothschild, *A Case of Black and White: Northern Volunteers and the Southern Freedom Summers, 1964–1965* (Westport, Conn.: Greenwood, 1982).

26. Charles Cobb, "Prospectus for a Summer Freedom School Program," *Radical Teacher,* Fall 1991, p. 36; SCLC, A:VII.

27. Sutherland, *Letters From Mississippi,* pp. 93, 96, 102. Rothschild, *A Case of Black and White,* suggests (pp. 95–96, 112–13) that the 1964 version of the schools was somewhat more traditionally academic and less political than had been intended, but that changed for those schools which remained through the winter of 1964 and the summer of 1965. The volunteers who stayed through that period, she contends, were more political than those available during the summer of 1964.

28. Holt, *Summer That Didn't End,* pp. 317–19.

29. Sutherland, *Letters From Mississippi,* pp. 100–101.

30. Ironically, the Freedom School in Shaw, despite its disastrous start, became a real model after it "so successfully joined its studies with political activity that it became the focal point of local organizing in Shaw." Rothschild, *A Case of Black and White,* pp. 109–10.

31. James Baldwin, *The Fire Next Time* (New York: Dial, 1963), p. 22.

32. Sutherland, *Letters From Mississippi,* pp. 48–49.

33. Raines, *My Soul Is Rested,* p. 253.

34. Watters and Cleghorn, *Climbing Jacob's Ladder,* pp. 372–73.

35. SCLC 155:34, Ponder, "Citizenship Education in the Heart of the Iceberg," 8/2/63; 155:26, Ponder, "Miss. Report to Annual Convention of the SCLC," 1963.

36. Myrlie Evers, *For Us the Living,* pp. 232–34.

37. Aaron Henry, *Inside Agitator,* Henry Papers, Tougaloo College, p. 162.

38. Patricia Hill Collins, *Black Feminist Thought* (New York: Routledge, 1990), p. 11

39. Robert Blauner, *Black Lives, White Lives: Three Decades of Race Relations in America* (Berkeley and Los Angeles: University of California Press, 1989), quotations from pp. 22–26. For other interviews with Black domestics touching on these themes, see John Gwaltney's *Drylongso* (New York: Random House, 1980).

40. Quotations from Blauner, *Black Lives, White Lives,* pp. 195, 66, 69.

41. "Gains in Mississippi," *New York Times,* October 6, 1964; "650 Whites Appeal in McComb, Miss. for Negro Equality," *New York Times,* November 18, 1964.

CHAPTER 11

1. Moses quotation from speech at Berkeley, circa 1965, excerpt in author's files; Baker quotation from HU, p. 80.

2. Black Elected Officials: A National Roster (Washington: Joint Center for Political and Economic Studies, 1991).

3. Pat Watters and Reese Cleghorn, *Climbing Jacob's Ladder* (New York: Harcourt, Brace and World, 1967), p. 7.

4. "We must keep on" quotation from Joanne Grant, "Mississippi Politics: A Day in the Life of Ella Baker," in Toni Cade, ed., *The Black Woman* (New York: Signet, 1970), p. 61. All others from Paul Good, *The Trouble I've Seen: White Journalist, Black Movement* (Washington: Howard University, 1975), pp. 172–73.

5. Andrew Kopkind, "Seat Belts for Mississippi's Five," *New Republic,* July 7, 1965; Michael Thelwell and Lawrence Guyot, "The Politics of Necessity and Survival in Mississippi," in Thelwell, ed., *Duties, Pleasures and Conflicts* (Amherst: University of Massachusetts Press, 1987).

6. "Minutes—Leflore County Convention," July 27, 1964, FDP 10:5. Rural areas seem especially likely to have been represented by Citizenship School teachers, perhaps because fewer other avenues existed there for developing leadership.

7. Mrs. Johnson to FDP Office, 11/15/65; "Greenwood Announces Black Easter Campaign," 1/13/66, FDP Papers, 10:5.

8. The description of the Greenwood Movement is based on my interviews with James Moore, Father Nathaniel, and Mary Boothe, as well as the interviews with William Wallace, Mary Boothe, and Mary Lane at Howard University.

9. Miss Pinkie Pilcher, Citizenship School Report, July 30, 1965. SCLC 155:1.

10. William Wallace interview, HU.

11. On the history of CDGM, see, in addition to Polly Greenberg, *The Devil Has Slippery Shoes: A Biased Biography of the Child Development Group of Mississippi* (London: Macmillan, 1969), the following *New Republic* articles by Andrew Kopkind: "Bureaucracy's Long Arm," August 21, 1965; "How Do You Fight It," September 3, 1966; "CDGM Muddle," November 12, 1966; "Shriver Comes Across," January 7, 1966.

12. James Farmer, *Freedom When?* (New York: Random House, 1966), p. 17.

13. Romaine interview, SHSW, pp. 7–8.

14. Annell Ponder, "Memo Re Adult Program," n. d., SCLC 155:35.

15. Long and Peacock from Dent Collection.

16. Michael Garvey, "An Oral History with Amzie Moore," *Mississippi Oral History Progam*, pp. 65, 67, 72.

17. Mary Lane interview, HU.

CHAPTER 12

1. Julian Bond in Howell Raines, *My Soul Is Rested* (New York: Putnam, 1977), p. 97; Elmore Moore interview, HU; Mrs. Hamer from the Anne Romaine interview, SHSW; Prathia Hall in Mary King, *Freedom Song: A Personal Story of the 1960s Civil Rights Movement* (New York: Simon and Schuster, 1964), p. 315.

2. Mary Lane interview, HU.

3. John Dittmer, "The Politics of the Mississippi Movement, 1954–1964" in Charles Eagles, ed., *The Civil Rights Movement in America,* (Oxford: University Press of Mississippi, 1986) p. 86.

4. Ibid., p. 89.

5. Mary King (in *Freedom Song,* p. 356), among others, argues that the Challenge had a great deal to do with the subsequent passage of the Voting Rights Act. She also notes that Martin Luther King was willing to accept the first, relatively weak version of the bill suggested by the administration had not SNCC changed his mind.

6. Ed King (University of Mississippi Medical Center) "The Struggle for Change in Mississippi: 1964–1970," unpublished.

7. Dittmer, "The Politics of the Mississippi Movement," p. 92.

8. Clayborne Carson, *In Struggle: SNCC and the Black Awakening of the 1960s,* (Cambridge: Harvard University Press, 1981), pp. 172–73.

9. Polly Greenberg, *The Devil Has Slippery Shoes: A Biased Biography of the Child Development Group of Mississippi* (London: Macmillan, 1969), pp. 29–31. On CDGM, also see the Fred Mangrum, Emma Sanders, and Mary Lane interviews, HU.

10. Greenberg, *The Devil Has Slippery Shoes,* pp. 523, 554–58. Since the New Deal, federal programs for the Delta poor have been controlled by the planter class, which typically used the programs to enrich themselves while ensuring the docility of their labor force. James C. Cobb "'Somebody Done Nailed Us on the Cross': Federal Farm and Welfare Policy and the Civil Rights Movement in the Mississippi Delta," *Journal of American History* (December 1990), pp. 912–36.

11. Johnson quoted in Bruce Hilton, *The Delta Ministry* (New York: Macmillan, 1969), p. 77; Machesky interview; Greenberg, *The Devil Has Slippery Shoes,*

pp. 601–03; Ed King, "The Struggle," pp. 15–18; "How Do You Fight It?" *New Republic,* September 3, 1966.

12. Dittmer, "The Politics of the Mississippi Movement," pp. 86–87; Fannie Lou Hamer and Aaron Henry interviews, Romaine Collection, SHSW; Pat Watters and Reese Cleghorn, *Climbing Jacob's Ladder,* (New York: Harcourt, Brace and World), pp. 291–92.

13. Greenberg, *The Devil Has Slippery Shoes,* pp. 605–06.

14. Carter, in a letter to the *Washington Post* argued that he and the other whites involved with MAP were motivated by concern rather than politics, supporting that contention with the observation that serving on any kind of biracial committee was certain to kill the political career of any white man. See Greenberg, *The Devil Has Slippery Shoes,* p. 639. Of course, that argument doesn't apply to those cases where the traditional enemies of the poor were serving on local MAP committees expressly to keep poor people from having too much influence. Nicholas Lemann's analysis of the War on Poverty—"a political failure mainly because it made enemies of local elected officials"—overlooks the fact that in much of the country elected officials were already the enemies of the poor. See *The Promised Land* (New York: Random House, 1991), p. 344. Whether talking about the North or South, he underplays the extent to which the antagonisms were real, not just reactions to the alienating style of poverty-program radicals.

15. Ed King, "The Struggle for Change in Mississippi."

16. "How Do You Fight It," *New Republic,* September 3, 1966; "CDGM Muddle," *New Republic,* November 12, 1966; Greenberg, *The Devil Has Slippery Shoes,* pp. 601–09.

17. Greenberg, *The Devil Has Slippery Shoes,* pp. 612, 649; Andrew Kopkind, "Shriver Comes Across," *New Republic,* January 7, 1967.

18. Polly Greenberg, "Evaluation of the CDGM Program for Children, Teachers, Parents and Communities," Tom Levin Papers, box 3:7, King Center, esp. p. 28; "Cleveland: Bolivar County: Edna Morton," FDP Papers, 1:30; Carole Merritt, "District II Report," n. d., box 1:30, Levin Papers; unsigned report, 1:36, Levin Papers; Greenberg, "Brief Program Report on the Greenwood Center at the American Legion Hut," 1:36, Levin Papers.

19. Polly Greenberg, "Evaluation of the CDGM Program," pp. 27–28; Carole Merritt, "District II Report," Levin Papers, p. 11. Even in the course of expressing her admiration for the way in which community people rallied behind the program, Greenberg suggested how little some of the people who worked with Black Mississippians understood about them: "Somehow or other, these desperately impoverished, *spiritually well-beaten human beings with nothing to call*

their own, managed to rise up" (emphasis mine), Greenberg, "Evaluation," p. 30.

20. Ed King, "The Struggle for Change"; Hollis Watkins interview.

21. Greenberg, *The Devil Has Slippery Shoes,* p. 610.

22. Mary Boothe interview, HU; Mary Lane interview, HU. Although the Catholics did ultimately receive substantial poverty funds, it does not appear that they were among the first groups in the state to do so. See Greenberg, *The Devil Has Slippery Shoes,* p. 610.

23. Susan Lorenzi Sojourner, "The 1967 Elections," unpublished. The 1967 elections had mixed results. Holmes County did elect a schoolteacher, Robert Clark, to the state legislature, the first Black to serve there since Reconstruction. Statewide, with Black voting strength up to 28% of the electorate, Blacks won only 1% of the available offices. The poor showing was largely the result of a series of changes in state election laws, enacted after the passage of the Voting Rights Act, which had the effect of diluting Black voting strength.

24. Both quotations from the Hurley interview, HU.

25. Worth Long and Owen Brooks interviews in Dent. Melissa Faye Greene's *Praying For Sheetrock* (New York: Addison-Wesley, 1991) is largely about similar processes of corruption in a Georgia county. William Hinton's *Fanshen* (New York: Random House, 1966), esp. pp. 222–40, details some remarkably similar stories against the backdrop of the Chinese Communist revolution.

26. Henry to Darden, June 20, 1962; Darden to Henry, June 22, 1922, NAACP "Mississippi State Conference: 1956–62," author's file.

27. See various correspondence in NAACP IIIA:230, "Gus Courts"; quotations from Current to Wilkins, September 26, 1956; Courts to Wilkins, April 18, 1957.

28. See the discussion of Marx in Jack Bloom, *Class, Race and the Civil Rights Movement* (Bloomington: Indiana University Press, 1987), p. 7.

29. Ed King, "The Struggle for Change in Mississippi." On Charles Evers, Theodore Henry interview, HU; my interview with James Moore.

CHAPTER 13

1. HU interview, p. 65.

2. "Black American Conservatives: An Exploration of Ideas," PBS Video, BL1K000. Underlying Page's comment is a dichotomy which still bedevils discussions of inequality: either something's wrong with "those people" or something's wrong with the social structure, a way of framing the issue which

would not make sense in the organizing tradition. Among the attempts to break out of an either-or paradigm are Cornell West, *Race Matters* (Boston: Beacon, 1993), my own *Getting What We Ask For: The Ambiguity of Success and Failure in Inner-City Schools* (Westport, Conn.: Greenwood, 1984), ch. 1, and Michael Williams, *Neighborhood Organizing for School Reform* (New York: Teachers College Press, 1989), ch. 3.

3. This chapter is only indirectly concerned with the decline of SNCC. Any full discussion of that would have to give greater emphasis to increasing federal repression, especially from the FBI. See Kenneth O'Reilly, *Racial Matters: The FBI's Secret File on Black America, 1960–1972* (New York: Free Press, 1989), pp. 180–94, 275–80. Also Clayborne Carson, *In Struggle* (Cambridge: Harvard, 1981), ch. 16; Mary King, *Freedom Song* (New York: Simon and Schuster), pp. 526–29; James Forman, *The Making of Black Revolutionaries* (Washington: Open Hand Publishing, 1985) pp. xv–xvi, ch. 57.

4. Both Baker quotations from her interview at HU, pp. 64 and 94.

5. Carson, *In Struggle*, pp. 138–39; Forman, *Black Revolutionaries*, pp. 416–19.

6. Mary King, *Freedom Song*, p. 484; Andrew Kopkind, "The Future of Black Power," *New Republic*, January 7, 1967.

7. Cleveland Sellers, *The River of No Return* (New York: William Morrow, 1973) pp. 130–31; Howard Zinn, *New Abolitionists* (Boston: Beacon, 1964), p. 10.

8. King, *Freedom Song*, p. 522.

9. HU interview, p. 81.

10. Carson, *In Struggle*, p. 149; Garrow, *Bearing the Cross*, pp. 488–89; Sellers, *The River*, pp. 130, 142–44; Jack Newfield, *A Prophetic Minority* (New York: Signet, 1966), p. 75; Forman, *Black Revolutionaries*, p. 477, also pp. 476, 481; King, *Freedom Song*, p. 520. For other examples, see documents in CORE Papers, reel 25, especially letters by Sellers and Marshall Ganz.

11. HU interview, p. 64.

12. King, *Freedom Song*, p. 524.

13. Sellers, *The River*, pp. 147–48; Carson, *In Struggle*, pp. 238–40. The rejection of rural people as an important constituency for the movement may have been partly a side effect of a struggle for ownership of the movement between earlier and later cohorts. Earlier cohorts had deep relationships with those people which later cohorts could not duplicate. By taking the position that the movement had moved beyond such people, members of later cohorts were countering their competitors' claim to special legitimacy.

14. Carson, *In Struggle*, pp. 231, 235; Forman, *Black Revolutionaries*, p. 477.

15. HU interview, p. 94.

16. All quotations from Charles Cobb, "Atlanta: The Bond Campaign," in Mas-

simo Teodori, *The New Left* (New York: Bobbs-Merrill, 1969), pp. 116–19. On the Bond campaign, see Carson, *In Struggle,* pp. 166–68; Sellers, *The River,* pp. 148, 150–51.

17. Zinn, SNCC, p. 186.

18. Joanne Grant, ed., *Black Protest* (Greenwich, Conn.: Fawcett, 1968), p. 417; Moses quoted in Dittmer, "The Politics of the Mississippi Movement," p. 88; Sellers, *The River,* pp. 184–6.

19. Garrow, *Bearing The Cross,* pp. 475–85; Carson, *In Struggle,* pp. 207–18.

20. Sellers, *The River,* p. 184; Carson, *In Struggle,* p. 230.

21. Carson, *In Struggle,* p. 234. See Robert Allen, *Black Awakening In Capitalist America* (New York: Anchor, 1970), ch. 6, for a description of the Black Panther Party as vacillating between concrete programs for its constituency and a media-oriented politics of rhetoric. See also Reggie Schell, "A Way to Fight Back," in Dick Cluster, *They Should Have Served That Cup of Coffee* (Boston: South End Press, 1979).

22. Quoted in Grace McFadden, "Septima P. Clark and the Struggle for Human Rights," p. 94, in V. Crawford, J. Rouse, and B. Woods, eds., *Women in the Civil Rights Movement: Trailblazers and Torchbearers, 1941–1965* (Brooklyn: Carlson, 1990).

23. HU interview, pp. 11, 69.

24. Ibid., pp. 66, 69.

25. Ibid., pp. 67, 79.

26. Zinn, SNCC, pp. 9–10; King, *Freedom Song,* p. 521–23; Carson, *In Struggle,* p. 137, 144; Forman, *Black Revolutionaries,* pp. 420–21. Sellers, in *The River* (p. 157), apparently referring to the 1965–66 period, puts the percentage of whites at over 25 percent, which seems high, especially at that period.

27. Gary Marx and Michael Useem, "Majority Involvement in Minority Movements: Civil Rights, Abolition and Untouchability," *Journal of Social Issues* 27, no. 1 (1971), pp. 81–104

28. Carson, *In Struggle,* p. 192; Sellers, *The River,* pp. 184–86; Grant, *Black Protest,* pp. 452–57.

29. Sellers, *The River,* p. 185; Carson, *In Struggle,* p. 238.

30. Carson, *In Struggle,* pp. 239–41. For some time after the vote, there was disagreement within SNCC about just what had been voted on. Danny Lyon, *Memories of the Southern Civil Rights Movement* (Chapel Hill: University of North Carolina Press, 1992), p. 175.

31. Sellers, *The River,* pp. 194–97; Lyon, *Memories of the Southern Civil Rights Movement,* pp. 176–81.

32. Carson, *In Struggle,* p. 195.

33. In an article surveying sociological literature on race, James Pitts notes that,

with some exceptions, "most of the research on black racial dispositions fails to collect and analyze data on the types of relationships among blacks and the social positions they hold in relation to one another." Instead, the emphasis has been understanding how Blacks feel about and relate to white people and vice versa. James Pitts, "The Study of Race Consciousness: Comments on New Directions," *American Journal of Sociology,* 80 (November 1974), p. 615.

34. It is likely that some of the frustration generated by the other conflicts spilled over into the discussion of race, a category more easily politicized.

35. Ella Baker interview, HU.

36. Letter to author from Wazir Peacock, October 26, 1992.

CHAPTER 14

1. Todd Gitlin, *The Whole World is Watching* (Berkeley and Los Angeles: University of California Press, 1980), p. 3.

2. Richard Kluger, *Simple Justice: The History of Brown vs. Board of Education and Black America's Struggle for Equality* (New York: Random House, 1975), p. 3.

3. Gitlin, *The Whole World,* p. 6.

4. Paul Good, *The Trouble I've Seen: White Journalist, Black Movement* (Washington, D.C.: Howard University Press, 1975), p. 59.

5. Mary King, *Freedom Song: A Personal Story of the 1960s Civil Rights Movement* (New York: William Morrow, 1987), p. 247.

6. Joyce Ladner, "A Sociology of the Civil Rights Movement: An Insider's Perspective." Presented at the 1988 meeting of the American Sociological Association.

7. Good, *The Trouble I've Seen,* p. 41.

8. Nicholas Von Hoffman, *Mississippi Notebook* (New York: D. White, 1964), p. 39.

9. Pat Watters and Reese Cleghorn, *Climbing Jacob's Ladder* (New York: Harcourt, Brace and World, 1967), p. 73.

10. Mary King, *Freedom Song,* p. 391; Watters and Cleghorn, *Climbing Jacob's Ladder,* p. 63.

11. David Garrow, *Protest at Selma* (New Haven: Yale, 1978), chs. 4, 5.

12. Good, *The Trouble I've Seen,* p. 255.

13. Southern Poverty Law Center, *Free At Last* (Montgomery, Ala., 1989), pp. 88–93. Howard Smead's contention that the 1959 lynching of Mack Charles Parker in Poplarville, Mississippi, was "one of the last lynchings in America" is at best misleading. Smead, *Blood Justice,* (New York: Oxford, 1986), p. xi. Emblematic of changing times, local white leadership in some of these cases— Jackson, White, and Dahmer—was aggressive about seeking the killers in

ways that would have been unthinkable a few years earlier. The traditional compact between "respectable" white leadership and white terrorists was eroding.

14. "Covering the South" Symposium, program brochure.

15. Good, *The Trouble I've Seen,* pp. 206–07.

16. Taylor Branch, *Parting the Waters* (New York: Simon and Schuster, 1988), p. 790.

17. Howell Raines, *My Soul Is Rested* (New York: Putnam 1977), pp. 154–55; Aldon Morris, *Origins of the Civil Rights Movement* (New York: Free Press, 1984), pp. 68–70; Anne Braden, "The History That We Made," *Southern Exposure* 7 (Summer 1979): 48–54.

18. For other examples of gilding the lily of King's leadership, see Charles Payne, "The Civil Rights Movement as History," *Integrated Education* 26 (April 1991). In a 1966 *New York Times* article, Gene Roberts refers to SNCC as having been "brought into being" by Dr. King, "who wanted an organization to coordinate the sit-ins" ("The Story of SNCC," reprinted in A. Meier and E. Rudwick, *Black Protest in the Sixties* [Chicago: Quadrangle, 1970]). There is also the tendency to introduce people significant in their own right by stressing their relationship to King. The limiting case of this may be the *Jackson Advocate,* Medgar Evers's hometown newspaper, introducing him as someone who had "worked with Martin Luther King in the Civil Rights March and other things."

19. Richard Lentz, *Symbols, the Newsmagazine, and Martin Luther King* (Baton Rouge: LSU Press, 1990).

20. Mary King, *Freedom Song,* p. 244. Watters and Cleghorn share King's opinion of Sitton and call *Newsweek's* Karl Fleming "outstanding." *Climbing Jacob's Ladder,* p. 73.

21. Gene Roberts provides an extreme example of the inability to take SNCC's viewpoint seriously. His 1966 "Story of SNCC" article contains not a sentence about developing community leadership, telling us instead that "unlike most radical organizations, which developed from a distinct philosophy, Snick grew willy-nilly out of the sit-ins and has been searching for a philosophy ever since." In Meier and Rudwick, *Black Protest,* p. 144.

22. Casey Hayden, "Sermonette on the Movement," *Southern Changes* 9, nos. 5–6 (December 1987), p. 29.

EPILOGUE

1. Moses quotation from Pete Seeger and Bob Reiser, *Everybody Says Freedom* (New York: Norton, 1989), p. 246. On the Algebra Project, see R. Moses,

M. Kamii, S. Swap, and J. Howard, "The Algebra Project: Organizing in the Spirit of Ella," *Harvard Educational Review* 59 (November 1989): 423–43; Alexis Jetter, "Mississippi Learning," *New York Times Magazine,* February 21, 1993.

BIBLIOGRAPHIC ESSAY

1. William Julius Wilson, *The Declining Significance of Race* (Chicago: University of Chicago Press, 1978), p. 135.
2. Steven Lawson, "Freedom Then, Freedom Now: The Historiography of the Civil Rights Movement," *American Historical Review* 96 (April 1991), pp. 456–71.
3. Clayborne Carson, "Civil Rights Reform and the Black Freedom Struggle," in Charles Eagles, *The Civil Rights Movement in America* (Oxford: University Press of Mississippi, 1986), pp. 24–25. Carson has an important discussion of the limitations of the term *civil rights* struggle, partly in an effort to focus less attention on the movement as an attempt to affect legislative change and more on it as a vehicle by which African American identity was being redefined.
4. Adam Fairclough, *To Redeem the Soul of America* (Athens: University of Georgia Press, 1987), p. 57. Fairclough might have noted that some of the local movements from which SCLC had been formed continued to be active during the late fifties.
5. In addition to Aldon Morris, *Origins of the Civil Rights Movement* (New York: Free Press, 1984), pp. 51–54, see Taylor Branch, *Parting the Waters* (New York: Simon and Schuster, 1988), pp. 120–38; David Garrow, *Bearing the Cross,* (New York: William Morrow, 1986), pp. 13–21; and Howell Raines, *My Soul Is Rested* (New York: Putnam, 1977), pp. 37–49; Rosa Parks with Jim Haskins, *Rosa Parks: My Story* (New York: Dial Books, 1992), chs. 5, 6, 9; Lewis Baldwin and Aprille Woodson, *Freedom is Never Free: A Biographical Portrait of E. D. Nixon, Sr.* (Atlanta: United Parcel Service Foundation, 1992), ch. 2. Mrs. Parks married a man she describes as the first real activist she had met; Parks with Haskins, p. 60. See Branch, *Parting the Waters,* p. 132, for a discussion of the controversy over how credit for starting the boycott should be divided. *Freedom Is Never Free* contains a useful discussion of how working the railroads politicized men like Nixon and how they in turn affected others. See chap. 1.
6. Frances Fox Piven, "Deviant Behavior and the Remaking of the World," *Social Problems* 28 (April 1981), pp. 489–508. Verta Taylor, in an article on the feminist movement, has suggested a way of emphasizing continuity between movement cycles by focusing on organizations that play the role of abeyance structures. Verta Taylor, "Social Movement Continuity: The Women's Movement in Abeyance," *American Journal of Sociology* 54 (October 1987), pp. 761–75.

7. Put another way, discourse about race is still troubled by the fact that most Americans have such a lowly embedded conception of what racism is. See Mark Chesler's "Contemporary Sociological Theories of Racism," in P. Katz, ed., *Toward The Elimination of Racism* (New York: Pergamon, 1976).

8. For one attempt at a balanced view of King's legacy, see Clayborne Carson, "Martin Luther King, Jr.: Charismatic Leadership in a Mass Struggle," *Journal of American History* 74, no. 2 (September 1987), pp. 448–54.

9. See Commentary in Charles Eagles, ed., *The Civil Rights Movement in America* (Jackson: University Press of Mississippi, 1986), p. 59.

10. David Garrow, *Bearing the Cross,* pp. 583, 591. Branch's narrative stops in 1963 before some of the changes in King's thinking had taken clear form.

11. Not only were large-scale demonstrations frequently coupled with boycotts but the turmoil they created often had the side effect of keeping white shoppers away from downtown areas. In several cases it is clear that businessmen were the first people willing to negotiate. On Birmingham, see Howell Raines, *My Soul Is Rested,* p. 180, and Aldon Morris, *Origins of the Civil Rights Movement,* pp. 269–73; on Saint Augustine, Paul Good, *The Trouble I've Seen* (Washington: Howard University Press, 1975), pp. 75–105.

12. In *Reaping The Whirlwind* (New York: Knopf, 1985), one normative interpretation seems curious. Robert Norrell maintains (p. 211) that by 1970, it was clear that Booker T. Washington's policies had worked, at least in Macon County, Alabama. Norrell's own analysis, though, centers on Black leaders who were far more aggressive in the pursuit of the vote than Washington advocated.

13. Reagon in Dick Cluster, ed., *They Should Have Served That Cup of Coffee* (Boston: South End Press, 1979).

14. For a study of Black activists reaching conclusions parallel to those of McAdams, see James Fendrich, *Ideal Citizens: The Legacy of the Civil Rights Movement* (Albany: State University of New York Press, 1993).

15. Joseph Sinsheimer, "The Freedom Vote of 1963: New Strategies of Racial Protest in Mississippi," *Journal of Southern History* 65 (May 1989), p. 243.

16. See Lawson, "Freedom Then, Freedom Now" for a fuller discussion of the role of women in civil rights historiography. On white women in Freedom Summer, see Doug McAdam, "Gender as a Mediator of the Activist Experience: The Case of Freedom Summer," *American Journal of Sociology* 97, no. 5 (March 1992), pp. 1211–40.

17. Paula Pfeffer, *A. Philip Randolph: Pioneer of the Civil Rights Movement* (Baton Rouge: LSU Press, 1990), pp. 50–53; Jervis Anderson, *A. Philip Randolph: A Biographical Portrait,* (New York: Harcourt, Brace, Jovanovich, 1972), ch. 16, pp. 264–65. In his discussion of the bluff issue, Herbert Garfinkel notes that

Randolph planned to have preliminary marches in several cities a week before the scheduled Washington march; it seems unlikely he would have run the risk of being embarrassed by low turnouts, suggesting that he at least believed he could produce sizeable numbers. *When Negroes March* (New York: Atheneum, 1973), p. 59. Randolph, by the way, is another who credits his own social consciousness to the racial pride of his parents. Pfeffer, p. 7.

18. Quoted in Anderson, *A. Philip Randolph,* pp. 266–67.

19. One of the interesting things about Randolph is the degree to which his influence over others rested on the belief in his integrity, even among those who disliked him or his tactics.

20. Lewis Killian, Preface (unpaginated), in Garfinkel, *When Negroes March.*

21. Pfeffer, *A. Philip Randolph,* pp. 124, 136.

22. Ibid., p. 138.

23. Ibid., ch. 4, esp. p. 141; Anderson, *A. Philip Randolph,* ch. 18.

24. Anderson, *A. Philip Randolph,* p. 280.

25. On Lowenstein, see Sinsheimer, "The Freedom Vote of 1963," p. 228–30. In the entire literature, perhaps the most ironic examples of pushing credit up the social ladder involve Bob Moses, since that form of thinking is so antithetical to his beliefs. The introduction to the Papers of the Freedom Democratic Party refers to Bob Moses having "introduced" the movement to Mississippi. Sean Cashman gives credit for the creation of COFO to Moses and Moses alone. *African-Americans and the Quest for Civil Rights,* (New York: New York University Press, 1991), p. 147.

26. Weisbrot maintains that "privately" Moses and Dave Dennis reached the decision that only white involvement would stimulate federal protection. The decision was anything but private.

27. Lewis in Carson, *In Struggle,* p. 136; Cleveland Sellers, *The River of No Return* (New York: William Morrow, 1973), p. 188. Weisbrot takes the Forman quotation from Peter Goldman, who also quotes Stokely Carmichael as saying that Malcolm wasn't saying anything of significance. Goldman cites no source for either quotation, so we can't get a sense of the context in which the remarks were made. Peter Goldman, *The Life and Death of Malcolm X* (New York: Harper and Row, 1973), pp. 142–43.

28. Henry Hampton and Steve Fayer, *Voices of Freedom: An Oral History of the Civil Rights Movement from the 1950s through the 1980s* (New York: Bantam, 1990), p. 353. See also Bobby Seale's comments, pp. 352–53.

29. *New York Times,* Feb. 28. 1965, p. 72. Attendance at the viewing and the funeral may have been affected by persistent and plausible rumors of violence. It is fair to say that Malcolm didn't live long enough for us to learn whether he could organize effectively outside the structure of the Nation of Islam.

30. For a particularly rich analysis of these questions, see Komozi Woodard, "The Making of the New Ark: Imamu Amiri Baraka (Leroi Jones), the Newark Congress of African People, and the Modern Black Convention Movement. A History of the Black Revolt and the New Nationalism, 1966–1976" (Ph.D diss., University of Pennsylvania, 1991).

31. See ibid.

32. Cultural nationalism is usually understood to mean nationalisms stressing the primacy of cultural values for social change and reconstruction, as opposed to the stress on power by political nationalist groups.

33. Thomas Hauser, *Muhammad Ali* (New York: Simon and Schuster, 1991) ch. 7, esp. p. 193.

34. Reviews of *Freedom Bound* include Ralph E. Luker, "Racial Matters: Civil Rights and Civil Wrongs," *American Quarterly* 43 (March 1991), pp. 165–71; Barbara Green, "Freedom Bound," *Antioch Review* 49 (Winter 1991), pp. 143–44; John Dittmer, "The Movement as History," *Reviews in American History* 18 (December 1990), pp. 562–67; David Garrow, "A Victory Half Won," *New Times Book Review,* December 17, 1989, p. 28; R. A. Fischer, untitled, *Choice* 27 (May 1990), p. 1575.

35. By and large, the various authors, myself included, citing factual errors in Weisbrot are citing different examples.

36. To see how much of an improvement Weisbrot represents, his work can be compared to some of what shows up in college textbooks about the movement, some of which I commented on in "The Civil Rights Movement as History," *Integrated Education* 19 (May–December 1981), pp. 54–60.

37. Vincent Harding, "History: White, Negro, and Black," *Southern Exposure* 1 (Winter 1974), pp. 51–62.

38. Elitism is also structured into the kinds of historical materials that have been preserved. It is simply easier to find material on a white liberal like Allard Lowenstein than an indigenous figure like Amzie Moore. The papers of every white moderate who ever lived in the South are enshrined in some archive somewhere.

39. Some COFO people and local people from McComb are currently participating in shaping a Hollywood movie about the McComb movement, so there may soon be one popular-culture representation of a grassroots conception of the movement.

40. Farmer, "The March on Washington: The Zenith of the Southern Movement," in A. Robinson and P. Sullivan, eds., *New Directions in Civil Rights Studies* (Charlottesville: University of Virginia Press, 1991), p. 35.

41. Karl Mannheim used *ideology* and *utopia* to refer to systems of ideas that are, respectively, order-serving or order-threatening. In that usage, traditional

movement histories are largely ideological—total ideologies, since they presumably reflect not more or less deliberate distortions but a relatively systematic way of thinking about the world and how it moves. These, though, are ideologies masquerading as utopias, since they purportedly describe how change has been made in the past and thus implicitly say something about how it might be made in the future. Mannheim, *Ideology and Utopia* (New York: Harcourt, Brace, Jovanovich), 1936.

42. Howard Zinn, *Peoples' History of the United States* (New York: Harper & Row, 1980), p. 570.

INTERVIEWS

Lou Emma Allen, Greenwood, 11/5/80
Howard Taft Bailey, Tchula, Miss., 6/22/81
John Ball, Greenwood, 5/21/81
Alberta Barnet, Greenwood, 12/5/80
B. L. Bell, Jr., Cleveland, Miss., 7/8/88
Freddie Greene Biddle, Washington, D.C., 8/14/88
W. J. Bishop, Greenwood, 6/19/81
Mary Boothe, Greenwood, 11/12/80
Rev. Thomas Benjamin Brown, New Orleans (by telephone), 7/11/93
Blood Bullins, Rising Sun, Miss., 7/3/81
Robert Burns, Greenwood, 11/8/80
Charlie Cobb, Washington, D.C., 8/22/88
Edward Cochrane, Greenwood, 6/23/81
Martha Cooley, Greenwood, 6/8/92
MacArthur Cotton, Kosciusko, Miss., 6/23/92
Homer Crawford, Cleveland, Miss., 7/7/88
Connie Curry, Atlanta, Ga., 7/31/91
Lee Davis, Greenwood, 7/3/81
Ivanhoe Donaldson, Washington, D.C., 8/21/88
Harold and Delleslyn Fleming, Carroll County, Miss., 6/27/88
Jefferson Eugene Fluker, Greenwood, 6/19/81

Albert Garner, Gary, Ind., 3/14/90

Dorothy Grady, Cleveland, Miss., 7/7/88

Ethel Gray, Sidon, Miss., 6/18/81

George Greene, Greenwood, 5/20/81

Lawrence Guyot, Washington, D.C., 8/20/88

Milton Hancock, Greenwood, 6/25/81

Alma and Nolan Henderson, Greenwood, 11/9/80

John Hodges, Knoxville, Tenn. (by telephone), 7/28/93

Emily Holt, Greenwood, 10/2/80

Ruth Howard Chambers, New York City, 9/21/88

Aaron Johnson, Greenwood, 11/19/80

Barbara Johnson, Greenwood, 10/4/80

June Johnson, Greenwood, 10/4/80

Waite Johnson, Greenwood, 11/22/80

David Jordan, Greenwood, 10/29/80

Dorie Ladner, Washington, D.C., 9/9/89

Joyce Ladner, Washington, D.C., 8/17/88

Father Nathaniel Machesky, Greenwood, 6/12/81

Rev. and Mrs. Archie Meadows, Greenwood, 6/28/88

James Moore, Greenwood, 6/29/88

Mary Lee Moore, Cleveland, Miss., 7/7/88

Ruth Moore, Cleveland, Miss., 7/8/88

Susie Morgan, Greenwood, 10/10/80

Bob Moses, Chicago, 8/25/93

Laura McGhee, Browning, Miss., 12/7/80

Silas McGhee, Browning, Miss., 12/5/80

Rev. B. T. McSwine, Greenwood, 6/6/92

Martha Prescod Norman, Atlanta, Ga., 10/14/88

Wazir Peacock, Jackson, Miss., 6/24/81

Floyd Peoples, Greenwood, 6/28/85

Beverly Perkins, Cleveland, Miss., 7/7/88

Herman Perry, Bolivar County, Miss., 7/9/88

Mattie Bell Pilcher, Greenwood, 6/20/81

Pinkie Pilcher, Greenwood, 6/12/92

Dorothy Pittman, Greenwood, 6/12/92

Rev. Louie Redd, Greenwood, 6/10/81

Mr. and Mrs. Willie Reynolds, Greenwood, 11/18/90

Clarence Robinson, Greenwood, 12/10/80

Mrs. Lillie Robinson, Cleveland, Miss., 7/7/88

Frank Smith, Washington, D.C., 8/30/88

Henry "Freedom" Smith, Greenwood, 11/3/80
Jean Wheeler Smith, Washington, D.C., 8/19/88
Rueben Smith, Cleveland, Miss., 7/7/88
Kwame Ture (Stokely Carmichael), Chicago, 4/18/88
Hollis Watkins, Jackson, Miss., 6/15/81
Richard West, West, Miss. (by telephone), 1/2/88
James Williams, Greenwood, 6/19/92
Arance Williamson, Greenwood, 6/12/81
Bob Zellner, New York City, 8/8/88

INDEX

ABC, 396, 399–400

Abernathy, Ralph, 76, 138, 256

abolitionism, outsiders involved with, 381–82

activism. *See* leadership; organizing; politics; social movements

Adams, Frank, 453n3

Adams, Samuel, 22

Adams, Wash, 9

Africa, rebellions against colonialism, 49

After Freedom (Powdermaker), 16–17

age: of Freedom School students, 302; and gender-related participation patterns, 266–67, 470n10. *See also* older people; youth

agriculture: cotton, 15–20, 133, 134, 159, 280; Holmes County, 280, 281–82; Leflore County, 134; modernized, 17–18. *See also* landowners; plantations; rural areas; sharecroppers

Agriculture Department, and Leflore County commodities program, 173

Alabama, 223; Black political party, 376; Lowndes County, 223, 315, 376; NAACP illegal in, 43, 353, 401; E. D. Nixon organizing in, 416; Selma, 3, 395, 396–97, 465n66; sharecroppers' union (1930s), 263–64; voter registration, 25–26, 463n42. *See also* Birmingham; Montgomery

Alabama Christian Movement for Human Rights, 401

Albany, Georgia, 394, 469n42

Albany, New York, NAACP, 87

Algebra Project, 409–11

Allen, Henry, 299–300

Allen, Lou Emma, 181, 192–94, 263, 271, *Plate 9;* attitude toward whites, 309; and CDGM, 330; in FDP, 323; now, 408

Allen, Louis, 123, 284, 285, 299–300, 396

Allen, T. A., 9, 21

Allen, Thomas, 192, 193

Allen, Tommy, 299

American Friends Service Committee, 45

American Quarterly, 437

Ames, Jessie Daniel, 20–21, 444n2

Amite County, Mississippi, 112–17, 120–21, 233, 236, 299. *See also* McComb

Anderson, Lula Mae, 299

Anderson, Reverend, 193

Antioch Review, 436–37

493

anti-war movement, 100, 375–76, 420

Arkansas: SNCC, 334. *See also* Little Rock

Arkansas Gazette, 399

arms. *See* gun ownership; military

Armstrong Rubber, 397

art: civil rights movement and, 256. *See also* music

Ashley, Stephen, 126

Association of Southern Women for the Prevention of Lynching (ASWPL), 11–12, 13, 20, 444n2

Atlanta, Georgia: demonstrations, 195, *Plate 21;* media and, 394; SNCC, 104, 110, 158, 162, 195–96, 294, 385–86

Atlanta Constitution, 78

Atlanta Journal, 399

Atlanta Project, 383–85

Atlantic City: Democratic National Convention (1964), 221, 285, 340–42, 344, 375, 399–400, *Plate 15*

Attala County, male leadership, 282–83

Bailey, Howard Taft, 278

Baker, Ella Jo, 4, 79–105 passim, 177, 363, 405; biographies, 425; and Black Power, 379–80; and Citizenship Schools, 75, 94–95; and class consciousness, 88–89, 186; and cooperatives, 82–83, 455n42, 458n3; death, 407; on degeneration of social movements, 379; on demonstrations, 93, 306; and direct action–voter registration compromise, 110–11; family, 79–81, 233, 457n60; FDP, 321; and giving people public recognition, 260; at Highlander, *Plate 5;* historiography and, 425, 437; and King, 91, 92–93, 95, 419, 457nn63,64; and leadership, 67–68, 92, 271, 277, 331–32; as Miss Baker, 5–6; and Moores of Florida, 238; and Moores of Mississippi, 45–46; Moses and, 4, 97–98, 101, 234, 236, 458n3; and NAACP, 45, 81, 84–91, 92, 456–57; in New York, 82, 302, 458n3; and nonviolence, 93, 95, 373; and organizational size, 369–70; on organizing, 83–89, 93–94, 369–70,

379–80; on participation vs. do your own thing, 371; seeing people in complexity, 199, 317, 375; SNCC influenced by, 67–68, 79, 95–102; and SNCC's decline, 367, 371; and southern/northern SNCC members, 385–86; on "spadework," 85, 264

Baldwin, James, 306, 310

Ball, John, 278, 279, 280, 472n25

Banks, Claude, 10, 12

Baptists: Cleveland New Hope, 34, 46; Greenwood, 140, 164, 170, 191, 197, 198, 229, 260, 322, 324

Baraka, Amiri, 436

Barnet, Alberta, 240, 251, 254, 277

Barnett, Ross, 55, 62, 165, 288

Barry, Marion, 71, 117, 119, 370

Bates, Bodie, 9

Battle, C. C., 40, 66

Bearing the Cross (Garrow), 419

Beasley. *See* Evers, Myrlie

beatings: CORE people, 126; Freedom Riders, 107, 108; Freedom Summer, 300–301; Guyot, 285; McGhees, 211–12; Moody uncle, 298; Shuttlesworth, 401; women in jail, 227–28, 270, 285, 309, 467n13; Zellner, 125

Beckwith, Byron de la, 288–89, 290, 322–23, 351, 407, 466n7

Bedford, Henry, 8

Belafonte, Harry, 260

Belfrage, Sally, 422

Bell, B. L., 65

Bell, Emma, 119, 167

Belzoni, Mississippi: boycott, 38; Lee and Courts shootings, 37–39, 40, 41, 66, 138–39, 208–9; NAACP, 36, 49, 66, 208; voter registration, 36–39

Bender, W. A., 66

Bennett, Myrtis, 126

Bevel, James, 71, 142, 154, 166, 197, 259, 291

Bible: Hurley using, 273; Jordan and, 140; Matthew 5:16, 1; Psalm 125, 265; slave Christianity and, 257; SNCC and, 258

Bilbo, Theodore, 24–25, 39, 112, 137

Bullins, "Blood," 157, 462n18
Burns, Robert, 156, 177, 181–85, 274, 280; and Block, 145, 147, 150, 151, 181, 182–83, 184
buses: Freedom Rides, 107–8; Montgomery boycott, 32, 72, 91, 92, 256, 415–18, 448n8

Cagin, Seth, 423
Campbell, Janie, 126
Campbell, Mr./Campbell's Cleaners, 157, 160–61, 177
Campbell College, Jackson, 125, 193, 461n37
Camus, Albert, 104
Canton, Mississippi, 176, 199–200, 238–40
canvassing, 115, 232, 244, 250–56, 468n27; Miss Baker's idea, 95; Greenwood, 165, 250–55, 294; for mass meetings, 261; rural areas, 130, 255; women, 268
Carawan, Candie, 71
Carawan, Guy, 71, 174–75
Carmichael, Stokely, 335, 376–78, 381; Alabama work, 315, 376; at Atlanta demonstration, *Plate 21;* Atlanta Project and, 383–84; and Black Power, 327, 376, 377, 379–80; and FDP, 322; and Dewey Greene, Sr., 224; jailed, 327, 377; and Malcolm X, 485n27; and March Against Fear, 376–77; Silas McGhee and, 240; and voting by affidavit, 291; and women activists, 470n5
Carrollton, Mississippi, massacre (1886), 178
Carson, Clayborne: on Camus, 104; and community studies, 414–15; *In Struggle,* 434; on "Let the people decide," 335; and Malcolm X, 434, 435; and SNCC decline, 370, 372, 378, 384–85; and term *civil rights* struggle, 483n3
Carter, Hodding, III, 341, 344, 477n14
Cashman, Sean, 485n25
Caston, Billy Jack, 116–17, 122

Caston, E. L., 114
Catholics: Greenwood, 324–25, 327, 349, 478n22; Mound Bayou, 43
Catledge, Turner, 399
Causey, John, 53
Cayton, Horace, 275
CBS, 400
CDGM (Child Development Group of Mississippi), 233, 318, 328–30, 338, 342–48, 359, 477–78
celebrity status: corrupting, 354–55; nationalist, 436. *See also* media
Central High, Little Rock, 109
Chafe, William, 414
Chaney, James, 301, 395, 396, 423, 451n51
character: of activists, 240–41, 243, 350–62, 370–71; and Black informants to whites, 135, 183–84, 230, 247, 290; corrupting processes, 350–62; courageous, 65–66, 401, 404; egotist, 351–52, 360, 387; and financial dishonesty of activists, 217, 222, 285–86, 294, 339, 350–54, 360; humanist, 314–15, 375; and local people's ambivalence about leaders, 336; vs. wealth, 405. *See also* ordinary people
charisma, 241–42, 388
Chestnut, Jerry T., 148
Chicago: female-dominated community organizations, 471n23; Garner projects, 409
Chicago Daily News, 394
Chicago Defender, 64, 182
Child Development Group of Mississippi. *See* CDGM
Chinn, C. O., 176
Choice, 437
Christianity, 256–58; activism related to, 272–74, 277–78; and Black attitudes toward whites, 308–9; liberation theology, 257; and mass meetings, 256–59; Moore and, 30–31; nonviolence, 373, 376, 383; slave, 257; SNCC and, 99, 257–58, 359. *See also* Bible; churches
churches, 249, 257, 359; burned, 34, 43, 46; Cleveland New Hope Baptist, 34,

community organizing, 1–4, 129–30,
236–64, 315, 365–90, 404–5; Miss
Baker's background in, 79–81, 82, 84;
and big dramatic actions vs. slow processes, 306, 366, 388, 392–93, 411;
building relationships, 143, 243–56,
264, 372–73; Carmichael in Alabama,
376; central theme, 392; COFO leaving
rural, 315–16; consciousness of,
419–20; developmental style, 68, 118–
31, 331–37; family for activists, 128,
194; and Freedom Schools, 302; Grier
in, 313–14; Highlander training, 70–
71, 142–44; historiography and,
413–17; identifying with people, 129,
143, 238–43; loss of tradition of, 285,
363–90; and media coverage, 403–4,
482n21; in Mississippi history, 23–24,
46–47; mobilizing vs., 156; for Montgomery bus boycott, 416–17; Moore's
background in, 30, 31–32, 33–34;
older people's strength in, 176–79,
190, 195–201, 207, 208, 225, 239–40;
by poor, 70, 76, 77; predisposition to
participation in, 177, 274–75, 281–83;
RCNL, 31–32; roots of tradition of,
67–102; SCLC and, 61, 76; sharecroppers', 21, 46–47, 253, 263–64, *Plate 2;*
and SNCC decline, 365–90; SNCC learn-
ings, 127–31; SNCC leaving rural, 315–
16, 372–73; SNCC themes carried on,
364, 409; urban focus, 315–16, 372,
374, 383; whites in the movement vs.,
297; youth relations with older
people, 64–65, 79, 176–79, 195–201,
225, 227, 231, 239–41, 254, 404. *See
also* canvassing; Citizenship Schools;
civil rights groups; demonstrations;
Greenwood; leadership; ordinary
people; rural areas; urban areas; voter
registration
Congress, U.S.: antidiscriminatory,
321–22; Courts testifying, 449n25;
FDP and, 321; Smith running for, 128.
See also laws; Senate, U.S.
Congress of Racial Equality. *See* CORE

constitution, Mississippi, voter registration and, 43, 115
Cooley, Martha, 462n18
Cooper, Owen, 344
cooperatives, economic, 82–83, 279–80,
425, 455n42, 458n3
cooptable networks, 63, 78, 141, 452n66
cooptation, and demoralization, 361–62
CORE (Congress of Racial Equality), 100,
101, 389; beatings, 126; in Canton,
176, 199–200, 238–40; in COFO, 62,
130; Farmer of, 170, 331, 440; Freedom Rides, 107, 108; March Against
Fear, 377; vs. NAACP, 62; SNCC absorption attempted by, 98; Suarez of, 176,
199–200, 238–39, 314, 425; and voter
registration, 129. *See also* Dennis,
David
Cornwall, Dr., 177
Cotton, Dorothy, 71, 294
Cotton, MacArthur, 117, 409; and Algebra Project, 411; building relationships, 243–44; and celebrity status,
355; and Freedom Summer, 297; and
gender of leadership, 282–83; and
Greenwood's older people, 178; jailed,
223; and local leadership, 194; with
MAP, 358; and southern whites, 381
cotton economy, 15–20; Holmes County,
280; Leflore County, 133, 134, 159
Cottonmouth Moccasin Gang, 397
Council of Federated Organizations. *See*
COFO
courage, 65–66, 401, 404
courtesy rituals, 404–5; titles, 6, 323
Courts, Gus, 36–40, 49, 450n37; Mrs.
McGhee's brother, 208, 217, 271, 356;
reconstruction as hero, 356–57; shoot-
ing, 39–40, 41, 66, 208–9
"Covering the South" symposium
(1987), 399, 401–3
Cox, Courtland, 96–97
Crawford, Homer, 65
Crawford, Vicki, 425
Cromwell, Oliver, 46
Crossley, Callie, 402

477n14; repression from, 42, 479n3; and voter registration, 34, 41, 43, 108–11, 116–24 passim, 141, 151, 171, 173–74, 245, 272, 360; WCC manipulating, 42. *See also* Congress; FBI; Justice Department; Kennedy administration; laws; military; Supreme Court

feminist movement, 63, 100, 402–3

FHA, WCC manipulating, 42

Field Foundation, 108, 347

fifties: as "awakening," 431; character of civil rights workers in, 353–54, 355–56; gender-related political participation, 266; Greenwood, 138–41; repression in, 35–59, 66, 113, 114, 121, 138–40, 194

finance. *See* economics

Fire Next Time (Baldwin), 306

Flanagan, R. Purdy, 9–10

Fleming, Harold, 109

Fleming, Karl, 399

"floating," 296

Florida: Moore family killed, 238; St. Augustine, 414

folk culture: southern, 71, 81, 101, 405, 455n38. *See also* music

food relief, Delta, 158–61, 167, 170–71, 173, 175, 351

Ford, Percy, 38

Forman, James: and Atlanta Project, 384; on Miss Baker, 79; and Black Belt Project, 367–68; Branch history on, 419; and Freedom Vote jailings, 296; on Greenes, 168; Mrs. Hamer and, 332; jailed, 169, 171; and McComb, 127; and Malcolm X, 434; on organization, 367; and SNCC decline, 370, 372; and SNCC northerners, 387; Weisbrot history and, 434, 485n27; and Zellner, 384

foundation funding, 108, 347, 410–11

Franks, Coleman, 8

Frazier, E. Franklin, 269

Free At Last? (Powledge), 418

Freedom Bound (Weisbrot), 426–38

Freedom Democratic Party. *See* FDP

Freedom Farm, 425

Freedom Riders, 107, 117; Block and, 142, 145–46; Ben Brown and, 397; COFO and, 461n45; Greenwood and, 178–79; Mrs. Morgan and, 231; NAACP youth chapter and, 187; Watkins and, 119

Freedom Schools, 301, 302–6, 329, 474nn27,30

Freedom Summer (Belfrage), 422

Freedom Summer (McAdams), 422–23

Freedom Summer Project (1964), 4, 285, 297, 300–16, 321, 329; and Black Belt Project, 367–68; historiography, 422–23, 432, 433–34; killings generating, 298; and local leadership, 335–36; media coverage, 315, 395, 396; normative thinking and, 422; and objections to outsiders, 297–98, 387–88; and SNCC decline, 368–69, 370; Watkins and, 297, *Plate 18*

Freedom Vote, 294–97, 396, 423–24, 433

Freeman, Jo, 63, 78, 141, 452n66

Frey, Dick, 295–96

Friends of Children in Mississippi (FCM), 346–47

Friends of SNCC, 158, 398

funding. *See* economics

Gaither, Tom, 129, 244

Gandhi, Mahatma, 52, 107, 180, 382, 430, 434

Ganz, Marshall, 236

Garfinkel, Herbert, 484–85

Garner, Albert, 166, 181, 185–88, 250, 358, 409

Garner, Dr. Mable, 177

Garrow, David, 3, 24, 237, 395, 419–20, 437

Garveyism, 234, 429

gender: and Black southern folk culture, 455n38; and decline in effective activism, 426; and leadership/activism, 76–77, 92, 141, 193–94, 266–83, 416–17, 425–26, 470–72; and trust, 275–76. *See also* men; women

Georgia: Albany, 394, 469n42; Bond running for House, 374; lynching rate,

Justice Department (*continued*)
    passim, 151, 171, 173–74, 212, 245,
    290, 315, 485n26; urban focus encour-
    aged by, 109. *See also* FBI

Karenga, Maulana, 436
Kemper County, Mississippi, and white
    vigilantes, 450n42
Kennard, Clyde, 55, 64, 66, 159
Kennedy, John: civil rights speech, 288;
    and Courts testifying before Con-
    gress, 449n25; and Head Start,
    185. *See also* Kennedy adminis-
    tration
Kennedy, Robert, 109, 459–60. *See also*
    Justice Department
Kennedy administration: civil rights dis-
    appointed, 124, 173–74, 218, 459–60;
    civil rights supported, 123, 288,
    459–60; and VEP, 108–9, 141; voter
    registration vs. direct-action support,
    108–9, 360. *See also* Justice De-
    partment
Kenya, Mau-Mau rebellion, 49
Kenyatta, Jomo, 49–50
Killian, Lewis, 429
killings, 205, 284, 285, 396–98, 451n51;
    Allen, 284, 285, 299–300, 396; Ben
    Brown, 397–98; Carrollton massacre
    (1886), 178; Cleveland, 31, 448n6;
    Dahmer, 398; death list, 40, 139,
    462n7; Evers, 205, 285, 288–90, 407,
    466n7; fifties, 35–58 passim, 138–39;
    Freedom Summer generated by, 298;
    Grier and, 313–14; Holman, 451n53;
    Wharlest Jackson, 397; Martin Lu-
    ther King, Jr., 326; George Lee, 37–
    38, 39, 40, 51, 138–39, 203, 432; Her-
    bert Lee, 122–23, 203, 233, 284, 298,
    299, 396, *Plate 13;* media coverage,
    20, 396–98, 403; Moore family (Flor-
    ida), 238; Natchez, 397, 403; Philadel-
    phia (Schwerner-Chaney-Goodman),
    301, 395, 396, 423, 451n51; Selma,
    396–97; Lamar Smith, 39, 41,
    449n24; Southwest Mississippi, 298–
    300; Till, 39–40, 44, 53–54, 139, 142,

192, 202; Turner, 58, 452n58; under-
    ground forms, 27; veterans, 31;
    White, 397. *See also* bombings;
    lynchings
Kimbrell, Elmer, 39
King, Coretta, 76, 266
King, Ed, 295, 341, 360
King, Lonnie, 109, 195–96
King, Martin Luther, Jr., 3, 61, 97, 100,
    193; assassination, 326; Miss Baker
    and, 91, 92–93, 95, 419, 457nn63,64;
    and Black Power, 377; and Citizen-
    ship Schools, 75; Cottonmouth Moc-
    casin Gang and, 397; historiography,
    417, 418, 419, 420, 440; Jordan and,
    140; and leadership conceptions, 76,
    92–93, 195–96, 417; Levison and Rus-
    tin with, 457n63; at mass meetings,
    260; media concentration on, 400–
    402, 482n18; on Parks, 416; Pritchett
    and, 394; sense of common human-
    ity, 314; and SNCC, 99; speech in de-
    fense of Daddy King, 195–96; and stu-
    dent sit-ins, 79, 96; and urban focus,
    109; and Vietnam War, 375, 376, 420;
    and Voting Rights Act, 476n5
King, Martin Luther, Sr., 195–96
King, Mary, 204; and Miss Baker, 97;
    and media, 393, 403; and SNCC de-
    cline, 368, 369, 371, 387; and Voting
    Rights Act, 476n5
King Lear, 29
Klineberg, Otto, 427
Kluger, Richard, 391–92
Knox, Reverend, 116
Ku Klux Klan: and *Brown* decision, 431;
    Clarksdale, 56; death list, 40; Delta
    hill counties, 112–13; and Greenwood
    Movement, 327; media coverage, 394;
    Mississippi (1940s), 27; purged from
    highway patrol, 316; and Turnbow
    bombing, 472n25; voter registration
    and, 112; WCC and, 34–35; White kill-
    ing, 397

labor: and Black population movement,
    18; in cotton economy, 16–18, 20; and

decline of racial terrorism, 41; Humphreys County, 36; Leflore County, 133, 134; migrant, 226; modernized plantation, 17–18. *See also* domestics; labor movement; sharecroppers

labor movement: Miss Baker working with, 83; Brotherhood of Sleeping Car Porters, 415, 416, 427–28; degeneration of, 379; Highlander and, 70, 416; media coverage, 403; E. D. Nixon and, 416. *See also* unions

Ladner, Dorie, 16, 63–65, 244; and Beckwith trial protest, 289; Dahmer's influence on, 64, 128, 398; Jackson boycott, 286

Ladner, Joyce, 54–55, 63–64, 389–90; Dahmer's influence on, 64, 128, 398; and emphasis on "Big Events," 393; Greenwood days, 168–71; Jackson boycott, 286; and SNCC arguers, 103; and SNCC northerners/southerners, 386; and Till generation, 54; on trust within SNCC, 366–67; and women's activism, 267, 268, 470n5

Lafayette, Bernard, 71

Lamb, Martha, 147, 150

landowners: community leaders, 141, 281–82; Holmes County Black, 278, 281–82; sharecroppers compared with, 281–82. *See also* planters; sharecroppers

Lane, Eddye, 322

Lane, Mary, 174–75; and boycotts, 349; with CDGM, 346; dissatisfactions, 336, 339, 340, 342, 348, 349, 353; FCM director, 347; with FDP, 322, 330, 340; and Freedom Summer, 336; and Greenwood Movement, 348; and leadership development, 335; on Moses, 240

Lang, Charlie, 13–14

Larry, Percy, 236, 238, 240

Lary, Curtis, 171, 175, 262, 296, 297

Laubach literacy method, 95

Lawrence, Ellet, 452n59

laws: anti-lynching, 9, 18–19, 20; and changing patterns of violence, 202; Civil Rights (1957), 113, 116, 120,

449n25; Civil Rights (1960), 116; Civil Rights (1964), 4, 210, 211, 217–18, 288, 315, 319–20; equal protection, 18; and media focus on violence, 395; Mississippi state election, 478n23; Public Accommodations (1964), 272, 320; public defiance of, 147; voter registration obstructed by, 43, 55; voting by affidavit, 290–91; Voting Rights (1965), 272, 398, 476n5, 478n23. *See also* Congress, U.S.; lawsuits; Supreme Court

law school, Evers and, 50–51

Lawson, James, 96

Lawson, Steven, 413–14, 415

lawsuits: Alabama antidiscrimination, 43, 401; Greenwood Movement, 327; NAACP, 43, 113

leadership, 4, 194–201, 237, 266; authoritarian/traditional, 67, 92–93, 180, 195–96, 268, 275, 334, 336–37; and Black student organizational titles, 363–64; collective, 67–68, 71, 77, 90, 93, 95–96, 180, 392, 417–18, 437; corrupting process, 350–62; gender and, 76–77, 92, 141, 193–94, 266–83, 416–17, 425–26, 470–72; Greenwood, 136–41, 152–53, 176–206, 229, 317–37, 349; historiography, 417–20, 437; Jackson, 288; landowner, 141, 281–82; media concentration on national, 400–402; by men, 66, 76–77, 92, 136, 141, 266–83, 425–26; NAACP training conferences, 89–90; now, 409; redefinition of, 180–206; secular, 141; by whites in the movement, 297, 382; by women, 92, 193–94, 266–83, 416–17, 425–26, 470–72. *See also* civil rights groups; local leadership; organizing

Lee, Bernard, 71

Lee, George, 36–38, 49, 66, 140, 409; Jordan and, 140; killing, 37–38, 39, 40, 51, 138–39, 432; and NAACP, 36, 37, 40, 449n18; wife, 41, 432–33

Lee, Herbert, 66, 121–23; funeral, 124; killing, 122–23, 203, 233, 284, 298, 299, 396, *Plate 13*

Lee, Herbert, Jr., 233
Lee, Rosebud, 41, 432–33
Leflore, Greenwood, 133, 170
Leflore County, Mississippi, 133–53;
    CDGM, 345–46; and commodity distri-
    butions, 158, 173; FDP, 189, 217, 229,
    233, 318, 322–25, 330, 342, 350; white
    SNCC workers, 381. *See also*
    Greenwood
Lemann, Nicholas, 477n14
Lentz, Richard, 402
Levin, Tom, 329, 330
Levine, Lawrence, 257, 469n44
Levison, Stanley, 45, 91, 457n63
Lewis, David Levering, 18, 414
Lewis, Ike, 119, 126
Lewis, John, 376; and federal help, 124;
    and Freedom Rides, 107; at High-
    lander, 71; on Malcolm X, 435;
    speech at March on Washington, 124,
    402; and voting by affidavit, 293
Lexington *Advertiser,* 279
liberal establishment: late and mid-
    sixties, 346, 375–76; media, 395–96;
    normative history and, 421–22; north-
    ern SNCC and, 387; racism's marks on,
    438
liberation theology, 257
library, Greenwood, 294
Like a Holy Crusade (Mills), 423–24
Lindsey, Merrill, 164
Lipset, Seymour, 470n3
literacy, 77; Laubach method, 95; voter
    registration and, 25, 75, 172–73. *See
    also* Citizenship Schools
Little Rock, Arkansas: Central High,
    109; Weisbrot history, 431
Liuzzo, Mrs., 396–97
local centers: civil rights movement, 78–
    79. *See also* rural areas; urban areas
localists, 101. *See also* community or-
    ganizing
local leadership, 3–4, 68–102, 129, 130;
    Birmingham campaign, 400–401;
    CDGM and, 343, 344–45; churches
    and, 92, 129, 141, 191–201, 232–33,
    249, 272; corrupting process, 350–62;

credentializing, 333–34; deacons, 196–
97, 249; decision-making by, 332, 335;
developing, 68, 118–31, 331–37; Greenwood, 136, 176–79, 194–201, 206,
229, 317–37, 349; Gregory on,
197–98; historiography and, 417–18,
422; identifying, 248–49; local
people's ambivalence about, 336; and
MAP, 344–45; media undervaluation
of, 393, 400–402; ministers and, 92,
164, 177, 191–201, 232–33, 340, 350; organizers' best kind of work with, 425;
St. Augustine, 414; SNCC's decline
and, 372; SNCC's measure of success
with, 318, 330–31; teachers, 129, 177,
199, 350; veterans, 13, 24, 30–31, 47,
56, 66, 136–37, 177, 181–82, 299, 404;
and whites in the movement, 297,
382–83, 387; youth relations with
older, 64–65, 79, 176–79, 195–201,
225, 227, 231, 239–41, 254, 404.
See also churches; community
organizing
Local People (Dittmer), 439
Lockett, Pig, 7
Lombard, Rudy, 239–40
Long, Worth, 262, 334, 354–55
Look magazine, 54
Lorenzi, Sue, 350
Los Angeles Times, 399
Lott, Hardy, 289
Louisiana, voter registration, 25–26
Love, George, 53
Love, Joe, 8
Lowenstein, Allard, 295, 433
Lowndes County, Alabama, 223, 315,
    376
Loyal Democrats, 341–42, 343–44, 358,
    360
Luker, Ralph E., 437
lynchings, 27, 450n42, 452n58; Georgia
    rates of, 444n2; law against, 9, 18–19,
    20; Mississippi rates of, 7, 444n2,
    460n21; 1920s, 18–19, 446n19; 1930s/
    1940s, 7–15, 19–21, 445n3; 1950s, 39–
    40, 48, 50, 53–54, 481–82. *See also*
    killings

media (*continued*)
379–80, 393, 402; and Black racism,
383; Blacks orienting toward, 376,
377, 379, 380, 388, 480n21; Bryant's library, 113; "Covering the South" symposium (1987), 399, 401–3; and Evers,
287, 482n18; focus on "Big Events"
and violence, 392–95, 403–4; focus
on dissension among civil rights
groups, 395–96; on former activists of
the sixties, 423; "framing," 392–404;
and Freedom Summer, 315, 395, 396;
and Freedom Vote, 297, 396; and
Greenwood Movement, 424; and
Mrs. Hamer, 258, 408; and Jackson
boycott, 286; King-focused, 400–
402, 482n18; lack of interest from, 4,
59, 161, 396; local leadership under-
valued by, 393, 400–402; lynchings
criticized in, 20; and police dog attacks in Greenwood, 169; and SNCC,
393, 398–99, 402, 403, 482nn18,21;
"tacit little theories," 403–4; whites
arousing interest of, 297, 396, 397,
403. *See also* newspapers; *individual
publications*
Meeks family, 159
Meier, A., 459n9
Melton, Roy, 39
men: economic dependency in Delta,
283, 472n30; leadership/activism by,
66, 76–77, 92, 136, 141, 266–83,
425–26; migrating, 268; political
alienation, 472; sexism of SNCC,
470n5; sexism of southern, 267. *See
also* leadership; ministers
Meredith, James: March Against Fear,
376–77, 395, 397; Ole Miss admission, 153, 178–79, 220, 233, 285
Metcalf, George, 397
Methodists: Greenwood, 146, 161–68 passim, 187, 191, 197, 221, 323, 344. *See
also* churches
MFDP. *See* FDP
middle class, 340, 414, 465n66; Miss
Baker and, 81; and domestics, 312;
FDP and, 350; Greenwood Black, 133,

177, 187, 340; Jackson Black, 52–53;
NAACP's orientation to, 87; organizing
and, 249–50; and repression tactics,
203, 205; SNCC, 237, 369, 372, 387;
women dominant in, 269. *See also*
ministers; teachers
migrations, 446n18; men, 268; population, 18, 19, 35, 40
Miles, Robert, 176
Mileston, Mississippi, 278–82; Plantation School, *Plate 1*
militance: historiography, 421; and social
elites in non-elite movements, 111. *See
also* Black Power; nonviolence; organizing; self-defense
military, federal, 42, 108, 203; National
Guard, 108, 326; segregation/desegre-
gation, 30, 429–30; Vietnam War,
375–76, 420; World War I, 18, 24. *See
also* veterans; World War II
militia, state, Colored Farmers Alliance
suppressed by, 46
Miller, Mrs. Hattie, 156, 157, 177, 274
Miller, Mike, 293
Mills, Kay, 425
Mills, Nicolaus, 423–24
Minds Stayed on Freedom (Rural Organizing and Cultural Center), 439
ministers, 177, 340; and Greenwood FDP
boycott, 323–24; and Greenwood
Movement, 348; with Greenwood
Movement, 350; in Hattiesburg, 246;
and Jackson demonstrations, 287,
288; and leadership, 92, 164, 177, 191–
201, 232–33, 340, 350; with MAP, 350;
slave, 257; SNCC attitudes toward, 97,
199. *See also* churches
Minnis, Jack, 164–65
Mississippi Action for Progress. *See* MAP
Mississippi Delta. *See* Delta
Mississippi Freedom Democratic Party.
See FDP
Mississippi Southern College, Kennard
application, 55
Mississippi state government: Robert
Clark in legislature of, 478n23; Col-
ored Farmers Alliance suppressed by,

Russell, Milton, 53
Rustin, Bayard, 35, 44, 45, 91, 104, 457n63

Sacks, Karen, 275
St. Augustine, Florida, Colburn on, 414
Salamon, Lester, 281–82
Salter, John, 286, 287, 288
Sampson, Charles, 135, 175, 203, 326, 328
Sanders, Cody, 187
Sanders, David, 177, 224
Scali, John, 399–400
schools: Algebra Project, 409–11; Black colleges, 43, 79, 81, 193; Black publicly supported, 302–3; Black sharecropper children and, 17, 49; Black student organizational titles, 363–64; Campbell College, 125, 193, 461n37; Clarksdale Black high school, 57; Freedom, 301, 302–6, 329, 474nn27,30; Greenwood Buckeye, 186–87; Greenwood junior and senior highs, 324; in Holmes County, 278; integration/desegregation, 28, 42, 55, 106, 109, 113, 153, 193, 286, 324; Little Rock Central High, 109; Mileston Plantation School, *Plate 1;* Nonviolent High, 125; segregation outlawed by Supreme Court (1954), 34, 42, 59, 72, 138, 391–92, 431–32, 454n14; separate-but-equal, 42, 52–53; in sixties, 77–78; traditional subjects in, 302–3. *See also* Citizenship Schools; education; Head Start; Highlander; teachers; University of Mississippi; youth
Schwartz, David, 472n29
Schwerner, Mickey, 301, 395, 396, 423, 451n51
Schwerner, Rita, 395
SCLC (Southern Christian Leadership Conference), 91, 100–101, 483n4; Miss Baker and, 91–93, 94–95, 96; Birmingham campaign, 174, 191, 400–401; Block and, 142; Citizenship Schools, 75, 94, 142, 153–54, 155, 166, 294, 378; Mrs. Clark with, 75, 76–77;

378; and direct action, 100; Evers and, 61, 452n61; fallow years, 415; formation of, 91; and Greenwood Movement, 326; Mrs. Hamer and, 155; Henry and, 61; King's frustrations with, 377; leadership conceptions, 76, 92–93; and local movement centers, 79; March Against Fear, 377; media coverage, 400–402; and money for Mrs. McGhee, 351; Morris on, 415; Moses with, 104; Ponder of, 166, 227; SNCC absorption attempted by, 98–99; and SNCC decline, 371; SNCC less southern than, 103, 458n1; and Sunflower County, 153–54, 155; and voting by affidavit, 293; Williams of, 71; and women, 76–77, 92. *See also* King, Martin Luther, Jr.
Sea Islands, 69, 72–74, 143, 282; Johns Island, 69, 72–74, *Plate 7*
segregation: Alabama Christian Movement for Human Rights and, 401; bus, 416–17; bus terminal (Supreme Court and), 107; and Democratic National Convention delegates, 341; military, 30; RCNL and, 32; school (Supreme Court *Brown*) and, 34, 42, 59, 72, 138, 391–92, 431–32, 454n14. *See also* desegregation; separate-but-equal doctrine
self-defense, 204–6, 450n42; Colored Farmers Alliance, 46–47; Dahmer, 398; Delaine, 391–92; Evers's guerrilla warfare idea, 49, 61, 314; Greene family, 168, 204, 221; Holmes County, 279; Mrs. McGhee, 204, 209, 213–14, 215; Mileston armed community patrol, 280; Wahalak community, 450n42. *See also* gun ownership
self-help, Black, 364
Sellers, Cleveland, 77, 105, 368–71, 383, 384, 435
Selma, Alabama, 3, 395, 396–97, 465n66
Senate, U.S.: Appropriations Committee, 343; Bilbo, 24–25, 39, 112, 137; Eastland, 153, 173–74, 343; Stennis, 343, 344, 345

Ture, Kwame. *See* Carmichael, Stokeley
Turnbow, Hartman, 204, 278, 279, 340, 472n25
Turner, Denzill, 58
Tuskegee Institute, 27, 414
Tyronne, R. J., 8–9

unions, 360; labor, 70, 415, 416, 427–28; sharecroppers', 46–47, 263–64, *Plate 2. See also* labor movement
United States government. *See* federal government
University of Mississippi, 203; "Covering the South" symposium (1987), 399, 401–3; Evers and, 50–51, 285; Greene admission attempt, 168, 220, 224, 244–45; Meredith admission, 153, 178–79, 220, 233, 285
UPI, 161, 402
urban areas: Algebra Project, 409–11; Atlanta Project, 383; Bond campaign, 374; churches, 191, 272; COFO moving to, 315–16; Democratic National Convention delegates from, 340; Freedom Schools, 304; Garner's experience organizing in, 409; organizing issues, 409; participation compared with rural areas, 280; rural areas chosen over, 109; SNCC moving to, 315–16, 372; Weisbrot history and, 433–34
Urban League, 109, 376–77
Useem, Michael, 381
U.S. News and World Report, 402
Ussery, Captain, 296–97
utopias, 486–87

VEP (Voter Education Project), 108–9, 130, 141–72, 232, 247
veterans, 30–31, 48, 87, 188, 404; change in attitudes of, 24, 47, 56, 177, 181–82, 404; leadership by, 13, 24, 30–31, 47, 56, 66, 136–37, 177, 181–82, 299, 404; and voter registration, 24, 47, 57, 137
Vick, Lee Chester, 126
Vietnam War, 375–76, 420

violence: media interest in, 393–95. *See also* racial terrorism; repression; self-defense
Virginia, NAACP branches, 86
Vivian, C. T., 71
Von Hoffman, Nick, 394
Voter Education Project (VEP), 108–9, 130, 141–72, 232, 247
voter registration, 1–2, 23–27, 108, 130, 247, 295–96, 459n9; Alabama, 25–26, 463n42; Belzoni/Humphreys County, 36–38; Boothe and, 349; canvassing for, 115, 165, 232, 244, 250–56; checklist of refusal excuses, 252; Citizenship Schools and, 43, 73–75, 153–54, *Plate 6;* Clarksdale, 56; Cleveland, 111, 460n18; Evers's son and, 407–8; federal government and, 34, 41, 43, 108–11, 116–24 passim, 141, 151, 171, 173–74, 245, 272, 360; Greenwood, 135–79, 182, 209, 214, 221, 230, 293, 424; Hattiesburg, 128–29, 144, 398; Highlander workshop, 142–44; historiography, 431; Holly Springs, 245–46, 253; Holmes County, 279; Jackson, 23–25, 60; Waite Johnson's view of, 251; on March Against Fear, 377; mass meetings and, 260; Mississippi politicians on violence around, 322; Moore and, 30, 34, 43, 106, 111, 459n9, 460n18; obstruction tactics, 26, 35, 43, 55, 116, 136; Parks and, 416; as prestige assignment, 305; RCNL and, 32, 59; Rolling Fork, 247–48; SCLC, 91–92, 94–95; SNCC, 105–6, 109–31, 141–79, 244; Sunflower County, 153–54, 155–56, 270, 291–92; VEP, 108–9, 130, 141–72, 232, 247; veterans and, 24, 47, 57, 137
voting: by affidavit, 290–93; Mississippi election laws and Black strength in, 478n23; mock elections, 294–97, 321–22; Northern Black, 18; white-only primary, 23–24, 57, 69. *See also* voter registration
Voting Rights Act (1965), 272, 398, 476n5, 478n23

Designer:	Nola Burger
Compositor:	Graphic Composition, Inc.
Text:	12/14.5 Garamond
Display:	Perpetua